General Editor's Introduction

The *Clarendon Studies in Criminology* was inaugurated in 1994 under the auspices of the centres of criminology at the Universities of Cambridge and Oxford and the London School of Economics. It was the successor to *Cambridge Studies in Criminology*, founded by Sir Leon Radzinowicz and J.W.C Turner almost sixty years ago.

Criminology is a field of study that covers everything from research into the causes of crime to the politics of the operations of the criminal justice system. Researchers in different social and behavioural sciences, criminal justice and law, all make important contributions to our understanding of the phenomena of crime. The *Clarendon Studies in Criminology* series tries to reflect this diversity by publishing high-quality theory and research monographs by established scholars as well as by young scholars of great promise from all different kinds of academic backgrounds. We especially welcome manuscripts representing theory-driven empirical research. The inter-disciplinary nature of criminology makes it apt for research that crosses disciplinary boundaries. We therefore also particularly welcome manuscripts that draw upon or integrate knowledge from different disciplines, for example, cross-level analyses of causes of crime or integrative approaches to criminal justice and crime prevention. Much criminological research is parochial in nature. There is a great need for more high-quality historic and cross-national comparative research that addresses, for example, the generality of criminological knowledge and the role of systemic factors for the patterns of crime and criminal justice. We welcome such contributions to the series.

In a globalised world the issue of international policing is an important topic. In his book '*Policing World Society*' Mathieu Deflem presents a long overdue comprehensive analysis of the history of international policing, with a particular focus on the history of international collaboration of the US and the German police. His main thesis is that 'the extent to which national police institutions acquire formal bureaucratic autonomy or institutional independence presents structural conditions favourable for international cooperation, regardless of whether the nation-states of those police institutions approximate one another in political, cultural, legal, and other respects' (p. 219). Deflem's book is informative, and at times provocative. It raises important questions about international policing, but also more generally, makes an important contribution to the understanding of the interaction between local and global processes. It will appeal to a readership that extends far beyond those narrowly interested in issues of policing.

Per-Olof H Wikström,
University of Cambridge &
Centre for Advanced Studies in the Social
and Behavioral Sciences, Stanford, (2002-3)
September 2002

Policing World Society

CLARENDON STUDIES IN CRIMINOLOGY
Published under the auspices of the Institute of Criminology, University of Cambridge,
the Mannheim Centre, London School of Economics,
and the Centre for Criminological Research, University of Oxford.

GENERAL EDITOR: PER-OLOF WIKSTRÖM (*University of Cambridge*)

EDITORS: ALISON LIEBLING and MANUEL EISNER
(*University of Cambridge*)

DAVID DOWNES and PAUL ROCK
(*London School of Economics*)

ROGER HOOD, LUCIA ZEDNER and RICHARD YOUNG
(*University of Oxford*)

Recent titles in this series:

Crime and Markets: Essays in Anti-criminology
Ruggiero
Paramilitary Imprisonment in Northern Ireland: Resistance, Management, and Release
McEvoy

Forthcoming titles:

Investigating Murder
Innes
Repair or Revenge: Victims and Restorative Justice
Strang
Accountability in Restorative Justice
Roche

Policing World Society

Historical Foundations of International Police Cooperation

Mathieu Deflem

This book has been printed digitally and produced in a standard specification in order to ensure its continuing availability

OXFORD
UNIVERSITY PRESS

Great Clarendon Street, Oxford OX2 6DP

Oxford University Press is a department of the University of Oxford.
It furthers the University's objective of excellence in research, scholarship,
and education by publishing worldwide in

Oxford New York

Auckland Cape Town Dar es Salaam Hong Kong Karachi
Kuala Lumpur Madrid Melbourne Mexico City Nairobi
New Delhi Shanghai Taipei Toronto

With offices in

Argentina Austria Brazil Chile Czech Republic France Greece
Guatemala Hungary Italy Japan South Korea Poland Portugal
Singapore Switzerland Thailand Turkey Ukraine Vietnam

Published in the United States
by Oxford University Press Inc., New York

Reprinted 2011

ISBN 978-0-19-927471-0

Printed and bound in Great Britain by CPI Antony Rowe,
Chippenham and Eastbourne

Opgedragen ter herinnering aan mijn vader,
Dedicated to the memory of my father,
Jozef Deflem (1925–1975)

Preface and Acknowledgements

Many of my debts in the history of this study defy acknowledgement. I am grateful to be able to thank friends and colleagues who have helped me in various ways with my research and the completion of this book. As always, I am most indebted to Gary Marx for enabling a person raised in Belgium to grow up in the United States. Gary has been with me professionally from the start of my career as an American sociologist, and his influence and support cannot be conveyed adequately in words. I am also grateful to Gary, as well as to Fred Pampel, Kirk Williams, Daniel Cress, and Paul Shankman for taking time to read through a prior version of this work that was presented as a doctoral dissertation in the Department of Sociology at the University of Colorado.

As I prepared this study and presented preliminary findings, I was fortunate to receive much needed feedback. For various critical and always helpful comments relating to this book, I owe thanks to Malcolm Anderson, Sharyn Roach Anleu, John Bendix, John Boli, Bruce Carruthers, Lewis Coser, Eve Darian-Smith, Kevin Dougherty, Richard Featherstone, Kenneth Ferraro, Cyrille Fijnaut, Peter Fitzpatrick, Tuviah Friedman, Philip Gorski, Terence Halliday, Steven Herbert, Jessica Kelley-Moore, Marc-Wilhelm Kohfink, Yunqing Li, Hsi-Huey Liang, William McDonald, Ethan Nadelmann, Detlef Nogala, David Rasmussen, Fritz Sack, Joachim Savelsberg, Steven Smith, Charles Tilly, John Torpey, Lode Van Outrive, Robert Waite, and Simon Wiesenthal.

For their kind hospitality during an extended period of data collection for this research in the Fall of 1995, I am grateful to Henri Meulemans in Leuven, the Nogala family in Hamburg, and Otto Diederichs in Berlin. Most members of staff at the archives and libraries I visited were very kind in assisting me. I acknowledge in particular the helpful services of Frau Wagner at the Police Library in Berlin, Kea Tielemann at the archives of the research group Civil Liberties and Police in Berlin, Frau Kock at the library of the Police Academy in Münster, John Taylor at the National Archives in College Park, Maryland, and personnel at the Library of Congress and the FBI Reading Room in Washington, DC.

Data collection for this research was supported by a grant from the National Science Foundation, division of Law and Social Sciences (#SBR–9411478). Opinions and statements in this book do not necessarily reflect the views of the National Science Foundation. Additional support, with regard to added research and teaching opportunities for this work, was provided under the Purdue Study Abroad programme for teaching at Oxford University; a Purdue-Hamburg Faculty Exchange grant for a one-month stay at the University of Hamburg; a grant from the Dean of Libraries of Purdue University for research at the Regenstein Library in Chicago; and a Dean's Small Grant Award from the University of Colorado for research at the National Archives in College Park, Maryland.

Additional support and audiences came from the Center for International Studies at Duke University, where I presented findings from my work at a conference on International Institutions; and from the Department of Criminal Justice at Indiana University, Bloomington, where I was invited to discuss related research materials. Papers based on this work were also presented at meetings of the American Sociological Association in 1996, 1997, and 1999, the American Society of Criminology in 1996, 1997, and 2000, the Law and Society Association in 1995, and the Academy of Criminal Justice Sciences in 1995. An earlier version of part of Chapter 1 appeared in *International Criminal Justice Review* (Deflem 1996) and shorter versions of Chapter 5 in *Law & Society Review* (Deflem 2000) and of Chapter 7 in *International Journal of Comparative Sociology* (Deflem 2002a).

I also have to thank John Louth, Editor at Oxford University Press, for his assistance in getting this work published. Likewise, I am grateful to the anonymous reviewers for their astute criticisms and useful suggestions that contributed towards making this book see the light of day.

Last but not least, I thank my friends and relatives who have supported me in many ways over the years. Their presence was far more important and dear to me than I had the courage to show. May we all live to see the dawn.

Contents

List of Abbreviations

AfK	*Archiv für Kriminologie* (Archive for Criminology)
BOI	Bureau of Investigation, US Department of Justice
DDP	*Die Deutsche Polizei* (The German Police)
DDPb	*Der Deutsche Polizeibeamte* (The German Police Officer)
DP	*Die Polizei* (The Police)
DPA	*Deutsches Polizei-Archiv* (German Police Archive)
DPP	*Die Polizeipraxis* (The Police Praxis)
FBI	Federal Bureau of Investigation, US Department of Justice
FNB	Records of the Office of Strategic Services, Foreign Nationalities Branch, National Archives
FOIPA	Freedom of Information/Privacy Acts Reading Room, Federal Bureau of Investigation Headquarters, Washington, DC
GFO	Records of the German Foreign Office, National Archives
IACP	International Association of Chiefs of Police
ICF	Investigative Case Files, Bureau of Investigation, National Archives
ICPC	International Criminal Police Commission
IKK	*Internationale Kriminalpolizeiliche Kommission*
IKP	*Internationale Kriminalpolizei*
IPC	International Police Conference
LN	League of Nations
MID	Records of the War Department, Military Intelligence Division, National Archives
NCLESJ	National Commission on Law Enforcement and Social Justice
NSDAP	*Nationalsozialistische Deutsche Arbeiterspartei* (National-Socialist German Workers Party)
OSS	Office of Strategic Services
PM	*Police Magazine*
RSHA	*Reichssicherheitshauptamt* (*Reich* Security Main Office)
RKPA	*Reichskriminalpolizeiamt* (*Reich* Criminal Police Office)
RLSS	Records of the *Reich* Leader of the SS, National Archives
SD	*Sicherheitsdienst* (Security Service)
SS	*Schutzstaffel* (Protective Squadron)
SA	*Sturm-Abteilung* (Storm Division)

Introduction
Historical Foundations of International Police Cooperation

It is 12 April 1946, the 106th day of the trials of major war criminals before the International Military Tribunal in Nuremberg, Germany. Ernst Kaltenbrunner takes the stand. Kaltenbrunner was the Chief of the Security Police and the *Reich* Security Main Office from 1943 until the fall of the Nazi regime. Charged with crimes against peace, war crimes, and crimes against humanity, he is interrogated by Rudolf Merkel, the defence attorney for the Gestapo. Lord Justice Lawrence presides over the hearings.

DR. MERKEL: Do you know of the so-called 'severe interrogations'? Are these in force in other countries, too?

KALTENBRUNNER: I was President of the International Criminal Police Commission, and in this capacity I had the opportunity to speak about this topic at a meeting in the autumn of 1943. From this conference and also from my reading of the foreign press over a number of years I gathered that the police system of each state also makes use of rather severe measures of interrogation.

DR. MERKEL: Could a State Police official . . .

THE PRESIDENT: What happened at some international police commission does not seem to be relevant to anything in this case.

DR. MERKEL: I only wanted to question him as to whether these 'severe interrogations' were applied not only in Germany but also in other states.

THE PRESIDENT: We are not concerned with that.

(*International Military Tribunal*, 1947–1949, Vol. 11, p. 312).

Policing world society

> A steady road leads . . . to the current position of the policeman as the 'representative of God on earth'.
> *Max Weber.*

Some books urge the reader to see old problems in a new light; others present fresh evidence. This work is of the latter sort, but not decidedly. It offers a sociological analysis of the historical antecedents of those police practices that transcend the boundaries of national states. This book has the dual task of uncovering empirically the relatively neglected aspects of the history of international policing and of developing and applying a theoretical perspective that can account for the nature and evolution of these developments. The empirical emphasis of this research is on international practices involving public police institutions from Germany and the United States in the period from the middle of the 19th century until the end of World War II. The selection of these specified time periods and police institutions is, as I hope this book will clearly show, based on their significance in the historical paths and turning-points of international policing leading up to its contemporary forms. The scope of the research, however, will by virtue of its international focus necessarily also involve police institutions from other nations. The thematic focus of this book includes, amongst other issues, the role of police institutions in the 19th-century development towards national independence; the evolution of international police cooperation initiatives from political to criminal enforcement tasks; the early history of international police organizations, including the origins of Interpol; the international implications of the Nazification of the German police; the rise of the FBI on the international police scene; and aspects of policing involved with World War II and its aftermath.

There is presently, at the dawn of a new century, much talk about such notions as the internationalization of social life, the new world order, the fluidity of boundaries, the permeance of temporal and spatial barriers, and many other aspects of a general globalization of society. This attention to developments beyond national states has also been of growing concern in the social sciences. In much of the contemporary discourse, the internationalization of social life is argued repeatedly to involve a decisive break with past societies. Yet, the scholarly attention to issues and developments that cross local and national boundaries has mostly not involved discussions of the function and institution of the police. To be sure, the internationalization of policing has increasingly been paid attention to by a range of social-science scholars, and, additionally, it has to some extent already begun to infiltrate the collective consciousness. Although relative to discussions of globalization in the economic and, to a lesser extent, political realm, international policing has not yet become central to theoretical debate and public policy, this situation may well be changing. Among the primary conditions of these ongoing transformations, I suspect, are contemporary developments in relation to certain well-publicized and increasingly more publicly recognized international police concerns, specifically in relation to the flow of drugs across nation-state borders, illegal immigration and related concerns of border control, the criminal opportunities enabled by an ever-expanding arsenal of computer technologies, and, since September 11, more importantly than anything else, the patterns and dynamics of international terrorism. What these international dimensions of crime and control have brought about is a more clearly and widely recognized urge to re-think our traditional, territorially-bound conceptions surrounding the locale of criminality and the appropriate jurisdictional authority of police control and judicial processing. With an increasing globalization and trans-localization of crime and police, these connections are much less fixed and clearly defined than they were before (Marx 1997). Moreover, at the very same time when problematic developments are taking place with respect to international crime and global security, our age has also been witnessing an unprecedented expansion of rights and freedoms, both nationally as well as internationally. At the world level, in particular, a normatively oriented debate without reference to human rights has become unthinkable.

It is in light of the undeniable relevance and increasing importance of concerns surrounding the international dimensions of policing in the modern era that this book hopes to make a distinctive and distinctly scholarly contribution. The aim of pursuing the research objectives of this book originated from the fairly straightforward idea that the recently discussed internationalization of society also pertains to the function and institution of the police, and that, moreover, the development of international policing is not a completely new phenomenon and must have its roots in history. Therefore, as a study in the historical sociology of social control across borders, this book seeks to present timely empirical data on, as well as introduce a theoretical model of, the history of international policing. To account for the historical transformations of international policing in the selected time periods and societies, in particular, this book will develop and apply a theoretical model of bureaucratization rooted in the sociology of Max Weber. Additionally, insights are taken from the globalization literature to account for the predominant forms under which the internationalization of policing has historically taken shape. Thus, the analyses of this book are situated in the sociological discourse on globalization, on the one hand, and the sociology of police and social control, on the other. These two intellectual traditions provide the contours of this book's analytical framework in which a more specific explanatory theoretical model of police internationalization will be situated.

The sociology of world society: Elements of orientation

It may cause little surprise that the scholarly interest in processes and structures beyond national states and other confined localities is not the invention of recent sociological reflection. Yet, because sociology is routinely associated with the rise of the national state, basic sociological premises and concepts have increasingly come under scrutiny to allow for a more dynamic approach to account for the transcendence of a variety of social forces beyond state borders. As such, it is no coincidence that globalization or internationalization, broadly conceived to designate the growing interdependence between dispersed social units, forms one of the prime challenges of contemporary social theory. However, a reading of the classical theories of the likes of Karl Marx, Max Weber, and Emile Durkheim brings to light that the founding fathers of sociology acknowledged that several dimensions of society were not restricted to the confines of the national state (Marx and Deflem 1993; Robertson 1992:108–114). Specifically, Marx (1846:181–186) addressed the territorial spread of capitalism and the formation of a global market economy; Weber (1922:520–527) discussed the fact that national states have a tendency to expand their powers geographically; and Durkheim (1900:28–41) acknowledged the tendency of nationalism to become engulfed in world-patriotic sentiments. In the course of modern sociology, too, there have been various manifestations of an attention for cross-border social phenomena. I will here not present a detailed intellectual history of these developments, but a brief review may suffice to indicate some of its basic elements.

Among the oldest sociological studies to focus specifically on internationalization are contributions by Charles Horton Cooley (1918) and George Herbert Mead (1929). Both scholars discussed the implications of the growth towards international society in the wake of World War I. Next to migration, warfare was indeed one of the first topics of sociological reflection that aroused an attention to the study of international issues.[1] It was the topic that was the primary motivation for sociologists L.L. Bernard and his wife Jessie to write a review of the sociology of international relations as early as 1934 (Bernard and

[1] A fairly extensive literature existed, especially in the years after World War I, which went under the heading of 'international police'. However, it dealt not with police institutions of criminal law enforcement, but with ways of establishing and maintaining international peace, in which meaning the term is sometimes still used today (e.g. Perritt 1999).

Bernard 1934). The theme of war further stimulated sociologists from Werner Cahnman (1943) to Louis Wirth (1948) and Talcott Parsons (1961) to discuss international phenomena. But apart from an interesting discussion with the likes of Pitirim Sorokin debating historical developments across dispersed societies (see Moore 1966; Bierstedt 1966; Sorokin 1966), the internationalization of society did not attract much sociological attention until the mid-1980s and particularly the early 1990s, when under the influence of such diverse developments as the computer revolution and the expansion of information technologies, the fall of communism, and the global development of a capitalist world-system, many contemporary social theorists began to address issues of globalization (e.g. Giddens 1990; Habermas 1992:632–660, 1998; Wallerstein 2000). Debated, in particular, has been the status of globalization as a new phase of modernity with more or less momentous implications for the sociological enterprise (Albrow and Eade 1994; Beck 2000; Robertson 1990; Robinson 1998). Increasingly, scholars have addressed globalization themes in relation to various dimensions of society, including culture (e.g. Boli and Thomas 1997; Featherstone 1990), law (e.g. Gessner 1995; Röhl and Magen 1996), politics (e.g. Deflem and Pampel 1996; Meyer et al. 1997), and market (e.g. Hirst and Thompson 1996). Furthermore, analytical models have been advanced to make theoretical sense of globalization (e.g. Albrow 1997; Robertson 1992; Robertson and Khondker 1998; Sassen 1996).

Foregoing a more detailed analysis,[2] there are at least two important analytical issues in the globalization literature that will prove relevant in the context of this book. First, globalization is a very broad concept covering a variety of events and activities in a multitude of social domains, often laden with strong normative connotations (Amin 1997; Silbey 1997; Woodiwiss 1996). In this book, globalization is understood in strict analytical terms as designating a degree of interdependence between geographically distinct social units, especially national states and their institutions. On the basis of this conception, two basic forms of globalization can be distinguished. On the one hand, some social developments are not restricted to any one national state or otherwise bordered social unit. The spread of capitalism, for instance, affects many societies at once and is as such a phenomenon supra-national to

[2] For overviews on the globalization literature, see the bibliographies in Albrow 1997; Boli and Thomas 1999; Featherstone 1990; Robertson 1992; Sassen 1996.

localities. On the other hand, other international patterns originate from one country or locality, or involve forms of cooperation and/or conflict between various entities. These forms of internationalization indicate, respectively, a trans-national intrusion across and an international relatedness between distinct localities.

Secondly, and relatedly, the globalization theme has often been addressed in terms of the relationship between international and national (or local) social structures and processes (e.g. Robertson 1992:124–125, 176–177). This relationship pertains to important issues of sovereignty and self-determination (or the loss thereof), and it entails analytically the question of whether internationalization and nationalization are conflicting trends, revealing tension and opposition (Ruggie 1993), or whether they complement one another in a more or less harmonious fashion (Amin 1997). These two questions are also at the heart of this study on the internationalization of the police function to consider the form under which international police practices take place and how a variety of such activities relate to local and intra-national police tasks and organizations. Before I offer a theoretical model of these issues, I will clarify relevant aspects of the sociology of social control, the second subfield in sociology in which this study is situated.

International policing and the sociology of social control

Although the sociology of law and social control can rely on a long history dating back to some of the discipline's most prominent founders (e.g. Durkheim 1893; Weber 1922:387–513), relatively little contemporary work of an explicitly sociological nature is devoted to uncovering institutionalized responses to crime and deviance, especially the function and institution of the police. While it cannot be denied that sociological research has successfully been devoted to the study of the police, both in terms of gaining a broad understanding of the role of the police in society as well as on more distinct aspects of policing (e.g. Bayley 1985; Black 1980; Bittner 1970; Jacobs and Helms 1997; Manning 1977; Marx 1988; Skolnick 1966), it is a truism indeed that, as Jacobs and O'Brien (1998) argue, coercion and the police remain conspicuously understudied by sociologists. Instead, there has been a trend towards the specialized treatment of the police outside the sociological mainstream, especially in criminal justice studies. No doubt pushed by social pressures (especially for police research to serve policy needs), this has brought about not only a fragmentation of knowledge, but also an instrumentalization of research questions in terms of administrative goals, a condition often and rightly lamented by sociologists in search of a more analytically justified outlook (Farrell and Koch 1995; Leo 1996). Regardless of whether this lack of attention to the police by sociologists parallels societal significance (for instance, the relative weight in national and world affairs of the polity versus the police), it has in effect impeded a maturation of social control and the police as serious sociological research themes. Perhaps most striking is the neglect of the police by political and comparative-historical sociologists, some notable exceptions notwithstanding (e.g. Tilly, Tilly, and Tilly 1975; Tilly 1986). It is especially remarkable that political sociologists have neglected the state's coercive apparatuses when we consider that Max Weber related his conception of the state explicitly to the institutionalized means of force. Weber defined the state in instrumental terms as 'that human community which within a certain territory . . . claims for itself (with success) a monopoly of legitimate physical coercion' (Weber 1919:506; see also Weber 1922:514–540, 566–567, 815–868). But despite Weber's explicit reference to the coercive agency of the police in his definition of the state, sociologists have mostly been interested in the state as the centre of political power over a territory, rather than in the bureaucratic apparatuses of legitimate force the state has at its disposal (but see Torpey 2000). However, in this book I do not seek to argue against a trend in political sociology. Yet, I do hope to demonstrate that the study of the police as a distinct theme of sociological analysis and reflection makes sound sense.

Corresponding to this book's intention to bring out the unique place of the function and institution of the police, the gradual delineation of social control as a separate theme of reflection has been the central development in the history of sociological theorizing on social control (Cohen and Scull 1985; Coser 1982; Liska 1997; Scull 1988). The concept of social control was since its 19th-century origins, especially in American sociology, at first virtually synonymous with social order, denoting the capacity of a group or society to regulate itself and secure harmony among its members. Since the 1950s, however, social control has come to be conceived more narrowly in relation to deviance and crime. Despite some attempts to redefine social control again more broadly (e.g. Janowitz 1991), social control has become a mainstay in this more restricted conception, referring to a variety of social processes and structures that—corresponding to the three dominant sociological theory groups (functionalism, social-constructionism, and conflict sociology)—redress, create, or reproduce more than crime and/or deviant behaviour (e.g. Cohen 1985; Deflem 1994b; Marx 1981).

The understanding of social control in relation to crime does not of course imply that social control is conceived only as reactive to crime or as being in one-to-one correspondence with the amount and intensity thereof. Nor does this conception imply the assumption that social control has no connection to broader issues involved with social order and integration, questions which, of course, any sociology must address. The notion of social control conceptually tied to crime and deviance only intends to take advantage of a methodological strategy that analytically disconnects various dimensions of society to analyse them separately, despite their empirical interconnectedness. It was precisely in this way that the most notable founders of our discipline were able to develop relevant theories of law and social control: Marx in criticizing the modern criminal justice system as contributing to, and justifying, conditions of socio-economic inequality (Marx 1846); Weber in his discussion of the formal rationalization of law in elective affinity with developments in economy, politics, and culture (Weber 1922:503–513); and Durkheim, perhaps most clearly, through a masterful analysis of quantitative and qualitative changes in law and punishment that, irrespective of the level and nature of crime, corresponded to changes in societal organization (Durkheim 1893:200–225, 1901).

Situated within the more delineated perspective of social control, sociological research has also been devoted to the institution and function of the police. The sociology of policing has, relevant to the present research, drawn considerable attention to the historical roots and transformations of modern police systems (Fijnaut 1979; Funk 1986; Liang 1992; Raeff 1975; Siemann 1983a). Among the critical topics of research on police history are the transformation of the police function, especially the relationship between the institution of the police and the political context of national states. In this respect, the gradual delineation of the police function to the enforcement of rules formally defined in criminal law, relatively independent of the political goals of established regimes, counts among the most interesting, yet also most problematic, developments. Further, it can be noted that most studies in the historical police literature are confined to developments at the urban and national levels. Scholars, moreover, have often treated issues of the police in relation to patterns of crime and/or as an aspect of formalized legal systems. These developments have hindered the development of the study of international police practices, and have additionally impeded the treatment of the police as a research topic in its own right.

Yet, although the history of international policing is a much neglected topic of sociological inquiry, an explicit focus on international dimensions of the police has been of growing scholarly concern. Among the growing sociologically oriented literature in the area are, to be mentioned especially in the context of the United States: Ethan Nadelmann's (1993) study of the role of US law enforcement in a global war on drugs; David Bayley's (1995, 1996, 1997) work on the role of US police in the promotion of democratic regimes abroad; William McDonald's (1997c, d) research of the policing of illegal immigration; Martha Huggins' (1998) work on US-controlled police training programmes in South America; Otwin Marenin's studies of police organizations' role in foreign policy (Marenin 2001; Cottam and Marenin 1999); and Dunn's (1996) and Kraska and Kappeler's (1997) analyses of the militarization of US police organizations. Also of growing concern in the context of the United States have been police issues involved with the control of the US–Mexican border (see, e.g. Andreas 1994, 1996, 2000; Deflem 2001, forthcoming). In Europe, international policing has been discussed in an even more flourishing literature, a trend that has been accellerated with the unification of Europe in the European Union (e.g. Anderson and Den Boer 1994; Benyon 1996; Fijnaut 1991, 1993b; Hebenton and Thomas 1995, 1998; Heindensohn 1997; Klosek 1999). Other investigations have focused on international police organizations and criminal developments in a global context (e.g. Anderson 1989; Deflem and Henry-Turner 2001; Findlay 1999; Fooner 1989; Koenig and Das 2001; Pearce and Woodiwiss 1993). In addition to these studies, comparative perspectives of policing have sought to learn from police experiences across the world (e.g. Bayley 1985, 1991; Maguire and Schulte-Murray 2001; Mawby 1990, 1999). Many studies on international policing are rather technical in nature or written from a legal perspective (e.g. Gibney 1990; Santiago 2000; Zagaris 1996), but other contributions offer more theoretically oriented and general discussions (e.g. Bayley 1996; Deflem 2000; Deflem and Swygart 2000; Marx 1997; McDonald 1997a, b; Sheptycki 1995, 1996, 1997, 1998b; Vagg 1993).

Clearly, as international police specialists James Sheptycki (2000b) and Monica den Boer (1999) argue, internationalization may be considered among the most critical challenges of policing today, though, as I will show, with considerable historical roots stretching far back in time. Research in the area of international policing has particularly centred on the mechanisms of interchange among national police forces, involving trends of standardization across nations as well as the development of informal and formalized cooperation among national police systems (Marx 1997). Among the critical issues addressed are the tensions and relationships between national and international police operations, concerning especially issues of sovereignty and legal jurisdiction (Deflem 1997b; Fijnaut and Marx 1995). Relatedly, a key issue revolves around the changing functions of national police systems with the appearance and increasing penetration of international dimensions of policing (Bayley 1996; Herbert 1997; McDonald 1997b).

The growing body of scholarship on international policing has done much to advance our understanding of various aspects of the historical and contemporary dimensions of international police structures and processes. However, while international policing is of growing scholarly interest, its historical antecedents have not yet been sufficiently researched. Among the most noteworthy exceptions are Fijnaut's (1979) comprehensive comparative study of national police systems in Europe, Liang's (1992) study of European police history, and Nadelmann's (1993:15–102) chapters on the history of the internationalization of US law enforcement. Yet, most studies of policing that have paid attention to the history of police systems have focused on state-internal developments, specifically the separation of the police from the military and the role of the police in maintaining autocratic political regimes. As such, this book hopes to fill a void in the contemporary literature by illuminating various aspects in the history of international policing.

International policing across and between Germany and the United States

This book investigates the internationalization of policing in the context of international practices that emanated from and took place between Germany and the United States from the second half of the 19th century until the end of World War II. While the rationale for the value of the delineation of my research topic will hopefully increase as the argument in this book unfolds, Germany and the United States present unique cases of national development, similar in some ways and contrasting in others, in terms of economic, political, military, and, indeed, police power. As I will explain in more detail in a later section of this chapter, among the most striking features is the fact that politically Germany did not turn to democratic government until the end of World War II, while the United States was built on the democratic ideal, however restrictively understood. Despite marked differences in the nature of political rule, both countries developed a federal structure of government and, perhaps most critically for this study, both Germany and the United States matured in political, military, and economic respects in roughly the same period—the second half of the 19th century—but with sharply different repercussions, culminating in both countries' antagonistic involvement in two world wars. In matters of policing, too, the respective and related histories of Germany and the United States may provide an interesting, empirically rich, and theoretically provocative field of inquiry. Despite my concentration on these two countries, I will traverse the fixed national-geographic borders to the extent that it serves the analysis of pertinent issues of international policing. The role of Germany in the history of Europe, and that of the United States on the American continent, may justify this broadening of the research perspective. Likewise, the time frame of police developments discussed in this book has no rigidly fixed boundaries. As a sociologist, I am interested, not in places and periods, but in issues of social significance that may or may not vary over space and time, to be illuminated with methodologically and theoretically appropriate instruments of analysis.

I conceive of international policing broadly as police activities that relate to citizens—investigators and/or suspects—or jurisdictions of different nations. Occasionally, I may also hint at other police activities which involve the breaking of some physical or social barrier and which can be more broadly understood as dimensions of cross-border policing, but only when they relate to international police practices. I centre attention, moreover, on various forms of internationalization which, on the basis of the typology of internationalization discussed above, ideally or typically involve the following: German and US police practices affected by similar conditions; police plans and operations originating either from Germany or from the United States that affect other countries or their nationals; and bilateral and multilateral international cooperation efforts, including joint German and US police practices.

I define the police as the institution formally charged by states to lawfully execute the monopoly over the means of coercion (Manning 1977:105). In identifying the police as an important dimension of social control, I do not define the category of the police beyond inclusion of all those functions, institutions, and activities which are so labelled in the societies at hand. My analysis, also, is mostly not about the police (in the plural) as a force of law-enforcement officials, but about the police (in the singular) as a function and/or institution. Emphasis will be on public police institutions that are formally sanctioned with the legitimate exercise of force at various levels of government in national states. Also, my analysis is not about coercion or violence, nor about the use of force, but about that organizational institution of states that has a legitimate right to use force under specified circumstances, a point more often than not obscured in the literature (e.g. Jacobs and O'Brien 1998:838).

Bureaucratization and international police cooperation

> In the modern state, real authority . . . rests necessarily and unavoidably in the hands of the bureaucracy.
> *Max Weber.*

I already drew attention to the fact that the relative neglect of the theme of the police in sociology is particularly striking in the light of the centrality of the bureaucratic apparatus in Max Weber's conception of the state. Besides conceptually incorporating bureaucracy in his definition of the state, Weber went as far as to equate modern power with bureaucracy: 'domination (*Herrschaft*) is in everyday life primarily administration (*Verwaltung*)' (Weber 1922:126). It is Weber's incorporation of a perspective of bureaucracy into his theory of the state that provides the foundation for the theoretical model of international police cooperation advanced in this book.[3]

To date, Weber's writings on bureaucracy have mostly been applied in normative terms and have relatedly served as a basis for conflict theories (Collins 1986). When bureaucratic theories are used in the study of social control, they similarly tend to emphasize the dangers involved with state agencies operating without sufficient democratic control (e.g. Benson, Rasmussen, and Sollars 1995; O'Reilly 1987; Gamson and Yuchtman 1977; Useem 1997). The relevance of these studies cannot be

[3] My reading of Weber's perspective of bureaucracy relies on the relevant sections from the posthumous collection *Wirtschaft und Gesellschaft* (Economy and Society) (especially Weber 1922:551–579, 815–837) and additional writings on bureaucracy in Germany (Weber 1918) and the political profession (Weber 1919). English translations can be found in Weber 1958, 1978.

denied, but based on the notion that critique cannot be constitutive of analysis, I follow a different route and develop a Neo-Weberian model to empirically uncover historical developments of the police. Let me first briefly repeat the key elements of Weber's perspective of bureaucracy.

Weber on bureaucracy and bureaucratic autonomy

Corresponding to Weber's perspective of societal rationalization as having gone in the direction of an increasing reliance on principles of efficiency in terms of a calculation of means (Weber 1920:13–17, 1922:514–516), Weber considered the modern state bureaucracy to be the most quintessential expression of formally rationalized societies (Weber 1922:551–579). Conceived as those institutional structures in charge of implementing policies decided upon in the polity, state bureaucracies of the modern type strive for an efficient management on the basis of the following organizational design: 1) bureaucratic offices are subject to a principle of fixed jurisdictional areas; 2) they are firmly and hierarchically ordered; 3) their activities are based upon written documents (files); 4) the public equipment of the official is divorced from their private property, and the executive offices are separated from the household; 5) specialized training is required; 6) the official activity is a full-time job; and 7) the management of bureaucratic offices is guided by general rules (Weber 1922:551–554). In addition to these organizational aspects, Weber specified various principles that guided bureaucratic activity. Most generally, Weber argued, the modern bureaucracy operates on the basis of a formal-rationality which entails that the technically most superior means are to be utilized. Officialdom operates without emotion on the basis of a 'formalistic impersonality' oriented at an equal application of rules and procedures to all, employing the most efficient, and only the most efficient means, given certain goals (Weber 1922:128, 561–566). Officials are appointed on the basis of their proven professional skills and the technical qualifications they acquired through special training (Weber 1922:124–130, 554). Bureaucracies are specialized, both from one another in terms of the various tasks they have to fulfil (e.g. collection of taxes, military protection, maintenance of order and crime control), and internally with respect to a specialized division of labor (e.g. investigations, evidence, personnel). Finally, with efficiency and specialization comes bureaucratic knowledge, including technical know-how (technical expertise) and official information (the knowledge accumulated in the exercise of official business) (Weber 1918:352–354). Next to the organizational design and *modus operandi* of bureaucracies, Weber devoted attention to analysing the social consequences of bureaucratization. Among them, Weber found most significant the trends towards bureaucratic autonomy, that is, the gradual formation of a bureaucratic machinery free from political and popular control.

I rely on Weber's theories to put forward the main thesis of this book that national police agencies can form international networks with wide international participation when they are sufficiently disconnected from their political contexts and have developed a specialized agenda for the control of international crime. However, according to Weber, it is also important to discuss the societal conditions under which bureaucracies were formed and developed. Conforming to his perspective of elective affinity, Weber linked bureaucratic rationalization to economic, political, and cultural conditions, particularly the development of a monetary economy and the rise of the modern state and mass political parties (Weber 1922:556–566). Yet, while Weber argued that these conditions facilitated the development of bureaucracy, they were 'not indispensable' preconditions and could not account for bureaucratic activity (Weber 1922:558). In fact, Weber argued, it was the technical superiority of the bureaucracy that was 'the decisive factor' for its spread as the most dominant form of organization (Weber 1922:561). In other words, the development of bureaucratic activity to apply principles of efficiency and calculability 'without regard for the person' was, according to Weber, more than any other factor accountable for the spread of bureaucratic rationalization (Weber 1922:562).

The primary regard for a purposive-rational execution in the modern bureaucracy is what accounts for its drift towards stability and independence, beyond and possibly even against political control (Weber 1919:541–542). Under those conditions, Weber argued, the bureaucratic apparatus becomes a permanent 'almost unbreakable formation,' while control of the bureaucracy is 'only limitedly possible for the nonspecialist: the specialist is in the long run frequently superior in getting his will done' (Weber 1922:570, 128–129). The officials are overwhelmingly powerful because of their expertise, knowledge, organizational skills, independent decision-making, and maintenance of 'secrecy of knowledge and intentions' (Weber 1922:572, 1918:333–342). Under these circumstances, then, the bureaucratic official has the real power and the political officeholder, whether democratically elected or not, is always in the position of 'a dilettante against the professional expert' (Weber 1922:572).

The bureaucracy of the police

It requires no great stretch of the imagination to conceive of public police institutions as bureaucracies. Formally sanctioned by states with the task of order maintenance and crime control, police institutions are arguably the most visible and concrete expression of the state's monopoly over the means of coercion. Weber himself put forward the conception of the police as bureaucracy when he specified among the functions of the modern state 'the protection of personal security and public order (police)' (Weber 1922:516). Weber also discussed as the most significant political factor that contributed to the furtherance of the bureaucratization process 'the increasing need, in a society accustomed to pacification, for order and protection ("police") in all areas' (Weber 1922:561). It was from then on, Weber continued, that the police had acquired the position of 'God's representative'.

Yet, despite the rather obvious relevance of Weber's bureaucracy and state perspective to police, it has not been very influential in research on social control. Instead of focusing on police organizations as bureaucratic institutions, several police scholars have defended a state-centred theory of social control and police (Busch 1995; Fijnaut 1979; Huggins 1998; Jacobs and O'Brien 1998). Such a perspective holds that the dynamics of policing and international policing are to be accounted for with reference to the political-ideological dictates and interests of the governments of national states. As an elaboration of these political theories, it has also been suggested that police and social control are determined by economic developments associated with the expansion of capitalism (Robinson and Scaglion 1987; Spitzer 1985). Such an economic perspective views the police as a tool in the suppression of the working classes, or more generally, in the control of labour.

Whereas political and economic perspectives share a commitment to explain developments of police and social control in terms of an overarching external variable, a contrasting perspective suggests that police and international police practices cannot be explained in terms of the political and economic conditions they are no doubt confronted with, but are instead determined by internal organizational developments related to a process of bureaucratization. I will here develop such a model on the basis of Weber's theory, but mention should be made of the fact that while a bureaucratic model has been far less applied in scholarly work on police and social control than political/economic perspectives, it has found some application in prior research (although not always with reference to Weber). Apart from the fact that many of these studies are rather limited in scope and apply to only one organization or singular aspect of policing (e.g. Ethington 1987; Ng-Quinn 1990; Theoharis 1992), they mostly find their primary relevance in a normative orientation to expose the negative impact of police discretion and lack of accountability (e.g. O'Reilly 1987; Skolnick 1966). This parallels a development in the sociology of organizations, where—often inspired by Weber's work (see Clegg 1994)—it has been a central concern to develop a critique of excessive bureaucratization (Jacoby 1969; Page 1985). In this literature, bureaucratization becomes virtually synonymous with dehumanization and oppression, and police bureaucratization is criticized in light of principles of democratic control and accountability. As mentioned before, my reliance on Weber serves purposes that are entirely analytical, using concepts from the Weberian bureaucracy perspective to construct a model that accounts for variation in empirical reality.

Finally, it should be mentioned that a more sustained development of studies of the police similar to the bureaucratic perspective has relied on the work, not of Weber, but of Michel Foucault, especially his theories of discipline and governmentality (Foucault 1975, 1978, 1982a, b). These studies have argued that various dimensions of social control are not justified in terms of a system of sovereign legality but are conceived as an efficient management of a depoliticized society of living subjects, irrespective of state and market (e.g. Simon 1988; Stenson 1993). Indeed, Foucault's governmentality perspective usefully brings out how certain modalities of power and social control cannot be accounted for with reference to formal legal systems and political orders. Foucault argued that the governmental form of power which developed since the 19th century did not rely on any justification in terms of a centred state or singular 'Prince', but was instead conceived in terms of an efficient economy directed at furthering the fertility of territories and the health and movements of the population. Governmentality broke with any form of state-sanctioned legalism: the legal system merely represented what was judged useful for, or harmful to, a society of living beings. In its effectuation, according to Foucault, governmentality relied on a triple alliance of criminology, statistics, and the police (see Garland

1985; Pasquino 1991b). Criminology provided the necessary knowledge about the regularities which criminal statistics had uncovered and upon which the police could act in both proactive and reactive ways. This perspective of the police, Foucault argued, was very broadly understood as 'a program of government rationality . . . to create a system of regulation of the general conduct of individuals whereby everything would be controlled to the point of self-sustenance, without the need for intervention' (Foucault 1982:241). In sum, these police activities were not intimately linked with and restricted to the dictates of formal legal systems but operated more independently on the basis of a broad, near total understanding of power.

A Foucauldian model can usefully bring out aspects of an autonomously operating technology of policing, but the theory has also been criticized, first, because it cannot deal satisfactorily with the ambiguous structures of law and social control in terms of justice as well as coercion (Habermas 1985:279–343), and, second, because it neglects the place of punishment and control in a broader societal context as well as the continued relevance of the formal legal order (Lacombe 1996; Smith 2000). Although there is some debate on the validity of these criticisms against Foucault (Deflem 1997a; Garland 1990, 1997; Simon 1994), it is clear that these two concerns were precisely of key significance from Weber's theoretical perspective. Indeed, on the one hand, Weber developed a theory of the effects of bureaucratization in addition to a descriptive-explanatory analysis of its course and outcome in a comparative-historical context, and, on the other hand, Weber developed a theoretical perspective that took into account the external conditions that favoured the bureaucratization process but that also emphasized its internal organizational logic (Albrow 1970:45–49; Page 1985:162–171; Mommsen 1987). Therefore, also, although a Foucauldian analysis can to some extent surely be complementary to a perspective based on Weber's bureaucracy theories, the model advanced in this book focuses attention on the dynamics that work towards bureaucratic autonomy without neglecting the external contexts in which bureaucratization takes place.

A Weberian model of international policing

Because my research on the internationalization of the police function centres on developments that accompanied the consolidation of Western national states since the middle of the 19th century, the model of international police that I introduce in this book rests on the assumption that certain societal, especially demographic, political, and economic conditions favoured the formation of specialized police institutions that are sufficiently formalized to conceive of them as bureaucracies. I cannot here provide an in-depth analysis of this development but briefly summarize the existing research (Bayley 1985:23–50; Manning 1977:41–71; Ng-Quinn 1990). Among the conditions favourable to the development of police bureaucracies can be mentioned a greater need for a specialized organization of crime control and order maintenance as societies grew in size and complexity. This relates to demographic developments (growing population size and density) as well as to increasing urbanization, industrialization, and technological progress. The most relevant political factor is that states concentrated ever more policy tasks in a centralized administration. Although these developments have not been accomplished evenly from one society to the next, bureaucratization tendencies are witnessed wherever national states have developed (Jacoby 1969:156–159; Parsons 1964:503–507; Torstendahl 1991).

Rationalization processes have historically influenced the bureaucratization of the modern police function across Western societies (Bayley 1985:23–52; Mawby 1990:16–33).[4] Despite national variations (which I will explain below in greater detail for German and US police institutions), modern police development has gone in the direction of the creation of a specialized bureaucratic apparatus in both functional and organizational respects (Bayley 1985:12–14; Manning 1977:109–111; Skolnick 1966:235–239). Functionally, public police institutions have gradually come to be responsible for order maintenance and crime control, tasks which are specified in a formal system of laws and for the fulfilment of which the police can legitimately resort to force. Organizationally, bureaucratization of the police is reflected in a variety of characteristics which closely follow Weber's typology: though separated from the military, police bureaucracies are hierarchically ordered with a clear chain of command and internal structure (discipline); agents are formally trained experts who, as full-time appointed officials (professionalization), perform specialized duties (division of labour); and policing operates on the basis of a legitimate

[4] The fact that my analytical model is rooted in theories of rationalization processes that have taken place in Western national states no doubt limits the generalizability of my research findings, and alternative models may be needed to account for non-Western developments, such as in the context of colonial policing (see, e.g. Deflem 1994a).

system of rules and procedures (professionalism); and is driven toward the use of technically efficient means, such as secrecy and force (purposive rationality).

Based on the view of police as bureaucracy, I will outline a two-tier model that differentiates between the structural conditions and operational motives of international policing. Structural conditions refer to a social environment that needs to be present for national police agencies to be in the position to move beyond the confines of their respective national jurisdictions. These conditions are necessary but insufficient for police institutions to engage in international cooperation. When the structural conditions are met, I argue, international police organizations need an additional motivational basis to become operational. The fact that national police agencies are in a position to cooperate internationally does not yet provide any reasons for collaboration if there are no organizationally defined goals that international police operations should fulfil. Relying on Weber, I will specify the structural conditions and operational motives of international policing in terms of two aspects of bureaucratic autonomy: 1) as a structural condition for cooperation across national borders, police institutions must have gained a sufficient degree of independence as specialized bureaucracies from their respective governments; and 2) international police cooperation plans can be operationalized when participating police institutions share a system of knowledge on international crime, including information on its empirical state and expertise for its control.

My first proposition relates to conditions that need to be fulfilled to create the structural opportunity of international policing. These conditions must be met regardless of whether created opportunities will actually lead to successful and stable cooperation. Peter Blau (1964:64–68) has specified conditions for exchange among collectivities by suggesting that inter-organizational exchange can occur when organizations are interdependent, for instance because of utilitarian-economic considerations in terms of organizational tasks and objectives. In the absence of supranational enforcement duties, police bureaucracies cannot be interdependent in practical respects in quite the same way as other organizations are in terms of a functional division of labour. However, given similarity in the institutional position of police bureaucracies across nations, formal congruence among police institutions in terms of their positions of relative independence from governments can be considered a condition for inter-organizational cooperation across national jurisdictions. Thus, as a corollary to the fact police institutions have become specialized and segregated from other state administrations such as the military (Manning 1977:111), I maintain that they can engage in cooperation with corresponding bureaucracies, i.e. other police institutions, from other nation-states, because of their similar high degree of detachment from their respective political centres. This detachment, I agree with Weber, is enabled by an increasing rationalization of police organization and police tasks in an instrumental manner that is primarily concerned with efficiency and impersonal calculability of means. The conditions of these rationalization processes are, as I will explain in this book, primarily technical in nature, related to advances in the means of criminal investigation and police technique (see Chapter 2). An important consequence of increasing rationalization in police institutions is that highly bureaucratized police institutions can function 'as a machine' and are 'capable of universal application' (Weber 1922:561, 126). Such universal applicability of police bureaucracies cuts across the boundaries of national states.

A high degree of bureaucratic autonomy will be indicated by a relative independence of police institutions from their respective governments in respect of the organization of those institutions and their field of operations. Bureaucratic autonomy is revealed by a commitment to professional standards of policing, rather than political loyalty, as reflected in the appointment process, police training and recruitment, and, most importantly, the planning and execution of strategies. If institutional independence is not or insufficiently achieved, police cooperation will remain limited with respect to international participation and will not extend beyond the confines of politically akin states, i.e. national states that resemble one another in ideological respects and/or that entertain close ties in international relations.

The notion of institutional independence does not imply an absolute autonomy or complete detachment of police institutions from the political centres of states. On the contrary, public police institutions are always agents of state control and as public institutions they can derive their legitimacy only from states. The institutional independence of the police, therefore, remains a matter of degree relative to the (historically variable) control from national governments. Yet, with these qualifications in mind, the condition of relative autonomy of police from the political powerholders of the state relates to the fact that police bureaucracies rely on a means–ends rationality to employ what are held to be the technically most efficient, not necessarily the politically most opportune means given set goals. The irony is that police institutions can then perform enforcement duties they were formally sanctioned to perform by the centre of the state in a manner that is no longer bound to its political dictates.

I focus on bureaucratic autonomy from politics although I discussed earlier political as well as economic perspectives of social control as alternatives to my model. Yet, it is to be noted that the economic model of social control is not far removed from a political outlook inasmuch as it views the state in instrumentalist terms as being controlled by the ruling economic classes. Indeed, when, as in this book, the focus is on public police institutions, there is an inherent imbalance between economic and political forces because only political states formally sanction the institutionalization of legitimate internal coercion. In other words, based on a state-centred theory, political élites control police institutions directly, whereas a neo-Marxian model would hold that economic élites exert influence via their control of the state. Therefore, my first proposition introduces independence of police institutions from the political context of nation-states.

> Proposition 1: *The greater the extent to which national police institutions have gained a position of institutional independence from their respective political centres, the greater is the chance that those institutions are in a position to engage in international cooperation.*

An alternative way of formulating this proposition is that police institutions are in a position to cooperate internationally when they have gained bureaucratic independence from the political centres of their respective states (formal bureaucratic autonomy). Or, conversely, a lack or low degree of institutional autonomy will impede the formation of international police structures. Police institutions that remain tied to the political centres of their states will either insulate themselves from international duties to stay within the boundaries of their national jurisdictions, or will engage in transnational activities that are intimately related to national tasks. International activities under these circumstances will not go beyond unilaterally conducted police operations abroad, temporary bilateral cooperation for specific duties, or limited international forms of cooperation among police of politically like-minded states.

My first proposition specifies structural conditions that allow for the possibility of international policing, but yet to be spelled out are the operational motives police agencies must develop in order to accomplish international cooperation. These motives form the basis around which to form a new field of activities that transcends the borders of national jurisdictions. In this respect, I rely on Meyer and Rowan's (1977) thesis that the operational rules and procedures of bureaucratic organizations function as 'myths' that define problems and specify solutions in terms framed by and for the bureaucracy (see, also, Crank 1994; Crank and Langworthy 1992). It is useful to call these cultural systems of knowledge myths, not to convey the notion that they are empirically false but that it is not primarily relevant whether or not they are. Together with the level of attained organizational efficiency, these myths influence the organization's legitimacy, activities, and resources, while minimizing external inspection and control.[5] In the case of policing, the organizationally defined myth that motivates police cooperation across national borders is provided by a professional interest in and conception of the control of international crime. The reasons the police can lay claim to define, and offer appropriate solutions to, the international crime problem relate to the fact that bureaucratic police institutions, as Weber (1918:352–354) argued about bureaucracies in general, accumulate specialized knowledge, including official information about the extent of and expertise to deal with international crime. Specialized systems of knowledge on international crime in terms of the proper means of objectives of international policing have operational consequences across national jurisdictions to the extent that they are shared among national police institutions.

> Proposition 2: *The greater the extent to which national police institutions can rely on a common organizational interest in the fight against international crime, the greater is the chance that those institutions will participate in international police cooperation.*

Formulated alternatively this proposition states that international police cooperation is more likely when police institutions have established sys-

[5] This resonates with a central theme discussed by organizational theorists. Mary Douglas (1986), for instance, has argued that an institution acquires legitimacy by showing how its rules and practices are the only answer to a problem it had itself formulated. In the case of police bureaucracies, Jerome Skolnick (1966:238) has spoken similarly of 'organizational interests' and 'official innovation' to indicate the tendency of modern police to set its own agenda.

tems of expert knowledge related to the fight against international crime (operational bureaucratic autonomy). Or, conversely, international police cooperation is unlikely to succeed—even if structural conditions are favourable—when participating agencies do not share an agenda in the fight against international crime.

Bureaucratization, professionalization, and international police cooperation

The first two propositions of my theoretical model point to the bureaucratization of police institutions as a critical determinant of international police cooperation, arguing that formal and operational bureaucratic autonomy increase the chances of international cooperation on a broad multilateral scale. This perspective attributes special significance to the expertise of police officials and their position, skills, and commitment as professionals. Based on insights from the sociology of organizations and professions (see Abbott 1988; Halliday 1987; Macdonald 1995), a brief excursion may clarify my theoretical position on bureaucratization and professionalization.

In the context of this book, a professional understanding of the police function with respect to means and objectives refers to conceptions of policing that are determined on the basis of claims to expertise in formal-rational terms, i.e. that are formulated in terms of efficiency standards irrespective of any ideological persuasions and other dictates of the governments of states. A professional conception of policing, in other words, is in contradiction with a notion of police as a mere extension of the power of the centre of states. My perspective harmonizes with police historian Samuel Walker's (1977) conception of police professionalization as involving, in the first instance, a claim to expertise and knowledge and, as a result, professional autonomy and a commitment to a service ideal. Expertise and knowledge concern techniques of the proper means of policing and information on the empirical conditions of police objectives. Professional autonomy involves control over access to and exercise of the profession (e.g. training, membership) as well as internal methods of supervision and control (e.g. for promotion). The service ideal, finally, relates to the police function as fulfilling a publicly recognized concern that is relevant to all of society, rather than to the members of the profession alone. Thus, the profession of policing is an ideal, but as an aspired ideal nonetheless clearly a reality with important consequences, which in terms of the history of international policing, as

I will show in this study, reveals that the 'emergence of nearly autonomous police bureaucracies is one of the main themes of modern police history' (Walker 1977:xi). In this tendency towards autonomy, professional claims to knowledge of technical expertise and accumulated information will be reaffirmed as the central driving force (see also Macdonald 1995:157–186).

As such, I defend a neo-Weberian perspective that conceives of police professionalization and police bureaucratization as two complementary processes, rather than two opposing forces. It is theoretically appropriate to argue that professionalization and bureaucratization go hand in hand on the basis of the Weberian perspective to conceive of these processes as manifestations of broader societal developments of rationalization (see Halliday 1983, 1987; Murray, Dingwall, and Eekelaar 1983; Rueschemeyer 1983). Within a Weberian framework, indeed, the emphasis of research is resolutely on the legitimation and exercise of power within a broader context of societal rationalization, which in the case of Western societies has taken the form of instrumental rationalization, and which organizationally has found its purest expression in the bureaucratic forms accompanying states and markets. It is in the specific institutional setting of the state bureaucracy that the police bureaucrat as professional is confronted with, and claims autonomy from, the political powerholder as amateur.

To be sure, sociologists of organizations and professions have shown that professionalization and bureaucratization do not necessarily go neatly hand in hand, especially when it concerns those professions that manage to gain autonomy and create their own culture of rules and network of relations separate from the institutional settings in which they practice their profession (Davies 1983). The legal and medical professions are exemplary in this respect (see, e.g. Engel 1969; Halliday 1987; Horobin 1983). However, in the case of public police institutions a separation between professional and bureaucratic components is not accomplished. For indeed, the profession of public police officials does not exist outside the institutional boundaries of the bureaucratic apparatus of nation states. On the contrary, as the evidence presented in this work will demonstrate, Walker (1977) is right to suggest that unlike the professions of law, education, and medicine, 'police service has evolved along bureaucratic lines' and that 'police careers are largely restricted to closed bureaucratic structures' (pp. x–xi). Unlike the free professions, then, police professionals have evolved from 'humble servants' to self-conscious experts within the setting of state bureaucracies (van Rhee 1999; see also De Lint 1999; Walker 1996).[6]

Relatedly, to the extent that police professionalization implies a (sub)culture of shared values and an accompanying network of officials, and in this sense includes a personal dimension, police culture and police bureaucracy mutually reinforce one another. In fact, in the internationalization of the police function, as this book will show, a global police culture emerged that not only did not hinder, but critically contributed to foster international ties among police institutions that were highly bureaucratized. Although it is no doubt true that Max Weber in his work neglected the informal aspects of bureaucracy (Herbert 1998; Heyman 1995), an inclusion of such considerations need not undermine the value of a perspective of (ideal-typically understood) bureaucracies, but can on the contrary contribute to unravel an additional important component in the bureaucratization process (see Blau 1955).

How can the concomitant professionalization and bureaucratization be accounted for theoretically as two complementary developments? The key, I argue, is that the tendency of state bureaucracies to gain institutional independence is itself already a paradoxical development. The very notion of bureaucratic autonomy is paradoxical inasmuch as it refers to an increasing independence of state institutions from the very centres that created them and from which they derive the legitimation of authority. My notion of institutional independence, therefore, should not be understood to imply that highly bureaucratized police institutions do not remain related to the governments of states, but only that they are autonomous in the planning and execution of their operations and strategies on the basis of professional considerations of expertise and knowledge. As such, any potential challenges from professional police associations to the strict code of conduct of bureaucratic authority (as well as the potential tensions between high-level and low-level members within the profession) hint at a tension that in the case of public police institutions can only operate within the bureaucratic context. Historically, indeed, the police profession did

[6] In respect of the liberation from institutional boundaries that marks the free professions, a parallel in the area of policing is found in the private police and security industry. The internationalization of private policing is a much more recent phenomenon, however. Although I will discuss some historical antecedents, it was indeed not until recent decades that the 'world' of private policing has acquired more than mere metaphorical meaning (see Johnston 1992, 2000).

not only emerge in the context of the bureaucratic state, the profession has in its further evolution not been dislodged from the institutional setting of state bureaucracies. In sum, the modern police institution must be conceived as a professional bureaucracy, their members as 'bureau-professionals' (Davies 1983:183). Therefore, also, the specialists of the internal and external coercion powers of modern states, in the institutions of police and military, respectively, complement one another as fellow 'professionals in violence' (Janowitz 1960:3).

The nationality of international policing

At the beginning of this Introduction, I discussed how globalization scholars have speculated on the various forms of globalization and its relationship with local and national processes and structures. In terms of the form of international police operations, I introduced the distinction between events that (supranationally) affect police institutions in nations across the globe, transnational police operations that are unilaterally instigated by one national police system, and international forms of conflict and cooperation. I have in the above outlined theoretical model of bureaucratization placed a premium on the form of international police cooperation because it involves an attempt to forge alliances among police systems jointly in order to transcend the jurisdictions of their respective national states. Cooperation, therefore, is quite unlike other forms of international police activities, specifically supranational processes affecting policing and transnational police strategies. Supranational events shaping police institutions in similar ways may not be recognized as such, although factual harmonization may be expected to increase the likelihood of cooperation. Transnational operations on foreign soil or against foreign nationals will not involve other police systems unless such operations become known (and often contested), again affecting the likelihood of cooperation. As such, international police cooperation and the formation of a police organization with broad international participation are clearly central among the various forms of international policing.

In terms of the relationship between national and international processes and structures, my theoretical perspective relies on insights from globalization scholars who have argued that even though there are certain trends of harmonization and supranationality (Albrow 1997; Meyer et al. 1997), global processes also impact upon nations and other localities differentially (Robertson 1995; Röhl and Magen 1996;

Yearley 1996). In terms of international cooperation across national states, this reaffirms those national states and their institutions as the central units of analysis inasmuch as they remain the participants in cooperation efforts. This viewpoint will in this book serve to defend the argument that international policing efforts are typically maintained as collaborative networks between national police systems, each of which separately also engages in unilaterally instigated transnational activities. These internal and external dimensions of policing, I argue, are to be conceived as existing side by side as two manifestations of the state-controlled monopoly of force. International police activities, therefore, typically do not conflict with national tasks, because international work is conceived explicitly as a dimension of the primary function of police to enforce the laws of the land (the police as representative of the state monopoly of force). Only in this way can police institutions make sense of the paradoxical fact that international police operations inevitably transcend the boundaries of the circumscribed national and otherwise localized jurisdictions police enforcement duties are formally subject to.

Proposition 3: *National interests remain paramount in the planning and execution of international police activities and organizations.*

This perspective conforms to the viewpoint that although national police institutions are not isolated from one another, they remain primarily involved with securing national-states' monopoly of legitimate coercion (Garland 1996; Herbert 1999). This is not only shown in unilaterally instigated transnational police activities responding to nationally defined police tasks, but also in international police cooperation efforts. Of course, planned and initiated cooperation efforts among police institutions across national borders represent a degree of attained internationality beyond the varied concerns of participating police. But even when united in joint organizational networks surrounding a common cause, as I will show, national police systems are influenced differently by, and variously react to, these global processes. Even despite collaborative activities and similarities in influencing factors, police systems across the world by and large keep their distinct traits based on national cultures and traditions and remain too varied in structure and activities to speak of a truly global trend of cross-cultural harmonization. I suggest an important persistence of nationality that researchers on police globalization must take into account.

The theoretical challenge of international policing

Before I proceed with my analysis on the basis of the outlined theory, a brief excursion may be useful to clarify my theoretical model relative to competing perspectives in the literature on international policing. Generally, it is clear that not only is international policing a relatively new and unexplored field of scholarly attention, many of its discussions are void of theoretical explorations and remain almost entirely or predominantly descriptive in nature (e.g. Anderson 1989; Benyon 1996; Fooner 1973, 1989). Of course, descriptively oriented empirical investigations do expand knowledge by exposing the hitherto relatively unknown dimensions and conditions of change and continuity of international policing. As such, these studies no doubt play a serious role in our scholarship. Complementary to this descriptive work are those contributions that seek to contribute to a better, more efficient, and/or more just state of international policing. These writings are, on the one hand, those that are technical in nature and attempt to contribute to the management and administration of international police strategies (see, e.g. contributions in Koenig and Das 2001). Although not meant to be scholarly, this work is at its very best surely informed by scholarship (e.g. Bayley 1995, 1997; Deflem 2001; Fijnaut 1991, 1995). On the other hand, normative issues in the world of international policing are addressed in work that focuses on concerns of justice involved with police internationalization and the potential or real threat in terms of human rights, democracy, and civil liberties (e.g. Brodeur 2000; Hebenton and Thomas 1995; Winer 1997). Such contributions play a critical role in a society's public sphere, but they cannot form the basis for, nor should they be confused with, explanatory and theoretical work on the conditions and consequences of international policing.

While descriptive, technical, and normative studies of international policing can justly claim their distinct if limited place in the literature, it is more troublesome for the state of our knowledge of the field that a-theoretical contributions sometimes naively adopt a bland functionalist model which assumes that international police operations are designed and executed in response to international crime (e.g. Duino 1960; Fooner 1975; Forrest 1955; Santiago 2000; Tullett 1963). Then, it is supposed, rather than researched—let alone proven—that international policing has assumed greater relevance because of 'the increasingly violent, crime-infested, and dangerous world of today' (Das and Kratcoski 2001:25). No arguments are made to explain the dynamics of such causalities, not to mention that, as I will show in this book, they can by and large not be supported by available empirical evidence. Functionalist explanations merely restate, and assume it is legitimate to transpose at the level of scholarly explanation, the internal motives of international policing operations as they are put forward by participating agencies and officials. But, naturally, the rationalizations of the participants cannot be confused with the conditions of their behaviour.

Relatedly, there are contributions that assume that the dynamics of international policing can be explained solely in terms of the enforcement of international dimensions of national and local legal systems and/or regulations of international law (e.g. Gibney 1990; Möllman 1969; Walther 1968; Zagaris 1996; Zagaris and Resnick 1997). In this context, international policing is intimately connected with formal systems of law to suggest that the harmonization of national criminal codes and the codification of international criminal law are the central driving forces of international policing. Treaties between the governments of national states are conceived as the necessary basis of international law enforcement. But, revealing a shortcoming similar to functionalist interpretations, such legalistic perspectives of international policing merely assume and never even question the linkages and dynamics between law and policing that scholarship precisely needs to address. My study here will precisely show that the association between policing and legal systems, as between police and crime, is more problematic and dissonant.

Among the theoretically more informed perspectives of international policing, as I have already mentioned, are state-centred and economic-deterministic perspectives. These theories suggest that the structures and processes of international policing are determined by the political–ideological dictates of the governments of states and/or, relatedly, the interests of those classes that control the free market. Economic theories have been less popular among scholars interested in the dynamics of international police strategies involving public police institutions, but the approach has been applied to the internationalization of private policing and has had some impact in the literature that focuses on security and information issues in international policing. Les Johnston (2000), for instance, argues that trends in global capitalism have brought about a global security market, which is aligned with the international dimensions of public police to refashion the global state of international policing in a fragmented way. With respect to the role of information in economics, Peter Manning (2000) has emphasized the role of information technologies in the constellation of international policing, and, relatedly, the changing world economy, the expansion of the free market, and the implications thereof for the flow of information across national borders. Information is thereby considered as having been commodified into a property, access to and use of which influences the planning of new, international methods of control (new methods of 'cyber-policing' are prototypical in this respect; see also Chan et al. 2001).

State-centred theories are a more common theoretical explanation of international police (e.g. Busch 1995; Fijnaut 1979; Huggins 1998). The popularity of this approach appears to be determined by the historical development that the institution of modern police was at its inception representative and protective of conservative political regimes and that 19th-century cooperation among national police systems, especially in Europe, was targeted primarily at the politically suspect opponents of established governments. The theoretically relevant implication, state-centred scholars argue, is that international police strategies are not only related to a nation-state's foreign policy, but are deliberately constructed and executed as a politically motivated contribution to a powerful state's international security agenda and quest for international dominance. Martha Huggins (1998), for instance, argues in favour of an internationalization perspective which posits that international policing, specifically in the form of assistance to police agencies abroad and operations on foreign soil, is 'one mechanism for a country to gain political control over another state' (p. 19). Thus, it is to be noted state-centred theories make a much stronger claim than political-science perspectives of international policing, which situate and research the dynamics of international policing in relation to a nation's foreign policy and the world of international relations between the governments of states (e.g. Anderson et al. 1995; Andreas 2000; Cottam and Marenin 1999; Fijnaut 1993b; Liang 1992). Here, international policing issues are related to the foreign policy of national states without necessarily attributing to their planning and implementation any sinister motives of global domination. Important trends such as 'imperialism' in international policing and the involvement of intelligence and military agencies in police tasks now become questions of research, rather than assumptions (Sheptycki 2000b:9). Most ground-breaking in this line of thought has been Ethan Nadelmann's (1993) study of the international aspects of US policing in the war on drugs. Arguing for a multi-causal perspective, Nadelmann is particularly interested in the diffusion of norms across national boundaries as influencing national policies of prohibition, including its impact on the institutions and practices of policing.

This book will show that the central problem of state-centred and economic perspectives of policing is that they fall short in terms of empirical adequacy requirements of constructing theoretical models that can account for variation in reality. Although some disagreement with respect to the analytical merit of their approach may remain, state-centred and economic perspectives take valid conclusions of research far beyond the immediate cases of their investigation to argue that all international police operations are politically motivated because certain developments in the 19th century were, or that interests of free-market control must be functionally implied in international policing because of the association of certain developments therewith, especially in more recent times. As such, only continued empirical research can strengthen our answers. Additionally, however, state-centred and economic theories are blinded by a hyper-normative understanding of their research subject and therefore fail to grasp the analytical strengths of a bureaucratization approach. Huggins (1998), for instance, writes that 'in every sense all policing is political' (p. 17). Such a proposition is not only conceptually meaningless, it can have no identifiable empirical usage. Instead, the variable connections and dissociations between the political centres of states, on the one hand, and the state's bureaucratic institutions, on the other, must be carefully examined. Thus, I agree with police scholar Neil Walker (1996), who formulated the conundrum of international policing very well: 'Policing is obviously influenced by political ideas and interests, but how does this influence tend to be expressed? In what sense, if at all, does the sphere of policing retain a degree of independence from wider political forms and developments?' (p. 251). As the evidence in this book will show, the answer is that police institutions cannot only maintain a considerable degree of independence in terms of means and objectives, but that such conditions of bureaucratic autonomy are indispensable for the planning and execution of successful forms of international police cooperation.

Importantly, to posit an institutional independence of police institutions does not mean that the police and policing are not related to wider societal, especially political conditions. On the contrary, formally charged with order maintenance and crime control, public police institutions are arguably the most visible and concrete expression of the state's legitimate monopoly over the (internal) means of coercion (see Bittner 1970; Melossi 1990; Reiner 1985). In fact, the proclaimed reliance of police institutions and other bureaucracies on principles of efficiency and their presentation in strictly professional terms are themselves important strategies of domination (Weber 1922:122–130). However, what is avoided in my theoretical model is a 'naive determinism' that commits the correlational fallacy that political influences on the police are all-explanatory of the dynamics of policing (Walker 1996:274). Instead, I suggest, the structures and mechanisms of international policing cannot be completely explained by the ideological dictates of the political centre of states, and, furthermore, that international police cooperation on a broad multilateral scale is driven precisely by developments of bureaucratization related to the means and objectives of professional policing.

The relative dissociation of the police from politics does not contradict the notion, which my theoretical perspective additionally defends, that the participation of police institutions in international initiatives continues to serve national policing interests. To conceive of these two components of my theory as contradictory, or to commit the mistake of not clearly differentiating between them, can only be based on a failure to distinguish between the two central components of nation-states as involving both a political and a cultural dimension. It need not concern us here that philosophers and social theorists from Hegel to Marx and Habermas have pondered the significance of a just connection between these two dimensions of nation and state (e.g. Habermas 1962), as to point out the relevance of the hyphen in nation-state and its consequences for the state's bureaucratic institutions. Indeed, paralleling my perspective that the process of bureaucratization is an essentially paradoxical development, my theory of international police cooperation argues against state-centred theories without neglecting the continued persistence of nationality. In this connection it is relevant to recall that nationalism historically refers not to a political claim of national governments but to a cultural claim of a people and its traditions. In similar vein, I argue that under influence of bureaucratization processes police institutions gradually break with the political centres of state, but without surrendering the traits and ambitions of their respective national cultures and traditions. Therefore, also, while international police strategies by definition transcend the boundaries of national states, nationally defined concerns continue to influence policing, even when they relate to supranational, transnational, or international (cooperative or conflictual) developments. International police strategies always cross but never erase boundaries. In the tracing of these developments from the middle of the 19th century up until the relatively recent period of World War II and its aftermath, therefore, a Weberian paradigm remains useful.

Finally, some comment is in order on those theories of international policing that build on the governmentality perspective developed by Michel Foucault (1978). As I stated before, this perspective also, like a Weberian viewpoint, argues for a 'relocation' of police 'away from the political centre' (Shearing 1996:286). However, governmentality studies of policing extend this ambition to defend a postmodern perspective. Indeed, especially as appropriated and popularized by Nikolas Rose and his devotees associated with the journal *Economy and Society* (see, e.g. Barry, Osborne, and Rose 1996; O'Malley 1997; Rose 1999), the governmentality theory of policing argues against a state-centred or otherwise localized theory of control in favour of an uncovering of the increasingly complex shifts and re-alignments among and between the various components of governance, including formal police institutions. Reminiscent of Foucault's (1981) statement that policing in the governmentality mode ultimately 'includes everything' (p. 248), governmentality scholars argue that the complexity of governmentality is such that it defies one model of explanation bringing logic to a constellation that is essentially a diversified patchwork. In consequence, to use the terminology of Jean-François Lyotard (1979), all that is left is a generalized 'incredulity toward metanarratives' (p. xxiv). In the area of international policing, James Sheptycki (1998a, b) has contributed centrally to a postmodern perspective, arguing that cross-border policing comprises such a multifarious hybrid of strategies and agencies that it defies clear-cut categorization, particularly in terms of assessing the rise of transnational policing and its role in diminishing or strengthening state power.

The theory I advanced in this work and its application in the coming chapters will show the merit of rejecting a postmodern approach to international policing on more than theoretical grounds alone. As an approach, postmodernist theorizing must ultimately abandon a rational foundation to resort to aesthetic posturing or, at best, a crypto-normativism (Habermas 1985). As a model of explanation, more importantly, a postmodern approach appears to totally abandon standards of scientific inquiry, especially in terms of empirical adequacy. But what I wish to show in this book is that increased complexity in the internationalization of policing need not imply that its historical antecedents cannot be empirically traced and its various components unravelled in terms of a theoretically founded comprehensive approach. My bureaucratization perspective offers such a model that can be falsified.

Because in this study I adopt a perspective of the police to include all those functions, activities, and agencies defined as such in the societies under investigation, it is worthwhile to describe the development of the police in Germany and the United States within their respective political contexts. For the important variations that exist in the political histories of Europe and America will affect the organization and function of national police institutions and influence their involvement in international policing initiatives. The following sections explain the basic elements of these national histories in order to offer a useful historical context for the in-depth investigations of international policing dynamics in the chapters to come.

'Omnes et singulatim': On the origins of the modern police

> Police is the state's system for order with respect to internal security, beauty, comfort, population, morality, and nourishment.
> *Carl Gottlob Rößig, 1786.*

> One cannot understand the difficulties [the police] meet without close acquaintance, and a closer acquaintance often shows that many of them are far wiser than the public knows. Yet it is equally true that many of them are ignorant, inefficient, simply bullies in uniform. They are often brutal, and the terror of the weak, rather than a terror to evil doers.
> *The Encyclopedia of Social Reform, 1897.*

Foucault's theory of governmentality holds that the police function is aimed comprehensively at administering everything that can contribute to the constitution of social life. Importantly, this peculiar police concept is not an analytical tool of Foucault's invention. Instead, as I will show in this section, the governmental notion of the police was historically part and parcel of a theory and practice of power rooted in the development of modern national states. Particularly in Continental Europe, a broadly conceived notion of the police influenced the establishment of police institutions that would gradually develop into bureaucratic agencies with more delineated tasks.

Police and politics in the process of German unification

The history of German police systems is marked by waves of decentralization and centralization corresponding to a process of German political unification (see Barber 1993; Carr 1991; Droz 1983; Holborn 1982; Hughes 1992). A unified German nation-state did not exist until the formation of the German Empire in 1871. Until the Vienna Treaty of 1815, Germany was a collection of several hundred dukedoms, free-towns, and principalities, loosely united in the Holy Roman Empire of the German Nation. Between 1794 and 1814, large parts of the Holy Roman Empire were brought under French control. In 1815, after Prussia, Austria, and Russia had successfully allied against the French armies, the Vienna Treaty formalized a unification of the German territories in the German Confederation (*Deutscher Bund*), a federal union that comprised thirty-eight states, with Austria and Prussia as the dominant powers.

Transformations of German police institutions followed the political unification process.[7] Initially, the police function in the German territories concerned the administration of all matters concerning the '*politeia*', i.e. the constitution of town or state. From the 16th century onwards, this conception of the police merged with a notion of '*politesse*' that conceived of policing in terms of the provision of order, welfare, and security (Loening 1910). In the 17th-century German states, this concept of 'good police' (*gute Policey*) concerned the observance and furtherance of all aspects of public life that affected the population's happiness (*Glückseligkeit*). This police concept, then, aimed very broadly at positively instituting and advancing happiness rather than merely responding negatively to adversities or breaches of law. From the 18th century onwards, the German police function would begin to include tasks related to the prevention of public dangers and other matters of internal security. A counterpart to the externally oriented function of the military, this police ideal was in the German territories first codified in the Prussian *Landrecht* Law of 1794, which defined the police as 'the necessary apparatus for the establishment of public peace, security and order, and for the deterrence of dangers facing the public or single members thereof' (in Liang 1992:2). However,

[7] Among the sources I used in this section are: Harnischmacher and Semerak 1986:1–71; Knemeyer 1978, 1980; Lüdtke 1982; Mawby 1990:16–33; Wolzendorff 1905, 1906.

although the police function was now conceived in terms of the dual tasks of order maintenance and crime control, police objectives were not defined with reference to formalized legal systems but were instead based on policies of life, health, and property, specified in a system of knowledge known as police-sciences (*Polizeiwissenschaften*) (Lüdtke 1992b; von der Groeben 1984:435–438).

In 1848, in the wake of a steadily growing capitalist system and the economic crises it produced, revolutionary unrest spread over Europe, aiming to overturn the dictatorial rules of Europe's autocratic governments (Holborn 1982:47–55; Langer 1971). Established regimes responded harshly and, in consequence, also strengthened their police. In Prussia, the police function was again comprehensively defined (e.g. Fallati 1844; Rau 1853). The Prussian Police Administration Law of 11 March 1850 stipulated as the tasks of the police: 'the protection of the person and of property; the care for life and health; the order, security and ease of traffic on public streets, roads and places, bridges, shores and waters; and everything else which from a police point of view must be included among the special interests of the towns and their members' (Harnischmacher and Semerak 1986:59).[8]

The unrest of 1848 did not at first affect the precarious balance of power between Austria and Prussia. This would change from the 1850s onwards when Prussia witnessed more favourable economic developments. Tensions between the two countries continued to mount after the accession of Wilhelm I to the Prussian throne in 1861 and, even more so, in the next year when Otto von Bismarck became Minister-President. Bismarck's aggressive foreign policy eventually led to the Seven-Weeks War between Austria and Prussia in 1866. Prussia's victory led the state to further strengthen its conservative rule and establish the North-German Confederation (1867), a federal union that excluded Austria. Provoked by Bismarck's tight control over Germany, France declared war against Prussia in 1870. A year after the French defeat, the German Empire was formed, uniting the northern and southern German states under Prussian dominance.

There was no one national police system in the German Empire. However, there were trends of harmonization of the police function throughout the Empire, particularly because Prussian police adminis-

[8] While this police conception is very broad, it should be noted that there were not many police agents in 19th-century German society. In Berlin, for instance, there were 400,000 inhabitants and only 204 police officers in the first half of the 19th century (Funk 1986:46).

tration served as a model for police reform in other German states. Police institutions in the Empire also became more distinctly limited to order maintenance and crime control. But despite an increasing emphasis on criminal police tasks, the German police function remained very comprehensive compared to other modern police systems. In the period before World War I, for example, the Berlin police issued ordinances regulating the colour of automobiles and the appropriate methods of purchasing fish and fowl (Fosdick 1915c:350–361).

Law and order in the American Union

The earliest systems of American policing were a hybrid of selectively appropriated models imported from various countries.[9] In colonial times, the local county sheriff was the main American law enforcer. In matters of crime control, the sheriff's duties were exclusively re-active, acting only upon a complaint or other information supplied by the public. Yet, as cities grew, more local police agencies were established and these eventually assumed the form of a force constantly present in society. American municipal police systems were largely modelled after the London Metropolitan Police, established in 1829 by the British Home Secretary, Robert Peel. The London Metropolitan Police was a civilian force with uniformed but unarmed agents, whose primary duties were crime prevention and maintenance of order. Borrowing selectively from the London system, American city police, too, began to emphasize patrol and crime prevention. But rejecting the professional representation of national government, American municipal police institutions were organized locally and varied widely from one city to the next. Importantly, US city police agents were appointed by representatives of local government on the basis of favouritism rather than skill. As a result, police corruption and political partisanship were widespread and impacted negatively upon the public perception of the agents. City police boards were created to improve police practices, but it would not be until the early 20th century that US police officers became more accountable to law than influenced by the whims of politicians.

Slowly, state and federal US police agencies also expanded, particularly when Progressive-Era concerns inspired plans to tackle a rising crime problem through expanded government powers. State police forces were organized from 1905 onwards to supplement inadequate

[9] This section relies on: Berman 1987; Eldefonso, Coffey and Grace 1982:14–26; Fogelson 1977:13–67; Johnson 1981; Sullivan 1977:18–43; Walker 1977, 1980.

law enforcement in rural areas and eventually became specialized in enforcing traffic laws. US federal law enforcement grew even more slowly than state police. Congress was reluctant to grant broad powers to federal police agencies, because national police systems were too closely associated with autocratic rule in Europe. Among the first federal agencies to be organized were the US Marshals Service and the US Customs Service, both created in 1789. In 1829, Congress founded a system of inspectors to enforce postal laws, and in 1836 Congress authorized the Postmaster General to pay expenses for agents who would later be called Post Office Inspectors. In 1865, the Secret Service was created in the Treasury Department to enforce counterfeiting laws. The Service gradually received more powers, and in 1902, a year after the assassination of President William McKinley, it was authorized to protect the US President.

Federal US police agencies would not acquire a significant role until several decades into the 20th century. The US Justice Department was created in 1870, but it was not until 1907 that US President Theodore Roosevelt—who between 1895 and 1897 had been Police Commissioner of New York City—asked Congress to legislate a federal detective force in the department. When Congress opposed the President's idea, Roosevelt created the force by executive order. The Bureau's jurisdiction included a variety of violations against federal laws related to interstate commerce, such as burglaries from shipments on interstate trains. The Bureau also responded to the need for police reform and professionalism and would eventually become the leading federal investigative agency in the United States, known since its name change in 1935 as the Federal Bureau of Investigation or FBI.

The dynamics of international policing

Although this study is not oriented at comparing police institutions across nations but at investigating actual connections between them, it must include a comparative focus on account of the fact that national police institutions are the participants in international activities. Characteristics of the police agencies that evolved in Germany and the United States will influence the intensity and form of their respective participation in international work. It is worthwhile, therefore, briefly to discuss their differences and similarities. [10]

[10] This section relies on the sources mentioned in footnotes 7 and 9 as well as on the comparative analyses in Bayley 1975, 1985; Fijnaut 1979; Liang 1992; Mawby 1990.

German and US policing in a comparative perspective

Comparing the historical patterns of German and US policing, the most conspicuous differences are with respect to the influences of the autocratic nature of political authority in the German tradition and the liberal-democratic ideals of government in the United States. In Germany, political autocracy was manifested in a strong police, which was granted very broad powers and was responsible (together with the military) for political tasks emanating from the centre of the state.[11] In the United States, on the other hand, democratic ideals of government—however limited in practice—prevented police from aligning closely with the political dictates of government. Separate police forces at different levels of government were responsible for well-circumscribed tasks that were rooted in formal systems of legality. But although US police agencies were in principle less representative of government, agents were historically less committed to professionalism and more dependent on political appointments.

While the distinct socio-political histories of Germany and the United States influenced variations in the function and organization of their police systems, there are also certain constants. In particular, the police function on both sides of the Atlantic developed gradually into a full-time profession involved primarily with maintenance of order and crime control. This trend towards police professionalization in Germany and the United States corresponds to a general rationalization process that took place across (Western) societies. Police in Germany increasingly developed on the basis of extra-legal systems of policing specified in the evolving *Polizeiwissenschaften*. In the United States, local police agencies became less influenced by political partisanship and more committed to professionalism. In Germany as in other parts of Continental Europe, police professionalization had already been taking place as early as the 17th century, whereas in the United States, police professionalization and, relatedly, police federalization were much later developments that did not mature until the early 20th century. Nonetheless, in both countries can be noticed a gradual move of police institutions away from political dependencies towards the adoption of professional standards of policing.

[11] Note that political policing in this context does not refer to intelligence activities organized in function of national security concerns, but to the powers of agencies of internal coercion to also investigate ideas and practices that are in conflict with the ideological persuasions of national governments.

Transformations of international policing: A look ahead

Differences and similarities between police organization in Germany and the United States will have repercussions for their involvement in international policing activities. Special attention must be given to the political conditions affecting the development of police institutions and their bureaucratization, for, as I explained earlier, public police agencies are formally sanctioned by political bodies of government. However, other factors besides politics, too, will shape international policing activities. A brief review of these conditions will bring out critical elements that the investigations in the coming chapters will focus on.

Among the most obvious influencing factors of international policing in Germany and the United States are matters of a socio-geographical nature. The European continent is characterized by a multitude of relatively small nations that are in close proximity to one another, marked by considerable differences with respect to custom, language, religion, and other aspects of historically evolved national cultures. The high cultural density of the relatively small space that marks Europe readily presents a situation that is conducive to concerns of an international nature, in police as well as other matters. On the American continent, however, the United States is bordered by only two nations, although the frontier demarcating the Union was not fixed rapidly in the course of national development. Furthermore, the United States also harboured considerable cultural and ethnic diversity within its borders, posing special problems for the maintenance of the social fabric. On the basis of these socio-geographical characteristics alone, one can anticipate that the need for police cooperation across national borders was higher among European than among American police. The geographical proximity of national states in Europe may be expected to have presented a strong need for cooperation efforts to transcend the limits of jurisdictional boundaries. In America, cooperation with foreign police would have been less at issue throughout much of the 19th century. Instead, border issues relating to the expanding frontier will initially have shaped international policing with US involvement.

Because of the strong control on police agencies by central autocratic command in Europe, one can anticipate that international police activities during the 19th century were largely instigated for political purposes, attempting to suppress organizations and people believed to threaten the order of established rule. Furthermore, it can be assumed that strong sentiments over national sovereignty will have prevented multilateral efforts to organize international cooperation formally for political purposes. Instead, international political police operations can be expected to have been largely transnational in nature, conducted secretively on the basis of unilateral plans. Whatever police collaboration that may have taken place in political matters will have been informal and temporary on the basis of specific needs, or otherwise limited in international scope to include only police institutions of states approximating one another in political–ideological respects. International policing in 19th-century Europe, then, will have reflected the many turbulent events in international relations on the political scene.

In the United States, police institutions were never aligned with the goals of government in any sense comparable to European police, although there were during the 19th century strong influences from local politics. However, the formal commitment to systems of law separating criminal from political duties can be considered to have excluded US police from involvement in the political activities that were prevalent in Europe. Also, the sharp differences in policing styles in Europe and America, particularly with respect to the acceptability of political tasks and the level of centralization, will have barred any significant degree of transatlantic collaboration before the turn of the century. And with only moderately developed means of transportation and communications, the sheer geographical distance between the two continents will have additionally prevented such cooperation from taking place until more recent times.

Because police institutions in Germany as well as the United States gradually became more committed to professional standards of expert policing, it can be anticipated that a condition of formal bureaucratic autonomy was gradually created that enabled international cooperation. In particular, as the police function from the late 19th century onwards gradually depoliticized, police institutions became more involved more independently with issues of the maintenance of order and crime control. As police agencies of different nations came to similarly recognize these tasks, opportunities for cooperation across the borders of nationally circumscribed jurisdictions will have opened up. One may anticipate this process to have first taken shape in Europe, where a relatively high level of police professionalization was reached earlier than in America. But as the 20th century proceeded in the direction of enhanced police professionalization across the continents, participation in international cooperation will have steadily increased, also enabling cooperation between the German and US police. Technological developments in the means of transportation and communication can be assumed to have further speeded up this process.

In sum, two central developments will guide my investigations of international policing in the chapters to come. First, in the early history of international policing, European police institutions may be expected to have initially taken on a leading role, specifically in terms of political tasks, while increasing police bureaucratization gradually enabled international work pertaining to criminal police duties. Secondly, accompanying this development is a transformation from intrusive to cooperative forms of international policing, replacing primarily unilateral and temporary plans with multilateral efforts to organize international cooperation on a more permanent basis.

Methodology and structure of the argument

The analyses in this study are based on a purposively selected sample of written documents gathered in a variety of libraries and archives (see Appendix 3). The collected documents contain primary and secondary sources, primary sources referring to documents produced as part of international police practices, and secondary documents offering interpretations thereof. Among the primary documents analysed in this book are internal police reports and correspondence, official government documents, proceedings of international police meetings, accounts written by police officials participating in international initiatives, and items published under the auspices of international and national police organizations. As an unobtrusive strategy, the document analysis will focus on naturally occurring instances of international policing. Following the logic of a case-based comparative strategy (Goldstone 1997), my research endeavours to obtain a theoretically informed understanding of international policing strategies. Data from various sources will be confronted to corroborate research findings. Detailed references to the collected documents will enable further testing of my findings.

I have chosen to present the analyses in this book in eight, more or less chronologically divided chapters. This division, however, is not meant primarily to indicate different historical time periods, but corresponds to the various phases and aspects of international police transformation that are relevant from the viewpoint of the theoretical perspective of this book. The chronological order is therefore not always respected. Each chapter will present relevant empirical evidence as well as theoretical reflections thereof. Also, I will typically start analysis with discussions of relevant developments in Germany and Europe, thereafter concentrating on the United States and the American continent. There is nothing principled about this choice other than that it harmonizes with the fact that international policing was at its beginnings in the 19th century more developed in Europe, where the bureaucratization of police institutions, too, relied on a longer history than in the New World.

The first two chapters examine the early forms of international policing from the middle to the late 19th century. This period roughly coincides with the decades leading up to and following the formation of the German Empire and the years of the American Civil War. In Chapter 1, I analyse selected European, especially German, international police initiatives that were mostly undertaken for political purposes. Also discussed are the efforts to formalize police cooperation through legal arrangements at the intergovernmental level of states, particularly in the areas of anarchism and white slavery. Chapter 2 discusses a variety of police tasks with a distinct cross-border dimension that took place during the 19th century in and across the United States. Special attention is devoted to the earliest forms of trans-Atlantic policing and the factors that enhanced the internationalization of social life, especially in police matters.

Chapter 3 deals with the most important development that was to come out of the 19th-century international police practices: the increasing efforts taken to establish multilateral police organizations that were explicitly oriented at criminal law enforcement tasks. I will discuss how and why such efforts were increasingly made from the late 19th century onwards and, especially, during the years before World War I, but, importantly, also why they failed. The turmoil of World War I presents an important, if temporary, break in the historical developments of international policing that had been taking place since the 19th century. Chapter 4 separately analyses the dynamics of international police activities in anticipation of, during, and immediately following World War I, including the impact of the Bolshevik Revolution in Russia.

Chapter 5 examines how during the 1920s, when a fragile international peace had been accomplished, renewed efforts were made to normalize international police activities and establish an international police organization with broad international participation in pursuit of criminal law enforcement tasks. Particular attention is paid to the formation of the International Police Conference in New York in 1922 and its (more successful) European counterpart, the International Criminal Police Commission, which was founded in Vienna in 1923. The creation of these organizations reflected a historical trend to formally structure international police cooperation on a multilateral basis. However, there still remained many initiatives taken by and originating from single national police systems on more restricted levels. Chapter 6 examines these unilateral and bilateral international police practices, devoting special attention to their transformation with the rise of Nazism in Germany and the federalization of law enforcement under direction of the FBI in the United States.

The last two chapters of this book are devoted to analysing the peculiar fate of the International Criminal Police Commission in the years before, during, and after World War II. Considering the Commission's scope and objectives, the multilateral police organization clearly emerges as a central outcome of prior historical developments. Chapter 7 analyses how US law enforcement formally participated in the organization and eventually clashed with the German membership that had come under control of the Nazi regime. In the final chapter, I discuss how the organization was refounded after World War II, eventually continuing to expand until today as the organization known as 'Interpol.'

There is only so much this book can hope to accomplish. While broad in thematic focus, my investigations are temporally and geographically framed. It would no doubt be fascinating to expand the research to a broader time frame and to include more police systems, but this is as impossible as it appears unwise. This study does not include investigations of present-day dynamics of international policing, but the findings of this work should be of more interest than mere historical curiosity in its uncovering of patterns and causes that are worthy of investigation beyond the immediate cases at hand. Also, although this study is conceived from an explicitly sociological standpoint, scholars from a broader variety of disciplines with similar or related interests may find food for thought in this book. In any case, I hope that the major achievements of this book lie in the questions it raises and the arguments it advances.

1

The Rise of International Policing

> Conspiracies of a comprehensive character are being hatched in certain back parlours, in certain back streets behind Mr. Cantelo's Chicken Establishment in Leicester Square. A complicated web of machination is being spun . . . against the integrity of the Austrian Empire, at a small coffee-shop in Soho. Prussia is being menaced by twenty-four determined Poles and Honveds in the attics of a cheap restaurateur in the Haymarket.
> *Charles Dickens, 1851.*

The theoretical model that I defend in this book holds that certain socio-political conditions determine the likelihood of police institutions engaging in various forms of international policing. In order to be in a position to cooperate beyond national boundaries, police institutions must have attained a sufficient degree of bureaucratic autonomy, irrespective of the dictates of protective national states. Developments in international policing during the middle of the 19th century are central in this respect, because, as this and the next chapter will show, police institutions began at that time to undergo crucial changes in terms of bureaucratization and professionalization. In consequence of these transformations, police institutions would gradually move away from the directives of their governments to independently plan and execute a variety of international activities. In this chapter, I discuss these developments in the context of Europe, focusing particularly on German police institutions. The next chapter will analyse separately these early origins of international policing in the United States and the rest of the American continent.

'Conspiracies of a comprehensive character': The international policing of politics

Reviewing international police practices throughout 19th-century Europe is a huge and practically impossible task, for it implies analysis of international involvement by the police from each of the many European national states. The participation of various nations' police institutions in international activities would have to be investigated separately, because, as I will show, most of the early forms of international policing were instigated unilaterally or involved bilateral, mostly temporary *ad hoc* forms of cooperation. However, although detailed investigations of the various participations in international police activities in 19th-century Europe are beyond the scope of this book, a broad review of themes may suffice to reveal the basic conditions and mechanisms of these early beginnings of international policing. Separate and more detailed attention is devoted to the Police Union of German States, a veritable organization of international police established in 1851, which may count as one of the first multilateral international police organizations in modern times.

Policing autocracy

Although the focus of this book is on developments of international police practices from the mid-19th century onwards, a few words can be said about their dynamics in Europe in the period before 1848 (Fijnaut 1979:798–843; Liang 1992:18–19, 33–34). Particularly worthy of mention is the introduction of French police systems across Western Europe, especially during the reign of Napoleon. The French police system was strongly centralized in a national Ministry of Police and it was devoted specifically to the protection of the security of the state (Stead 1983:40–43). As a corollary to European unification brought about under French control, the centralized French police model initiated police reforms in many European states, either because the French system was adopted as an exemplary model in national states oriented at maintaining autocratic rule, or because it was imported forcefully alongside of French occupation.[1] In the period of restoration after 1815, special attention should go to the impact of Metternich, the powerful Austrian statesman who engineered and controlled much of Europe's system of international relations until 1848. Metternich's policy was intended to curb any form of political dissension through censorship, espionage, and other means of suppressing revolutionary movements. In a very definite sense, therefore, Napoleon and Metternich can be seen as among the first to bring about a Europeanization of the police, establishing the beginnings of developments that were to mature in the latter half of the 19th century.

[1] The German security police, for example, was imported by the French during the occupation of the Holy Roman Empire (Fijnaut 1979:798–803; Rupieper 1977). After 1815, the security police was redirected against French (and German) espionage activities, and later it functioned internally to gather information on the political mood (*Gesinnung*) of the German population.

The revolutionary year of 1848 served as a critical catalyst in launching a new chapter in international police practices in Europe. Broadly speaking, two forms of international policing took place in the wake of 1848. First, in the period following that revolutionary year, autocratic political regimes in all major European countries, such as Austria-Hungary, Russia, France, and Prussia, followed a conservative course aimed at suppressing any further threat to the established reign. As one of the central strategies towards achieving this reactionary ambition, police institutions were reorganized and reinforced (Fijnaut 1979:107–145; Liang 1992:18–82). As such, 1848 brought about not only reforms of various national police powers but also a *de facto* standardization and harmonization of police organizations across Europe. At least in respect of strengthened control and centralization, the police institutions of various European countries so began to approximate one another more closely than ever before.

Secondly, the revolutionary period also led to an increase in more distinctly international police activities justified in terms of political objectives aimed at suppressing liberal-democratic movements. International political policing occurred in the form of intelligence work abroad and/or by means of increased cooperation for shared purposes of political suppression (Fijnaut 1987:33–35). Covert political police operations abroad were by their very nature typically unilaterally instigated without the knowledge of the police or other authorities of the country where the activities took place, closely akin to espionage activities but undertaken by institutions of internal coercion whose functions comprised political dissent. Typically, these political functions were conceived as part and parcel of criminal duties, or they were defined broadly without distinction. Lacking formal jurisdiction abroad, such police operations were conducted secretly. Unlike transnational policing, international police cooperation for political purposes involved bilateral and even multilateral efforts to organize information exchange, either through establishing contacts between police officials (the so-called personal correspondence system) or through the distribution of printed information on wanted suspects (published in search bulletins). Whereas the correspondence system was initiated *ad hoc* by the police of one nation on the basis of a specific need for assistance (e.g. following an assassination attempt on a monarch or statesman), the bulletin system represented a more permanently organized form of international information exchange.

Multilateral forms of police cooperation for political purposes would not be accomplished easily during the turbulent 19th century. Indicative of this, for instance, is the manner in which international police investigations took place during the International Industrial Exhibition in London in October 1851 (Auerbach 1884:22–32; Smith 1985:89–93). A display of recently developed products and their manufacture, the five-month exhibition symbolized the triumph of capitalist free trade, technological progress, and British industrial supremacy. Among political and police circles it was widely believed that the London Exhibition would attract a large number of social democrats, liberals, and communists from all over Europe, who would seek to unite their efforts to overthrow Europe's conservative regimes. In response, the Chief of the London Metropolitan Police, Richard Mayne, attempted to organize international police cooperation on the occasion of the Exhibition and sent a memorandum to the British Minister of the Interior, Lord Palmerston, suggesting that police from Paris, Brussels, Vienna, Berlin, Frankfurt, and Cologne be invited. Although not unaccustomed to a considerable foreign presence in London, where since 1848 many revolutionaries had been seeking refuge, Mayne feared that the Exhibition would attract 'some good specimens of Socialists and men of Red colour' (in Smith 1985:89). Minister Palmerston followed up on Mayne's request and invited several police officials from abroad.

Some thirty-five foreign police officials were present at the London Exhibition, among them agents from Berlin, Brussels, Paris, Vienna, and New York. However, it is more likely that they were there at their own initiative and not because of the British request. The British embassy in St. Petersburg, for instance, found out that a Russian agent had been sent to London, but Russian police had not been invited. In Prussia, King Friedrich Wilhelm personally appointed Wilhelm Stieber, the head of the Berlin Criminal Police, to observe the foreign and German communist presence at the exhibition. Although the Prussian monarch expressed the wish that Stieber would work in 'intimate cooperation with the London police', Prussian and other police from continental Europe in fact faced much resistance from their British counterparts (Siemann 1985:377–378). British police pointed out the constitutional constraints posed on police practices under English law, while their colleagues from the European continent objected to the British use of German-speaking émigrés as translators in police inquiries. Such dynamics of international policing are indicative of the limits of political police cooperation, because political objectives tend to remain closely aligned with the various ideologies represented by the political centres of national states and the factions and frictions in international relations that are associated with them. Nonetheless, even during the turbulent times of the 19th century there were attempts to formally structure police cooperation for political purposes. One of the earliest international organizations of the police with a more or less permanent structure was established as early as 1851, when the Police Union of German States was founded.

'Absolutely formless and noiseless': The Police Union of German States, 1851–1866

Responding to the revolutionary unrest of 1848 and the continued threat of an increasingly internationally organized political opposition, the Police Union of German States was formed when the police of Austria and the German territories of Prussia, Sachsen, Hanover, Baden, Württemberg, and Bavaria united their political policing efforts in an international organization.[2] The central driving force of the Police Union was Karl Ludwig Friedrich von Hinckeldey, the ultra-conservative head of the Berlin police. Von Hinckeldey had responded to the unrest of 1848 by establishing a new and separate political police division and by organizing a system for information exchange on political opponents for all of Prussia. Beyond centralizing political policing in his state, von Hinckeldey also initiated a plan to organize police cooperation against the political opposition at the international level. On 3 April 1851, von Hinckeldey sent out letters to police officials in Hanover, Dresden, and Vienna, to propose that the political opposition should be policed jointly and that an international intelligence system should be established to collect and exchange information on liberals, communists, and nationalists. To arrange the practical details of this cooperation, von Hinckeldey suggested to hold a 'joint, absolutely formless and noiseless conference' (Siemann 1983a:22).

Von Hinckeldey's initiative was followed up by a police conference in Dresden on 9 April 1851, attended by representatives from Austria,

[2] The Police Union of German States has received minimal attention in the secondary literature (Haalck 1959–1960; Rupieper 1977; Siemann 1983b, 1985, 1990). Two volumes of primary sources have put scholars in a position to analyse the organization more thoroughly (see the selection of documents in Siemann 1983a, and the reports of all of the Police Union's conferences in Beck and Schmidt 1993). This section is revised from Deflem 1996.

Prussia, Sachsen, and Hanover. Within a year, the police of the four states negotiated with representatives from Bavaria, Württemberg, and Baden, to form the seven-member 'Police Union of the more important German States,' as the organization was called formally (Siemann 1983a:2). Instead of seeking to enhance police powers of investigation and arrest, the Union was concerned primarily with establishing swifter modes of information exchange. In the first instance, information was exchanged during the meetings the Police Union organized every year between 1851 and 1866—with two meetings in 1851, 1853, and 1855, and three in 1852—and, additionally, the Union relied on a newly instituted system of printed magazines, containing information on political opponents, that were to be published and distributed weekly (Siemann 1985:260).

The activities of the Police Union were directed against people, organizations, and events that were believed to threaten the stability of the established political order. International cooperation between the police was considered necessary because political dissenters were thought to be conspiring from London, Paris, and other capital cities in Europe in order to 'unite, unify and convince present unsatisfied elements of the idea of solidary harmony among all revolutionary forces', as a police memorandum at one of the Union's 1855 conferences stated (Siemann 1983a:129, 131). The revolutionary opposition was considered to be organizing its efforts in a collectivity referred to as the *Umsturzpartei* (Overthrow Party), but political opponents were broadly defined to include communists, social-democrats, migrants, religious groups, Freemasons, gymnastics groups, labour organizations, and student movements. The Union focused attention separately on the policing of press activities, including the surveillance of bookstores and publishing companies and the confiscation of politically subversive writings.

Although it is difficult to determine to what extent the Police Union was an effective instrument of international policing, the Union maintained throughout its existence a very active system of information exchange on various political movements and kept track of the activities of some well-known political dissidents, among them Karl Marx and Friedrich Engels (Beck and Schmidt 1993:339–340). The Union's intelligence activities were very comprehensive, including communist extremists as well as moderate social-democrats, and extended geographically beyond German and European borders to cross-Atlantic investigations of revolutionaries that had fled to the United

States.[3] Information exchange continued throughout the Union's existence but, ultimately, international political events would catch up with the police organization. As antagonisms between Prussia and Austria mounted from the early 1860s onward, the Police Union gradually reduced its scope of operations against political dissidents. Ultimately, with the outbreak of the Seven-Weeks War in 1866, the Union was dissolved, and would not be revived after the separation of the North-German Confederation and the Austro-Hungarian monarchy.

The politics of international policing

The early dimensions of international policing that I have discussed so far are of special significance in this study, because they form the historical basis of the processes and structures that the remainder of this book will investigate. This is not to imply that the history of international police is marked by continuity more than change, only that every present condition is inevitably but variably shaped by prior circumstances, the dynamics of which this book seeks precisely to uncover. Separate theoretical reflections upon these early beginnings of international police practices, therefore, are in order before later developments during the 19th century will be analysed. Taking as a guide the analytical framework advanced in this work, I therefore focus on the cause and course of the internationalization of the police function following the revolutionary year of 1848 and the manner in which international policing was influenced by socio-political conditions.

The internationalization of political policing

The historical evidence shows most critically that international police efforts after the 1848 unrest were concerned primarily with the control of the alleged political opponents of established autocratic regimes. The police responses to the situation of unrest took on several forms, most essentially involving a harmonization of policing styles in different national states and various kinds of international police operations.

[3] For instance, the Police Union gathered intelligence on Karl Schurz, a German social-democrat, whom the Union's members considered to be a dangerous communist. In 1852, Schurz migrated to the United States, where he became a confidant of President Lincoln, US ambassador to Spain, a General in the Union armies, US Senator, and ultimately Secretary of State. Apart from Germans migrating to the US after the revolutionary year (the so-called 'Forty-eighters'), the Union's policing activities towards the United States also included the German-language press printed in the United States (Siemann 1983a:157–158).

Harmonization of police institutions across European states was not the result of a planned policy by a supranational body of law or government, nor deliberately planned by the various national police institutions or their governments, but was instead a *de facto* consequence of various national reforms of the police. Following the 1848 revolutions, indeed, the police institutions of all major states in Europe were reorganized in a manner that was conceived in order to avert the danger of political disorders, therefore leading particularly to strengthen and expand political police powers (Fijnaut 1979:113–117, 127–130; Mawby 1990:39–42). In Prussia, for example, police reforms took place immediately after the unrest in 1848, specifically with the appointment of von Hinckeldey as Police President of Berlin, and in France they occurred a few years later after the *coup d'état* of Louis-Napoleon Bonaparte in December 1851 and his elevation to Emperor Napoleon III in the following year. Though implemented for nationally defined concerns and not oriented strategically at cementing international relations, factual standardization of police organizations and activities across national states contributed to the creation of a commonality of the police across national states. This commonality could be favourable for the establishment of international cooperation, providing at least that socio-political conditions did not intervene in police institutions aligning with one another. Importantly, these conditions were initially not accomplished.

Beyond a factual harmonization of the police across Europe in the 19th century, the most dominant form of international political policing remained unilaterally planned and transnationally executed operations, only minimally supplemented by international cooperative efforts. The widespread practice of transnational political police operations testifies to the critical concerns over sovereignty in 19th-century Europe. Socio-political conditions also influenced the fact that efforts to establish international cooperation between the police were predominantly instituted on a temporary basis and/or limited in international scope. The Police Union is no exception, for although the organization could count on unprecedented broad support, it remained very limited in international appeal. Specifically, the Union remained restricted to German-language states united in the German Confederation and was not able to garner support from the police in other national states, even if and when those institutions were as committed to the international policing of politics. Indeed, the political distance between Prussia and the other states of the German Confederation, on the one hand, and France, on the other, are well reflected in the Police Union. Originating from the offices of von Hinckeldey, the Union was a Prussian initiative and despite its international ambitions it is best conceived of as an extension of national police concerns to which other participating forces were aligned. This Prussian aspiration posed no special problems for the other German states, nor for Austria. Socio-political conditions allowed for Austrian participation in the Union despite it being a Prussian initiative because Austria was politically aligned with Prussia in the German Confederation. As no political or other obstacles prevented collaboration, the police of Prussia and Austria—both particularly well developed in terms of political duties—could establish cooperation because of similarity in objectives and attained expertise. As I mentioned earlier, Austrian police institutions had since the first half of the 19th century established systems of international policing in which they were rivalled only by the accomplishments of the Prussian political police after 1848. The French national police system was as sophisticated in respects of technological means and as politically oriented in terms of objectives as its Austrian and Prussian counterparts. France had since the reign of Napoleon developed a remarkably powerful centralized police system, separated organizationally between political (high) and criminal (low) police (Stead 1983:44–53). In Germany and Austria, high and low policing tasks also existed, albeit as a functional specialization within an over-arching police apparatus. However, antagonisms in international political affairs prevented French participation in the Police Union. In terms of objectives, the police institutions of all these conservative states shared a common enemy in the liberal-democratic political opposition, but the antagonisms between the countries in international political affairs proved a stronger dividing force, placing even police with similar objectives and expertise against one another.

Thus, political conditions pertaining to Europe's fragile order of national states and their quest to consolidate conservative rule help explain why it was that the Prussian initiative of the Police Union could count on the support of the police from Austria but not from France and many other European countries. Originally, von Hinckeldey had hoped to establish an international political police organization across all of western Europe, but that plan met with strong opposition. Under the Police Union's supervision, a German police officer was appointed at the German embassy in London and other agents were placed in Paris, London, Brussels, and even in New York. But these agents abroad were involved predominantly in transnational operations that were conducted secretively and could not count on cooperation from the local police (Rupieper 1977:340). National differences in political-ideological respects combined with sovereignty concerns to make police cooperation with broad international representation impossible. This confirms that socio-political conditions may prevent police institutions from establishing cooperation across national states. Therefore, also, it causes no surprise that with the rise of Bismarck and his uncompromising foreign policy, the Police Union's activities gradually began to decline and that the Union collapsed when war broke out between Prussia and Austria.

Political police activities after 1848 were conducted across national boundaries because the political opposition was perceived to be organizing at an international level, aiming to overthrow not only one national monarchy or autocratic system of government but all of Europe's established autocracies. The notion of an international organization of the liberal-democratic opposition thus provided the common ground for the police to work transnationally abroad or—socio-political conditions permitting—to participate in international cooperation schemes. Importantly, I do not defend the functionalist argument that international police operations respond to an internationalization of crime, but that the necessity of international police practices in response to an internationalization of the political opposition reflects the understanding defended by the police authorities themselves. In the invitation for the Police Union's founding conference, for example, von Hinckeldey referred explicitly to the international organization of revolutionary forces, the centres of which he perceived to be in Paris and London.[4] National political police duties were therefore to be complemented by international tasks. Apart from an assumed internationalization of the political opposition, what also motivated an international police response was the fact that politically motivated threats against an autocracy within a national state were perceived to have implications across national borders. The failed assassination attempt against Emperor Napoleon III by the Italian Felice Orsini on 14 January 1858, for example, led other monarchs in Europe to fear similar

[4] Von Hinckeldey also stated that he was convinced of the international organization of the *Umsturzpartei* because of a message he had received from Alexis-Guillaume Baron de Hody, the head of the Belgian secret service, that confirmed that the revolutionary forces were organizing across national borders (Beck and Schmidt 1993:5). De Hody, incidentally, had been responsible for the arrest and extradition of Karl Marx in Brussels in 1848.

actions against their lives. The incident reinvigorated political police activities across Europe and served as a catalyst to revive the Police Union's activities.

Additionally, it was widely believed among police and government authorities that the internationalization of political protest was aided by recent technological developments in the areas of communication and transportation. The relevance of technologies of communication for international police practices is particularly well reflected in the fact that many of Europe's political police institutions focused special attention on the printed press. At a time when weekly magazines and daily journals constituted the prime source of information, the relevance of the press as a forum for the distribution of ideas was explicitly recognized among the police. Because the press and printed writings more generally could be oriented at affecting public opinion across national borders, police would likewise have to operate beyond the confines of national jurisdiction.[5] An indication of the powers of the written word is the fact that the press formed one of the Police Union's specifically defined fields of inquiry and that the clandestine opening of letters was a favoured method of political policing across Europe (Huber 1967:153–154).

Next to the technologies of writing, developments in the means of transportation also affected international policing. In particular, the development of the railways was considered to have potentially troublesome implications for police activities. The total number of railway lines increased exponentially from the middle to the late 19th century, with a total of some 4,000 kilometres of railway lines across Europe in 1840 and nearly 50,000 kilometres in 1860 (Pounds 1985). In the German territories, railway lines were introduced in 1835 and expanded greatly in the following decades. Whereas only 469 kilometres of railway lines connected different cities within the German Confederation's territory in 1840, this number had risen to 7,826 in 1855, and 13,900 in 1865. As with the internationalization of political protest, the opportunities of mobilization enabled by the expansion of the railroads were relevant because they were recognized as having

[5] The relationship between police and press in relation to public opinion is discussed by Jürgen Habermas (1962) in his historical analysis of the public sphere in capitalist democracies. Habermas argues that police and press were closely related institutions during the early development of capitalism inasmuch as 'good police' (in the cameralist sense of policy or administration) concerned the public market, whereas the press concerned public opinion, neither one of which is spatially bound to confined regions (Habermas 1962:77–79).

consequences for the development of crime by police initiating international activities. As early as 1855, for example, Police Union member Häpe of Sachsen explicitly referred to the expansion of traffic, which 'accelerated through the railways, [had] since about 10 years particularly benefited the overthrow parties of the different states in their common organization and dangerous cooperation' (Siemann 1983a:28).

Because it was accepted among the police that the political opponents of established regimes were organizing at an international level and were aided in their plans by evolutions in the technologies of communication and transportation, international police activity with political objectives underwent a considerable upsurge in the aftermath of 1848, an increase in international police activities not witnessed since the days of Napoleon and Metternich. Yet, although an internationalization of political movements was seen as necessitating police practices that likewise employed international means, there were limits to the international scope of these activities. As already mentioned, transnationally planned and confidentially executed police practices dominated over international cooperative efforts, which themselves remained limited in international participation because of political antagonisms and concerns of sovereignty. As such, police developments within nations shape the form and outcome of international policing, because transnational police operations can be seen as an extension of intra-national policing tasks, while the limited scope of international initiatives indicates that socio-political conditions affecting national states and their interrelations may prevent police cooperation with broad international appeal. Additionally, there is an important limitation to the scope of international police plans that even the most broadly international plans of collaboration had to deal with. The limitation is that an international police organization established in a cooperative form reaffirms the police institutions of different national states as the key players in the international arena and, in consequence, strengthens local powers of police forces that are locked into an international network of institutions. The fact that participation in an international cooperative organization does not imply a surrender of local control within nations can be seen in particular from a closer look at the Police Union, at this time the most internationally ambitious police organization yet. Aimed at enhancing information exchange across national borders, the Union's organizational structure implied that the participating police forces had established and/or would establish adequate internal intelligence systems. This involved, minimally, that within each of the participating states, a police officer or a ministerial employee was appointed to deal with this task. In the absence of plans to create a new supranational police force out of the participating institutions, the cooperative model of the Police Union reaffirmed the dominant role of Prussian and Austrian police institutions, because their intelligence systems were particularly well developed, especially in technical respects. The Austrian political police transmitted weekly reports (*Polizei-Wochen-Rapporte*) between some thirty-one police directions across the Austrian territory. The police of Vienna, particularly, in the 1850s and 1860s, published a two-weekly 'Central Police Bulletin' (*Central-Polizei-Blatt*) in which was printed information on wanted suspects, with information on extradited foreigners listed separately (Schaefer 1977:31–32, 1979:57–58). In Prussia, likewise, the police of Berlin and other cities had instituted central intelligence bureaus and transmitted information to one another via 'Weekly Reports for the Interior' (*Wochenberichte Inland*). Because von Hinckeldey had in the aftermath of 1848 managed to secure elaborate financial means for an expansion of the Berlin police, it must have met the Police Union's requirements in a most ideal fashion (Funk 1986:67ff; Siemann 1985:340ff). Thus, although the Police Union attained an unprecedented level of international participation, its cooperative structure nonetheless implied that local police powers were strengthened and expanded at the same time when, and precisely because, regional forces were locked into an international network and that nationally variable characteristics of participating police systems determined to what extent international police plans could be attained successfully (Siemann 1990:53). Throughout this study, I will show that this persistence of nationality in international policing will remain an essential concern at all times when international police cooperation plans have been discussed and introduced.

The political origins of bureaucratic policing

Reflecting the dynamics of national and international political conditions, police institutions during the 19th century played a central role in the quest of national autocratic governments to consolidate conservative political rule. As such, it is clear that although police agencies were separated institutionally from the military, they both remained closely aligned as the two central state organs of coercion (Fijnaut 1979:127–130). In consequence of their primarily political focus, international police operations during the 19th century were predominantly transnational in kind or of a cooperative nature that was limited in functional respects (initiated for a specific purpose and terminated after it was achieved) and/or in international scope (bilateral or multilateral between police of politically akin states). However, although these international political police operations were dominated by the political dictates of national governments, I maintain that they also contained and enabled the origins of a bureaucratic autonomy of police that would characterize later developments of international policing as beyond political control. The reason for this peculiar development lies in the fact that while political autocratic governments in the 19th century ordered police institutions to engage in various modalities of international political work, accepted rules of international diplomacy in respect of national sovereignty prevented those orders from being made public. Instead, political policing powers were delegated to police agencies who were charged with arranging and executing all appropriate measures at the administrative level. Therefore, although these international police activities were oriented towards tasks that were not only political in nature but also dictated by the governments of national states, the manner in which those political tasks were executed operationally was to be decided upon by police professionals. Because of the confidentiality of their assignments, moreover, police institutions could determine the means of political policing independently of political and/or legal control and irrespective of the boundaries of jurisdictional authority. This attained level of organizational independence is the one critical implication of the relinquishing of administrative power from central governments to the institutions of internal coercion that would further propel a process of police bureaucratization that would ultimately also influence the objectives of international policing.

Unilaterally conducted transnational policing on foreign soil had to be conducted secretively because it readily violated jurisdictional restraints, but agreed upon international police plans, too, were kept confidential. Bilateral police activities were typically not based on formal international agreements between states, while multilateral cooperation efforts were likewise not legally sanctioned. The Police Union, for instance, was not sanctioned by a formal intergovernmental accord. Instead, the heads of state of the participating police agencies approved silently of the arrangement. In München, Bavaria, for instance, Prime Minister von der Pfordten had been informed about von Hinckeldey's plan to create the Union via the Austrian ambassador. The Bavarian Prime Minister notified Minister of the Interior von Zwehl, who informed King Max II, who approved of his state's participation in the plan. But though sanctioned confidentially, concerns over sovereignty prevented the Police Union from operating on the basis of an explicit treaty between the governments of the participating states. For indeed, although the Police Union's participating states were loosely united in the German Confederation, they recognized explicitly each other's political sovereignty. It was no surprise, when Austrian and Prussian police made a joint request to the German *Bund* to formally sanction a centralized federal police system, that the plan failed (Siemann 1990:43–65).

Although concerns over national sovereignty prevented participation in international political police initiatives from being made public, such restrictions did not apply to cooperation between police institutions at the administrative level. This can be gathered from both the structure and operations of international political policing. International police structures, indeed, were designed purposely to circumvent the provisions and restrictions of international law, especially with respect to jurisdiction and extradition. This involved, in particular, the elaboration of systems of information exchange that would bypass legal provisions of information exchange between the police of different states. To conform with legal provisions throughout the 19th century, a request for information from the police of another state would first have to go through the Ministry of the Interior and the Ministry of the Exterior in the requesting police institution's own state. Then the message would have to be passed on to, successively, the state's embassy in the foreign state where information was requested, its Ministry of the Exterior, Ministry of the Interior, and, finally, the appropriate police agency. To follow up on the request, the entire route had to be followed backwards. But with the establishment of bilateral and multilateral systems of information exchange—however limited in scope—the exchange of information could take place directly from police to police.

In the case of the international system established by the Police Union, it is particularly clear that international police cooperation was in structural and operational respects conceived to circumvent the provisions of formal law and jurisdictional authority. In terms of its structure, the Police Union was concerned exclusively with establishing systems of direct police communications. The Union went as far as to redefine jurisdictional limits by dividing responsibilities of the police of the seven participating states over four newly created districts, in each of which a police office was designated to administer centrally the exchange of information (Siemann 1985:260). And throughout its existence, the police measures and operations implemented under supervision of the Police Union proceeded in the same 'formless and noiseless' manner in which the organization was created. Typically, for instance, when in the late 1850s the Union's members took charge of policing a ban which the Prussian Minister of the Interior had declared against all German-language American newspapers and magazines, a public announcement of the ban had 'not been judged expedient' (Siemann 1983a:158). Furthermore, although the Union's conferences after 1862 could not always count on the attendance of the police from all participating states, even in the midst of growing antagonisms between the governments of national states there were attempts to formalize police collaboration for all of Europe. Austrian police authorities, in particular, were still attempting to expand the Union's international membership and formalize a European-wide police organization on the basis of intelligence exchange and agreements on the pursuit of fugitives (Liang 1992:151–153).

Thus, although conducted primarily on the basis of political orders received from governments, international police operations in the second half of the 19th century were in their implementation left to the expertise of police. The fact that police institutions were given such generous administrative powers in international (and national) activities was enabled by important developments at the national level. Most importantly, as police institutions were reformed and expanded after 1848, they had gradually also been able to gain control with respect to their organization. The most influential development in this respect had already been launched in 1796, when a separate Ministry of Police was created in France (Stead 1983:38–40). The French example was much envied by police authorities in other countries of Europe, where a similar system of self-control was aspired to—sometimes successfully. In Prussia, most notably, von Hinckeldey had succeeded in persuading Friedrich Wilhelm IV to appoint him to General Director of Police (*Generalpolizeidirektor*), a new position independent from the Minister of the Interior (Fijnaut 1979:128–130; Funk 1986:60; Schulze 1955). But with or without taking control from above, police participating in international political initiatives had been delegated the authority to establish the proper means of policing. And, especially through the cooperative forms of international political policing, whether more or less permanent and more or less wide in international scope, relationships between police authorities across Europe could at a personal level be established effectively. When von Hinckeldey invited the police from various states to jointly form the Police Union, he envisioned a conference of 'men . . . who in their difficult profession know one other as reliable and have learned to appreciate one another' (Beck and Schmidt 1993:5).

As perhaps the most important consequence of the relative independence granted to police at the administrative level, police officials cooperating across national borders started to develop a common culture that could further cement and build international relations, irrespective of the dictates of political governments. By the second half of the 19th century, strong political antagonisms and nationalist sentiments may still have interfered with the development of a common police culture, but there were clearly the beginnings of such a European police culture. In the case of the Police Union, for instance, this is indicated by the fact that while after the rise of Bismarck the Union's activities declined, they then also changed qualitatively rather than just diminishing in quantity. Most crucially, during the 1860s the Police Union focused more and more on issues of criminal policing, in relation to traffic, commerce, ethics, health, and various non-political offences. This refocusing on criminal police tasks indicates not only that political duties had become too precarious to be policed jointly by institutions from politically increasingly hostile states, but additionally that police officials had begun to set their own agenda of tasks, independently from their respective governments. A next step would be to have these police arrangements sanctioned by law. This occurred on at least one occasion, when in 1863 the governments of Prussia and Austria agreed on an international convention to collaborate in matters concerning the suppression of common crime and vagrancy. Under the provisions of the convention, Prussian and Austrian police were given the right to cross the border to pursue dangerous fugitives, while police in neighbouring districts of the two countries could contact each other and organize joint patrols (Liang 1992:31–32).

The peculiar paradox of these developments is that political conditions enabled the police to gain independence from politics and enabled the creation of an independent police culture based on professional expertise. Though international police cooperation for political purposes was mostly bilateral or limited in international participation, cooperation allowed for the establishment of personal contacts between officials who could increasingly recognize one another as fellow experts. The implication is that by charging police with the administrative handling of political duties, national governments granted police the powers to develop the appropriate means of policing based on professional standards of expertise. And increasing opportunities of police professionalization in terms of the expert means of policing also accelerated a process by which police institutions gradually began to define the proper goals of policing. As such, police institutions during the 19th century began to develop from merely determining the means to execute an agenda to additionally instituting its goals. The irony is that national governments were responsible for the development of police institutions working irrespective of politics beyond national borders. For what started as a mere administrative issue at the level of officialdom would gradually become a basis for the police to lay claim to develop independently international plans on the basis of professional expertise and irrespective of the dictates of national governments.

The legacy of 1848 and the origins of European police culture

International policing for political goals would continue to be the dominant concern of European police institutions throughout the latter half of the 19th century. Strong sentiments over national sovereignty and jurisdictional authority as well as important political hostilities between many of Europe's national states prevented any long-lasting attempts to formalize international police organizations with broad international representation. Unilateral and confidential transnational actions and temporary and bilateral cooperative forms remained the preferred strategies of international policing. Detailed inquiries of all of these are beyond the scope of this book, but illustrative case materials may indicate the essential dynamics of these developments.

In light of earlier developments, it is not surprising that Prussian, Austrian, and French police continued to play a critical role in international political police activities in the latter half of the 19th century. Building on the elaborate police structures developed since the Habsburg dynasty, the Austrian political police further elaborated systems of international intelligence gathering and information exchange. Copies of Austrian police bulletins were from the 1860s onwards sent regularly to the police in Prussia, and by the 1880s, the bulletins were distributed across Europe (Liang 1992:32). Similar strategies were developed by German police agencies. The police of Frankfurt, for example, published

English, German, and French versions of an 'International Criminal Record,' with information on the whereabouts of criminals reported by various police across Europe. In the German Empire, however, it was particularly the Berlin powers that continued to be expanded (Funk 1986:72; Huber 1967:158–162; Siemann 1985:371ff). In 1850, the new division of Criminal Police in Berlin was given explicit enforcement duties without geographical restriction. The head of the division, Wilhelm Stieber, would become one of the most colourful characters of international policing in the second half of the 19th century, especially after he had been appointed by King Friedrich Wilhelm to observe the communist presence at the London Exhibition. On the basis of Stieber's investigations in London and elsewhere, several German communists were trailed and convicted in Cologne in 1852.[6] In return for his valuable contributions, Stieber was able to steadily expand his personal command over Prussian intelligence work. In 1860, he became the head of a newly created *Zentral-Nachrichtenbüro* (Central News Office), a Berlin police office that centralized information on international anarchists and communists. During the 1860s, Stieber combined his duties in Berlin with intelligence work for the Russian secret police (Huber 1967:162; von der Groeben 1984:448).

Continuing a development established since 1848, *ad hoc* and mostly political police tasks forged international police alliances within limits determined by socio-political conditions throughout the second half of the 19th century. Police relations between Prussia and France, for instance, remained strenuous before and after the war of 1870.[7] But in other cases, cooperation could be achieved. For example, when in response to Bismarck's proclamation of an anti-socialist law in 1878 the German police were responsible for the banishment of socialists to other countries in Europe, foreign police would often assist their German colleagues with intelligence activities. The Swiss police, for instance, observed meetings of the German socialists in Switzerland and sent reports of their investigations to German police (Funk 1986:150–153; Liang 1992:104–112).

[6] Stieber's inquiries in London, incidentally, included an undercover investigation of Karl Marx, the amusing details of which are recounted in Stieber's posthumously published memoirs (Stieber 1980:25–38). In some writings, Marx criticized Stieber and von Hinckeldey for their role in tracking down communists (e.g. Marx 1853).

[7] A popularized account of the Prussian secret police was published by the Swiss novelist Victor Tissot in 1884 (Tissot 1884). The book was very popular among the reading public in France, although it offered criticisms that were just as applicable to the French political police.

With regard to limited forms of cooperation, mention should also be made of the practice of courtesy visits between police officials. These visits were typically not planned for any investigative purposes, but instead served to learn of one another's police experiences, share thoughts on the proper means of policing, and build relationships at a personal level. Such courtesy visits became more and more common during the 19th century. In 1879 and 1889, for instance, high-ranking Japanese police officials visited the Vienna police on an informal inspection tour. When Berlin Police President von Borries assumed office in 1903, he notified the police chiefs of all European capitals, as did Arkadiy Harting when in 1905 he became Chief of the Okhrana Foreign Bureau (Liang 1992:151–155).

Beyond limited and *ad hoc* forms of cooperation, attempts were made to more broadly formalize international police cooperation in the latter part of the 19th century. Initially, however, sovereignty concerns would typically continue to prevent multilateral police cooperation from being established and sanctioned at the intergovernmental level. In 1881, for example, negotiations between the German Kaiser, Russia's Alexander II, and the Austrian monarch Franz Joseph failed to produce an agreement on a common anti-anarchist policy (Fijnaut 1979:1007–1012). A trilateral treaty could still not be agreed upon even after the assassination of Tsar Alexander II later that year had proven the usefulness of such an accord. But what could not be achieved intergovernmentally was accomplished—if in somewhat more restricted form—at the level of policing, when interventions by the Russian consul in Berlin led to the establishment of a limited form of cooperation between the Prussian political police and its Russian counterpart, the Okhrana. The Okhrana had been created in the aftermath of the assassination of the Russian tsar (Andrew and Gordievsky 1991:17–37; Conquest 1968; Fischer 1997). Continuing a long tradition of political policing in Russia dating back to the Oprichnina founded in 1565 by Ivan the Terrible, the Okhrana established a vast international political police network with headquarters in Paris where a Foreign Bureau was created in 1883. The Foreign Bureau established liaison with the French national police and hired French, British, and other detectives. To police revolutionary activity organizing abroad against the Russian Empire, additional offices were created in Berlin, London, and other European cities. Growing resentment among liberal-minded French politicians would eventually lead the Russian government to formally close the Paris Bureau in 1913. The office thereafter continued a clandestine existence under the cover of the private detective agency 'Agence Bint et Sambain', a proprietor of which had served in both the Okhrana and the French political police.

Next to unilaterally conducted practices, bilateral and limitedly multilateral forms of cooperation for political purposes remained the dominant cooperative forms of international policing until the early 20th century. Cooperative forms of international policing did not always rely on a clearly developed agenda of common objectives shared by all participating police institutions, as these objectives were mostly of a political nature and so remained dependent on nationally variable ideological conceptions of justice and legality. However, police authorities participating in various forms of cooperation shared a commonality of expertise on the means of policing around which a network could be formed through which the legitimacy of one another's work could be recognized. Such mutual recognition among police professionals was far from trivial, as it indicates the beginnings of a common culture of police experts across national borders. Indeed, however limited agreements were in time, scope, and enforcement duties, they did establish personal and concrete relationships between police authorities of different national states. And it was during these activities of contact and cooperation that the professionals of policing found the opportunity to begin to recognize one another as fellow experts, similarly oriented at executing enforcement tasks and equally specialized and professional in employing expert means of policing. From here on, a common culture based on professional expertise in police technique could be extended to also include the proper objectives of policing. Under those circumstances would it become possible for police authorities to organize independently international police cooperation on a multilateral basis.

Enforcing international law: The social defence against anarchism and white slavery

I have argued that international political police activities in 19th-century Europe were restricted in scope and failed to endure in multilateral form because they were influenced by concerns pertaining to national sovereignty. Though at the administrative level international operations clearly extended beyond a traditional legal framework rooted in national jurisdictional authority, governments secretly ordered but did not openly sanction police cooperation in political matters by means of a formal international treaty. It may come as somewhat of a surprise, then, that a broadly multilateral effort to establish European-wide police cooperation would be attempted at an international conference held in 1898 that was organized at the intergovernmental level and focused specifically on anti-anarchist measures. Unveiling the causes and implications of the anti-anarchist conference, however, will help explain this paradoxical development and will also clarify the dynamics of similar international treaties, specifically in the area of prostitution.

The Anti-Anarchist Conference of Rome, 1898

In the final decade of the 19th century, violent incidents inspired by radical political ideas once again shook the foundations of established autocratic regimes in Europe and accelerated international police activities with political objectives. Partly in response to this renewed threat to persisting autocratic rule, attempts were again made to establish relatively permanent measures of international police cooperation with wide international representation in a form that would overcome earlier complications related to national sovereignty. Again, in many ways these attempts were unsuccessful, but they also signalled an important transformation in the objectives of international police cooperation, the consequences of which would affect the dynamics of police internationalization during the first half of the 20th century.

The 1890s witnessed a revival of anarchist activities and, in response, police actions directed at suppressing them (Liang 1992:155–163). Between March 1892 and June 1894, eleven bombing incidents killed nine people in Paris alone. In 1893, there were plans to assassinate Emperor Wilhelm II and Chancellor Caprivi of Germany, information about which was intercepted by the French police and passed on to the police in Berlin. In the same year, following bombings in Paris and Barcelona, negotiations were held between the French and Spanish governments to establish an international police organization against anarchism. But although authorities from Great Britain, Austria, and the German Empire indicated an interest in joining the plan, it never came to fruition. Other anti-anarchist police measures were restricted to bilateral agreements. In 1898, for instance, French and Italian police exchanged information through their respective consulates about the possible connections between a bombing in Milan, a bank robbery in Paris, and a dynamite theft in Switzerland. On 10 September 1898,

Empress Elisabeth of Austria was murdered by the Italian anarchist Luigi Lucheni, again intensifying concerns over the anarchist threat. A week after the assassination, the Austrian foreign minister, Goluchowsky, proposed to his Swiss colleague the formation of an 'International Police League' against anarchists. The Austrian–Swiss plan remained unexecuted, but a few weeks later, on 29 September 1898, the Italian government sent out invitations for an international conference to be held in Rome later that year in order to organize the fight against anarchism.

The 'International Conference of Rome for the Social Defence Against Anarchists' was held from 24 November to 21 December 1898, and was attended by fifty-four delegates from no less than twenty-one European countries, including all major powers (Jensen 1981; Fijnaut 1979:930–933; Liang 1992:163–169). The gathering attracted mostly government representatives, diplomats, and ambassadors, but also present were police officials from the participating countries. Discussed at the Conference were the development of an appropriate concept of anarchism and the establishment of international anti-anarchist police measures. Following a proposal of the representative of Monaco, the Conference agreed to define an anarchist as a person who had committed an act 'having as its aim the destruction through violent means of all social organization [*toute organisation sociale*]' (Jensen 1981:327). Other resolutions were passed to introduce legislation in the participating countries that prohibited the illegitimate possession and use of explosives, membership in anarchist organizations, the distribution of anarchist propaganda, and the rendering of assistance to anarchists. It was also agreed that governments should try to limit press coverage of anarchist activities and that the death penalty should be the mandatory punishment for all assassinations of heads of state.

On matters of practical policing, the delegates at the Rome Conference agreed to encourage their governments to have police keep watch over anarchists, to establish in every participating country a specialized agency to achieve this end, and to organize a system of exchange between these national agencies. Great Britain was the only country to abstain from this otherwise unanimously approved provision. All Conference attendants, except the British delegates, also agreed to introduce in their countries the '*portrait parlé*' method of criminal identification. The *portrait parlé* (spoken picture) was a refinement of the anthropometry or bertillonage system, invented by the French anthropologist Alphonse Bertillon, which classified the identification of criminals on the basis of certain measurements of parts of their head and body and the colour of their eyes, hair, and skin. Measurements based on the bertillonage system were expressed numerically to be transmitted from one state to another by telephone or telegraph, a practice which the Conference encouraged to be further developed. Finally, the Conference also approved a provision to extradite any person who had attempted to kill or kidnap a sovereign or head of state. The provision was referred to as the '*attentat*' or Belgian clause and had first been introduced in Belgium following the failed assassination attempt on Napoleon III.

The assassination of US President McKinley by an anarchist in September 1901 provided Russian authorities with a concrete ground to revive the anti-anarchist programme of the Rome Conference. Co-sponsored by the German government, Russian officials sent out a memorandum to hold an international meeting to the governments of various European countries and the United States. The initiative led to a second anti-anarchist meeting, held in March 1904 in St. Petersburg, then the capital of Russia, where the representatives of ten countries, including Germany, Austria-Hungary, and Denmark, agreed upon a 'Secret Protocol for the International War on Anarchism'. The United States government had refused to participate in the meeting and was not involved in the final agreement. France and Great Britain did not sign the St. Petersburg Protocol, but the authorities of these countries did express their willingness to provide assistance with other states on police matters relating to anarchism.

The suppression of the white slave trade

The implications of white slavery or prostitution had occupied private groups, governments, and police institutions at national and international levels for some time in the 19th century.[8] In 1869, Austrian authorities requested information from a number of European governments about their laws regarding the transportation of prostitutes across national borders. The effort aimed to harmonize anti-prostitution laws in Europe, but it was not successful. Subsequent private plans to organ-

[8] Data on the policing of prostitution reported in this section are taken from Dressler 1933:361; Hagemann 1933a:744; League of Nations (hereafter: LN) 1927; Mander 1941:72–76; Palitzsch 1926a:26–31; Reinsch 1916:64–66; Schmitz 1927:25–27. Studies on the history of prostitution provided additional materials (Bristow 1983; Decker 1979; Petrow 1994).

ize international efforts to control prostitution included the 'International Congress on the White Slave Traffic' organized by the National Vigilance Association in London in 1899. The meeting led to the creation of an 'International Bureau for the Suppression of White Slavery' in London, and produced a follow-up meeting, the 'Second International Congress on the International Fight Against the White Slave Traffic', held in Frankfurt, Germany, in 1902 (Phillip 1928:1146).

An anti-prostitution initiative was taken at the intergovernmental level when an international conference was organized by the French authorities in Paris on 15 July 1902. The participants of the Paris meeting agreed upon a final protocol that criminalized prostitution and specified extradition treaties and several administrative arrangements on the issue. The recommended police measures included provisions for governments to organize the surveillance of procurers and suspicious foreigners in railway stations and ports (Petrow 1994:163–164). At a subsequent meeting in Paris in 1904, the 'International Agreement for the Suppression of White Slave Traffic' was signed by the governments of twelve European countries, including France, Germany, Great Britain, and Russia. Other, non-European states, among them Brazil, China, India, and the United States, did not sign the accord but nonetheless agreed to adhere to its provisions (LN 1927:197). The nine-article Paris Agreement specified, amongst other things, that governments should police all persons involved with organizing prostitution at railway stations and ports. It was also decided to create intelligence bureaux on prostitution in all participating countries and for these bureaux to be in direct contact with one another. Finally, the agreement provided that governments should arrange to report foreign prostitutes in their respective countries to the authorities of the prostitutes' country of origin and to repatriate them upon request from foreign authorities.

At a follow-up meeting in Paris on 4 May 1910, the 'International Convention for the Suppression of the White Slave Traffic' was signed by thirteen nations, including most of the countries that signed the 1904 Agreement, as well as Austria-Hungary and Brazil. The United States was among the countries that no longer adhered to the programme of the Convention (LN 1927:197–200). The Convention reaffirmed the provisions of the 1904 Agreement, additionally regulating a system of information exchange between the participating states. Specifically, it was recommended that international police communications on prostitution be conducted either through diplomatic channels or directly between the appropriate police authorities.

International policing—from politics to crime

I explained earlier how international police practices in Europe during the 19th century were largely aimed at political objectives and, influenced by national sovereignty sensibilities, were mostly of a transnational and/or limited cooperative form. However, towards the end of the 19th century the objectives of international police activities began to be disassociated from the dictates of national governments to become oriented towards matters of a more distinctly criminal nature. Also, while bilateral and *ad hoc* agreements remained the dominant forms of international police collaboration, attempts to structure police cooperation on a more broadly international basis increased in number. To be sure, international policing with specifically criminal objectives had as yet only developed in very moderate ways and, likewise, the attempts that had been made to build police cooperation on a broad international level were not very successful. But the fact that political objectives in international police plans declined in favour of criminal tasks and that multilateral attempts became more numerous than before does indicate important transformations in the dynamics of international policing, the full consequences of which were yet to be realized. It is therefore worthwhile to contemplate briefly the dynamics of these transformations as well as the conditions for their relative failure.

The depoliticization of international policing

The anti-anarchist conference of Rome and its follow-up meeting in St. Petersburg occurred at a time when international police cooperation for political purposes had slowly but steadily been in decline. In order to explain this paradoxical situation, I will consider more precisely the manner in which the topic of anarchism was treated at the intergovernmental level and the actual consequences of the intergovernmental treaties in terms of legislation and police practice.

The fight against anarchism was evidently a matter of a decidedly political nature, most especially because it included policies reaching beyond the control of criminal incidents inspired by anarchist motives. But the meetings in Rome and St. Petersburg reframed the problem so as to conceive of anarchism in all its manifold dimensions as an entirely and strictly criminal matter, the enforcement of which was to be handled at the administrative level by police institutions. The Italian government's invitation to the meeting downplayed the delicate and divisive issues involved with devising appropriate legislation and instead emphasized the practical police aspects involved, for which reason, the invitation stated specifically, the necessary 'technical and administrative staff' would be invited to attend the meeting (Liang 1992:162). Remarkably, the delegates at the Rome Conference nonetheless spent considerable time disputing a proper definition of anarchism and settled ultimately on a broad and imprecise concept that sought to avoid associations with political ideology. In the Final Protocol of the Conference, it was emphasized that anarchism had 'no relation to politics' and could not 'under any circumstance be regarded as a political doctrine' (Liang 1992:163).

However, although anarchism was formally depoliticized in order to accommodate many, politically diverse national states, and although the Conference attendants promised to enact in their respective countries appropriate legislation, only few countries actually passed laws based on the provisions of the Rome and St. Petersburg protocols. The aspiration to treat anarchism as a criminal matter could evidently not be maintained at the level of the various national governments where the international treaties had to be ratified, because there the initiatives were injected into the ideological battles that dominated intra-national governing. The official response from the French government to the Rome Conference, for instance, declined to approve an intergovernmental accord sanctioning international police cooperation on anarchism because of difficulties 'from the political point of view' (Jensen 1981:345).

Next to the failure of the Rome and St. Petersburg treaties to influence anti-anarchist legislation in the various participating states, ideological divisions in international political affairs also imposed limits upon international police cooperation in the fight against anarchism. Most clearly, the participants of the Rome and St. Petersburg meetings failed to agree upon the creation of a central anti-anarchist intelligence bureau through which the exchange between the various national bureaux could be coordinated. The reason was that, as before, divisive nationalist sentiments in Europe were too intense to accept the creation of a central bureau that would put the one country in which it was to be located at a marked advantage, as the central bureau, indeed, would be the only office connected with all other national bureaux. Instead, only a system of direct facilitation exchange between the various participating states was agreed upon. As such, then, ideological differences and political antagonisms between the countries of Europe not only prevented legislation at the national levels from being passed, they also imposed limits upon the practical systems of international police cooperation that were devised.

It is therefore correct to claim—as historian Richard Jensen (1981:340) does—that the international anti-anarchist treaties failed to influence legislation in the states that signed the accord, because 'national self-interests and rivalries edged out international concerns'. Yet, it is equally important to observe in what manner the Rome and St. Petersburg meetings did contribute effectively to enhance the practices of direct police communication across nations, the necessity of which was widely recognized. It is typical, for instance, that although the British government formally abstained from the provision to institute an international system of information exchange, one of the British representatives at the Conference, Howard Vincent, the former head of the Criminal Investigations Division at Scotland Yard, also acknowledged that direct police communications were beneficial 'if only by forming reciprocal friendships leading to greater cooperation' (Jensen 1981: 332). Among the few realities that harmonized with the agreements reached at the meetings, indeed, was the fact that anti-anarchist intelligence bureaux were set up in the various participating states and exchanged information with one another. The police of Italy and Greece, for example, had such systems of information exchange up and running until the eve of World War I. The fact that the international treaties were relatively successful at the level of police practices is explained by the fact that the suggested system of information exchange was to be instituted and coordinated at the administrative level by police agencies. These provisions were conceived in technical and bureaucratic terms and not coined in the legal language of most of the other provisions. Indeed, while the delegates at the Rome and St. Petersburg meetings were mostly diplomats and other government representatives who negotiated with one another in a language of formal systems of law rooted in jurisdictional authority, the anti-anarchist methods of information exchange that had successfully been worked out had been decided upon by police officials at meetings they held separately during the Conference (Jensen 1981:331). The success of the administrative means of the international fight against anarchism, therefore, was possible more because of the attained level of expertise and organization of police institutions, nationally and internationally, than because of a willingness on the part of the governments of national states to legislate anti-anarchist policies. In light of previously discussed police developments, it is not surprising, for example, that the anti-anarchist bureau of Austria was most successful in gathering information on anarchists from all over Europe, having collected information on some 3,000 anarchists by 1914 (Liang 1992:168).

A further indication that international anti-anarchist intelligence was influenced more by established international police culture than by intergovernmental treaty is the fact that the two provisions of the Rome Conference which applied to all crimes and not specifically to anarchism—the *portrait parlé* system of identification and the Belgian clause of extradition—were among the few Conference proposals that were effectively put into law in several European countries in the years following the meeting (Jensen 1981:331–333). Legislation on these international police activities could be accomplished successfully because of developments in matters of international police organization and police technique that had already begun many years before. For as preceding sections in this chapter have revealed, whether more or less specifically focused on anarchism, police institutions had been exchanging information on a regular basis throughout the 19th century, forging a network of international police experts and developing technical know-how on international police methods. The fact that practical police measures were legislated effectively in the aftermath of the international treaties shows that police authorities had succeeded in having those matters perceived by their respective national governments as purely administrative in nature. As such, the conclusion is that the Rome and St. Petersburg treaties benefited the development of international police practices which they did not initiate but that had already been set up by police institutions.

The anti-anarchist conference of Rome in 1898 and its follow-up meeting in St. Petersburg in 1904 represent remarkable threshold cases in the transformation of international policing in Europe. On the one hand, these efforts clearly have a foot in the 19th century as they remained largely framed in a politically sensitive framework of national governments and international formal law. Yet, on the other hand, they also reveal the growing influence of a developing European police culture that was moving towards the institution of international police practices on the basis of professional expertise. It is for this reason appropriate to consider the international treaties on white slavery in the same context as the anti-anarchist accords. For, indeed, while the international agreements on white slavery dealt with a non-political issue, the agreements reached in Paris in 1904 and 1910 were, like those on anarchism, decided at the intergovernmental level and framed in the language of formal international law. And unlike the Rome Conference on anarchism, the international meetings on white slavery had no police authorities discussing separately issues of practical police control, but instead subsumed all policy measures, legislative and administrative, under one accord of international law. In consequence, although available information on the effects of the Paris agreements is sparse, it appears that they did not impact upon international police strategies and other practical aspects of prostitution policy (Decker 1979). Likewise, the various private initiatives on prostitution were not successful in influencing an international police response. Private groups may be assumed to have been even less capable of influencing police responses than intergovernmental accords, because the moral language in which they condemned prostitution was even further removed from the realities of policing than the legal language in which governments framed treaties of international law. Actual police activities in the area of white slavery, in any case, developed as part of national policies and the international exchange networks police institutions had established without intergovernmental accords.

In sum, late 19th-century international developments concerning anarchism and prostitution need to be framed in terms of the complex dynamics of the relationship between intergovernmental arrangements and international police cooperation practices. Socio-political conditions at the turn of the 20th century prevented broad support for intergovernmental agreements attempting to formalize international police cooperation at the level of international law and, additionally, also set boundaries to the scope of administrative police objectives which remained too closely tied up with the directives of national governments. Accomplishments in effective practical cooperation between police, even when it was achieved in the wake of formal intergovernmental treaties, was not governed top-down by governments and the treaties they had been able to agree upon, but was worked out from the bottom up at the level of a developing European police culture of experts. Thus, it is significant to observe that the Rome and St. Petersburg agreements failed to shape an international police response against the anarchist threat, while they did provide an arena for heads of police to formalize developments of international policing in matters of police technique that had begun many years earlier. The ironic conclusion is that a formalization of police cooperation was achieved in criminal matters after it had originally been conceived in relation to the political issue of anarchism. It is in this context additionally ironic that the anti-white slavery agreements appear to have been unsuccessful in fostering international police cooperation, although they concerned a non-political crime. But the international accords on white slavery were directed by governments at the level of international law without much regard for the practical issues of policing. It is in this light that conclusions on the enforcement of the international laws on anarchism and white slavery must focus on the relative success of the Rome Conference (in a non-politically reoriented fashion) and the relative failure of the anti-white slavery initiatives (despite their focus on a criminal matter).

The internationalization of society

Anarchism and white slavery share the one central characteristic that they were perceived by government and police authorities to be problems that were essentially international in nature, providing grounds on which to build international cooperation at the level of international laws between governments and, at the administrative level, of police institutions. But aside from the varying success of these reactions, it is also important to consider the manner in which international cooperation was conceived, particularly in terms of the relatively successful efforts to forge police collaboration across national borders.

Earlier, I discussed how the political opponents of established regimes were conceived as organizing their efforts internationally, as a sort of pioneering practitioners of the creed to 'think globally and act locally'. This conception of internationality was applied by police and government officials to communists and, especially in the late 19th century, to anarchist movements, the philosophies of which often indeed included explicit attacks on nationalism and the very existence of national states. When after the assassination of Empress Elisabeth of Austria, the Austrian foreign minister called for the establishment of an international police league, he referred to anarchists as 'wild beasts without nationality', who were a menace 'not only to sovereign rulers but to all persons' (Liang 1992:160). The broad international representation at the Rome Conference, with countries as diverse in ideological persuasion as France, the German Empire, and Switzerland, testifies the extent to which the notion of anarchism's internationality was widespread. Even Great Britain sent delegates to the Rome Conference, because although traditionally committed to relatively liberal policies of tolerance towards ideological diversity, the country had all too often served—in the words of one of the British delegates at Rome—as a 'dumping ground' for radical refugees from Continental Europe (Jensen 1981:332).

White slavery, likewise, was perceived primarily from the viewpoint of its international dimensions. The very terms 'white slavery' and 'white slave trade' are meant to indicate that 'movement between brothels was at the very heart of the system' (Bristow 1983:29). Regular clientele demanded variety in supply, venereal diseases caused unemployment and required replacement, and deliberately moving women away from their familiar surroundings strengthened the control powers of their employers. During the 19th century, the traffic in prostitutes had indeed increasingly assumed an international scope, within Europe as well as beyond, especially towards South America (Decker 1979:63–66).[9] Furthermore, the trafficking in prostitutes was recognized to have become an international business that was to be condemned. In a book published in 1904, the President of the Austrian League for the Suppression of White Slavery stated: 'There exists an international organization which in many places of the earth has its general terminals; the export is so regulated that women of particular countries of origin are always sent to those centres where they are especially appreciated' (Schmitz 1927:13).[10]

However, although there was broad support for the notion that that anarchism was an international threat affecting several countries, and although the worldwide trafficking in prostitution was widely condemned, the various policy and police responses were nonetheless

[9] Statistics provided by Schmitz (1927:121–122) reveal that of all prostitutes registered for health purposes in Buenos Aires in the years from 1889 to 1901 about 24% were from Argentina, 19% from Russia, 14% from Italy, 11% from Austria-Hungary, and 10% from France, next to females from Germany, Spain, Switzerland, and several other countries. At that time, some 200 foreign pimps were at work in Buenos Aires (Bristow 1983:29–35, 111–117). Occasionally they would fall victim to the vigilance of police. In 1879, for instance, some thirty-nine procurers, among them Romanians, Poles, and Hungarians, were deported from Brazil back to Europe.

[10] Also relatively widespread was the idea that procurers and prostitutes were predominantly Jewish (Näcke 1913). In consequence, some of the oldest anti-prostitution organizations were also Jewish (Petrow 1994:160). In Warsaw, the Jewish Federation was established in 1897 to unite working-class Jews against criminality, especially organized prostitution. One night in May 1905, Federationists rampaged through brothels and attacked pimps and prostitutes alike. A few years later, the riots were studied by two experts on international prostitution, Marcus Braun, an American immigration inspector, and von Treschow, the head of the German anti-prostitution police (Bristow 1983:58–63).

shaped by local, nationally varying conditions. The suppression of anarchism and other politically deviant ideas was more forcefully conducted in some countries than in others. National policies on prostitution varied even more widely, from outlawing the practice to regulating only its harmful side-effects, especially in terms of health concerns. The globally perceived conditions of anarchism and white slavery affected nations differently.

Furthermore, it is in this respect critical to note that the international police initiatives that were developed in response to the international threats of anarchism and white slavery were so designed that they necessitated the participation of police institutions within national states. Indeed, both the anti-anarchist accords and the treaties on white slavery contained propositions to create intelligence bureaux for information exchange in each of the participating nations. In other words, the suggested systems of international policing entailed the formation of a cooperative structure between existing police institutions within nations, without even the additional advantage of a central bureau linking the various bureaux. Such a system of cooperation avoided the creation of a supranational investigative or intelligence agency and instead reaffirmed the various institutions within nations as the actors in an international network. As I already discussed in the case of the Police Union of German States, this characteristic of international police structures reveals an important persistence of nationality despite the recognition of police objectives as being essentially international in kind.

Finally, the extent to which nationally variable conditions remained relevant and affected the form and scope of international systems is also shown from the fact that international police efforts radiating from Europe had by and large not yet included participation by police agencies from the United States of America. Throughout the 19th century and for a considerable time in the 20th century, indeed, international police activities on the American continent had mostly followed a separate path of development.

2

The Expansion of World Society

> For a long time the leading race elements in the New York police force have been, as they are now, Irish, German, and native American, with a sprinkling of almost every other race under the sun.
> *Theodore Roosevelt, 1897.*

> In the poorer quarters of our great cities may be found huddled together the Italian bandit and the bloodthirsty Spaniard, the bad man from Sicily, the Hungarian, the Croatian and the Pole, the Chinaman and the Negro, the cockney Englishman, the Russian and the Jew, with all the centuries of hereditary hate back of them. They continually cross each others' path. It is no wonder that altercations occur and blood is shed.
> *The Independent, 1907.*

The history of international policing in the 19th century is clearly European history. The manifold instances and various forms of international policing that dominated Europe were simply absent in the context of the United States. However, this is not to deny that police in the New World, too, faced certain challenges of a distinctly international nature, dating back to as early as the first decades after the proclamation of American Independence. As this chapter will make clear, most of the international policing issues posed in the early history of the United States were very specific to that country, although some matters were not without parallel in the developments that I have discussed in the European context. And though one cannot speak of any truly developed structures or processes of trans-Atlantic police cooperation until in much more recent times, there were even in this early period certain problems and opportunities that brought US law enforcement institutions into contact with their counterparts in Europe.

'Every race under the sun': The internationalization of US policing

Ethan Nadelmann's (1993) study of the dynamics of US participation in international policing focuses primarily on present-day conditions and recent developments in the context of international drug enforcement. But Nadelmann's thorough analysis also contains a detailed historical investigation of US participation in international policing activities from the late 18th century onwards (Nadelmann 1993:15–102). I will therefore restrict my analysis in this section to a brief discussion of the issues Nadelmann has so meticulously unravelled and focus in more detail on the distinct traits of international policing with US involvement as well as those dimensions of US law enforcement which involve connections with the police from Europe. Following the theoretical model spelled out in this work, I will analyse these aspects in terms of the dimensions of form and scope of police internationalization which I previously applied in the European context.

Slaves, immigrants, and the frontier

Among the international issues that occupied the early efforts of US policing, those most distinctly characteristic and different from the European situation were related to slavery and the slave trade, immigration and ethnic diversity, and the expanding frontier of the American Union. These issues are very dissimilar both in nature and in the degree to which they influenced responses from police institutions. Also, as I explained earlier, the organization of US policing was such that law enforcement responses could be extremely varied in terms of local conditions. Yet, despite these variations in enforcement duties and local police conditions, certain police issues emerge that share features of an international kind.

The African slave trade was criminalized as early as 1807, when President Thomas Jefferson signed 'An Act to Prohibit the Importation of Slaves into any Port or Place Within the Jurisdiction of the United States' (Nadelmann 1993:31–46). Although the prohibition was only minimally and irregularly enforced, it did produce some police activities, such as in the 1850s when four steamers were sent to patrol the Cuban coast and apprehend slave traders. While the slave trade was an early target of police actions, slavery itself was not, at least not until the constitutionally guaranteed abolition of the practice in 1865. In fact, until the ratification of the Thirteenth Amendment to the US Constitution, the most critical cross-border police activity pertaining to the American institution of slavery involved Southern slave patrols pursuing slaves who had escaped to free states and foreign jurisdictions where slavery was prohibited. As these slave patrols were also in charge of maintaining discipline among slaves on plantations and preventing slave insurrections, they may count among the first US institutions that were endowed with policing duties.

Related to issues of migration and ethnicity in the context of the United States were cross-border police efforts involved with the variously tolerant immigration laws, the perception of a link between crime and migration, the policing of ethnic riots and unrest, and the ethnic composition of the various US police forces (Fogelson 1977:18–19, 36–39; Millspaugh 1937:64–68, 83–85, 177–204). Violations of migration laws were typically treated as civil affairs, yet certain provisions were handled as matters of criminal law. For instance, the Chinese Exclusion Act of 1882 prohibited the importation of Chinese into the United States and was enforced by a special group of customs agents, the so-called Mounted Inspectors, who were employed along the Mexican border. These inspectors were later replaced by agents of the US Immigration Service, who in 1924 were organized institutionally in the Immigration Border Patrol.

The connection between crime and migration counts among the oldest as well as most contested of criminological explanations (e.g. Abbott 1915). The association between crime and conditions relating to immigration and ethnicity was most influential in instigating police actions as a result of the ethnic riots that erupted throughout the history of the United States. Ethnic unrest, for instance between Anglo-Saxon Protestants and Irish Catholics, were among the most common causes of riots throughout much of the 19th century. Furthermore, police and government authorities responded to the criminality that was associated with recently arrived non-Anglo migrants, especially in the larger cities. Police agencies would even direct activities specifically against alien or foreign-born groups, such as in 1909 when the New York police established a service to deal with the Italian-born criminal. A final association between ethnicity and police is posed by the fact that US city police forces, especially in larger urban areas, reflected the ethnic diversity of the population they were to police. For example, in his capacity as Police Commissioner of New York from 1895 to 1897, Theodore Roosevelt was proud to proclaim that 'the leading race elements' in his city's police force were 'Irish, German, and native American, with a sprinkling of almost every other race under the sun' (Roosevelt 1897:395). Roosevelt and other police leaders presented ethnic diversity in the police as the result of conscious efforts to secure representation of the population at large. Yet, it is more likely, as sociologist Robert Fogelson (1977) argues, that the overrepresentation of non-Anglo immigrants in law enforcement was a consequence of economic and social conditions being such that recently arrived migrants were more drawn into the low-prestige career of law enforcement.

Finally, the expanding frontier of the United States and the protection of its national borders with the neighbouring states were also of special concern to US law enforcement agencies. Foreshadowing contemporary conditions, US relations with Canadian law enforcement were much less problematic than with the Mexican police (Nadelmann 1993:60–76). Because of the difficult and occasionally hostile international relations between the United States and Mexico, police collaboration and governmental treaties between the two countries were never easily achieved. Yet, there were exceptions, such as in 1882 when a treaty was agreed upon that allowed US and Mexican troops to pursue fugitive bands of so-called 'savage Indians'.

In the context of US border controls, separate mention should be made of police efforts that pertained to smuggling activities. The control of smuggling was assigned to the Treasury Department and was considered a primary challenge of law enforcement, as customs duties were among the federal government's most important revenues. Not surprisingly, the Treasury Department's Customs Service was together with the US Marshals Service one of the first federal US police agencies created in 1789. Among its international tasks, the Customs Service would engage in cooperation strategies with foreign police or station agents abroad. At the turn of the century, US Customs agents were placed in at least five cities in Europe.

Across the Atlantic

As the international activities of the US Customs Service indicated, there were even as early as the 19th century some instances in which the range of US police operations would extend into Europe. Next to the Customs Service, other federal US police agencies also engaged in foreign liaison work. Specifically, the US Marshals Service and the Secret Service were assigned enforcement duties with international dimensions. US Marshals were in charge of pursuing and returning fugitives from justice between America and foreign countries, an activity that until the advent of more sophisticated means of transportation was largely restricted to the American continent. The Secret Service established connections with foreign police primarily in matters of counterfeiting, but occasionally extended its enforcement duties into other matters too. In the 1880s, for instance, Secret Service agents cooperated with Scotland Yard's Criminal Investigation Division against terrorists fighting for Irish independence.

For a considerable time in the period before World War I, more important than the international liaisons established by federal US law enforcement were those initiated through private police agencies. The Pinkerton National Detective Agency, most notably, had managed to expand its activities at home and abroad after its founder, Allan Pinkerton, had been appointed by the federal government to head the Secret Service and conduct espionage work during the Civil War (Pinkerton 1883; Axelrod 1992). During most of the 19th century, the Pinkerton agency in effect fulfilled the role of a *de facto* national US police which could cooperate with police abroad. By the 1890s, the detective agency had opened several offices across Europe.

Additional law enforcement connections between the United States and other parts of the world were established through intergovernmental initiatives, specifically in the areas of prostitution and narcotics. In terms of the regulation of the white slave trade, the United States was at first but minimally involved by agreeing to adhere to the provisions of, though not actually signing, the 1904 Paris Agreement, and soon withdrew from these international treaties altogether when the 1910 Convention no longer received US support (LN 1927:197). Instead, efforts to control the trafficking of prostitutes into the United States were largely conducted from within the country. As early as 1870, the US Attorney General had hired investigators to inquire about allegations concerning the transportation of European women to the United States for immoral purposes (Sullivan 1977:28). In 1908 the US fight against prostitution was truly launched, when the Immigration Commission conducted an investigation on the 'Importation and Harbouring of Women for Immoral Purposes' (LN 1927:7). The results of the inquiry produced an amendment to US immigration laws and the passing of the White Slave Traffic Act by the US Congress on 23 June 1910. Introduced in Congress by Representative Mann, the federal law came to be known as the Mann Act and its enforcement was assigned to the Justice Department's Bureau of Investigation.

Another matter of law enforcement that established trans-continental connections between US and foreign law enforcement in the period before World War I was the control of narcotics. In fact, next to the suppression of the white slave trade and anarchism, the regulation of the production, use, and traffic in narcotics was also regulated by international treaties agreed upon by the governments of national states.[1]

[1] On the history of international drug laws, see Bruun, Pan and Rexed 1975:7–27; Millspaugh 1937:79–83; Reinsch 1916:61–62; Renborg 1942; and Walker 1991:1–61.

The use and import of opium had occupied governments and private groups off and on from the 18th century onwards. Originally tolerated, narcotics use in the United States was in the latter half of the 19th century increasingly subjected to criticism over its harmful medical effects. A first intergovernmental effort on the matter was made in 1909, when delegates of thirteen states convened at the International Opium Commission in Shanghai. Initiated by a proposal of the US Secretary of State, an Opium Conference was held in the town of The Hague in the Netherlands in 1912. The meeting produced a 'Convention for the Suppression of the Abuse of Opium and Other Drugs', signed by the governments of fifty-seven countries. The Convention stipulated that the participating countries were to enact laws to control the production and distribution of raw opium and make efforts to restrict the manufacture, sale, and use of morphine and cocaine for medical and other legitimate purposes. In 1914, the US Congress enacted several relevant laws, among them the Harrison Narcotics Act, which in agreement with the Convention drawn up in The Hague restricted the production and distribution of narcotics.

The boundaries of the new world

Although US police agencies were since the formation of the American republic engaged in a variety of international tasks, US involvement in international policing during the 19th century is clearly dwarfed by the frequency and intensity with which European police institutions were at the time involved in international policing efforts. As Ethan Nadelmann (1993:15–18) argues, the present-day status of US law enforcement as a leader on the international policing scene did not begin to develop until as recently as the end of World War II. Nadelmann attributes US insularity from international policing outside of the American continent to a number of factors, including the isolationist approach of US foreign policy, the geographical isolation of the United States, and the slow development of US federal policing agencies (Nadelmann 1993:15–18). These factors are indeed among those that shaped the distinct nature of international policing with US involvement, but it is useful to estimate the relative impact of these factors in terms of a distinction that can be drawn between the specificity of many of the international duties of US law enforcement, on the one hand, and the relative insularity of US policing from international cooperation, on the other.

The borders of international policing

A discussion of the characteristics of international policing practices in the United States during the 19th century cannot avoid considerations pertaining to the socio-geographical conditions that characterized the American continent. As a whole, the American continent never possessed the geographical proximity of national states that to this day characterizes Europe and there much more acutely brought about opportunities for international police cooperation. The United States since its founding covered a large territory and gradually but steadily expanded its frontier. Unlike the countries of Europe with their manifold national borders that could justify an immediate need for international police operations, the United States is bordered by land by only two nations, separated from the rest of the world by two vast oceans. US involvement in international policing activities beyond the American continent, therefore, could only be minimal in the years considered here, most obviously because technological developments in the means of transportation and communication were throughout the 19th century not yet sufficiently advanced to bridge the huge distance between America and the world's other continents effectively. Instead of international concerns shared across the continents, therefore, intra-national developments mostly determined the objectives of US law enforcement. As such, the equivalent of international police cooperation in Europe was inter-state cooperation between local law enforcement in the United States (Nadelmann 1993:16).

A majority of the internationally oriented issues that US police agencies were involved in throughout the 19th century concerned specific tasks associated with slavery and the slave trade, migration and ethnic diversity, and the expansion of the frontier. These issues were not altogether dissimilar in terms of their cross-border dimensions from some of the conditions that existed in Europe and other parts of the world. But in the absence of any concrete connections with the experiences in other countries, US involvement in these tasks remained limited in international scope. Whatever forms of cooperation that were achieved in these matters were mostly limited to the United States' neighbouring countries. In terms of the pursuit of fugitive slaves in the decades before the Civil War, international initiatives with US involvement on the matter predominantly involved unilateral work in the form of US agents working abroad or bilateral forms of cooperation between the United States and its two neighbouring states. The peculiar history of migration and the high degree of ethnic diversity in the United States are also unique to the country, with remarkable influence on the ethnic composition of US police forces. And in terms of the fight against the slave trade, too, developments in the United States were more significant than international arrangements. Typically, for instance, when in 1890 a conference in Brussels led to the creation of coordination offices in Zanzibar and Brussels to oversee the enforcement of an international agreement outlawing the slave trade and African slavery, the United States was not involved (Mander 1941:53–65; Reinsch 1916:64).

Border control presents a final international policing task that specifically occupied the United States since the country's independence. To be sure, border control duties can be assumed to be relevant in the context of much international policing across the world, because borders demarcate nations from each other. At the same time, however, national border regions are by definition restricted to the areas of particular nations where police actions are to be conducted. In the United States, border control assignments were in the first instance shaped by the expanding frontier shifting the boundaries of national jurisdiction. Also relevant in the history of US border control were tasks related to smuggling activities that sought to circumvent customs regulations. As early as 1845, for instance, an agent was dispatched to the US–Mexican border territory to detect smugglers trying to evade customs provisions that were in effect since the annexation of Texas. In fact, dating back to at least 14th-century England when a 1351 Statute of Treasons criminalized the importation of counterfeit money, smuggling counts among the oldest criminal violations instigating internationally oriented policing (Deflem and Henry-Turner 2001). In the US context, there was historically a strong emphasis on the enforcement of smuggling laws, indicating that relatively new national states place a particularly high premium on taxation laws and the protection thereof. It comes as no surprise therefore that the US Customs Service was among the first federal US police forces to be created in 1789 and that Treasury agents were among the first to engage at an international level in protective strategies aimed at enforcing revenue laws (Nadelmann 1993:22–31).

The insularity of US policing

Beyond the socio-geographical conditions that led the majority of international police operations in the United States to be specific to that country, certain characteristics of US police institutions and their participation in international police activities further contributed to the relative insularity of US policing from international involvement beyond the American continent. In terms of the organization of law enforcement in the United States, the most striking features are the generally poor state of US policing and the slow development of federal police institutions.

The fact that US police forces were inadequately organized and that police responses were very pragmatic contributed directly to restrict the operational field of US policing. Given the limitations of US police organizations in terms of competence, personnel, and enforcement powers, there simply was not much opportunity to engage in the outwardly oriented tasks of international policing. As Ethan Nadelmann argues, because of the severe practical limitations facing most US police agencies, a fugitive criminal fleeing abroad could very well mean the end of the case (Nadelmann 1993:17). Also, as a result of the poorly developed state of public police agencies, several international police functions were in the United States carried out by other institutions, particularly military forces and private detective agencies. Navy and Army troops, indeed, at times complemented their function of external coercion with the likewise outwardly oriented duties of international policing, for instance to enforce the prohibition on the slave trade (Nadelmann 1993:20). Of all US police organizations, private detective agencies were during the 19th century most involved in international police cooperation. Private agencies were relatively well organized and had attained a considerably higher level of professional standards than public police forces. Also, because they were less subject to government control, large private detective agencies like the Pinkerton Agency could collaborate with foreign police more easily than official US police. Until the turn of the century, private police agencies in the United States provided the law enforcement link with Europe and other parts of the world (Nadelmann 1993:55–60).

The fact that US police organizations during the 19th century were poorly developed may also have contributed to the fact that international law enforcement duties in the United States were comparatively more subject to international treaties reached between the US and foreign governments. In the absence of much actual cooperation between law enforcement from the United States and abroad, the US government tried to fill the void by formalizing international regulations and their enforcement in a number of areas, particularly with respect to the international rendition of fugitives (Nadelmann 1993:404–411). Initially, the US government was reluctant to engage in treaties with governments abroad, but in 1848 the US Congress passed an extradition law and in the following decades the US government signed some thirty-three extradition treaties with countries all over the world, especially in Europe. Yet, much as I argued to be the case in the European context, there are no indications that these formal intergovernmental accords were able significantly to influence policing activity or actual extraditions. In his analysis of the international functions of US law enforcement, Ethan Nadelmann (1993) provides little empirical evidence to indicate otherwise. The relative ineffectiveness of the extradition treaties signed by the US government is all the more telling since all these treaties from the 1840s onwards included explicitly a 'political offence' exception, a regulation that was far from insignificant considering the broad functions and sweeping practices of Europe's police regimes (Nadelmann 1993:419). Also, when extradition treaties proved inadequate or were not available, US police officials often relied on foreign extradition laws or on the willingness of foreign officials to deliver fugitives without formal treaty. For instance, between 1842 and 1890, over 200 people were extradited to the United States, and more than 200 were delivered to foreign countries, but these renditions may include many that were not based on a formal treaty (Nadelmann 1993:436–437, 401). It is, then, extremely unlikely that formal accords between the US and foreign governments shaped international police operations in the United States. Not only were these intergovernmental treaties framed in the traditional language of jurisdictional authority which law enforcement typically sought to circumvent, they could in the US context also not rely on a level of police organization sufficiently developed to provide the necessary resources, personnel, and expertise to implement whatever arrangements governments had agreed upon.

The absence of well-developed federal US police institutions not only contrasted sharply with the situation in Europe, but was a direct reaction against European conditions. Throughout history, the US Congress repeatedly argued against the creation of a national police system because it was reminiscent of the centralized police models that were associated with the repressive political regimes of Europe (Nadelmann 1993:48). As a result, there was in the United States during the 19th century no federal police institution that was sufficiently evolved in organizational and functional respects to participate in international cooperation efforts on a level equal to the European police. The oldest federal US police institutions—the Customs Service, Postal Inspection Service, and Marshals Service—were but very small forces with limited police powers. The Secret Service and the investigative branches of the Justice Departments, which were later created, were initially also too restricted in terms of enforcement duties and resources to be able to provide a link with the European continent. The fact that US policing styles had been imported from Europe—if more from Britain's civilian police rather than the semi-military style that dominated continental Europe—did not lead to a *de facto* standardization of US and European police practices, because the importation of policing styles in the United States (as in colonial territories, in general) was piecemeal in fashion and adjusted to local conditions.

Among the most important local conditions that initially shaped US policing was the influence of partisan politics, particularly through the control of appointments of top-rank positions. The political dependence of the police in the US context concerned a local control over law enforcement by 'political machines', an association of the police with politics that was anything but equivalent to the European situation of policing developments in function of central governments (Fogelson 1977:13–39). On the contrary, as a result of strong sentiments against the political associations of European police systems, the connection between national police systems and repressive political regimes in Europe effectively limited cooperation across the Atlantic, particularly—though not only—in political police matters. For example, on the occasion of the London Exhibition in 1851, several city police forces in the United States were invited by the British government to attend the Exhibition to check on 'criminal and dangerous characters' and even politically suspicious subjects who could 'act as propagandists of their principles' (in Smith 1985:90). But although some US police officials were sent to London, they did not cooperate with continental police and restricted their activities to criminal law enforcement duties, such as the observation of pickpockets from New York (Smith 1985:90–91). A further indication that international political policing schemes in Europe could not count on US support is the fact that the US government was not involved in the anti-anarchist meeting at St. Petersburg in 1904, although the meeting was directly inspired by the assassination of US President McKinley by an anarchist in 1901. The only politically oriented international dimensions of US law enforcement in the 19th century took place under very exceptional circumstances, specifically when there was a temporary redefining of law enforcement duties in times of war. For instance, the Secret Service was engaged in espionage matters during the Civil War of 1861–1865 and the Spanish-American War of 1898, but those activities were aborted as soon as peace was restored (Nadelmann 1993:50).

Finally, US insularity from international police cooperation is also reflected in the fact that US involvement in intergovernmental treaties of international law was typically restricted to bilateral agreements. Indeed, consistent with the isolationism of US foreign policy before World War I, the US government typically refrained from participation in intergovernmental arrangements with (and without) law enforcement implications that were organized at a multilateral level. For instance, the United States did not participate in the regulation that was worked out to suppress the slave trade, when in 1841, Prussia, Austria-Hungary, and Russia joined the agreement that the governments of Great Britain and France had signed in 1833 (Mander 1941:53–65; Reinsch 1916:64). Instead, the US government agreed upon bilateral accords, such as the 'Treaty Between United States and Great Britain for the Suppression of the Slave Trade' signed in April 1862. Likewise, other matters of criminal law recognized by the international community of governments, such as white slavery, could typically not count on support from the United States. Remarkably, in the international regulation of drugs, the United States did not only participate but actually led the effort, when the US State Department in 1912 organized the Opium Conference of The Hague. However, US involvement in the initiative clearly responded to intra-national concerns over the drug habit and mainly to ensure that the international drug trade would not affect the United States. The State Department's Opium Commissioner was careful to emphasize that the United States had taken on a leading role in the international anti-drug effort 'not as a result of pressure from foreign states, but as a matter of international courtesy' (*New York Times* 1909).

In sum, US involvement in international police practices during the 19th century was limited in scope because it was restricted to specific duties with a cross-border dimension and because US law enforcement was by and large excluded from international cooperation beyond the American continent. On the one hand, most law enforcement concerns with an international dimension were specific to the US situation and remained localized to the American continent. On the other hand, until the first decades of the 20th century, US law enforcement was not heavily involved in international cooperation for a variety of reasons: the geographical distance from the European mainland presented a physical barrier which could not be easily transcended with available means of transportation and communication; the United Sates did not possess a national police force sufficiently developed to collaborate with foreign national police institutions; European international policing was during the 19th century too heavily motivated by political objectives to appeal to US law enforcement; and US isolationism in matters of foreign policy prevented involvement in multilateral intergovernmental treaties with law enforcement implications. The influence of these factors again demonstrates that socio-political conditions of various kinds may impose limits upon international police cooperation in a manner that differs from one nation to the next. Although certain police duties of an international nature were recognized in the United States during the 19th century, it would still take considerable time for conditions to change in order to ensure more developed forms of US law enforcement participating in international work beyond the American continent.

From national sovereignty to international society

Inasmuch as 19th-century efforts to establish international police organizations were still framed in terms of international law and the diplomatic relations between states, they mostly failed to influence actual police practices. At the same time, however, ongoing efforts in the internationalization of policing paved the way for later developments that were to be more successful. Two transformations in the form and organization of 19th-century international policing are in this respect critical. First, there occurred a gradual shift in international police practices from covert transnational operations and limited collaborative plans to more structured and multilateral forms of cooperation. This reveals a growing recognition that the police across various countries shared a common task, while the preferred cooperative form preserved the traits and authority of participating national police institutions. Secondly, there occurred a change in the objectives of international policing from the control of political opponents to the enforcement of criminal violations. Early forms of international policing, especially in Europe, focused on anarchism and other politically suspect movements, but gradually made way for the control of more distinct criminal activities such as white slavery and narcotics. In the

United States, most international police duties had always been of a more distinct criminal nature, but with a poorly developed federal police system and considering the rather specific nature of most law enforcement assignments on the American continent, US involvement in international efforts remained restricted throughout the 19th century.

These developments in the area of policing did not take place in isolation but were part of a broader trend of a growing internationalization of society. Of special relevance to this development in the area of policing were certain advances in technology and accompanying systems of knowledge in the area of criminal investigation.

The rise of international society

With increasing pace during the 19th century, international processes were taking place across various dimensions of social life (Boli and Thomas 1997; Meyer et al. 1997). According to one observer, more than 2,000 international meetings were held between 1843 and 1910 (La Fontaine 1911:244). The same period also witnessed the founding of a multitude of international organizations, such as the Universal Postal Union in 1874, the World Union of Wireless Telegraphy in 1909, and the International Institute of Sociology founded by the French sociologist René Worms in 1893. And in the areas of law and crime, too, a variety of international initiatives were taken besides the police developments focused on in this chapter. For example, the Institute of International Law was established in Paris in 1873 and the International Union of Criminal Law in 1888. International Prison Congresses had been held since 1846 when a first meeting convened in Frankfurt, Germany.[2]

The internationalization of the police function during the mid to late 1900s, then, was clearly part of a broader pattern of a globalization of social life. However, historical evidence indicates that there were by and large no institutional connections between the international efforts in the areas of criminal law and penology, on the one hand, and the various practices and organizations of international policing, on the other. International organizations of criminal law and penology rarely discussed policing issues, which were typically viewed as mere administrative matters. And when aspects of policing were brought up, they

[2] On the international prison congresses, see Teeters 1949; Butler 1926; Conti and Prins 1911; AfK 1925b, 1934b, 1935b; Gault 1929; Henderson 1910, 1911; Lyon 1931; Reinsch 1916:56–59. On international organizations of criminologists, see AfK 1938c, 1938e; Bischoff 1931.

were discussed in a framework that remained rooted in terms of formal systems of law. For example, the International Union of Criminal Law or *Internationale Kriminalistische Vereinigung* (IKV), an important European association of legal scholars founded by Franz von Liszt, Adolphe Prins, and Gerardus van Hamel, devoted some attention to issues of international policing (Bellman 1994; Radzinowicz 1991). At the eighth meeting of the IKV in Budapest in 1899, preventive and repressive measures against the white slave traffic were suggested (Schmitz 1927:26). And at the tenth IKV meeting in Hamburg in 1905, it was decided to promote the establishment of central agencies in various countries to collect and exchange information on international criminals. However, these initiatives found no support among police officials, who were developing appropriate models of international cooperation separately.

Thus, although initiatives in the areas of international criminal law and punishment did not always originate from state or legal authorities but also from private associations of legal scholars, they all remained framed in the formal legal terms which police experts had gradually begun to abandon in favour of a depoliticized and extra-legal practice of policing and international police cooperation. Indeed, as I have already repeatedly indicated and as the remainder of this study will confirm, in wake of an increasing bureaucratization of the police function, efforts to forge international police cooperation did not rely on principles of international criminal law. Although the precise contours of international criminal law are difficult to draw, in the 19th century even more so than today, this body of law is based on the systems of criminal law recognized by national states as well as the bilateral and multilateral treaties they maintain with one another (Bassiouni 1997, 1999; McRae and Hubert 2001). International criminal law regulates both (supranational) violations of the global order of states (e.g. crimes against humanity, and war crimes) as well as (transnational) crimes that affect more than one nation (e.g. drug trafficking, and smuggling). Additional regulations of international law govern the manner in which international crimes are administered and enforced, including, for example, the organization of international courts and the procedures of extradition and mutual legal assistance across nations. However, as this and the previous chapter showed, police institutions would increasingly begin to develop an expert practice of policing and international police cooperation that was not based on formal systems of international criminal law, not even when they concerned transnational crimes and their enforcement.[3] On the contrary, international police strategies would often be designed purposely to circumvent the formal regulations of international law. This extra-legality of police is most clearly shown by the various efforts to establish direct international police communications and the influence of professional police conceptions of the internationalization of crime. This development, it will be shown at various stages throughout this study, was aided critically by important technological innovations.

Technology and knowledge in the internationalization of policing

Instrumental in the development of international police cooperation from the middle of the 19th century onwards were a number of technological innovations that facilitated the gathering and transmission of information on criminals and suspects across the borders of national states. Among these technologies were initially various forms of printed media containing information and pictures of wanted suspects and criminals. The transmission of published information on wanted suspects was especially well developed among the political police of Europe, but the practice was also widely used for criminal purposes and would remain a favoured method of police communications until well into the 20th century. After the first picture of a convict had been taken in a Brussels prison in 1843, the police of Paris were the first to set up a collection of pictures of criminals in 1874. By the end of the 19th century, photographic identification services were established among all major police institutions in Europe and the United States. In the 1880s, the New York City police department established a picture collection of international rogues and exchanged information with police in Europe (Nadelmann 1993:82–83).

Perhaps most important among the technological innovations that influenced the internationalization of the police function were the bertillonage and fingerprint systems of identification (Brown and Brock 1953; Cole 2001; Hagemann 1933a:744; Nadelmann 1993:82–85; Sullivan 1977:38–40). The bertillonage or anthropometry system was

[3] Violations of the global order regulated by international law find their counterpart to the policing of international crimes not in any operations of (civilian) police but in military interventions, specifically so-called 'peace-keeping' missions, which are at times referred to as 'police interventions' or efforts of 'international enforcement', but such terminology is clearly metaphorical at best, misleading at worst (see, e.g. Eliot 1953; Welsh 2001).

developed by Alphonse Bertillon in 1870 and first adopted by the French government in the 1880s. In 1890, the Chicago police was the first to implement the system in the United States. In the same year, it was suggested at a meeting of the International Prison Society in Berne, Switzerland, that the method could be used to track down fugitive criminals abroad. When the World's Fair was held in Chicago in 1893, the local police department showed its bertillonage system to visiting foreign police. The Fair itself also proved a testing ground for the new method, because 'the temporary influx of strangers from every quarter of the globe' on occasion of the exhibition was expected to present a 'problem of international significance' (Bonfield 1893:714; McClaughry 1893).

The application of fingerprinting techniques for criminal investigations was first suggested in the 1880s by British anthropologist Francis Galton, who in his book *Finger Prints* argued for the individuality and permanence of fingerprints (Galton 1892). In the 1890s, police official Juan Vucetich of Argentina and Edward Henry of Scotland Yard were the first to introduce fingerprint classification systems for the purposes of criminal identification. In 1891, the Argentinean Police adopted a criminal identification system based on Galton's classification, and the system was revised and introduced at Scotland Yard in London in 1901. To ease cross-border exchange, fingerprints were expressed numerically on the basis of certain selected characteristics and transmitted telegraphically. The fingerprint system would rapidly become internationalized to remain among the most important methods of criminal identification to this day. In 1902, Henry P. DeForest introduced the dactyloscopy system in the New York Civil Service Commission. A year later, the New York state prison adopted the system, and in 1904 the St. Louis Police Department organized its fingerprint bureau with the help of a Scotland Yard sergeant. In the same year, a detective of the New York Police Department travelled to London to inspect the application of the method by Scotland Yard. By the early 1900s, the system had also been introduced in Germany, though in France the bertillonage system remained in force for some time after that (Schneickert 1904, 1911).

Technologies of identification were accompanied by other developments of efficient policing responding to the threat of the internationalization of crime, especially in the area of transportation. Considered particularly troublesome—as already noted, for instance, by the members of the Police Union—was the development of the railways. As early as 1893, a German scholar devoted an entire book to the criminal, legal, and police implications of the railways (Loock 1893). Later, cars and planes were added to the list of means of transportation relevant for use by criminals seeking refuge abroad and, consequently, by police in their pursuit (Hanna 1927; Roenneke 1936; Schneickert 1922; Weiß 1919). These technological developments were in the first instance considered to represent an increase in the general mobilization of society, enhancing opportunities for criminal wrongdoers to seek refuge in foreign countries beyond the jurisdiction and competence of the national police.

While it was not until the 20th century that technological innovations were to be broadly consequential for the international organization of policing, related developments in the science of criminology had already been strongly influential from the middle of the 19th century onwards. The internationalization of police practices, indeed, could rely on developments in the 19th-century criminal sciences, specifically the growing popularity of the positivist perspective of criminology which located the causes of crime in a society of living beings, not in a formal system of law (see Deflem 1997a; Foucault 1978, 1982a, b; Garland 1985:121–125; Pasquino 1991a). Crimes, the positivist criminologists argued, were committed by people who were causally determined to act criminally for various reasons related to their body, psyche, or social environment. Earlier perspectives of the classic school of criminology defended the notion that criminals had to be considered in terms of the consequences of their actions, i.e. as persons who violate a law. With the discovery of the causes of crime and its statistical regularities, however, the focus of attention shifted from the national jurisdictions of legality to a borderless society of dangerous criminals (Foucault 1974). And as society knows no boundaries, the criminal sciences and criminal justice agencies that base their practices on them should know no boundaries either (Deflem 1997a). This helps explain how the two most critical transformations of international policing in the 19th century—the shift towards cooperative organizations with wide participation and towards criminal enforcement duties—went hand in hand: given the shared perspectives of the nature and development of crime across nations, international police organizations appealed to a broader base of representation, while its objectives gradually de-politicized.

Indeed, as one important element of the new sciences of crime, there would be expressed, time and time again from the mid-19th century onwards, the idea that international crime was on the rise as a consequence of a general modernization of social life. In the late 19th century, the famous French social psychologist Gabriel Tarde claimed that criminals used 'more intelligently than the police the resources of our civilization' (Marabuto 1935:30). In 1893, the German criminologist Franz von Liszt expressed the similar idea that criminals specializing in monetary crimes had begun to roam the world and that the police response against them should be coordinated internationally (Fooner 1973:10, 1989:29; Marabuto 1935:15). Under such a developing commonality in the targeting of police culture, it would become possible for police authorities to organize international cooperation on a broadly international basis. Then, as criminologist Cyrille Fijnaut (1997) has argued, slowly but steadily an international brotherhood of police was formed that developed into 'a fraternity which felt it had a moral purpose, a mission, to perform for the good of society' (p. 111). In consequence, the increasing attention given to the international criminal since the second half of the 19th century also implied a societalization or de-politicization of crime and its suppression beyond the formal legal systems of states. As the coming chapters will show, this recognized commonality among the police in terms of expert means and objectives would become more and more significant in organizational respects during the earlier half of the twentieth century.

3

Towards an International Criminal Police

> Police co-operation is more prompt and thorough throughout the world than ever before . . . We find the finger print of England and the finger print of United States filed within the police cabinets of the principal cities of these two great countries. The photographs and measurements of the criminals of Paris may be found in the galleries of the department in Washington, and vice versa.
> *Police Chief Richard Sylvester, 1905.*

> We live in an age of constantly expanding traffic. With the railroads one can move about quickly all over Europe. Travelling criminals take advantage of that! But our police methods—and this is the major problem, my dear Meunier—still hail from the Middle Ages . . . That has to change! . . . I will as soon as possible organize an international conference in Monte Carlo, a police congress or something like that.
> *Albert I, Prince of Monaco, 1914.*

Until the early 20th century, international police cooperation was not yet structured on a broad international scale in a more or less permanent organization. In the United States, police duties with cross-border implications were related to very specific circumstances associated with slavery, immigration, and the founding of national borders on the American continent. Although local law enforcement agencies were heavily influenced by partisan politics, democratic ideals prevented the police from formally pursuing political tasks. Collaboration with European and other police outside the United States occurred therefore, as well as for reasons of geographical distance, only on very sporadic occasions. In Europe, international police practices were comparatively much more developed, but remained typically organized on a rather limited international basis and/or primarily pursued political tasks. Such was the case, most clearly, with the Police Union of German States, which could appeal internationally only to the police of nations with a close ideological and political affinity. Other efforts to formalize cross-border police collaboration, specifically the Anti-Anarchist Conference of 1898, likewise remained too closely tied to the political constitutions of national states to garner broad support. Additionally, the Anti-Anarchist Conference, as well as similar schemes on matters of non-political criminality, specifically prostitution and narcotics, were organized at the formal level of international law. These efforts involved the signing of formal treaties between governments, but they failed to build any structures of practical cooperation between police institutions. To be sure, such agreements could affect reorganizations of national police institutions and occasionally also served as catalysts for instituting reforms of existing international police practices. Successful reorientations of international policing, however, were typically arrived at through informal agreements by police officials established separately from the provisions of formal treaties.

International collaboration in the policing of political crimes and efforts at cooperation instituted at the level of international treaties between governments share the characteristic that they both by necessity mirror the political conditions of international affairs among national states and the characteristics of their respective systems of law. Such forms of cooperation impose severe limitations upon the scope of their international potential and do not allow the participating police to move beyond the legal authority sanctioned by national states and the political dictates of their governments, regardless of whether international agreements take place for political or criminal purposes. However, as the previous chapter showed, a trend emerged during the latter half of the 19th century to focus the attention in international policing schemes away from political crimes towards more distinctly criminal police functions. An indication of this is the failure to build an anti-anarchist police network, while non-political policing tasks started to attract more attention. Yet, until the turn of the century, cooperation practices in criminal police matters mostly took place on an informal and temporary basis. Such informal contacts were rather innocuous in themselves, but they may have functioned as factors contributing to form the beginnings of a common culture of the police across nations. It is this commonality of the police across nations in respect of function and practices, and its explicit recognition among the police, I argue, that would form the basis on which new, more structured organizational forms of international collaboration could be built from the early 20th century onwards. This chapter will indeed show that there were since the turn of the 20th century various attempts undertaken to establish a veritable organization of international police cooperation. Unlike informal and *ad hoc* forms of police cooperation, an international police organization typically has a clearly specified structure (often including a procedure on acquiring membership and the assignment of leadership positions), agreed upon goals in terms of investigative tasks (e.g. criminal matters in general, or selected offences), specified means to reach those goals (e.g. standardized methods of police investigation, detective work and information exchange, a central headquarters, and a functional division of labour between participating police), and it is set up ideally as a permanent organization.

This chapter will review the earliest attempts to establish international police organizations with wide international appeal and the conditions that affected their success or failure. From the discussion in the previous chapter it will be no surprise to learn that of these efforts the one with the broadest international representation took place in Europe, specifically when the 'First Congress of International Criminal Police' was held in Monaco in 1914. Remarkably, however, before that time several efforts to formalize international police cooperation had already been undertaken on the American continent.

'International comity'—'*Conferencia internacional*': International police cooperation in the Americas

The first effort to structure international police cooperation on the American continent did not concern the development of an international police organization with investigative powers, but was instead oriented at extending on an international level the scope of a professional association of police officials that had been established in the United States. The formation of a nation-wide police association in the context of the United States, however, is in itself not without parallel in developments of police internationalization, for US policing was after all a predominantly local affair, so that nationalization in the United States—like internationalization in Europe—implied enhanced cooperation between the police agencies of different localities. In Latin America, the fostering of police cooperation was taken a step further and also involved attempts to form an organization of police with goals related explicitly to criminal investigation on a truly, if limited, international scale.

The international association of chiefs of police

The internationalization of a US police organization emanated from the creation in 1893 of the National Police Chiefs' Union, a professional association of police intended to foster cooperation between the various local police agencies in the United States. Similar attempts to enhance police cooperation across the municipalities of different US states had already taken place on several occasions, first at the National Police Convention organized in St. Louis, Missouri in October 1871.[1] Attended by over 100 police officials from twenty-three US states, the St. Louis convention aimed at police cooperation nationally in the United States, and also appealed to foreign police officials to join the effort. As an 'act of international comity', the police of various European countries were invited to attend the meeting, and American embassies in Europe were requested to pass on information on local crime conditions (National Police Convention 1871:vii). However, the international response to these requests was minimal. While the US ambassadors of several European countries provided the meeting organizers with information on crime and policing in their respective host countries, none of the invited foreign police attended the convention.

The St. Louis Convention and similar efforts in later years did not have any lasting impact until the National Police Chiefs' Union was founded in 1893. At the suggestion of Washington, DC Police Chief Richard Sylvester, then President of the organization, the Union was in 1901 renamed the International Association of Chiefs of Police (IACP), under which name the organization still exists today. Although Sylvester wanted the police organization to develop on an international scale, the association would have only limited international appeal. Despite the name change, the IACP was then—and would continue to be until this day—a predominantly American affair, with very few foreign, mostly Canadian, members. Although European police officials were regularly invited to attend the IACP annual conventions, they would usually not attend. At the association meeting in Washington, DC in 1905, Sylvester once again called for international cooperation, remarking that police communications 'throughout the world' had much improved thanks to an international exchange of information

[1] This section relies on an official report of the St. Louis convention (National Police Convention 1871) and additional observations from police officials (McCaffrey 1913; Sylvester 1912, 1914). See also Marabuto 1935:22–23; Nadelmann 1993:84–87; Walker 1980:133–135.

(Nadelmann 1993:86). But the appeal had little or no effect. As one of the few accomplishments in terms of international collaboration for investigative purposes, the Association set up a National Bureau of Criminal Identification that collected Bertillon cards of convicted and suspected criminals to be exchanged with foreign police. In the 1920s, however, the identification bureau was handed over to the Justice Department and eventually brought under the supervision of the Bureau of Investigation.

Latin-American police cooperation

Remarkably, Latin-American police were among the first to plan the formation of an international criminal police organization. But, like their counterparts in North America, these initiatives did not produce any lasting results.[2] At the 'Second Latin-American Scientific Congress' in Montevideo in 1901, Juan Vucetich, Police Chief of La Plata, Argentina, voiced the idea of organizing international police cooperation through the establishment of Intercontinental Offices of Identification in Europe, South America, and Northern America. The offices would be in contact with one another and transmit dactyloscopic data on international criminals. Vucetich's plans did not produce any concrete results, but at the Third Scientific Congress, in Rio de Janeiro in July 1905, it was decided to follow up on Vucetich's idea and arrange an international police congress to formalize an agreement on the matter. As a result, an international meeting of police was held in Buenos Aires in October 1905, leading to the signing of an 'International Police Convention' by the police of Buenos Aires, La Plata, Montevideo, Rio de Janeiro, and Santiago de Chile. The convention sought to enhance means of information exchange between the police and develop a common system of defence against criminals crossing national borders.

Information on the collaboration schemes among the police of Latin America is very scarce, itself symptomatic of the fact that the initiatives were not very successful. A further indication of the lack of impact of these schemes, similar ideas for enhancing police cooperation in Middle and South America would be repeated for several years after 1905. In 1910, at the 'International American Scientific Congress' in

[2] Information on international police collaboration in Latin America is taken from discussions in AfK 1939b; Fooner 1989:29–30; Lindsey 1910; Marabuto 1935:26–27; Reinsch 1916:66–67.

Buenos Aires, a student of Vucetich proposed the creation of a Universal Police Union (Marabuto 1935:26). Additional meetings of the Latin-American police were held in Sao Paolo in 1912 and in Buenos Aires in 1920 where the '*Conferencia internacional sudamericana da policia*' was held from 20 to 27 February. Although by 1922, reportedly, seven countries had joined the convention first drawn up in 1905, these Latin-American schemes give no indication of successful implementation (Fooner 1989:29). As late as 1931, Luis Almandos of Argentina again argued for the creation of an International Identification Union on the basis of the plans Vucetich had originally developed in 1901, proposing the establishment of a permanent 'International Commission' and 'intercontinental bureaux' in every continent of the world (Almandos 1931:179).

'Springtime ravings at the Côte d'Azur': The First Congress of International Criminal Police

From the discussion in Chapter 1, it may cause no surprise that a European counterpart to the Latin-American attempts to structure international police cooperation would be able to attract broader international participation. Yet, the 'First Congress of International Criminal Police' ('*Premier Congrès de Police judiciaire internationale*'), held in Monaco in April 1914, would also be ineffective in establishing a viable organization of international police cooperation.[3] The Monaco Congress attracted about 300 magistrates, diplomats, lawyers, law professors, and police officials from twenty-four countries. Nearly all European countries were represented, including France, Germany, Italy, and Russia, as were several nations outside Europe, such as Persia, Algiers, Cuba, and Mexico (Roux 1914:4–5). Some officials attended the Congress as official delegates of their respective governments, others were present as private observers.

The Congress discussed various ways to enhance the international exchange of information among the police in matters of criminal, non-

[3] Information on the Monaco Congress is taken from the published minutes of the Congress (Roux 1914), articles by some of the meeting's participants (Finger 1914; Heindl 1914b, 1914c, 1914e; Locard 1914; Schneickert 1914), and other contemporary reports (Journal de Monaco 1914; Journal du Droit International Privé 1914: Deutsche Strafrechts-Zeitung 1914). See, also, the analyses by Marabuto 1935:2–3; Liang 1992:153–155; Möllmann 1969:38–40; Palitzsch 1926a:40–44; Schmitz 1927:88–89; Stiebler 1981:11–14; Walther 1968:11–16.

political violations. Specifically, four thematic sessions were held that dealt with general police questions, means of identification, a central registration system, and extradition procedures (Roux 1914:66–198). The systems of police information exchange that were suggested were to be executed directly from one police agency to another, with the aid of postal, telegraphic, and telephonic means of communication. Also proposed were a universal system of identification of fingerprints and photographs, the distribution of an international publication containing search warrants, an international clearing house, and the introduction of Esperanto as the universal police language.

At the end of the five-day meeting, the participants eventually adopted resolutions that specified that direct police communications should be developed and improved and that the various national governments should allow the police free use of postal, telegraphic, and telephonic communications for matters pertaining to international criminals. French was chosen as the language for international police communications. At the suggestion of the representative of the Romanian government, a follow-up meeting to evaluate and improve international police methods was to be held in Bucharest in 1916.

The rise and fall of international police cooperation

The multitude of schemes made to organize international police cooperation during these years indicates a continuation of internationalization processes that had started in the latter half of the 19th century. Specifically, police institutions across the industrialized world had come to recognize more and more the commonality in their tasks and planned cooperation on a relatively large international scale in the form of a permanent organization oriented at criminal violations. The number of those and related efforts in the area of international policing clearly increased in the years leading up to World War I. Worthy of mention alongside the schemes I have already discussed, for instance, are an international meeting of police in Madrid in 1909 (Schmitz 1927) and the formation of the 'International Esperanto Society of Police Officials' at an international meeting in Antwerp in 1911 (Roux 1914:34). The lack of data on the organization and implications of these and other schemes is indicative of their ineffectiveness. Still, the remarkable increase in attempts to organize international police cooperation on a formal basis manifests a more general trend of internationalization in cultural and organizational domains that had been taken place in various institutional spheres since the 19th century (Boli and Thomas 1997; Meyer et al. 1997). However, in matters of policing, these international schemes, especially the efforts to organize international police cooperation on the American continent and in Europe, were still facing certain conditions inherited from the 19th century which, like their predecessors, prevented them from being successful.

The boundaries of American policing

The IACP was established to enhance coordination between various local police agencies in the United States with the explicit purpose of introducing and furthering standards of professionalism in policing. Not surprising, considering the typical problems confronting US police agencies since the late 19th century, police professionalism was defined primarily in terms of the elimination of the influence of local politics and the adoption of scientific methods of criminal investigation. This was a distinctly American problem, and the calls for international cooperation are to be seen as part of remedies for the deficiencies of US policing. For, indeed, the suggestions to develop international cooperation emanating from the IACP contained no references to an internationalization of crime. Posing the need for police cooperation against problems of international crime in the context of the United States during the earliest decades of the 20th century would have required a far greater stretch of the imagination. After all, the United States was bordered only by Canada and Mexico and, as I discussed in Chapter 1, the establishment and protection of the border required mostly unilateral or limited bilateral police collaboration, not cooperation on a widely international scale. Also, technological means of communication and transportation had not sufficiently developed for there to be any real concern that international criminality was taking place between the Southern and Northern parts of the American continent, let alone between America and Europe.

The calls in the IACP promoting international cooperation between police, then, did not form part of an agenda related to the fight against international crime, but were instead part and parcel of the quest for police professionalism, particularly through the police reform movement that sought to fight off political partisanship and corruption and enhance professionalism in policing (Walker 1977). The quest for police professionalism in the IACP also entailed efforts to improve police relationships, between the police and the public as well as between US law enforcement and police from other nations. Particularly from the European police, it was thought, scientific methods and professional standards of policing could be adopted. Alongside of these unique objectives of US police cooperation, the particular nature of police conditions on the American continent may also explain the dynamics of international policing in the United States, as well as in Latin America. The insularity of American policing brought about by conditions of geographical and socio-political distance contributed to the failure of international police cooperation in Latin America. Restricted to only a limited number of countries, Latin-American appeals to organize police cooperation on a broadly international basis lacked a sufficiently realistic basis.

Perhaps more puzzling than the failure of Latin-American attempts to foster international cooperation are the reasons why police officials from such countries like Argentina and Brazil were nonetheless involved in establishing such plans. The relative lack of data in this matter does not prevent informed speculation. It could be that Latin-American police officials were particularly involved in seeking cooperation due to the fact that they shared specific investigative duties of an international kind, particularly in the area of prostitution. Indeed, the internationally organized trade in prostitutes in the late 19th and early 20th century largely followed routes from Europe to the major cities in various countries of Latin America, especially Montevideo and Buenos Aires (LN 1927). A 1924 government report from Argentina, for instance, stated that a majority of women of 'loose character' in the country originated from Poland, France, Italy, and other European countries (LN 1927:50).

While the white slave trade may have contributed to the internationalization of the police function in Latin America, the dynamics of policing should never be too readily accounted for as responses to developments in crime. As sociologists of social control and policing have uncovered in a variety of contexts (Marx 1981), police practices are often justified explicitly on the basis of professional myths related to a rise in crime, although such self-stated goals cannot be taken at face value. It may therefore be more plausible to attribute the origins of Latin-American police cooperation plans to the peculiar enterprising efforts of Argentinean police official Juan Vucetich who instigated those plans. Vucetich was indeed a very prolific and innovative leader in Latin-American police circles. Under his direction, methods of modern policing, especially techniques of criminal identification, were particularly well advanced in the police agencies of Argentina and other Latin-American countries. As I mentioned in Chapter 1, Vucetich had introduced a fingerprint classification system in the Argentinean police in 1891. As Vucetich played a key part in the development of technically advanced police methods and as he was also at the forefront of international police cooperation in Latin America, it is plausible to argue that these cooperation plans were inspired by Vucetich's ambition to spread the use of advanced techniques of policing and enhance the standards of professionalism among the police of other states in South and Middle America, in addition solidifying his reputation as a policing expert. Given the insignificance of Latin-American police cooperation in investigative respects, it is not realistic to maintain—as did a participant at the International Congress in Buenos Aires in 1910—that Vucetich was 'the real creator of the international organization of social defence against the activity of criminals' (Marabuto 1935:26). However, because the dactyloscopic system—as other technological developments—indeed served as a useful basis for establishing systems of information exchange between the police across national borders, the schemes to organize international police cooperation in Latin America may indeed have contributed to introduce scientific methods in, and thus enhance the professionalism of, participating police. But in the absence of any real concerns over international criminality, Vucetich's dreams of establishing an international police organization for criminal identification and investigation purposes could not be realized.

The politics of European police cooperation

On 28 June 1914, two months after the Monaco Congress was held, the heir to the Austro-Hungarian throne, Archduke Franz Ferdinand, and his wife, the Duchess of Hohenberg, were assassinated in Sarajevo. The killing was perceived as an act of Serbian-nationalist aggression against Austria-Hungary, although police investigations could never prove Serbian involvement.[4] Pressured by the German government, the Austro-Hungarian monarchy declared war on Serbia on 28 July 1914.

[4] Soon after the beginning of the war, the Head of the Sarajevo Criminal Police who was in charge of investigations into the assassination concluded that the Serbian Crown Prince Alexander had ordered the killing (Iwasiuk 1915). In reality, however, police investigations failed to prove Serbian involvement in the assassination. An official of the Austrian Ministry of Foreign Affairs went to Sarajevo in July 1914, but found no evidence of involvement by the Serbian government. Despite assistance from police authorities in Turin, Bonn, and Berlin, Austrian police officials were likewise unsuccessful (Liang 1992:182–189).

The outbreak of World War I prevented any practical implications of the Monaco Congress. However, despite the fact that the war effectively meant the failure of the Congress, I would defend the argument that the effort could not have succeeded—even in the absence of international warfare—because the manner in which the meeting conceived of the organization of international policing did not take into account developments in police bureaucratization, relying instead on an outdated model of international policing inherited from the 19th century. In particular, although, as described earlier, police experts had by the early 20th century already developed a common culture on the means and goals of professional policing, the Monaco Congress was still rooted in principles of national politics and formal systems of law. This can be seen, first of all, from the fact that the Congress was from its inception not an undertaking organized by police officials. Instead, the initiative to organize the Congress was taken by Albert I, Prince of Monaco. The meeting may have been an attempt by the Prince to enhance Monaco's international prestige in world political and cultural affairs (Bresler 1992:18–20), or it may have been inspired by the Prince's awareness that the status of the principality as a resort for the wealthy posed particular problems of property crime (Walther 1968:11). But regardless of the Prince's precise motives and despite the Congress's explicit focus on criminal and not political police tasks, it is in any case clear that the meeting was not instigated nor organized by police bureaucrats. In fact, despite the explicit focus of the Congress on cooperation between police, most attendants at the Monaco Congress were magistrates and government representatives, not police officials. Furthermore, because of the over-representation of legal experts and diplomats, the discussions at the Congress took largely place within a legal framework, mostly debating formal arrangements of international law, such as extradition procedures. To be sure, the Monaco Congress also devoted specific attention to international measures of policing, but only as one and the least discussed of four conference themes (Roux 1914:66–198). There was even wide consensus at the Congress that diplomatic formalities hindering international police operations would have to be abandoned in favour of improving direct police communications (Roux 1914:25–36). Nonetheless, the Congress's resolutions were dominated by a framework of formal law and proposed policing measures only in function thereof.

The Congress worked on the basis of a model of formal systems of law that could not but mirror the many differences that existed between national jurisdictions. Recognizing existing variations between national legal systems across the countries of Europe (and the world), the cooperation plans of the Monaco Congress would be difficult to accomplish unless the police system of one nation were adopted at the international level. And that was precisely what the delegates at the Congress attempted to do, specifically by suggesting that participating states should adopt the techniques and principles of the French system of policing in all international operations. The famous criminalistics expert R.A. Reiss of the Police-Technical Institute at Lausanne, for instance, suggested the creation of an international police bureau that would not only collect information about international criminals but also have at its disposal an international mobile police force, modelled after the French mobile units. Although Reiss's suggestion was not approved, the participants at the Congress spoke very favourably about instituting French systems of criminal identification and investigation at the international level. Eventually, the Congress decided, for example, that the Paris criminal identification service would serve as central international bureau and that French was to be used in all international police communications (Roux 1914:200–201). These arrangements patently placed French participation in international police cooperation centre stage. Not surprisingly, the French delegates at the Congress by far outnumbered the representatives of other nations (Roux 1914:4–5). And while French-speaking delegates attended the Congress as official government representatives, the governments of other countries, including, most notably, Germany, Austria-Hungary, Great Britain, and the United States, did not send official representatives. Rather, delegates from those countries were present in a private capacity as observers and did not take part in the discussions (Roux 1914:4–5).

The seemingly broad international representation of the Monaco Congress, then, could not conceal the fact that officials from France and French-minded countries dominated the meeting. And the frictions between these and other nations haunted the Congress's plans to formalize international police cooperation even though it focused explicitly on criminal and not political police matters. As historian Philip Stead (1983:156–157) remarks, the Monaco Congress may well have been conceived from the very start on the basis of the French notion of policing as '*surveillance du territoire*' or counterespionage, i.e. as an extension of a centralized concept of policing directed at the protection of the boundaries of nation states (Stead 1983:156–157). Indeed, considering the volatile nature of international political affairs in Europe during the early part of the twentieth century, not least of all in terms of German–French relationships, the conception of the Monaco Congress as a French national, rather than a truly international initiative, harmonizes with the critical reactions the meeting received from the two German attendants (Finger 1914; Heindl 1914a, b).

The German delegates at the Monaco Congress bemoaned the fact that the meeting was primarily an affair of 'Latin' countries and that it had adopted the French language and French systems of identification in international policing (Finger 1914:268; Heindl 1914a:649). Robert Heindl, the Police President of Dresden, in particular, criticized the suggestion of adopting the anthropometric system of identification as 'nonsense' (Heindl 1914e:649). These criticisms betray deep-seated German–French conflicts in police technique and administration, because the anthropometric bertillonage system of criminal identification (measuring characteristics of the body) was implemented nationally in France, whereas the dactyloscopic system (of fingerprinting) was used in Germany.[5] Therefore, the choice over which identification system would be adopted at the international level was not a mere technical matter, but would necessitate the reorganization of all other participating police systems. At the root of the problem, the German delegates argued, was the view voiced at the Congress that conceived of that 'newly invented buzzword'—international policing—as a separate supranational police force, instead of trying to institute a cooperative network between police institutions that would preserve their respective national traits (Heindl 1914e:647). A decade after the meeting was held, Heindl again dismissed the Monaco Congress as 'dangerous dreams! Congressional fantasies! Springtime ravings at the Côte d'Azur' (Heindl 1924:20).

In sum, the many instances of international police initiatives at the beginning of the twentieth century clearly indicate an acceleration of the internationalizing trend that had been taking place across many dimensions of society. Yet, for various reasons these initiatives of international policing failed to attract a wide international base. In Latin and Northern America, most international police practices were

[5] Heindl's criticism of the dactyloscopic system harmonized with conclusions reached at the Second Police Conference of German State Governments held in Berlin in 1912 (Borosini 1913b; Schneickert 1912a, 1912b, 1913). At the Berlin conference—organized not only to coordinate policing practices in Germany, but also to enhance international communications—Heindl was among the most active participants to suggest the creation of a centre for police information exchange on the basis of fingerprint files.

relatively distinct in nature, restricted to concerns that affected only the continent, revolving specifically around police professionalism and modern investigative techniques. In Europe, the Monaco Congress failed to establish an international police organization because the meeting did not take into account the developments of police bureaucracies and their accomplished degree of autonomy from the political centres of national states at the turn of the 20th century. The Congress was still conceived on the basis of a model of formal law and politics that was rooted in 19th-century conceptions of sovereignty and national jurisdiction. It thereby conflicted with the attained level of bureaucratization of police institutions that were already prepared for the 20th century by having developed knowledge systems of the expert means and goals of policing, nationally as well as internationally. As discussed earlier, a European police culture had begun to develop that conceived of the proper means and goals of policing in terms no longer based on legality but on professional information and expertise. This also implied a mutual recognition among police officials that the only viable form of police cooperation with broad international participation could not have political objectives and should not aim to institute a supranational police, but would instead have to be a cooperative police organization whose objectives involved only criminal matters. This trend was already beginning to take shape from the late 19th century onwards and would become influential at an organizational level in the 20th century.

4

War and Revolution

> Thus, when the Germans invaded Belgium, they thought that they were penetrating on a territory which was a kind of *res nullius* and which they expected they could in some way make theirs. Of course, they promised that they would evacuate it once the hostilities had ended; but we know what their promises are worth. In any case, there are many different ways to submit a state to servitude.
> *Emile Durkheim, 1915.*

> The danger of communism is nil. There is more danger of disturbances from the Right radical elements under the leadership of Hittler [*sic*]. Any disturbances from these elements, however, will be only local and it is not believed that they would have any serious reaction anywhere outside of Bavaria.
> *From a US military intelligence report, 10 April 1923.*

The argument I advanced in the previous chapter that the outbreak of World War I did not primarily cause the failure of the Monaco Congress to establish an international police organization is of course not meant to deny the impact of the war on the organization and role of the police in the countries involved. In fact, the irony is that just when criminal police cooperation initiatives were sharply on the rise in the first two decades of the 20th century, there occurred a sudden and drastic return to politically oriented police practices because of the outbreak of World War I, soon followed by another major international disturbance: the Bolshevik overthrow of tsarism in Russia in 1917. The First World War unsettled international relations on an unprecedented scale, and the Russian revolution, too, would send shock waves across much of the world for the better part of the 20th century. Both events were primarily political in nature but had important effects across a variety of aspects and institutions of society, including indeed the function and organization of the police.

'Different ways to submit a state': Policing World War I

The dynamics of policing during periods of war are exceptionally complex and cannot be done justice in the space of a short section in this one chapter. However, here I wish to bring out critical aspects of the reorganization of German and US police activities related to the outbreak of World War I in order to provide an adequate picture of the police institutions that in the post-war period would be involved in founding an international criminal police organization.

The outbreak of the war affected critically the organization of German police functions, both at home as well as abroad (Heindl 1926; Kamps 1918; Liang 1992:182–236). By the Order of 31 July 1914, German police institutions were formally brought under control of military command, assigning police with new enforcement tasks related to changed international military and political conditions and other matters that acquired special significance because of the war. Domestically, German policing duties during the war included the control of espionage and sabotage as well as the supervision of bridges, railways, and factories. In terms of German police strategies in occupied Europe, different policies were implemented in the eastern and the western occupied countries. In the western territories, such as in Belgium, the occupying force only minimally interfered with police duties in the hope of gaining tolerance from the local population and of importing German culture. In the occupied countries of eastern Europe, on the other hand, assimilation of the subjugated population was not sought and, instead, martial law was rigidly imposed with the aid of a mounted military police.

The United States did not enter World War I until 6 April 1917, but the war in Europe had in the preceding years already affected US law enforcement (Lowenthal 1950:22–35; Ungar 1976: 40–43; US Attorney General 1918; Wilcover 1989). In the years before 1917, a variety of police and military agencies were involved in the enforcement of US neutrality laws and the control of Imperial German sabotage activities in the United States. After the United States entered the war, law enforcement duties related to the war were entrusted to several federal agencies, particularly the detective branches of the military departments and the Treasury and Justice Department. Warfare-related police assignments mainly included enforcement activities pertaining to national security, such as the control of espionage and the supervision of war plants and waterfront installations (Goode 1994). Among the most relevant federal enforcement agencies to be mentioned are the Secret Service, which was in charge of observing groups and individuals who opposed official US war policy, and the Bureau of Investigation (BOI) in the Justice Department, which was assigned responsibility for the investigation of espionage and sabotage activities, the observation and control of enemy aliens and pro-German organizations, and the enforcement of violations of the Conscription Act and the detection of draft-law invaders.[1]

On 11 November 1918, Germany accepted the armistice conditions offered by the Allied Forces. The outcome of the war would directly and significantly affect German police organization, particularly after the declaration of the German republic—the so-called Weimar Republic—and the acceptance of the Treaty of Versailles in June of 1919. The institution of the Weimar Republic brought with it the prospects of a democratic government and a constitution guaranteeing liberties and rights that were unprecedented in German history. The Versailles Treaty included, *inter alia*, a reduction and disarmament of the Germany military force as well as restrictions on the number of police and a clear separation of civil police organizations from the military (League of Nations 1919b). Under conditions of a democratic constitution and the restrictions imposed by the Versailles Treaty, the German police institutions of the Weimar Republic were confronted with the difficult task of securing crime control and the maintenance of order under conditions of respect for democratic rights and ideals (Bessel 1987, 1992; Fijnaut 1979:164–176; Harnischmacher and Semerak 1986; Liang 1970; Zaika 1979). Although several changes in German police organization were introduced, the democratization of the police during the Weimar Republic would never be adequately achieved. Most importantly, German police (and military) institutions never fully complied with the Versailles Treaty. In 1920, for example, a new Security Police (*Sicherheitspolizei* or Sipo) was created along military lines to deal with public disorder. In response to demands from the Allied Powers, the Sipo was formally abolished but in actuality never completely disbanded.[2] Furthermore, the national government decreed on 21 July 1922 that the various local criminal police organizations across

[1] The extent of the BOI investigations aimed at German-Americans can be gathered from the Bureau's 'Investigative Records Relating to German Aliens,' which amount to no less than 400,000 pages (see National Archives, *Records of the Federal Bureau of Investigation [Record Group 65]: Investigative Case Files of the Bureau of Investigation, 1908–1922* [ICF]).

[2] See National Archives, *Collection of Foreign Records Seized, 1941- (Record Group 242): Records of the German Foreign Office Received by the Department of State*, microfilm T–120, roll 3,627; *General Records of the Department of State (Record Group 59): Records of the Department of State Relating to Internal Affairs of Germany, 1910–1929*, microfilm M–336.

Germany would be harmonized. This meant that despite the pressures from the Allied powers, German police institutions had emerged from the war as strong as ever.

'The danger of communism is nil': Policing the Bolshevik world revolution

In Chapter 1, I discussed how the perceived threat of political subversion, especially from anarchist and communist movements, served as one of the most significant instigators of international police practices and collaboration in the second half of the 19th century. A revival of such political policing efforts with international implications was to take place almost immediately after the end of World War I, prompted by developments in the previous year. The overthrow of the tsarist regime and the Bolshevik revolution in Russia in November of 1917 triggered a substantial reorganization of police activities across Europe. The perceived threat of communism would also extend across the Atlantic to the United States, formally providing common ground to the operational domain of police institutions in Europe and the New World.

The return of Euro-communism

The fear of communist rebellion in the aftermath of the revolution in Russia spread across European police institutions as soon as the end of World War I allowed a renewed focus on the domestic situation in the various countries of Europe.[3] Most national governments in Europe would respond by strengthening and expanding existing police powers and, additionally, by forging alliances with foreign police institutions, displaying a remarkable resemblance to the situation following the unrest of the mid-1850s. In Switzerland, for example, the police observed vigilantly the Bolshevik presence that had concentrated in the capital city of Berne and that was thought to be encouraged by the success of the revolution in Russia. In Austria, the communist presence was considered to be particularly significant because the Bolshevik

[3] This section relies on the US Military Intelligence files concerning the German police situation in the years after World War I (see National Archives, *Records of the War Department General and Special Staffs [Record Group 165]: Military Intelligence Division Correspondence, 1917–1941* [MID]). See, also, Critchley 1967:176–222; Stead 1983:73–81.

movement emanating from the Soviet Union focused special attention on the newly founded republic, the political instability of which was believed to provide fertile ground for furthering the revolutionary cause. The Austrian police was therefore engaged with exceptional intensity in anti-communist activities.

The police in other countries in Europe faced along with the threat of communism additional, local concerns in the aftermath of the First World War. In Great Britain, for example, there were some concerns over a spread of communist ideas across the Channel, but police reorganizations were mostly necessitated by discontent among British police over their labour situation. Resembling the situation on the European mainland, British police reorganization involved centralization of police duties and the creation of a national police under the auspices of the Home Office.

In Germany, the policing situation was shaped additionally by internal developments after the armistice. The military defeat and collapse of the German monarchy had brought about growing unrest among the German population, which the proclamation of the republic alone could not subdue. Spurred increasingly by protest and violent uprisings, a forceful response from the German police took place on different fronts. As mentioned, a new Security Police was created specifically to handle popular unrest, while the *Sicherheitspolizei* was formally abolished but in actuality never fully dismantled. Among the reasons why, as an official German police report stated, was the concern that only a separate force such as the Sipo could effectively suppress the rebellions that were 'arranged from Moscow with the German communists' (GFO 319881). Similarly, in August 1923, the German government justified the military-like housing of police forces in barracks as a means necessary 'to keep the force free from communist or reactionary influence' (MID 2016–889). German communists and emissaries from the Soviet Union were additionally policed by various private militias and military units. The militias, such as the *Freikorps* (Free Corps) and the *Einwohnerwehr* (Civic Guards), were ultra-conservative armed groups that had been organized since 1919 with the explicit purpose of suppressing the communist movement (Jones 1992). The addition of military units under the control of political policing was influenced ironically by the enforced demilitarization of the German police under conditions of the Versailles Treaty. The Treaty stipulated that the German army was to be solely responsible for matters pertaining to internal security and border control, thus opening the way for the army to take up political policing duties directed at German citizens.

Because the internationalism of the Bolshevik movement was an important problem recognized by several European police institutions, there were various instances of international police cooperation against the communist threat (Fijnaut 1979:161–210; Liang 1992:213–236). The Swiss police, for example, passed on information on the communist movement in Switzerland to the French police authorities and allowed French, British, and American agents stationed at their respective embassies in Berne to observe the communist presence. Seeking to revive the internationally recognized prestige of the former Habsburg monarchy, Austrian police officials defended the centrality of their country's efforts against the Bolshevik revolution in Europe. The Viennese Federal Police were indeed well-suited to function as an international centre of political policing, particularly because of its extensive collection of files on political dissidents in a Central Clearing House (*Zentralevidenzstelle*), which could, as in previous times, be consulted by foreign police.

The suppression of communism also motivated German involvement in international police activities in the post-war period. From 1919 onwards, German and Swiss police exchanged information on communist movements and organized courtesy visits to their respective headquarters. Anti-Bolshevik arrangements were also worked out between the German and Viennese police, the common cause aided additionally by anti-Semitic sentiments. As stated in a German military report of 10 October 1919, the notion prevailed among police circles that communist, socialist, and other left-wing groups were supported by money obtained 'both from the interior and from abroad (Jews)' (MID 2512–124). In July 1919, a Swiss military intelligence officer similarly spoke of the Bolshevik funds as being 'handled by Israelite bankers in Vienna', while a list of fifty Soviet government officials drawn up in Berne in 1920 explicitly identified forty-two of them as Jewish (Liang 1992:218).

'The International Struggle Against Bolshevism' Conference, Munich 1920

As the previous sections indicated, international policing with anti-communist objectives was not structured formally in an international police organization but mostly took place at a unilateral and bilateral level and was largely *ad hoc*, establishing short-term cooperation arrangements. However, on 10 December 1920, an international police meeting was held in Munich, Bavaria, at the initiative of German police officials, with the intent of formalizing international cooperation in the policing of European communism. This meeting deserves separate discussion, not only because the conference has to my knowledge not been discussed in the literature, but because it is the only documented attempt in this period to structure international police cooperation against communism in the form of a permanent organization.[4]

Officially held under the heading 'The International Struggle Against Bolshevism: An International Trouble,' the anti-Bolshevik conference of Munich was attended by twenty-four police officials from Germany, Austria, Czechoslovakia, Switzerland, the Netherlands, and Italy. Presiding over the meeting, Munich Police President Pöhner emphasized the strictly confidential character of the gathering. The participants of the conference first reviewed the state and development of the communist threat in Europe. Most delegates agreed that there was no real danger any more of a communist uprising in their respective countries, arguing that the communist threat had been averted by a successful implementation of police methods and because of changes in government policies aimed at satisfying popular demands for political rights and economic comfort. A Swiss police delegate even spoke of 'the shortly expected breakdown of communism in Soviet Russia' (MID 10058-L–36). Only the delegates from Italy and Austria expressed some continued concerns over the communist presence in their countries.

Although participants at the meeting concluded that there was no real danger of a communist uprising in Europe, the resolution was reached that police authorities attending the conference would stay 'in constant touch' and exchange information about the communist movement in their respective countries (MID 10058-l–36). The exchange was to involve confidential transmissions of personal data of suspects, if possible with the inclusion of photographs and fingerprints. Furthermore, it was agreed upon that police authorities visiting foreign countries to study the local communist movement would be granted

[4] I discovered information on the anti-Bolshevik conference in Munich in the Military Intelligence files at the National Archives (MID 10058-L–36/1–3). Relevant documents include an English translation of a report of the meeting drafted by one of its attendants, Vienna Police President Hans Presser, and an accompanying letter of the military attaché at the American embassy in Vienna to whom the report was sent.

'every possible assistance and support' (*ibid.*). The Italian delegate and one of the German conference participants suggested the formation of an international intelligence bureau to centralize the collection and exchange of information. The idea was discussed at some length but eventually rejected because it was believed 'to have no special value' (*ibid.*). A further meeting—the date and place of which would still have to be decided—was planned to evaluate the effectiveness of the agreed upon system of information exchange.

American communism and the 'Red Raids'

Much like the Bolshevik revolution had prompted reorganizations of police in Europe, law enforcement in the United States, too, would not be left unaffected by the purported rise of the world communist movement. At the end of World War I, US military intelligence was—as a supplement to the operations directed against extremist groups in the United States—also involved in surveillance of the Bolshevik movements in Europe (MID 2512–98). But from 1921 onwards, US concern for the development of communism in Europe declined, and in January 1923, a military intelligence report concluded that the danger of European communism was 'nil' (2657-B–603). However, by then, the ghost of communism was perceived to have spread from Europe to the United States.

Soon after the Russian revolution, the Bureau of Investigation was engaged in investigations of Bolshevik and other socialist activities in the United States. Based on observations from BOI agents and information provided by local police and private citizens, the Bureau started to observe communist groups in the United States only a few days after the Russian revolution (ICF 446, 98219, 672, 258421). Targeted especially were the radical labour union Industrial Workers of the World and the two American communist parties which in 1921 merged into the United Communist Party of America.

One of the most dramatic police actions against American communism took place few years after the end of World War I. In the post-war years, the United States faced a soaring cost of living and rising unemployment. As a result, labour unrests and strikes took place on an unprecedented scale, with no less than four million workers on strike in the United States over the course of 1919. A time of popular protest, it was also a period of intense reaction. Most drastically, in January 1920, Attorney General A. Mitchell Palmer organized a major crackdown against radicals who were to be arrested and deported under the provisions of the Alien Act passed by US Congress in 1918 that allowed for the deportation of radical aliens (Preston 1963; Lowenthal 1950:147–236; Walker 1980:162–163). At the time known as the 'Red Raids' and since named after the Attorney General who organized the operations, the raids were directed at some 60,000 foreign-born radicals whom Palmer claimed threatened the stability of American democracy. Based on a list compiled by the Bureau of Investigation, no less than 6,000 arrest warrants were obtained. On 2 January 1920, simultaneous raids in thirty-three cities led to the arrest of some 2,500 suspects, and on 6 January, additional raids brought the total number of arrests of alien radicals to about 10,000. Involving serious violations of constitutionally protected rights, the raids received a great deal of attention in the media and provoked much popular criticism.

A rebirth of political policing?

As argued time and again throughout this book, the perspective I defend does not deny the impact political and other societal conditions can have on international police developments. Against state-centred and economic deterministic theories, however, my perspective of bureaucratic autonomy maintains that these conditions cannot account for the dynamics of cooperation initiatives between the police, although they do affect the degree of institutional independence of the police from the political centres of their respective states, in turn influencing the success of international cooperation efforts beyond short-term bilateral plans and cooperative forms between the police of like-minded states. In this context, World War I and the Bolshevik revolution present two critical events that impacted upon international policing in very dramatic fashion. Having reviewed the empirical dimensions of these occurrences, it is useful to contemplate their dynamics and relevance for the state and evolution of international policing.

Dynamics of warfare policing

Sociologists of war often express regret over the relative neglect of their specialty in the discipline (Dandeker 1992; Roxborough 1994; Scruton 1987). The critique is not without substance because periods of warfare between and within nations represent momentous occasions of extreme upheaval that like no other circumstance affect societies in very profound ways. Though the impact of war on police institutions deserves an analysis more detailed than presented here, in terms of the theme of this book it is clear that the key implication of war for the possibility and modalities of international policing is that the institutional independence of police vis-à-vis the political centres of their respective states can no longer be maintained. This condition may generally apply to all circumstances of extreme societal upheaval, particularly when it involves struggles over political power, be it internal (such as a civil war) or external (warfare between nations). Such a retreat of police institutions back to the political powers of national states can be observed to occur irrespective of the fact that a relatively high degree of bureaucratic autonomy had been accomplished during earlier periods of relative stability. As such, police institutions across societies will find themselves formally in similar circumstances, but confronting one another antagonistically or forging alliances as determined by their varied national positions in the struggle that caused their re-politicization. As perhaps the most critically disturbing period in international relations between societies, the global event of war thus affects nations differently, each confronted with the distinct circumstances of their respective involvement in the international confrontation.

Hence, it can cause no surprise that the function and organization of the police is profoundly affected during periods of war. Typically, the impact of war on police institutions functionally implies an expansion of police duties to include new tasks intimately related to the war effort, while organizationally police forces are given new and improved means in terms of equipment, personnel, and budget. In functional and organizational respects, also, police institutions are during periods of war closely (re-)aligned with the military. However, while warfare brings about an abrupt loss of the bureaucratic autonomy of police, this re-politicization is specific in kind and largely temporary, related to the circumstance of war and restricted to the period of military combat. This does not mean that the wartime reorganization of the police can have no effects that endure after peace has been established. In this respect, World War I presents a unique situation inasmuch as the Versailles Treaty implied very different circumstances in Germany from the rest of the world. In the newly founded German republic, specifically, police organization was subject to imposed arrangements determined by the Allied Powers. Although the German police never fully complied with the dictates of the Versailles Treaty and managed to retain much of its pre-war powers, the resentment that came with the international imposition would not be without consequence in the years leading up to the Second World War. Elsewhere in Europe as well as in the United States, the end of the war meant primarily a normalization of the policing situation and a return to the peacetime conditions that existed before the war. Organizationally, police institutions may be expected to have come out of the war stronger than before to the extent that newly acquired means were not relinquished during peace time. But functionally, these added means of policing could again be applied to duties of law enforcement applicable under conditions of relative stability. In terms of international police activities in Europe, this also implied a return to the gained achievements in respect of institutional independence necessary to foster an international organization of criminal police, while police institutions in the United States would again be largely shaped by circumstances related to professionalism and a continued process of federalization.

Policing global communism

The spread of communism that was thought to emanate from the Bolshevik revolution in Russia across the world occupied police institutions in Europe and the United States as soon as World War I had ended. However, although there were instances of cooperation between police in the control of communism, anti-communist sentiments failed to become a basis for the formation of an international police organization. The response to communism in the United States was too distinct in kind to forge cooperation with the European mainland. As public police institutions in the United States remained formally committed to uphold democratic ideals, an alliance with political implications was excluded with a European police strongly associated with a highly centralized government (Nadelmann 1993:100). A further indication of the distinctiveness of the US reaction against the communist threat, as historian William Preston (1963) has argued, the Palmer Raids are not primarily to be seen as a reaction against the turmoil created by World War I and the fear of the Russian revolution, but were also a more indigenous, if excessive outgrowth of American nativist sentiments. As such, the early 20th-century suppression of radicalism and political subversion in the United States—like manifestations thereof before and after that time—was fuelled as much by ideological persuasion as by the notion that communism was a force that originated from abroad, imported by recently arrived immigrants and as such representing a threat that was, in the strict sense of the word, un-American.

Furthermore, in terms of consequences for the development of law enforcement, the policing of communism in the United States was also specific in nature. As John Noakes (1996) argues, the Palmer Raids reveal at least three critical transformations in US law enforcement: an expansion of non-military control in the maintenance of public order; a decrease of overt violence in favour of generalized surveillance; and, most importantly in the present context, a centralization of law enforcement. Indeed, although various law enforcement agencies and xenophobic vigilante groups were also involved, the Palmer Raids were led by federal law enforcement agencies in the Department of Justice. Among the most zealous of participants in the raids was the head of the General Intelligence Division of the Justice Department, J. Edgar Hoover. As the coming chapters will reveal, the centralization of law enforcement in a strong federal agency and the earlier discussed hostility against foreign elements would be among the most important factors affecting US participation in international police cooperation through the first half of the 20th century.

In Europe, shared ideological sentiments against communism could more easily have cemented cooperation between police of various countries, more accustomed as they historically were to political police schemes and mutual assistance and collaboration. Yet, the political issue of communism failed to become a basis for the establishment of an international police organization on a broad multilateral scale. The predominant form of anti-communist policing would remain unilaterally conducted transnational work and confidential cooperation at a limited bilateral level. As such, it can again be noted—as was the case with the anti-anarchist initiatives some years before—that sovereignty concerns combined with a growing dedication to democratic ideals and a depoliticization of police duties to make political police cooperation with broad international representation impossible.

The largely ineffective anti-Bolshevik conference of Munich confirms most clearly that police institutions in Europe were again unable to establish an international police organization with political objectives. The conference managed to attract police representatives from only six nations, with half of the participants coming from Germany and the one Italian delegate attending the meeting only informally. The police from many other nations in Europe were not present, although they cannot be expected to have been any less committed to anti-

Bolshevik policing objectives. A British delegate, it was stated at the conference, had been prevented from attending the meeting because of 'technical difficulties', but other police officials did not participate because of the volatile political conditions that marked the post-war period (MID 10058-l–36). When at the end of the conference the suggestion was made to invite police from other states to join the initiative, the delegates agreed that participation of police from France was in any case 'undesirable' (*ibid.*). The discussions at the conference also revealed the limited possibilities for co-operation in anti-communist police operations. Though the delegates provided one another with relevant information, there was at times considerable animosity during the meeting. At one point, Bernhard Weiss, the representative of the Police Presidency in Berlin, refused to provide information on the communist presence in his city and stated that he had only come to the meeting to gain information. The other delegates criticized Weiss's actions and, referring to the newly instituted leftist government in Berlin, accused him of being 'an envoy of the Prussian Social Democrat Minister Severing' (*ibid.*). Also, the resolutions reached at the conference and their practical implications were rather limited in organizational respects. The idea of establishing an international intelligence bureau to collect information from the various participants was rejected in favour of exclusively confidential bilateral arrangements of information exchange. Likewise, mutual assistance of police during operations abroad was agreed upon only inasmuch as it concerned activities that remained 'unofficial' (MID 10058-L–36). As such, the meeting merely agreed to continue existing practices of cooperation, while socio-political conditions prevented the elaboration of a common agenda in political policing matters on the basis of which an international organization of police could be formed.

In sum, although World War I and the threat of communism following the Russian revolution represented two highly disruptive events in international political affairs, they only temporarily implied a return to political police duties. In matters of international police cooperation, accomplished developments in bureaucratic autonomy and the evolution of a common police culture outweighed the sudden disruptions caused by the war and the Bolshevik threat. Not long after the end of the war, indeed, police institutions would again pick up where they had left off in 1914 in moving towards the development of a cooperative organization that focused on criminal enforcement duties.

5

The Origins of Interpol

> Ours is not a political but a cultural goal . . . It only concerns the fight against the common enemy of humankind: the ordinary criminal.
> *Vienna Police President Hans Schober, 1923.*

> They don't know what we are doing . . . We do the work.
> *New York City Police Commissioner Richard Enright, 1923.*

The culmination of the evolution of police institutions seeking to forge international cooperation in matters of criminal law into the form of a cooperative structure would be organizationally accomplished in 1923, when the International Criminal Police Commission was established at the International Police Congress in Vienna. Refounded after World War II, the Commission was in 1956 renamed the International Criminal Police Organization, abbreviated as ICPO-Interpol, under which label it has acquired worldwide fame. Not only because of its remarkable endurance, growing eventually to an international organization currently representing 179 nation states, but also because of the conditions of its founding and the goals and means of its organization, the International Criminal Police Commission is among the most important developments in the internationalization of the police function. This chapter will discuss these developments in the light of my theoretical model of bureaucratic autonomy, investigating comparatively the International Police Conference, which was founded in New York at about the same time as the ICPC, but which failed to develop as a durable organization of international cooperation.

Interpol is arguably the most discussed and least understood international police organization. Most writings on the organization focus on its growth and involvement in spectacular cases, with much praise for its noble goals and presumed achievements, and minimal explanation, let alone understanding, of its history (e.g. Duino 1960; Fooner 1975; Lee 1976; Noble 1975; Reader's Digest Association 1982). Studies devoting attention to Interpol's historical antecedents mostly present descriptive internal perspectives, written by police officials or crime news reporters (Fooner 1973, 1989; Forrest 1955; Tullett 1963; Walther 1968). Corresponding to Gary Marx's (1988:xiii) contention that studies on policing are often either informed but uncritical or critical but uninformed, most of the historically oriented writings are relatively instructive and entirely uncritical, whereas other historical studies are more critical than the presented evidence can support (e.g. Garrison 1976; Greilsamer 1986).[1]

Academic studies on Interpol are few in number and, interestingly, most are doctoral dissertations (e.g., Hoffmann 1937; Marabuto 1935; Möllmann 1969; Schmitz 1927; Stiebler 1981). However, most of these dissertations, as well as other more or less academic works, are largely written from a legalistic perspective and the viewpoint of the police authorities themselves, that is, as contributing to international police strategies by means of exploring their merits and limitations in controlling international crime. As such, these studies have much in common with the publications on the ICPC and/or Interpol that were written by participants in the organization, for which reason these writings have to be treated chiefly as primary sources (e.g. Dressler 1931, 1933; Heindl 1924; Palitzsch 1926a, b; Schober 1926, 1930). To complement the secondary literature, a considerable number of internal reports, congress proceedings, and official correspondence on the ICPC and Interpol are available and will be relied on heavily in this and the following chapters.

'From almost every state of the earth': The International Police Congress at Vienna, 1923

From 3 to 7 September 1923, the International Police Congress was held in the headquarters of the Criminal Police of Vienna.[2] The Congress was initiated by Johannes Schober, the Police President of Vienna,

[1] Among the critically oriented works on Interpol, the books by Meldal-Johnsen and Young (1979), the National Commission on Law Enforcement and Social Justice ([hereafter NCLESJ] 1977) and Schwitters (1978) stand out. These writings were published as part of activities instigated by the Church of Scientology, which in the early 1970s claimed to be under investigation by Interpol and which persuaded the US Congress to hold hearings on the US participation in Interpol (US Comptroller General 1976; Garrison 1976:208–212).

[2] This section relies on a German version of the proceedings of the Vienna Congress (*Internationale Kriminalpolizeiliche Kommission* [hereafter: IKK] 1923) and reports of the Congress by some of its participants (e.g. Dressler 1933; Heindl 1924; Schmitz 1927:91–94). The Congress is also discussed in several secondary studies (see, e.g. Anderson 1989; Fijnaut 1979:398–408; Fooner 1973:13–15, 1989:6–9; Forrest 1955:27–29; Marabuto 1935:20–22; Möllmann 1969:40–43; Schwitters 1978:13–17; Stiebler 1981:15–28; Tullett 1963:24–25).

who with the assistance of Robert Heindl of Germany had sent out invitations to some 300 police officials (Bresler 1992:22–23). The list of participants published in the proceedings names 131 persons, with several more unnamed officials present at the Congress (IKK 1923:3–4). Some guests represented their respective governments as official delegates, while others were present in a private capacity as observers. The participants represented all major European states, including Austria, Germany, France, and Italy, as well as Egypt, Japan, China, and the United States. Although the police from Washington, Chicago, and New York were reportedly invited to the meeting (Meldal-Johnsen and Young 1979:41), the only US delegate, attending privately as an observer, was Samuel G. Belton of the New York City Police.

In his opening speech, Schober stated that he had first developed the plan to establish some form of international police collaboration about a year after the end of the World War, but that he had then left the initiative to Captain van Houten, whom he thought to be more appropriate because he was from the 'neutral' Netherlands (IKK 1923:8). Van Houten, Captain of the Royal Marechaussee (the Dutch criminal police), had indeed sent out a letter as early as 10 December 1919, inviting police officials of various countries to establish an international organization of criminal police, complementing the recently established League of Nations (the letter is reprinted in a German criminology journal, see van Houten 1923). Van Houten suggested the formation of an international police organization that would study criminality across the world, make plans to control crime effectively, distribute information on international criminals, and facilitate international communications between the police. He also stressed that the letter was a personal initiative and that his suggestions excluded the policing of political crimes. Referring explicitly to Robert Heindl's criticisms of the Monaco Congress (see Chapter 3), van Houten also stressed that the suggested international police organization should have no executive powers and would only seek to enhance the direct exchange of information between the police of different nations. There are no sources to determine which police authorities van Houten's letter was sent to, nor which, if any, responded. It has been suggested that most of the contacted police were excited about the plan, but that during the confusing days immediately following the end of World War I no agreement could be reached about where to hold a meeting to organize such matters (Walther 1968:15; Schwitters 1978:14). Van Houten discussed the issue with Basil Thomson, the Chief of the

Security Police London (Thomson 1923), and on 16 September 1921 met in Amsterdam with Robert Heindl (Möllmann 1969:39–40; Schwitters 1978:14; Stiebler 1981:14). Heindl and van Houten reportedly decided to organize an international meeting of police, but it was not until Schober took charge of the initiative that the meeting in Vienna was organized.

The discussions during the five-day Congress dealt with various issues of international police cooperation, including the fight against international crime, extradition, the development of an international police language, and technical issues of criminal developments and criminal investigation. The discussions proceeded in an enthusiastic atmosphere of approval and camaraderie. A recurrent theme was the need to develop better cooperation between the police because of the increase in crime, in general, and in international crime, in particular. The creation of a permanent international police organization was proposed that would have central headquarters and national offices in the participating countries. Closing the meeting, Schober gratefully extended best wishes and warm thanks to the 'members of our congress from almost every state of the earth' (IKK 1923:196).

Eventually, the Congress passed a series of resolutions (IKK 1923:197–202). Recognizing that the fight against international crime could only be carried out successfully through collaboration between the police of all 'civilized states' (*Kulturstaten*, p. 197), the Congress first of all, and most importantly, decided to found the 'International Criminal Police Commission' (*Internationale Kriminalpolizeiliche Kommission*), the goal of which was to establish and enhance mutual assistance between all police within the frame of the laws of their respective states and to establish all institutions suited to the fight against 'ordinary crime' (*gemeine Verbrechertum*) (*ibid.*). Cooperation between the police was encouraged, in particular, through the exchange of information on fugitive criminals and assistance in police training. The Commission was to have its headquarters in Vienna and organize international meetings every year. Countries not present at the Congress were invited to nominate their representatives, which could be either individual police officials or formal police institutions. The Commission's leadership was to consist of an elected President, along with five reporters and a secretary. The Commission members were encouraged to have their governments sign treaties that would sanction (and pay the costs of) international police practices. It was also decided that requests for arrests to a foreign police authority could only be made on the basis of an extradition order, though the police were allowed to observe fugitives until such an order would come through. The development of international extradition agreements was encouraged in order to simplify and expedite the procedure. The Congress recommended the use of German, English, French, and Italian for all international police communications, while a study group would investigate the use of Esperanto.

'Good things in economic and cultural respects': The elaboration of the ICPC, 1923–1934

Between the ICPC's formation in 1923 and 1934, the organization progresses steadily with respect to its membership, the development of the international headquarters in Vienna and the national offices of participating police, as well as various means of police technology and information exchange. These accomplishments were discussed and decided upon at the international meetings and congresses which the Commission organized on a regular basis until the advent of the Second World War. It will serve to substantiate the theoretical arguments of this book in the case of the ICPC to review briefly these various components of the Commission's success.[3]

The precise development of the ICPC membership is difficult to determine, in part because the Commission accepted member status from both private individuals and police institutions. Clearly, however, the ICPC membership expanded steadily, though it hardly reached beyond the borders of Europe. The membership grew from twenty-two representatives at the time of the Commission's founding to fifty-eight members (of which forty-six represented their countries officially) in 1934, when together with the police from almost all European countries the police from Egypt, China, and Japan were also

[3] This section relies on a variety of documents which provide information on every ICPC meeting and congress held in the considered period and the various resolutions that were reached (see the resolutions of the meetings held between 1924 and 1928: IKK 1924, 1926b; Daranyi and Daranyi 1927:299–301; IKK 1927, 1928b; the proceedings of the International Police Congress in Berlin: IKK 1926c; reports of the meetings from 1926 to 1931: Palitzsch 1926c; Schober 1926, Dressler 1927; Palitzsch 1927a; Schober 1928; Palitzsch 1928; Schober 1930; Dressler 1931; and related articles in police magazines and criminology journals: *Archiv für Kriminologie* [hereafter: AfK] 1924b, 1930b; *Die Polizei* [hereafter DP] 1930a; Baerensprung 1931b). Additional information is taken from the second edition of the ICPC handbook (IKK 1934), some older studies on the ICPC (Dressler 1933, 1943; Marabuto 1935; Palitzsch 1926a; Schmitz 1927), and the sources mentioned in footnote 2.

represented. Although a US police officer privately attended the Vienna Congress, the United States did not officially become a member of the ICPC until 1938 (see Chapter 7).

The leadership of the ICPC consisted of a President, several Vice-Presidents, and an Executive Committee (IKK 1934:19–21; Marabuto 1935:83–87). The first ICPC President, Johannes Schober, occupied the post from 1923 until his death in 1932 when he was replaced by Franz Brandl. Originally, the President was to be elected for a period of five years, but in 1934, the ICPC Presidency was placed permanently with the Police Directorate at Vienna, in which year Michael Skubl replaced Brandl who had retired as President of the Viennese police. The system of Vice-Presidents was instituted in 1930 and expanded in 1932, from when onwards the President was assisted by six Vice-Presidents (Marabuto 1935:225–228). The positions of the Vice-Presidency rotated regularly from one country to another, although European police officials always dominated the posts. The day-to-day affairs of the Commission were taken care of by an Executive Committee, which initially consisted of five reporters, a permanent reporter, and a secretary, and which by 1934 had expanded to nine reporters, two permanent reporters and a secretary-general, all appointed by the President (Dressler 1927:293; IKK 1934:23–24). The posts of permanent reporter and secretary (in 1930 renamed secretary-general) were from 1923 taken up by Bruno Schultz and Oskar Dressler, respectively. In 1932, the Belgian Florent Louwage was appointed as the second permanent reporter. Schultz, Dressler, and Louwage would hold their positions until World War II.

In terms of organizational accomplishments, the ICPC headquarters in Vienna occupied a strategic position, because it centralized information on a variety of police matters, especially notices of wanted criminals that were received from the participating police institutions. The organization of a headquarters had already been decided at the Vienna Congress in 1923 and elaborated further at the following meetings. An international fingerprint division was located originally in Copenhagen, under the supervision of a police official, Hakon Jörgensen, who had devised a system to express fingerprints in a multiple-digit number which could be transmitted telegraphically (Borgerhoff 1922; Jörgensen 1922, 1923a; Schneickert 1921). But in 1928, at the ICPC meeting in Berne, it was decided to discontinue use of the Copenhagen bureau—probably because Jörgensen had died the year before—and incorporate a fingerprints division in the Vienna headquarters (Marabuto 1935:101–113). By

1934, the Vienna headquarters had expanded to include the following four divisions: 1) the 'International Central Office for the Suppression of Falsification of Currencies, Cheques and Securities'; 2) the 'International Dispatch of Fingerprints and Photographs of International Criminals'; 3) the 'International Central Office for the Suppression of Falsifications of Passports'; and 4) the International Bureau, which consisted of three subdivisions: the 'International Register' (or 'Information Service on International Criminals'); the 'International Warrant Register'; and the 'International Register of Persons Dangerous to Society' (IKK 1934:19–20, 31–81; Tenner 1932; Schultz 1932; Heindl 1932d). Importantly, because of the organizational design of the international registers, which relied exclusively on information compiled and transmitted by the members, the Vienna headquarters had to rely on specialized offices in the various member states. This system of special offices for international police cooperation in the various participating countries—today known as National Central Bureaux or NCBs—had already been set up in 1926 when a proposal by a French police official to create 'National Central Offices' in the participating countries was received with approval at the international congress in Berlin. ICPC members would either establish a new office specializing in international policing or authorize an already existing police office to specialize in the task. The latter option was chosen by most countries.[4]

Next to the Vienna headquarters, various means to enhance direct international police communications constituted the most important institutional achievement of the ICPC. Among the means instituted to facilitate communications between the police were a coded telegraphic system, a radio network, and various publications. Plans to establish an international system of telegraphic police communications were already made at the Vienna Congress in 1923 when it was decided that a study group would explore the matter. At a 1926 meeting, it was decided that coded telegraphic communications should be instituted, and a year later a German version of the 'International Police Telegraph Code' was completed (IKK 1926a). In 1928, the code was translated into French, and by 1931, it was available in German, Bulgarian, English, French, and Czech, with a Romanian edition in the

[4] By 1927, for instance, a national office, the '*Nederlandsche Centrale inzake Internationale Misdadigers*' (Dutch Centre on International Criminals), was established in the Netherlands (IKK 1927). By 1928, the Judicial Police at Brussels and the Federal Police Directorate at Vienna were chosen as their respective countries' national central offices (IKK 1928; DP 1930a).

making. The organization of an international radio or wireless communications system was less easily achieved. The idea was first expressed at the Amsterdam meeting in 1927 when a special subcommittee was formed and members were encouraged to attend the 'Radio-Telegraphic Conference' in Washington, held later that year, in order to secure certain wave lengths for police communications. At the Vienna meeting in 1930, Commission members were again urged to appeal at the 'International Radio Congress,' which would be held in Madrid in 1932, to secure fixed wavelengths for police communications. At its 1931 meeting, the Commission declared that an international police radio network would take effect by January 1932 (Marabuto 1935:163–180).

The ICPC transmitted various forms of printed information among its members. At the 1924 meeting in Vienna, it had already been decided that relevant information was to be distributed through a periodical called '*Internationale Öffentliche Sicherheit*' *(International Public Safety)*, which was to be published in German, English, French, and Italian editions (AfK 1924a, 1925c; Marabuto 1935:158–163). The periodical was to appear monthly with information on wanted criminals and statistics on international crime. A trial printing was published in November 1924, and the first issue appeared on 15 January 1925 as an appendix to the Austrian police magazine *Öffentliche Sicherheit* (AfK 1924c, 1925e). It contained articles on police matters and warrants requesting the arrest of fugitive suspects (Bresler 1992:33–40). Most of the following issues, appearing regularly in the period before 1935, would likewise include such warrants. In 1926, the periodical was expanded with an appendix specializing in falsifications of currencies, but in the same year it was decided that the magazine would no longer be published in English and Italian because so few copies were being distributed to the USA, Great Britain, and Italy. Apart from the periodical, the Commission also published a dictionary of criminal investigation, a book with the addresses of the police from across the world, and a handbook on international policing (IKK 1928a, 1934).

The ICPC also organized several international police meetings. Together with the various publications, the meetings counted among the organization's most tangible achievements in its formative years. Between 1923 and the beginning of World War II, the ICPC organized fourteen regular meetings in various capital cities throughout Europe, plus two international police congresses in Berlin, in 1926 and in

Antwerp in 1930. The regular meetings were attended by the members who occupied the various leadership posts, while the international congresses were very elaborate and festive occasions to which the police from all over the world were invited. Most importantly, the regular meetings were used to plan and institute the various organizational achievements of the Commission. The meeting in Paris in 1931 stands out for the particular reason that it was organized in collaboration with the International Police Conference, an organization that had meanwhile been established in New York City. The Paris meeting was the first—and would for some time remain the only—formal meeting between a European-based international police organization and a similar organization originating from the United States.

'The premier police association of the world': The International Police Conference

The International Police Conference was established in New York in 1922, a year before the Vienna Congress, at a police meeting organized by Richard Enright, the Commissioner of the New York City Police Department.[5] In 1921, Enright had organized a national police meeting in the United States to foster collaboration between the various municipal police departments in the United States, but a year later the initiative was expanded to an international gathering. Although the meeting was attended mostly by US police officials, with only five foreign delegates (from Great Britain, Belgium, Argentina, Canada, and Denmark), it was decided to establish the International Police Conference (IPC) as a formal organization of police from across the world. The goals of the IPC were to: 1) promote cooperation among police; 2) disseminate information regarding new methods of police practice and police procedure; 3) improve the effectiveness of policing; and 4) study the causes of crime and ways to deal with them.

Both in terms of operational scope and international membership, however, the International Police Conference was a very limited enterprise. The Conference planned to establish a 'National Police Bureau' in New York City and similar offices in foreign countries with IPC

[5] The International Police Conference has rarely been discussed in the secondary literature (e.g. Marabuto 1935:22–23). This section relies on articles written by IPC members and official IPC publications (see Enright 1925a; Hart 1925; International Police Conference [hereafter: IPC] 1923; Jörgensen 1923b; *Police Magazine* [hereafter: PM] 1925; Schmitz 1927:90; Welzel 1925c).

representation, but no such offices were ever created. Instead, the Conference mostly concentrated on a better coordination between local police agencies in the United States. Among the IPC's few tangible achievements was the creation of a 'Foreign Police Commission', a group of four New York police officers who organized research visits to Europe to study the organization and methods of the police in various cities (e.g. Belton 1924a, b; Belton et al. 1924a, b, c, 1925a, b, c). The Conference was also responsible for various publications, such as the proceedings of the 1923 meeting (IPC 1923), a list of the IPC membership (IPC 1925), an 'International Police Conference Code' (IPC 1924), as well as a periodical published under auspices of the Conference by the New York Police Department, the *Police Magazine*. The periodical appeared monthly from May 1924 onwards, was later renamed *Police Stories*, but was already discontinued as early as October 1925. Unlike the periodical published by the International Criminal Police Commission, the IPC magazine contained no data on wanted criminals or other investigative reports.[6]

The IPC was from the start and would during its brief period of existence remain a predominantly American organization and mostly promoted a coordination of US law enforcement agencies, with some additional participation from Canadian law enforcement. Although Enright planned the IPC to foster 'the closest cooperation between the law enforcement organizations of the civilized world' (IPC 1923:15), the IPC was surely not 'the premier police association of the world' (Hart 1925:55), as one of its members would have it, even though additional meetings organized in 1923 and 1925 attracted more foreign delegates.[7] By 1925, police officials from thirty-nine countries were represented in the Conference, but an overwhelming majority of the IPC membership, numbering some 800 officials, were from the United States (IPC 1925). Only the IPC's Honorary Presidents were all foreign police officials, giving perhaps the only significant concrete form to the international character of the Conference.

[6] The *Police Magazine* mostly covered essays on the organization of foreign police systems (e.g. Harbord 1924; Zaturenska 1925; Cowell 1925; Beard 1924) and visits by US police to colleagues abroad (e.g. Enright 1925b, 1925c; Welzel 1925c).

[7] Among the 365 delegates attending the 1923 IPC meeting were foreign police officials and diplomatic delegates from twenty-four countries (IPC 1923; Jörgensen 1923c; Belton 1924a:42–43; Schmitz 1927:90–91), while the 1925 meeting was attended by seventy-eight foreign police from forty-five different countries (*Archivio di Antropologia Criminale, Psichiatria e Medicina Legale* 1925a, 1925b; Draper 1931; Schober 1925; van Houten 1930; Welzel 1925a).

One of the few tangible attempts to make good on the international aspirations of the Conference took place when a joint meeting was organized with the International Criminal Police Commission in Paris in September 1931 (Baerensprung 1931b; Draper 1931; Dressler 1931; Marabuto 1935:24–25; van Houten 1930). However, though held in the same buildings of the Sorbonne, the gathering of the International Police Conference, attended by only few foreign delegates, was held separately from the ICPC meeting. A joint committee of the two police organizations was set up, but their resolutions were passed separately at both meetings. The resolutions provided for more cooperation between the two organizations with respect to the control of three kinds of international criminals: people convicted in one of the two continents, Europe or America, who were born in the other continent; those arrested in one continent who had already been sentenced in the other continent; and those convicted in one continent who intended to travel to the other (Baerensprung 1931b:522). An international police bureau was to be set up in the United States to maintain contacts with the ICPC headquarters in Vienna and it was decided that both organizations would send delegations to their respective meetings. A subsequent joint meeting would discuss the creation of a 'World Organization of Police', but no other joint meetings were organized after the gathering in Paris. In 1932, the IPC was brought under the direction of Barron Collier, a wealthy retired businessman who cultivated a keen interest in international police cooperation and tried to put new life in the organization.[8] However, apart from police meetings in Chicago in 1933 and in Montreal in 1937 (both with only about half a dozen European delegates), it seems that all that ever came of Collier's ambitious plans was an office in the New York City Police Department with 'International World Police' written on the door and a full-time secretary inside (Nadelmann 1993:91).

In sum, the International Police Conference and the International Criminal Police Commission represent two very different attempts to formalize cooperation between police of different nations in a permanent organization. Both initiatives went beyond the cross-border plans and operations instigated by national police systems but were very different in terms of their practical impact. In the next sections, I will clarify this differing impact in terms of the suggested theory of bureaucratic

[8] On the role of Collier, see Marabuto 1935: 24–28; Meldal-Johnsen and Young 1979:39–41; Nadelmann 1993:90–91; Söderman 1956:270–271.

autonomy and argue that the structural conditions necessary for international police cooperation were achieved both in the case of the International Criminal Police Commission as well as the International Police Conference. However, in terms of a motivational basis to operationalize international policing, I will argue that what the International Police Conference in the United States missed was a practical playing field on which effectively to organize the fight against international crime. The International Criminal Police Commission originating from Europe, on the other hand, could successfully defend a professionally conceived myth of a rise in international crime in the aftermath of World War I.

The success of the International Criminal Police Commission, Part I: The organization of 'purely technical matters'

Relating to my proposition on formal bureaucratic autonomy of police institutions as a necessary condition for international cooperation, a variety of circumstances surrounding the formation of the ICPC indicate that this condition of institutional independence was achieved and explicitly relied upon. There is first of all the fact that ICPC was formed at a meeting convened independently by police officials, not as the result of a diplomatic initiative. Though the original initiative by van Houten failed to formalize international cooperation immediately, it was but five years after the end of World War I that the Vienna Congress was organized by Hans Schober of Vienna and Robert Heindl of Germany, the latter of which had earlier met with van Houten, who so, at least indirectly, had contributed to the seminal meeting. Indicative of van Houten's influence, also, is the fact that he had already in his 1919 letter suggested that an international organization of police should have no executive powers and focus exclusively on criminal matters, two issues that the ICPC adopted in its programme (van Houten 1923). As I argued in the previous chapters, the conception of an international police organization in the form of a cooperative network with criminal enforcement goals was indeed what police officials had come to recognize as an acceptable and appropriate form of cooperation across national borders. That this conception corresponded to a professional notion of bureaucratic police experts is well demonstrated when Schober during his opening speech at the Vienna Congress proclaimed that he realized the boldness of the meeting's plan but also hoped that 'even in the midst of oppositions between the nations of the earth' the Congress would unite police 'above the political battle', because police cooperation, he argued, was 'not a political but a cultural goal' (IKK 1923:1, 9, 2).

The somewhat delayed gathering of the Vienna Congress after World War I demonstrates that the degree of institutional independence of police bureaucracies is not unaffected by broader societal developments. Indeed, the immediate implications of the war were obviously considered too weighty in political respects to allow for international police cooperation. Van Houten's and Schober's plans to create an international police did not materialize instantly because they were aware of the turmoil that marked international relations at the end of the war (IKK 1923:8). Yet shortly thereafter, in 1923, circumstances had already sufficiently changed. Among the conditions that then allowed police institutions to take advantage of their acquired degree of bureaucratic autonomy was the period of relative tranquillity and pacification in world affairs that had begun after World War I. Of course, as history would dramatically show, this condition of post-war stability was more presumed than real, but it was nonetheless of sufficient reality in perception that it effectively enabled police institutions to take advantage of structural conditions that allowed them to engage in international cooperation.

Importantly, the acquired independence of police institutions participating in the ICPC did not imply a surrender of national sovereignty. On the contrary, the ICPC was set up explicitly—and Interpol still operates today—not as a supranational force but as an inter-national network enabling direct communications between police of different countries (Anderson 1989:168–185). As ICPC President Schober emphasized, the Commission would not strive for 'something [as] impossible' as 'supranationality' and would instead 'hold on to the national individuality of all participating states' (in Archiv für Kriminologie 1925:72; see also Dressler 1933:361). Sensitivity about nationality questions was also reflected in the composition of the ICPC executive committee, where the various posts of the Vice-Presidents carefully rotated from one country to another. The only accepted imbalance in terms of the various nationalities being equally represented in a cooperative partnership was the placement of the ICPC headquarters in Vienna and the appointment of the Presidency and the secretary-general of the Commission with the Viennese criminal police. The reasons why this Austrian advantage was acceptable among the

ICPC membership relate to the fact that Austrian police systems and organization were particularly well advanced, especially in technical respects. Indeed, as I explained in Part I, the Austrian police had a long-standing history of collecting files on, and specializing in the fight against, international criminals, particularly in developing technically sophisticated systems of information exchange (Liang 1992:18–34; Möllmann 1969:41; Stiebler 1981:15). Dating back to the days of the Habsburg dynasty, several attempts had been initiated by Austrian authorities to establish a European police system. And while these plans were unsuccessful, they do indicate a special preoccupation of Austria in international police practices, which must inevitably have benefited the expertise and technological means of Austrian police in international matters. Relieved from any political associations, the acquired expertise, means, and technical prowess of Austrian involvement in international policing could be put to good use after World War I, especially for criminal enforcement duties. Additionally, the technically dominant position of the Viennese police in the ICPC was also accepted because the police from the smaller European countries lacked the necessary resources to maintain an international office and because participants from Germany and France were unacceptable in any leadership position given their antagonistic positions during and after World War I.

To further secure the individuality of the police institutions participating in the ICPC, the Vienna headquarters were so designed that they enabled exchange and cooperation among national police systems without amalgamation into one central force. The headquarters only collected information forwarded by participating police institutions from various countries and could pass on requests from one national police force to another. The headquarters had no separate force that would initiate its own investigations but only functioned as a facilitator of police communications between national systems (Anderson 1989:168–185). International communication by telegraph, radio, and printed media likewise enabled interaction between police, as did the meetings, without the formation of a supranational force.

Perhaps the clearest indication of the achieved independence of the police from politics is that the ICPC was established without the signing of any international treaty or legal document. All ICPC activities were planned (mostly at the meetings and, additionally, through personal correspondence) and executed by and for the participating police without input or control from their respective governments. In fact, the

Commission had no internationally recognized legal status and no legal procedure was ever formalized to acquire membership in the ICPC.[9] Importantly, the Commission did strive for governmental and legal recognition of its established structures and appealed for formal sanctioning from the League of Nations (Palitzsch 1927b; Skubl 1937). Van Houten had already suggested that an international police office should be established as an institution within the League of Nations. However, such appeal for political-legal approval occurred only after the Commission was developed and its structures were already in place, for, as van Houten expressed, the League of Nations was not considered capable of handling 'such purely technical matters' (van Houten 1923:46).

Throughout the 1920s and 1930s, the ICPC tried to establish ties with the League of Nations, in the first instance by inviting League representatives to the Commission meetings. The ICPC first invited a representative from the League of Nations to attend the International Police Congress in Berlin in 1926. Although the League decided not to send a representative, further information was requested about the Commission's activities (Dressler 1927:293). At the Berlin Congress, President Schober declared that the League consented to the ICPC proposal that diplomatic formalities in international criminal investigations should be eliminated (in Palitzsch 1927a:384). In its resolutions, the Commission declared that the League would be notified of the ICPC's international bureau to suppress the falsification of currencies. The next ICPC meeting, in Berne in 1928, was attended by a delegate from the League. The resolutions at the Berne meeting, as of later meetings in Vienna and Antwerp in 1930, specified the Commission's explicit approval of the international police schemes developed by the League of Nations (Broekhoff 1933). However, as a non-governmental organization, the ICPC was never very successful in having its activities formally sanctioned by the League of Nations, precisely because the League organized various aspects of policing independently, especially in matters of white slavery, narcotics, and falsifications of currencies (themes on which the League held several meetings and passed international

[9] Membership in the ICPC would be *de facto* granted to individuals or government-approved police institutions simply upon presenting some kind of written request. Factual participation in the ICPC was thereupon regarded as binding (Stiebler 1981:15–16, 18–19; Möllmann 1969:42–43).

resolutions throughout the 1920s and 1930s).[10] As late as 1937, then ICPC President Michael Skubl again argued in favour of the common cause of the Commission and the League (Skubl 1937), but any formal connection between the two organizations always remained more fiction than fact. More successful was the ICPC's pursuit of approval from the national governments of the various participating police agencies. Specified in one of the resolutions at the Vienna Congress as a desirable goal of cooperation (IKK 1923:201), by the 1930s nearly all ICPC members were officially sanctioned by their respective governments and could often rely on additional funds and personnel to set up specialized offices needed to maintain international communications with the Vienna headquarters. As such, what is witnessed is an international police network seeking to obtain legal and governmental approval after the organization had already been established and elaborated independently on the basis of professional police conceptions and without regard to political and legal considerations.

The failure of the International Police Conference: The boundaries of international crime

Turning to the internationalization of the police function in the United States, the International Police Conference was definitely not a successful organization, though it was created under structural conditions favourable for international cooperation. Like the ICPC, the Conference was organized independently by police agencies, especially the New York City Police and its commissioner Richard Enright, that were sufficiently professionalized to operate independently from governmental control. As Enright remarked at the IPC founding meeting, police professionals were in charge of 'the work' of law enforcement, matters on which the politicians were not knowledgeable (IPC 1923:341). Police cooperation in the IPC was also intended to be formalized without the signing of a legally binding document, while—

[10] The Covenant of the League of Nations contained the stipulation, under Article 23c, that the members of the League would entrust the organization 'with the general supervision over the execution of agreements with regard to the traffic in women and children, and the traffic in opium and other dangerous drugs' (LN 1919a:168). On the control of narcotics, the League drew up several conventions in the 1920s and 1930s (Bruun et al. 1975:15; LN 1919a:168). The suppression of the white slave traffic was likewise a matter the League of Nations and the ICPC devoted much attention to (AfK 1929a; Lyttleton 1928; Marabuto 1935:134–141; Schmitz 1927:28–45).

again paralleling similar attempts by the ICPC—the Conference did strive for legal-political recognition once the organization had been formed. Indeed, while IPC President Enright recognized the Conference as but 'an unofficial league', it was also desired that its resolutions be politically and legally sanctioned (Enright 1925a:21). In particular, the IPC's plan to create a National Police Bureau in New York was to be approved through appropriate legislation in the US Congress. Bills to that effect were entered in the Senate in December 1922 and in the House in February 1923 (IPC 1923:19; MID 2045–739/3). But the plan did not succeed and no central police bureau was ever formed, despite the fact that its creation had reportedly been approved by President Coolidge (Hart 1925:107).

Thus, structural conditions for international cooperation were in terms of formal bureaucratic independence as favourable in 1922 in the United States as they would be a year later in Europe when the ICPC was formed. However, in terms of my second proposition as to the operational motives of international police cooperation, what the International Police Conference lacked was a practical playing field on which to effectively organize police cooperation against international crime. Instead of responding to a professional myth on the internationalization of crime, the IPC needs to be situated in the more distinct and delineated context of the evolution of law enforcement in the United States, particularly the quest for and gradual development of police professionalism.

In terms of the objectives of the International Police Conference, the self-stated and publicly proclaimed motives of the organization's founders were clear: the organization had to reach beyond national jurisdiction because 'the enemies of society, organized or otherwise, are international in their scope—for boundaries and flags mean nothing to them' (Enright 1925a:89). This internationalization of crime, furthermore, was believed to have been brought about by the rapid social changes after World War I, especially 'the numerous and rapid means of transportation which are now available' such as 'the automobile and the wireless' (Enright in IPC 1923:15; Collier 1932:545; see IPC 1923:14–15; Hart 1925:54). In reality, however, any internationalization of crime with sufficient implications for the development of a professional myth that would justify the creation of an international police organization was at this time still missing in the United States. To be sure, US law enforcement had, as I explained in Chapter 2, to some extent already been involved in international tasks for many years, but because of the geographical distance from Europe and in the absence of a well developed federal police, law enforcement in the United States remained relatively insulated from the rest of the world. Also, technological means of communication and transportation were until the mid-20th century not sufficiently developed for there to be any real concern about international criminality between the American and European continents. Police tasks that related to an increasing mobility in social life in the United States were either handled locally (e.g. the policing of immigrant groups) or remained mostly restricted to interstate matters (e.g. white slavery) (Woelfle 1939). And, as I earlier discussed, from the late 19th century onwards these duties were handled by federal US law enforcement agencies, such as the US Customs Service and the US Immigration Service.

Why then was the International Police Conference nonetheless established with the intent of fostering cooperation across national states? Rather than viewing the formation of the International Police Conference in terms of a professionally conceived myth of the internationalization of crime, the organization should be considered in light of certain policing developments in the United States, particularly the police reform movement that sought to fight off political partisanship and corruption and enhance professionalism in policing (Walker 1977). This increasing quest for professionalism also entailed an effort to improve police relations, primarily with the public, but also with the police of other nations. The IPC explicitly represented itself as promoting international cooperation, but not in order to respond to any growing concern over an increase in international crime. It is striking, in this regard, that there is no empirical evidence that any international investigation ever originated from the IPC. Although the International Police Conference held meetings and published a periodical (like the ICPC), these initiatives were mostly meant to foster personal relationships between the police across the world. The short-lived IPC magazine, for instance, covered many articles on foreign police systems but never contained any investigative information.

Instead of being oriented toward fighting international crime, the IPC served as an organizational 'presentation of self' relative to other professional police forces across the world, especially in Europe. For this reason, it was important for founder Enright to argue that the IPC brought together the police from all 'civilized nations, states, and municipalities of the world' (IPC 1923:15), even though an overwhelming majority of the organization's membership was from the

United States. However, as a professional association, the IPC could not compete with the International Association of Chiefs of Police (IACP), which since 1893 had contributed to advance professionalism among local US police agencies (Nadelmann 1993:84–91). There were in fact competing interests between the IPC and the IACP, as the result of inter-agency conflict between the New York City Police, which founded the IPC, and local and federal law enforcement agencies in Washington, DC, which controlled the IACP. Positioning itself explicitly as an advocacy group, the IACP could make good on its ambitions of professionalism much more readily than the IPC on its aspirations to fight international crime. Police officials from Europe, also, found that the IACP was a more significant organization, better suited for cooperation across the Atlantic (van Houten 1930).

In sum, the fate of the IPC was sealed in the absence of any significant concerns about an internationalization of crime that would justify a transatlantic police organization, while in terms of concerns over inter-state crimes within the United States as well as with respect to the forms of international crime that at this time occupied US law enforcement, the IPC could not compete in any significant way with the United States' expanding federal police agencies, in particular the investigative force in the US Justice Department that since 1935 was called the Federal Bureau of Investigation (FBI). Indeed, especially during the 1930s, the FBI would under the direction of its famed Director, J. Edgar Hoover, successfully gather the means, personnel, and budget to virtually monopolize all international law enforcement duties emanating from the United States (see Chapter 6).

The success of the International Criminal Police Commission, Part II: The fight against 'the common enemy of humankind'

Whereas the International Police Conference in the United States could not successfully develop a myth of international crime, the International Criminal Police Commission in Europe was in this respect successful. The motivational basis of the ICPC was in the first instance provided by a cross-national rise and internationalization of crime which police officials argued had taken place after World War I and which was seen as necessitating expanded control beyond national borders. This operational myth for international police cooperation was formed on the basis of a specialized knowledge on the internationalization of crime as well as the professional means to deal with it. Moreover, knowledge and skills were justified in terms of an expertise that sidestepped legal arrangements and focused not on violations of a political nature but the ordinary or common criminal.

In the secondary literature is repeated over and over again the theme that the end of the war had brought about dramatic increases in crime which needed invigorated efforts on that part of the police. The end of the war, it is argued, brought with it a 'crime wave of unprecedented proportions' (Tullett 1963:24) and 'floods of dejection and disillusion . . . accompanied by a widespread contempt of the social order' (Forrest 1955:27). The war's end had created 'a happy hunting ground for forgers, swindlers, and black marketeers' (Fooner 1973:13). It was a time of 'immorality, greed and vice' (Garrison 1976:52). However, the validity of this argument is based on a functionalist notion of law enforcement as responding to developments in criminality. My perspective of a professional myth providing the motivational basis for policing, however, holds that regardless of whether or not the view of a spectacular crime wave at the end of World War I is empirically valid, the notion that it had occurred and should serve as the basis for international police cooperation corresponded to the self-declared motives of the participating police. This professional police understanding of an increase in criminal violations at the war's end occurred in two forms. First, there was the idea among police authorities that the general level of crime had increased dramatically after the war. The Dutchman Captain van Houten had already expressed the notion of a spectacular influx in crime in many nations at the war's end to justify his initiative in 1919 (van Houten 1923) and Schober reiterated the theme at the Vienna Congress (IKK 1923:8–10). The reports and statistics provided by officials at the meeting confirmed the necessity of an adequate police response and the commonality of the task among European police.[11] Secondly, there was also believed to have occurred an epidemic spread of a particular new class of criminals that abused the modernization of social life and the increase in mobility after the war. They were the money swindlers, the passport, cheque and currency forgers, the hotel and railway thieves, the white slave traders and the drug traffickers (AfK 1928b; Hagemann

[11] The idea of a spectacular rise in crime after World War I was also supported by the empirical findings from contemporary criminal justice research (Auer 1916; Hirsch 1916; Travers 1915; Rosenbaum 1917). Later reflections by police participating in the ICPC reaffirmed the significance of 'the rise in crime in all countries after the war' (*Die Polizeipraxis* 1933:224; Dressler 1933:359).

1933b; IKK 1934:82–129; Pella 1928; Schmitz 1927). With the latest technologies of communication and transportation at their disposal, these criminals had in common a unique capacity to transcend the boundaries of time and space in disregard of the national jurisdictions that police institutions were traditionally subject to.

The preoccupation in the ICPC with these technologically influenced crimes is well illustrated by the fact that a separate division on the falsification of currencies was created at the very first meeting and that later meetings continued separate discussions on these and other typically modern crimes. This new class of criminals, also, was not percieved to be politically minded but seen as typically motivated by material pursuits. The ICPC, as Schober stated at the Vienna Congress, therefore had to focus on the suppression of the 'ordinary criminal' (IKK 1923:1). Thus, what police officials organizing the ICPC cited in order to justify collaboration across national borders was a new class of criminals appearing in all countries undergoing rapid social change and technological progress, including particularly mobile criminals transcending nation-state borders. The adequate police response was conceived as a well-organized international network that would foster cooperation as an efficient means of enforcement. A French newspaper reporter cited in the German police magazine *Die Polizei* (1933d) expressed this notion very well when he argued that police institutions should adjust to 'modern development, which in all respects is directed toward organization across states' (p. 146). Given the cooperative structure of the ICPC as facilitating exchange between participating police institutions from different countries with respect for their distinct traits, the recognition of the rise of international crime among police did not lead the ICPC to develop a clear-cut definition of international crime and/or international criminals. The matter was an issue of some controversy at several ICPC meetings, and no one conception was ever formally adopted.[12] However, no one legally valid definition had to be accepted by the Commission, for, as ICPC reporter Louwage of Belgium proclaimed, only the practical police implications mattered, not any legal arrangement (Dressler 1933).

[12] At the Antwerp Congress in 1930, for instance, a distinction was made between criminals who committed a crime in a place other than where they resided, and those who sought refuge in a place other than where the crime was committed (AfK 1930b; AJPS 1930). But when in 1930, Prussian police officials joined the ICPC, they used a different definition, one which also applied to people who had a 'criminal tendency' (AfK 1930a:59–60).

The professional police conceptions of international crime and their significance for the organization of the police across national borders were not just a matter of discourse among police officials. This is clear from a closer look at the organizational innovations the ICPC introduced. Primarily, as noted, the ICPC was concerned with a coordination of investigative information as well as of technical know-how through a variety of newly instituted means of international police communications. The Commission therefore established systems of technologically advanced means for international communication, specifically a telegraphic code, a system of wireless (radio) communications, and printed publications, which next to the meetings served most importantly as efficient means of direct international cooperation, unhindered by legal procedure and diplomatic formalities. The ICPC publications contained information on international criminals and articles on the latest police techniques, written by police professionals in the various participating states. The meetings were likewise planned and attended by police officials and experts in criminal investigation, rather than by political dignitaries or judicial administrators. The primary concern for the efficiency of methods of international police operations is also well reflected in the organization of the international headquarters at Vienna, which were divided functionally in terms of expert goals and means of enforcement (e.g. fingerprints, falsifications, wanted notices). The organization of the headquarters, in other words, was based on expert police knowledge, not on categories of criminal law, and reflected technical know-how on the means of policing, not procedures of international law or politics.

Perhaps most clearly exemplifying the impact of a professional understanding of international policing beyond politics and legality were the criticisms among ICPC members of existing political-legal means to control international crime, the most prominent expression of which was extradition. Extradition was by far the most addressed issue among the ICPC membership during the organization's formative years. Particularly criticized were the many formalities involved with, and the slowness of, official extradition procedures. At the Vienna Congress in 1923, the Commission had already decided that participating police forces should develop measures to expedite extradition procedures and that under some circumstances the police could exchange suspects without formal governmental approval (IKK 1923:200–201; Marabuto 1935:203–208). At later meetings, the Commission members similarly criticized extradition as an inadequate tool in the fight against international crime (e.g. IKK 1926b; 1927, 1928b). The procedure was not criticized in terms of jurisdictional sovereignty but because of its inefficiency in fighting international crime, which, as an ICPC resolution of 1928 declared, had been developing 'in a manner alarming to mankind as a whole' (IKK 1928b). At a meeting in 1930, the Commission eventually determined to bypass extradition procedures altogether, deciding that ICPC members could make provisional arrests of suspects on the basis of information in the ICPC periodical, even in the absence of an international treaty that sanctioned this provision (AfK 1930b). Criticizing extradition as an inefficient tool of international police practices, what the ICPC instead suggested were various expert police methods to tackle efficiently the international crime problem. As the resolutions at the Vienna Congress specified (IKK 1923:197–202), the establishment of direct police-to-police communications and a swifter exchange of information were the primary tools for cooperation across national borders. Considerations of efficiency dominated in the choice of adequate police techniques, not concerns over legality or justice. Instead of trying to construct an internationally valid legal definition of international crime, the ICPC organized the international headquarters in Vienna on the basis of practical matters of crime detection and international police activities and sophisticated means of police technique and identification, such as fingerprints and photographs. For similar reasons communication systems through telegraph, radio, and printed documents were also instituted, while meetings were organized for the police to interact on a person-to-person basis.

In sum, just as the increase in international crime was, among the ICPC members, understood in expert terms, the means to handle the problem were conceived professionally on the basis of a purposive-rational efficiency in the Weberian sense. Technological developments, ironically, were instrumental in both stimulating concerns over international crime and in enhancing the means of law enforcement. For while technological progress brought about increasing opportunities for cross-border criminality, it also led to a growing expertise in the means of policing and criminal investigation. Thus, technically sophisticated means of crime detection were important factors that enabled police bureaucracies to develop effectively a myth of international crime that went beyond a mere discourse among experts.

Bureaucratic autonomy and international criminal police cooperation

I have explained the success of the International Criminal Police Commission and the failure of the International Police Conference to formalize police cooperation in a permanent organization on the basis of a theoretical model of bureaucratic autonomy. In terms of my first proposition, I argued for the relevance of the structural condition of formal bureaucratic autonomy of police institutions participating in international efforts. In the case of the ICPC as well as the IPC, formal bureaucratic autonomy was most clearly evidenced by the fact that both organizations were established independently at the initiative of police officials. Certain conditions had to be met for police institutions to become detached from their political centres. In the case of the ICPC and the IPC, political conditions of pacification and stability clearly enabled the trend towards bureaucratic autonomy of the police in the inter-war decades of the 1920s and 1930s. This confirms, as Weber argued, that the bureaucratization of the police is particularly accelerated in a 'society accustomed to pacification' (Weber 1922:561).

My thesis on formal bureaucratic autonomy underscores the argument that structural differences in independence from politics accounted for the fact that some national police systems could and others could not participate in international police organizations such as the ICPC. This suggests that formal bureaucratic autonomy is a determining factor of police internationalization irrespective of the political ideologies of the nations involved and irrespective of the nature of their relationships in matters of foreign policy. This thesis contradicts perspectives that suggest that the ICPC (and other international police organizations) are to be explained as efforts to advance the political goals of certain powerful states. Authors defending such perspectives have in the case of the International Criminal Police Commission alluded to the ideological persuasion of the police officials who founded and participated in the ICPC and, relatedly, the political objectives the ICPC was supposed to accomplish under the guise of crime control (Bresler 1992:21–52; Busch 1995:264–274; Greilsamer 1986:21–52). Political motivations would be most clearly revealed in the case of Johannes Schober, the main initiator and first President of the ICPC (Heindl 1932a, 1932b; Hubert 1990; Schultz 1930). Schober was also Chancellor of Austria on two occasions, in 1921 and 1929, and served as Austrian Minister of Foreign Affairs from 1930 to 1932. Given the ambitions of Schober in matters of international politics, it has been suggested that he founded the ICPC as an instrument of Austrian foreign policy, particularly a tool to revive Austria's international prestige after the country had been left in a state of instability after the war. Relatedly, it is argued that the ICPC served as an organizational bastion to fight the spread of communism, fear of which had gripped political élites in Europe (and the United States) since the Russian revolution of 1917 (Bresler 1992:21–26). All countries participating in the ICPC had at the time instituted anti-Bolshevik policies and were experienced in the control of socialist and communist organizations (Fijnaut 1979:399). The fact that police from Russia and, later, the Soviet Union did not participate in the ICPC is advanced as the strongest evidence for this perspective.

However, the evidence indicates that a political perspective has serious flaws in accounting for the formation of the International Criminal Police Commission. Specifically, what a state-centred approach cannot account for is that the ICPC not only explicitly dealt with criminal, rather than political activities, but that any preoccupation with political issues at this time actually prevented various efforts to foster police cooperation across national borders. Indeed, during the 19th century police institutions were typically still representative of conservative political regimes and, hence, international police cooperation, particularly in Europe, was targeted primarily at the political opponents of established governments (Bayley 1975; Liang 1992). But by the early decades of the 20th century such political ambitions were delegated to separate intelligence forces and no longer guided the international organization of bureaucratic police institutions. It is true that in the years between the two world wars there were still attempts to foster international police cooperation with explicitly political goals—especially with the purpose of controlling communist movements—and that some of these political ideals were also held among certain members of the ICPC. Yet, these political policing efforts were never implemented successfully in an international organization. As I argued in Chapter 2, the revival of political policing duties during and after World War I and the Bolshevik revolution did not lead to the establishment of an international police organization.

Against state-centred interpretations of international policing, therefore, I suggest that certain police institutions, including those of Communist Russia, could not cooperate in the ICPC not because of any political motivations among the membership of the ICPC—however real political antagonisms were at the level of national governments—but because of the structural condition that those non-participating institutions remained too closely linked to their respective political centres. It was not the ideological nature of the political regimes of participating police, but the formal separation of police bureaucracies from their respective governments (whatever their ideological disposition) that enabled their participation in international organizations. This explains not only why the police from Russia did not take part in the ICPC because of its strong attachment to the Communist dictatorship, but also why the police from other nations could and did participate in the same police organization although they were not closely akin in ideological respects and entertained anything but amicable political relationships. The strongest evidence supporting this argument is the cooperation in the ICPC of the police from countries that were as politically hostile during those years as France, Great Britain, Italy, and Germany. The adoption of a political programme, such as the fight against communism, may well have broken up such a diverse grouping of police institutions (Fijnaut 1997:119). Political processes, then, cannot be considered constitutive of international policing, although the structural condition of formal bureaucratic autonomy is influenced by historically variable circumstances which in turn are shaped politically. The fate of the ICPC in the build-up towards and during World War II will offer clear evidence of how political conditions can impede police from attaining or maintaining formal bureaucratic independence (see Chapter 7).

Among the implications of the fact that police institutions are in a position to cooperate internationally once they have gained formal bureaucratic autonomy is that cooperation can take place between police of national states that may be very different in terms of political, legal, and other conditions. In this respect, my analysis reveals that despite the formation of an international police organization, the cooperative structure of the ICPC nonetheless reaffirms the various national police systems and their variable characteristics. The ICPC was in its very foundations built explicitly on an ideal of respect for nation-state sovereignty and the 'laws existing within the individual states' (IKK 1923:197). It was therefore precisely no coincidence that the organizers of the 1923 Congress in Vienna did not conceive the meeting as a re-organization of the Monaco Congress, which a decade earlier had failed to recognize the advantages of a cooperative organization. Still, the very creation of the ICPC remains remarkable taking into account the great political and cultural heterogeneity that marked the European continent, dividing the region for hundreds of years. But putting aside any divisive issues, national police institutions participating in the ICPC could cooperate because of shared professional standards and objectives beyond state politics (Fijnaut 1997:111–114).

With the structural conditions for international cooperation fulfilled, the motivational basis of international police operations across national jurisdictions in the case of the ICPC was a professional myth of a cross-national rise and internationalization of crime since the end of World War I. The IPC, on the other hand, could not effectively uphold this myth, while as a professional association it could not compete with the IACP. But in the ICPC, the goals as well as the means to deal effectively with the problem of international crime were framed in professional police terms. With its emphasis on technically sophisticated means of policing, best exemplified by the functionally specialized headquarters and instituted mechanisms of police-to-police communications, the ICPC so accomplished what Weber with a witty quip directed at Marx once called a 'concentration of the means of administration' (Weber 1922:567).

Based on the myth of international crime, the elaboration of the ICPC involves a formal rationalization in terms of efficiency. Of course, it is not primarily relevant whether the proclaimed views on the nature and level of international criminality were empirically accurate, but that they were accepted to be valid among the police and motivated international cooperation effectively. As such, police knowledge systems are seen to operate actuarially in establishing certain harmful possibilities that can be predicted and proactively responded to. Negatively, this perspective is supported by research that finds that crime rates historically had little or no effect on the development of police institutions (Gillis 1989). The International Criminal Police Commission is in this respect an exemplary case in that it was a myth of international crime that enabled police institutions to participate in the international organization on the basis of professional crime conceptions that were formed irrespective of any political and legal concerns. For as sociologists Blau and Meyer (1971:50–59) argue, bureaucratic myths not only mobilize members around organizationally defined causes, they also insulate the organization from control and criticism. This also confirms, as Weber maintained, that state and market do not determine the relative strength of the bureaucracy versus the political rulers (Weber 1922:128–130,

615). Instead, it is the level of technical expertise attained by the officials and the amount of official information they accumulate that propel the bureaucracy to take on a course of its own.

My perspective implies no conclusions as to whether a rationalization of policing is more efficient or effective. I do not argue that the ICPC was a more efficient instrument in the control of international crime, but instead that it was motivated by, and designed explicitly to accommodate, a professional conception of efficiency. In fact, evidence indicates that the ICPC was not very effective in terms of handling international crime. Based on the minimal evidence available, some 870 cases were handled during the first three years of the ICPC's existence (Walther 1968:19). Between 1922 and 1927, the identification bureau in Copenhagen received some 7,000 fingerprints from thirty-two countries (Marabuto 1935). By 1928, the 'International Register' reportedly contained information about some 1,100 people, while the 'International Bureau for the Suppression of Falsifications of Currencies' was said to be communicating with twenty-nine countries (Palitzsch 1928). Those numbers are not impressive compared to the information collected by most other participating and comparable national police systems, which at the time were steadily being expanded (see Chapter 4). The relative ineffectiveness of the ICPC in investigative respects harmonizes with Weber's insight that the actual power of a bureaucracy in influencing the social structure it acts upon is empirically variable (Weber 1922:572). Instead of effectiveness in investigations, the fostering of professional relationships between police officials, especially through the personal contacts established at the meetings, may well have been among the ICPC's most concrete realizations. These personal relationships, moreover, may also have fuelled additional bilateral cooperation between the police complementing the structures of the ICPC. The notion that cooperation in the ICPC was enhanced through personal contacts parallels Peter Blau's famous theory on the role of informalism in organizations (Blau 1955).

Among the implications of the development of a professional myth of international crime in the ICPC is that expert systems of police knowledge emphasize a particular conception of, and an efficiency to control, international crime in extra-legal terms. In fact, police officials in the Commission criticized legal conceptions of crime and existing arrangements of international law, because they remained bound to national jurisdictions and were time-consuming and inefficient. And scholars of international law in the first half of the 20th century conceded that 'unofficial organizations,' such as the ICPC, had been much more successful in establishing cooperation in the fight against international crime, irrespective of, and contrary to, intergovernmental regulations between states, at which level a uniform system of international criminal law had not been accomplished (Kuhn 1934). Indeed, what the members of the ICPC emphasized instead were developments in crime influenced by societal factors (modernization, technological progress), not violations of formal legal systems. In terms of means, also, it was a strong emphasis on efficiency—in the Weberian sense of purposive rationality—that led to the establishment and elaboration of the ICPC's organizational facilities and accelerated its progression irrespective of legal arrangements and without supervision from political authority. The ICPC facilities and activities were planned and executed as efficient responses that were conceived to be as technologically sophisticated as the achievements of their targets. And only after the structures of international policing were already in place, were appeals made to legally and politically sanction what expert police bureaucrats had already established by themselves.

6

Policing Across National Borders

> German orderliness is proverbial. The streets and parks of German cities are spotless. A hundred thousand people bring their lunches to the *Grunewald* near Berlin every pleasant Sunday and leave it as clean and clear of rubbish as when they entered.
> *Raymond Fosdick, 1915.*

> There are certain sections of New York, Major, I wouldn't advise you try to invade.
> *Richard Blaine to a German military officer, Casablanca, 1942.*

> The Director [of the FBI, J. Edgar Hoover,] is fond of jotting pungent notations on the borders of memorandums, and the filling of all four borders is known as a 'four-bagger'. Once, he was irked by a memo that left little room for his scrawlings. 'Watch the borders', he wrote in his characteristic green ink. Uncertain of what he meant and afraid to ask, officials carried out the dictum to the letter. For over a week, agents were staked out along the Canadian and Mexican borders, unsure of what they were watching for.
> *A retired FBI agent.*

The formation of the International Criminal Police Commission in 1923 was the outcome of a process of bureaucratic autonomy begun in the second half of the 19th century, when police institutions gradually began to develop schemes for international cooperation beyond unilaterally instigated and *ad hoc* bilateral schemes. The acquired institutional independence of the police enabled the creation of a multilateral organization with large international appeal, crystallized around a newly defined operational domain that united the police from various countries around shared objectives. The form which this collaboration took was a cooperative structure that brought police institutions in direct contact with one another, without the formation of a supranational force. Among the permanently instituted structures that facilitated cooperation were a central headquarters and various technical means of direct police communication. The objectives of cooperation were limited to criminal police duties and excluded political violations.

At the outset of this book, I explained that the formation of an international police organization, providing a structure of cooperation, is a distinct accomplishment relative to transnational and temporary bilateral police cooperation. Participation in a pre-structured international organization relies on a shared commitment to a common cause that is not intimately bound to any one police institution and its agenda as a coercive organ of a single national state. However, as the previous chapter showed, the establishment of a cooperative organization such as the International Criminal Police Commission did not occur at the expense of concern for nationality issues. On the contrary, a national persistence is witnessed in the very way in which international police organizations such as the ICPC are set up as cooperative structures that enable communications and exchange between police institutions of various national states.

While an international organization of police cooperation is critical from an analytical viewpoint, the establishment of such an organization can by definition not be expected to exhaust all police duties with an international dimension. In other words, an international police organization does not necessarily absorb all international police functions, and the relative weight of participation in an international organization, on the one hand, and (a continuation of) other international police practices such as transnational activities and *ad hoc* and bilateral cooperation, on the other, is a matter that remains empirically variable. An investigation of international police cooperation, therefore, can never be at the expense of continued attention to the nationalization of policing, including the role of transnational police operations and cooperation of an *ad hoc* and/or limited bilateral character. This chapter will show that there continued to be many forms and occasions when modern police systems—despite their participation in an international organization—continued to engage in transnational or limited cooperative operations during the first half of the 20th century. While it is impossible to discuss all their empirical manifestations, the central characteristics of these developments will be revealed in this chapter in the context of Germany and the United States.

The expansion of national police systems

Continuing on the same path of bureaucratization that had already evolved for several decades, modern police institutions continued to grow in the first half of the 20th century in respect of the quality of their expertise and means of enforcement as well as in quantitative terms related to personnel, budget, and other forms of growth (Bayley

1985:23–52; Mawby 1990:16–34). These developments took place across western societies, but with certain local variations in organization and scope. In the case of Germany and the United States, critical differences existed, in particular, with respect to the socio-political context in which police institutions developed during the first half of the 20th century and the manner in which they would have a dramatic effect only conditions in world society.

The collapse of the Weimar Republic and the rise of the Nazi police

On 30 January 1933, President Paul van Hindenburg appointed Adolf Hitler to the German Chancellorship. On 29 February that year, the day after a fire had destroyed the building of the German national parliament, the *Reichstag*, and the Nazis had blamed the communists for the fire which they had set themselves, Hitler declared a permanent state of emergency and governed without parliamentary control. After the death of von Hindenburg in August 1934, Hitler completed his dictatorial conquest of Germany by merging the offices of Chancellor and President in the newly created position of '*Führer und Reichskanzler*'. Soon after Hitler's appointment, a policy of '*Gleichschaltung*' (coordination or Nazification) was implemented in order to bring all German social institutions in line with Nazi ideology (Fischer 1995:278–284; Thamer 1996; Winkler 1976). This Nazification process included control of labour and politics, the manipulation of public opinion, the passing of nationalist and racist legislation, and the control of bureaucratic institutions, including law enforcement. The Nazification of the German police involved three components: first, the removal of all unwanted personnel; secondly, the establishment of organizational connections between existing German police institutions and relevant NSDAP organs such as the SS; and, thirdly, a harmonization and centralization of all police offices in Germany. Most conspicuous was the fact that many police officers were neither particularly committed nor opposed to the Nazis and could therefore often hold their functions. Of the 85,000 police in Prussia in 1933, for instance, only 2,668 were dismissed.

The history of the Nazification of the German police dates back to the very beginning of the Nazi party, when para-military and semi-police forces were created within the NSDAP.[1] The first to be established were

[1] This section relies on discussions of German policing published during the Nazi regime (Best 1941; Daluege 1936; Grauert 1934; Liepelt 1938; Nebe and Fleischer

the SA (*Sturmabteilung*) or Storm Division, a private Nazi military force that was headed by Ernst Röhm, as well as the *Stosstruppe-Hitler* (Assault Force) and the *Stabswache* (Staff Guard). In 1925, the latter two were merged into the *Schutzstaffel* (Protective Squadron) or SS, a force which at first was in charge of protecting the leaders of the NSDAP and guarding the party against armed attack. In January 1929, Heinrich Himmler assumed leadership of the SS in his function of *Reichsführer-SS* (*Reich* Leader of the SS), and the force, strengthened to some 50,000 men, was now assigned to protect the Nazi party against internal and external attempts at overthrow. Also created was a separate SS intelligence service, the *Sicherheitsdienst* (Security Service) or SD, which became an additional source of rivalry with the SA and its intelligence service, the *Nachrichtendienst* (Information Service) or ND.

From 1933 onwards, the SA and SS were institutionally related to existing German police organizations. The SA was connected with the *Schutzpolizei* (Protective Police), and the SS was linked with the political police in the Gestapa (*Geheimes Staatspolizeiamt*, Secret State Police Office), which in 1936 was renamed Gestapo (*Geheime Staatspolizei*, Secret State Police). The leadership of all major police posts was also placed under Nazi control. The *Reich* Leader of the SS, Heinrich Himmler, first became Police President of Munich in 1933, then headed the police for all of Bavaria, and in January 1934 acquired leadership over the political police in all of Germany. On 30 June 1934, during the so-called 'Night of the Long Knives', the leaders of the SA, including its head Ernst Röhm, were liquidated by the Nazis, because Hitler feared that the force could become a threat to his position and the Nazi quest for control of Germany.

The Nazification of German police institutions also involved a nationalization of police. The Versailles Treaty prohibited the formation of a national police in Germany, but, as a first step towards centralized Nazi control, Heinrich Himmler had in 1934 acquired leadership over Germany's political police offices. In June of 1936, the completion of the Nazi-controlled nationalization of German police was symbolized by the appointment of Himmler to *Reichsführer-SS und Chef der deutschen Polizei* (*Reich* Leader SS and Chief of the

1939; Palm 1934; Richter 1941; Roschorke 1937, 1939; Werner 1942) and some helpful secondary studies on the Nazi police (see Aronson 1971; Browder 1990; Delarue 1962; Duprat 1968; Engelmann 1949; Gellately 1992a, 1992b; Graber 1978; Graf 1983; Harnischmacher and Semerak 1986:92–109; Koehl 1983; Krausnick et al. 1968; Riege 1966:41–57; Reitlinger 1957).

German Police). The criminal police and the Gestapo were united in the *Hauptamt Sicherheitspolizei* (Main Office Security Police), while the *Gendarmerie* and *Schutzpolizei* were brought together in the *Hauptamt Ordnungspolizei* (Main Office Order Police). In 1939, the Security Police and the SD were united in the *Reichssicherheitshauptamt* (*Reich* Security Main Office) or RSHA. The RSHA would become one of the most powerful Nazi police institutions, for it combined, amongst other agencies, the Security Services (for interior and foreign affairs), the criminal police (*Kriminalpolizei* or Kripo), and the Gestapo. The criminal police was centralized and institutionally brought under one office, the *Reichskriminalpolizeiamt* (*Reich* Criminal Police Office) or RKPA.

The progressive era and the rise of the FBI

In the United States, the first two decades of the 20th century witnessed reform movements in various areas of society, including criminal justice and law enforcement.[2] The impetus to reform in the areas of crime and the police mostly implied a continuation and intensification of developments that had been taking shape since the later decades of the 19th century, specifically in terms of the critique of police corruption and the inefficiency of policing. The need for police reform was responded to by various local and national commissions comprised of experts, in order to study and rectify the problems. In 1929, President Herbert Hoover initiated the National Commission on Law Observance and Enforcement, the so-called 'Wickersham Commission', named after Attorney General George W. Wickersham. The Commission researched the policing situation in the United States, and the fourteen reports it published exposed an abundance of problems. Other initiatives of reform rested with private organizations and were launched by major police experts, such as Arthur Woods, August Vollmer, Bruce Smith, and Raymond Fosdick. As will be discussed later in this chapter, there were distinct international dimensions involved with this otherwise typical US process of police reform. From the perspective of the organization of US police institutions, the reform movement of the 1920s and 1930s involved efforts aimed at a scientification of policing and a professionalization of the various forces. This implied an emphasis on the adoption of new technological developments, such as patrol cars, police radios, and

[2] On the police reform movement, see Center for Research on Criminal Justice 1977:32–42; Fogelson 1977:93–113; Vollmer 1922, 1930, 1932, 1933, 1936; Walker 1977, 1980:169–193.

fingerprint files, and a claim to independence from (local) politics. Additionally, the move to professionalism also implied some degree of harmonization, coordination, and/or centralization between various local police agencies. In this particular sense, the ultimate ideal of the police reform movement would be the development of a well-organized federal police that would, independent of petty local politics, implement scientific methods of criminal investigation across the United States.

Corresponding to the ideal of a professional federal police, the Bureau of Investigation, later called the Federal Bureau of Investigation or FBI, would from the early 1930s onwards come to represent the most significant federal police institution in the United States. Created in 1908, the Bureau was originally responsible for only relatively few criminal violations.[3] The initially limited jurisdictional competence of the Bureau was mainly determined by the fact that there were only few federal criminal laws. Four developments, in particular, were beneficial for the expansion of the Bureau: the passing of new federal laws; the appointment of J. Edgar Hoover as Director; the gangster era of the 1930s; and the policing implications of two world wars. With regard to the growth of the Bureau's jurisdictional field through the expansion of federal legislation, the passing of the Mann Act in 1912 provided the initial impetus for the development of the BOI, when the Bureau was assigned to control violations of the anti-prostitution Act (Langum 1994). After participating in war-related activities during World War I, the enactment of the National Motor Vehicle Theft Act in 1919 further extended the BOI's jurisdiction. However, by the early 1920s the Bureau still shared with other US police agencies the usual problems of corruption and incompetence. To rectify the image of a scandal-ridden Bureau, Attorney General Harry Daugherty and BOI Director William Burns were forced to resign, whereupon the newly appointed Attorney General, Harlan Fiske Stone, brought in John Edgar Hoover to turn the Bureau into a professional

[3] The literature on the FBI is extremely extensive, much of it concentrating on the excesses of the Bureau under, and the abuse of power by, its famous Director, J. Edgar Hoover. These works serve a critical function in the US democratic public sphere, but they are often less than valuable in terms of analytical perspective (e.g. Theoharis 1995; Theoharis and Cox 1993; Tully 1980; Turner 1993). Other contributions on the FBI focus on the person of Hoover and interpret the history of the FBI in light of his psychology (e.g. Gentry 1991; Powers 1987; Sumners 1993). Other writings provide internal perspectives written by FBI agents or published under the supervision of the Bureau (e.g., Comfort 1959; FBI 1945b, 1974, 1994a, 1994b; Look 1954). While a solid scholarly history of the FBI remains to be written, some thoughtful accounts on the Bureau were valuable from the perspective of this book (see Keller 1989; Lowenthal 1950; Overstreet and Overstreet 1969; Poveda 1990; Robins 1992; Ungar 1976).

and accountable organization. As head of the General Intelligence Division, J. Edgar Hoover had been involved in the Palmer Raids of January 1920. Despite the criticism he had then received, he was in 1921 appointed Assistant Director of the BOI under Director Burns. After the latter was ousted, Hoover was in May 1924 appointed Acting Director and in December that year confirmed as Director, a position he would hold until his death in 1972. Professionalization of police, especially a thorough reliance on modern science, as well as a strong executive leadership independent from any political influences, were to become the key elements of Hoover's policy.

The crime wave of the 1920s and 1930s provided the first opportunity for Hoover to present the Bureau as the leading federal crime-fighting agency. Partly as a result of the lack of effective law enforcement in the era of Prohibition, a new type of criminal—the gangster—had appeared. While prohibition violations were the responsibility of the Department of the Treasury, many of the criminal activities that went along with it fell under the jurisdiction of the BOI. The Bureau's involvement in some heavily publicized criminal cases—which were actually not representative of any broader crime patterns—stirred public hysteria and captured the public's imagination. These were the days of the kidnapping of the son of Charles Lindbergh, the organization of crime and racketeering activities by the likes of Al Capone, and the ruthless exploits of John Dillinger, Pretty Boy Floyd, Ma Barker, and Bonnie and Clyde. Hoover responded by manipulating the media and presenting the Bureau's special agents as professional and dedicated heroes. By the mid-1930s, the Bureau had clearly become the most powerful of all federal US law enforcement agencies.

'American ideas are German ideas as well': A dialogue on policing in two countries

National police developments do not occur in isolation from one another but are in varying degrees interconnected, establishing concrete relations between and borrowing selected elements from one another. The police and criminological literature that appeared in Germany and the United States in the first half of the 20th century presents an interesting source from which these respective views of the police and criminal justice situation in the two countries can be studied (see Appendix 2). While not providing a complete picture, an analysis of these writings in the specialized journals can offer important insights into how the German and US police and criminal justice officials conceived and evaluated one another's organization and functions, the relations that were established between them, and how their perceptions and interactions affected their respective participations in international practices and organizations of police cooperation.

In general terms, it can be noted that of all collected writings published between 1900 and 1945 in Germany and the United States that discuss explicitly the police and criminal justice situation in their respective countries, the total number of German documents (142) by far exceeds the number of US items (53). This disparity displays the fact that police and criminal justice developments in Germany relied on a much more intellectually oriented tradition than in the USA. Indeed, as I argued in the Introduction, German police organization was sustained theoretically by a well-developed scientific activity, while the law enforcement situation in the United States developed in more *ad hoc* ways in response to various practical conditions. Unlike German theorizing in the tradition of the '*Polizeiwissenschaften*', the US pragmatist orientation in policing did not allow for much intellectualizing. The difference in the development of a specialized literature on both sides of the Atlantic, therefore, is no coincidence.[4]

The German discovery of the New World, 1900–1943

Of all the German documents I collected that discuss aspects of the US criminal justice system, about as many deal with policing (70) as with crime and criminal law (73).[5] Among the noteworthy observations is

[4] The different state of the policing literature in Germany and the United States was in fact addressed in one of the collected documents. Specifically, the German police official Robert Heindl (1930a) announced the publication of the *American Journal of Police Science* in a 1930 article in a German criminology journal. Praising the new journal for providing for the first time in the United States an outlet for police studies much like those that were already available in many European countries, Heindl argued that German criminologists could benefit from the journal to become better acquainted with the experiences of their US counterparts. The US journal itself immediately reprinted Heindl's favourable article (Heindl 1930b).

[5] The most important German sources are the criminology journal *Archiv für Kriminal-Anthropologie und Kriminalistik*, later renamed *Archiv für Kriminologie*, and the police magazines *Die Polizei* and *Der Deutsche Polizeibeamte*, later renamed *Die Deutsche Polizei*. The *Archiv* was founded in 1899 and was mostly oriented towards a readership of criminologists and law professors, rather than police officers. The police magazines *Die Polizei* and *Der Deutsche Polizeibeamte*, on the other hand, mostly lacked academic articles and offered very practical information on everyday aspects of policing. *Die Polizei* has been published since 1904 by the Prussian Ministry of the Interior and still appears today. *Der Deutsche Polizeibeamte*, after 1938 *Die Deutsche Polizei*, was published by the SS from 1933 to 1945.

that forty-four, or nearly 63 per cent, of the articles specifically dealing with police issues were published in the 1930s. Before the 1920s, the German literature on US criminal justice was sparse and most of it was written from a theoretical–legal rather than from a practical policing perspective, concerned thematically more with US crime and criminal law than with police. The few articles that in the early 20th century discussed police conditions in the United States (e.g. Hatschek 1910, 1911) were written from a legal viewpoint without contemplation of any implications for police organization. One of the few pieces dealing with more practical policing issues was a German translation of William Pinkerton's (1905) address at the meeting of the International Association of Chiefs of Police in St. Louis. William Pinkerton and his brother Robert at the time headed the famous private detective agency named after, and founded by, their father Allen.

A series of articles by forensic expert Hans Fehlinger published in the first two decades of the 20th century reveals many of the characteristics of similar accounts that would be published in Germany in the years to come. First, these articles were predominantly technical in nature and provided mostly descriptive information on a wide variety of issues, such as the level of crime among 'negroes' and foreign-born immigrants (Fehlinger 1906, 1919), the number of prisoners in the USA (Fehlinger 1908), unlawful marriages (Fehlinger 1910), crimes of women and children (Fehlinger 1912), and the US practices of the sterilization of criminals (Fehlinger 1915). Among Fehlinger's few reflective commentaries were his defence of a biological theory of crime, arguing that it was 'confirmed more and more that criminal tendencies are predominantly the result of inborn abnormities [*sic*]' (Fehlinger 1912:203). Biological crime theories, of course, were far from atypical in Fehlinger's days and remained prevalent, along with environmental crime causation theories, for quite some time to come. Fehlinger (1915) also spoke with approval of US legislation on the sterilization of criminals, a topic which would remain of interest to German criminal justice professionals for some years (Hofman 1913; AfK 1935a).[6]

More striking, especially from the viewpoint of this book, is the relative intensity of German discussions on US policing during the 1920s

[6] Relatedly, many articles in the German criminology literature dealt with 'negro' criminality (Näcke 1909; Burchardt 1940b; *Die Polizei* 1940c) and lynchings (Spitzka 1903; Raper 1932; DP 1933c, 1936f, 1936h; Heindl 1933). Typically, the commentaries on lynching were very negative, but not so much because it was a racist practice as because 'lynch justice' (*Lynchjustiz*) was considered an inefficient form of popular vengeance.

and 1930s. During this period, in fact, German police officials travelled frequently to the United States to learn first-hand about the US police situation (e.g. Paetsch 1928a, 1928b, 1929; Paetsch and Voit 1927; Voit 1928, 1931; Welzel 1922a, 1922b, 1926). Many of the reports of these travels and other contributions on police practices and organizations abroad featured in a series called 'About Foreign Police' ('*Aus fremden Polizeien*')—from 1933 onwards called 'Police Abroad' ('*Polizei im Ausland*')—that from about 1930 appeared in *Die Polizei* (e.g. DP 1933a, 1933b, Monfigny 1931; Riege 1930a, 1930c, 1931a; Ratcliffe 1932b, 1932d). On the police situation in the United States, most reports were predominantly of a very technical and descriptive nature. However, whenever German police officials offered evaluations of the police experience in the United States, they commented very favourably. Police experts, such as Robert Heindl (1914d, 1927a, 1927b), noted, in particular the increasing attempts to professionalize and coordinate policing, developments that the police reform movement had rightly anticipated as more acutely necessary because of the rise in criminality in the major US metropolitan areas (Heindl 1921, 1932c, 1935a; Palitzsch 1930; see Waite 1992:193–196).

After the Nazi seizure of power, German police experts continued to report mostly technical descriptions of the US police situation (e.g. AfK 1936c, 1937c, 1939a; Ratcliffe 1932a, 1932e; DP 1936a, 1940a; Burchardt 1937d). But commentaries became more critical of US police methods and organization, particularly during the later half of the 1930s. Criticized in particular were problems of police corruption, the prohibition of alcohol, and the sensationalist press coverage of police and crime issues (Riege 1931b, 1931c; Meyer 1938; PPD 1938). The only aspect of US police discussed in a more positive light were the (Federal) Bureau of Investigation and its Director, J. Edgar Hoover. The leadership of Hoover (Welzel 1926:353) and the FBI's use of scientific methods of criminal detection (Burchardt 1937a; Peirhal 1939) and its fingerprint collection (AfK 1929b; AfK 1935c; DP 1936d; Burchardt 1937f) were commented upon favourably. As late as 1938, several articles by J. Edgar Hoover that commented very positively on the FBI's efficient use of fingerprints were published in the *Archiv für Kriminologie* (Hoover 1938b, 1938c, 1938d). And in 1940, at a time when the racial and sterilization laws of the United States were commented upon favourably by German legal experts (Waite 1992:207–211), Hoover's opposition against parole and the FBI's methods of controlling white slavery also received German approval (DP 1940c). Other reports, however, criticized various aspects of the US criminal justice system, such as trials by jury (Meinert 1939a,b), the use of lie detectors (Burchardt 1940a), and the lack of implementing the death penalty (Burchardt 1940b). Once the United States had joined the War, articles in the German police literature on the situation in the United States were so much dictated by the Nazi ideology that they no longer contained discussions of police issues at all, but formed an intrinsic part of the Nazi war propaganda against the United States, particularly targeting the worldwide conspiracy of 'the Jew and the Yankee' (DDP 1943e:328; see also DDP 1943e, 1943f, 1943g, 1943h).

US perspectives of German criminal justice, 1900–1945

The specialized literature published in the United states discussing German criminal justice is, as noted, much less elaborate than the corresponding German material.[7] Nearly 40 per cent of the collected US documents are reviews of German books and journal articles, indicating again that criminal justice in Germany was oriented more towards theoretical reflection. Most documents deal with German criminal law (32) and less with police (21). Also, US interest in German criminal justice was more intense before than after the First World War, when more than half (53%) of the reviewed articles were published. In the period before the war, US observers mostly combined a scepticism about the powerful scope of the German criminal justice system with positive evaluations of the reliance on scientific methods. The German centralized autocratic system was criticized because it clashed with US conceptions of self-government, but it was also recognized that certain German procedures, such as the registration system and the use of identity papers, were very efficient (James 1910; Garner 1911). One of the few accounts published in the United States which outlined more parallels than differences between the German and US criminal justice systems was actually written by a German lawyer from Berlin, who

[7] The most frequently discussed US periodical in this analysis is *The Journal of the American Institute of Criminal Law and Criminology* (hereafter: JAICLC), in 1931 renamed *The Journal of Criminal Law and Criminology*. The *Journal* was published by the American Institute of Criminal Law and Criminology which was a product of a national conference held in Chicago in 1909. The conference was organized by the law faculty of Northwestern University and brought together scientists and professionals interested in criminal justice. Although the editorial board of the journal, which is still published today, consisted mostly of university professors, the publication was mostly practical in orientation. Also relied upon are articles in the *American Journal of Police Science*, a short-lived publication which only appeared from 1930 to 1932, whereafter it was absorbed into *The Journal of Criminal Law and Criminology*.

claimed that '[t]he American ideas of criminal law are frequently discussed in Germany. They are German ideas as well' (Hartmann 1911: 350).

Early US views of German police institutions were similarly critical of the unnecessarily broad powers granted to police and approving of the use of scientific methods of investigation. Adoption of these methods in the United States, it was argued, could lead, in particular, to redress the public distrust of the police (Albrecht 1911a; Fuld 1911, 1912a, 1912c; Gault 1913, 1915). The positive evaluation of the use of scientific methods of criminal investigation in Germany also motivated US police officials to travel to Germany and other parts of Europe. In 1902, for instance, Avery Andrews, a former Police Commissioner of New York, studied the European police forces, especially those of Paris and London, with the purpose of reforming the New York Police Department (Andrews 1903). Before World War I, Arthur Woods, William McAdoo, and Raymond Fosdick, all of New York, made similar trips to Europe in order to learn about effective police methods that could be implemented fruitfully in the United States (McAdoo 1909; Fosdick 1915a, 1915c). Fosdick's (1915a) judgment of the European police as 'an excellent piece of machinery' (p. 37) was especially well received in the United States, which in turn met with approval in Europe (Heindl 1922b).

As part of the reform movement that sought to establish and enhance police professionalism in the United States, police visits to Germany and other European countries continued during the 1920s (Nadelmann 1993:87–88). It was in 1923 that the members of the 'Foreign Police Commission' of the International Police Conference traveled to Europe (see Chapter 3) and several others followed (e.g. Gollomb 1926; Goddard 1930). Among the travellers were also the famous criminologist Sheldon Glueck, then a student at Harvard, and his wife Eleanor, who—at the request of Arthur Woods, the Police Commissioner of New York and a major figure in the police reform movements—studied the police forces of several of Europe's major cities (Glueck 1926). However, from the late 1920s onwards, US interest in the European police was clearly waning and only few, mostly technical reports on German criminal justice were published (JAICLC 1928, 1929), sometimes written by German professionals (Viernstein 1932; Exner 1933). As one of the last US police trips to Germany organized before World War II, police chiefs of the cities of Rochester and Wichita visited Germany in June and July of 1933, as part of a sixteen-member group which, funded by a private German–American organization, was tasked with studying the administration of selected German cities. The US observers commented very favourably on the state of the German police and approved particularly of the disciplined organization and use of scientific crime detection methods (Kavanaugh 1933; Wilson 1933). The favourable judgments of the US police chiefs were welcomed proudly in *Der Deutsche Polizeibeamte*, the Nazi police magazine (Hartmann 1933, 1934).

As US attention for German and European criminal justice and policing declined, negative reports began to appear in the US criminal justice literature about the Nazi reformation of the German criminal justice system. Especially criticized were the abolition of earlier instituted progressive reforms in German criminal law and the establishment of an all-powerful state (Cantor 1934b; Honig 1936). Also negatively perceived was the German law of June 1935 that stipulated that every crime to which no law was directly applicable would be punishable by the law whose basic idea was most closely related to the crime (Preuss 1936). Enacting this law, the Nazi regime had replaced the principle of *nulla poena sine lege* (no punishment without law) by what was referred to as 'the higher and more powerful legal truth—*nullum crimen sine poena*' (no crime without punishment) (in Preuss 1936:848). The few reports that in the late 1930s and early 1940s appeared in the US literature were invariably critical of the Nazi policies on criminal justice issues, disapproving specifically of the system's racist and autocratic nature, the abolition of the separation of powers, the harsh forms of punishment, the destruction of individual rights, and the submission of science to politics 'in order to produce an Aryan criminology' (Cantor 1937:793; Ploscowe 1936; Kirchheimer 1938; Landecker 1941). In 1938, the *Journal of Criminal Law and Criminology* published an interview with the director of a German prison, who candidly revealed that the Nazi regime had instituted a separate legal system for Jews, 'since a contemptuous attitude towards them is not only a right but a duty' (Leiser 1938: 350–351). Though always critical, accounts about the Nazi criminal justice system appeared only sporadically in the US police and criminological literature. It was not until the very end of World War II that a critical report was published, written by a German refugee, that condemned the 'Law for the Protection of German Blood and Honour' of September 1935 which had deprived all Jews in Germany of German citizenship (Hoefer 1945). The article also deplored the end of judicial independence in Nazi Germany, the removal of all non-Aryans and anti-Nazis from the German police, and the existence of the concentration camps.

'Our constant battle': The internationalization of national policing

Apart from the police visits and exchange of information and evaluation of police methods and organization in the specialized literature, a host of other international policing activities—more or less closely related to actual criminal investigations—continued to be initiated by various, national and regional police institutions in Germany and the United States despite those and other countries' participation in more organized forms of cooperation. As was the case with such operations in the 19th century, these activities did not involve any formalization or permanent organization of international cooperation and served distinctly nationally or regionally defined goals. Yet, much like the cooperative organizational forms, these unilateral and short-term bilateral international plans also became more prevalent and tended to focus more on criminal enforcement duties in the decades between the two world wars of the 20th century. Towards the end of the 1930s, however, with international tensions mounting in the build-up towards World War II, international police activities again acquired a distinctly political character. In the present section, emphasis is on those dimensions of international policing with German and US involvement that are a continuation of developments set in during earlier decades. Police efforts in the move towards World War II will be discussed in the next chapter.

From democratic inclusion to dictatorial control

I discussed earlier how the German police during the Weimar years were reorganized unsuccessfully by the Versailles Treaty and remained a strong force with extensive powers inherited from an autocratic past. Nonetheless, the German police in the Weimar years was, at least publicly and formally, dedicated to fulfilling its role in the newly created democratic republic, internally by developing standards of accountability and externally through participation in international cooperation initiatives and otherwise attempting to be accepted in the international community of police professionals. Hence, the German police participated in the ICPC and occasionally even took on a leading role, such as with the anti-Bolshevik conference of Munich.

Further revealing the intent of having the German police (re-) accepted in the international community after the embarrassment of World War I, two rather spectacular international police conferences were organized in Germany in the 1920s: the International Police-Technical Exhibition in Karlsruhe in June 1925, and the Great Police Exhibition in Berlin in 1926.[8] The Karlsruhe Exhibition attracted police officials from several European countries as well as delegations from the ICPC, the International Police Conference, and the Bureau of Investigation. Beyond serving as a meeting to exchange information on methods of criminal investigation, the Exhibition also led to the establishment of the 'German Criminal Police Commission' (*Deutsche Kriminalpolizeiliche Kommission*). The Commission was formed as the formal representative organ of German police in the ICPC and would also seek to enhance cooperation between the criminal police offices in the different German states, focusing specifically on the 'travelling criminal' within the borders of Germany (Palitzsch 1926d). As such, the German Commission fulfilled a coordinating role and contributed to a nationalization of policing in much the same way as the IACP and IPC attempted in the United States.

The Great Police Exhibition in Berlin in 1926 was even more clearly organized with the purpose of enhancing the international prestige and acceptance of the Weimar police institutions. The Exhibition was a very elaborate affair, organized in conjunction with the third ordinary meeting and second International Police Congress organized by the International Criminal Police Commission. As the first ICPC meeting to be held in Germany, eight years after the end of World War I, the Berlin gathering was clearly an occasion for the German authorities to demonstrate their return to the international community of nations. In his opening speech at the Congress, the German Minister of the Interior emphasized that the international meeting would serve to promote the 'greater ideal of the general understanding of nations' (in IKK 1926c:13). Similarly, German ICPC member Palitzsch commented that the decision to hold the meeting on German soil was an indication that the 'prejudice and reservations against Germany' had vanished (Palitzsch 1926c:354).

[8] On the Karlsruhe Exhibition, see AfK 1925a, 1925d, 1925f, 1925g; Gundlach 1925; Jung 1926; Wolz 1926. On the Berlin Exhibition, see Abegg 1926; Daranyi and Daranyi 1927; Hirschfeld and Vetter 1927; Polizei-Ausstellung Berlin 1926a, 1926b; Schober 1926. See also the reports on foreign policing by some of the Berlin delegates, Dressler 1927; Keffer 1927; Palitzsch 1927b; Schlanbusch 1927; Tilgner 1927; Weiß 1927.

The Karlsruhe and Berlin exhibitions did not stand alone as manifestations of the German aspiration to participate on an equal footing with other democracies in international policing matters during the 1920s. For example, the German police also took part in the Police-Technical Exhibition held in Zoppot, Poland, in July 1924 (AfK 1925e). Organized by Police President Froböá of Danzig and attended by representatives from Hungary, Warschau, and Germany, the meeting promoted the exchange of information on methods of criminal investigation. Other cooperation schemes were actually organized by the German police. Next to the anti-Bolshevik conference in Munich in 1920 (see Chapter 4), mention can also be made of the proposal by Bernhard Weiß, the head of the Berlin criminal police, to establish an international police bureau (Weiß 1922), and a German police official's proposition to create an international police labour union (Siering 1931). With the steady expansion of the ICPC, however, none of these schemes were successful.

Next to police cooperation initiatives, the German police throughout the 1920s and 1930s also maintained their involvement in a host of other international police operations. A major impetus for these activities was the preoccupation of German police with foreigners and, relatedly, practical matters of extradition.[9] German police institutions, in fact, contained specialized divisions of 'Foreigners Police' (*Fremdenpolizei*). During the Weimar years, these agencies focused on the registration of foreigners in Germany and enforced compliance with regulations concerning passports and work permits. After the Nazi seizure of power, these police tasks were redefined in terms of the dictatorship's racist policies.[10] As early as 1933, an article in *Die Polizei* discussed the 'East-Jewish question' as a problem for the Foreigners Police and argued that only the German people could expect police protection, while Jews would first have to prove their 'undangerousness' (*Ungefährlichkeit*) (Müller 1933).

[9] On the German police perspectives of foreigners and extradition during the Weimar Republic, see AfK 1931b; DP 1922a, 1922b, 1924a, 1924b, 1925, 1926, 1930, 1932; Isay 1923; Maürer 1925; Usinger 1929.

[10] On the Nazi view on the policing of foreigners, see DP 1937a; Hein 1935; *Der Deutsche Polizeibeamte* 1935b, 1937; DDP 1941b; Warth 1938. An extremely interesting source revealing the transformations involved in the Nazification of the German police are the *Amtliche Nachrichten* (Service Reports) issued by the Berlin Police Presidency (see Der Polizeipräsident von Berlin). While these internal reports, published since 1899, apply only to the policing of Berlin, they provide an excellent inside account into the practical issues involved with the policing of foreigners and cooperation with foreign police in Germany's capital city.

Gradually but steadily from 1933 onwards, the Nazification of the German police was reflected in a radical sharpening of the control of foreigners under direction of a Nazi-controlled centralization of all international police practices with German involvement through the German Foreign Office (see Chapter 7).

The FBI as an international police

Beyond the organization of the International Police Conference and other relatively inconsequential involvements in international cooperation plans, the US police during the 1920s and 1930s continued to be involved mostly in a variety of international police activities that were already prevalent before World War I. Continued, in particular, were the control of immigrants, the policing of criminality among specific ethnic groups, mostly of newly arrived immigrants, and international enforcement duties in matters of narcotics.[11] Narcotics control provided a major impetus for the development of US police operations abroad. In the 1930s, for instance, agents from the Federal Bureau of Narcotics (FBN), an agency in the Treasury Department, were stationed in Europe and held meetings with narcotics officers from other countries, including France, the Netherlands, and Nazi Germany.

Also aiding the internationalization of US policing was the police reform movement that sought to enhance professionalism in policing and, partly therefore, established contacts between police agencies in and outside the United States. From the 1930s onwards, the reform era also witnessed initiatives for police reorganization and proposals related to cross-border police issues that began to be formulated in terms of a new, cross-border crime problems (e.g. Black 1938; Interstate Conference on Crime 1935; Wigmore 1937; Wood 1937). The International Police Conference was relatively unsuccessful in responding to these issues, mostly because of inter-agency conflicts with, and the more successful organization of police coordination by, the IACP and, more clearly still, the FBI.

The IACP, as noted in Chapter 3, always remained a largely American affair, but the organization did foster some cooperation with

[11] On crime and immigration in the USA, see Hacker 1929; Lancaster 1932; Lind 1922; *Police Chiefs' News Letter* 1936; Police Magazine 1925; Roberts 1925; Ross 1937; van Vechten 1942. On the policing of ethnic minorities, see, for instance, Ronquillo 1934 and Cahir 1932 on the Chinese in Chicago, and Beynon 1935 on Hungarians in Detroit. And on international dimensions in the control of narcotics, see Nadelmann 1993:93–99; Tullett 1963:62–63.

police officials from outside the North-American continent, if mostly on an informal basis.[12] As noted before, these personal contacts between the police across national borders helped to develop a common culture of police experts, recognizing one another in their common task. Because of such contacts, US police experts like Collier may indeed have had good reasons to argue that '[f]oreign police officials . . . are our friends, our comrades, our fellow-workers in our constant battle against crime' (Collier 1937). However, as a professional advocacy group, the IACP remained largely focused on police professionalism and coordination in the United States. From the mid-1930s onwards, it was the FBI that would become the leading federal US law enforcement organization, in terms of federal offences as well as with respect to international crimes.

At the heart of the development of the Bureau of Investigation was what is essentially an issue of cross-border policing, as the Bureau was put in charge of violations of the White Slave Traffic Act of 1910 and other federal offences related to inter-state commerce (Millspaugh 1937:78). Throughout the 1930s, the Bureau's powers continued to grow through an expansion of the number of violations that were regulated by federal law, the effective portrayals of a rising crime problem, and the pro-federal regulation policies of President Roosevelt. With the expansion of its operational domain, the FBI was increasingly responsible for cross-border and international crimes, such as violations of immigration laws and the prostitution trade. The FBI also took part in international programmes that were inspired and organized by the police reform movement. J. Edgar Hoover chaired the Committee on Foreign Relations in the IACP, and FBI Special Agent E.P. Coffey conducted an inspection tour of European police in the late 1930s (*FBI Law Enforcement Bulletin* 1938a, 1938b, 1938c, 1938d, 1938e, 1939).

Enabling its broadened functions, the FBI was successful in acquiring a variety of sophisticated technological means.[13] In 1930, the Bureau assumed responsibility of the Uniform Crime Reports, the (currently still

[12] On the role of the IACP in the 1920s and 1930s, see International Association of Chiefs of Police 1924, 1925, 1926, 1929; Draper 1937; Hoover 1937, 1938a; *Police Chiefs' News Letter* 1934, 1938, 1939; Quinn 1937; Sullivan 1939.

[13] On the international functions of the FBI since the 1930s, see Goddard 1930; Lowenthal 1950:368–387; Powers 1987:148–158; Ungar 1976:55–56. Also helpful were the annual reports of the US Attorney General (1918–1946) and reports published by the FBI, especially its official magazine, the *FBI Law Enforcement Bulletin* (1936a, 1936b, 1937a, 1937b), and the FBI annual reports (Federal Bureau of Investigation 1938, 1939, 1940, 1941a, 1943, 1945a).

existing) nation-wide collection of criminal data in the United States, and in 1935, a professional training facility was established in the National Police Academy. Perhaps most important among the means aiding the FBI's international police efforts was the vast machinery of its fingerprint system in the Division of Identification, later called the National Division of Identification and Information. In 1924, the Identification Division contained 810,188 fingerprints, a number which would rise exponentially to about one million in 1926, two million in 1930, five million in 1935 and thirteen million in 1940. Through this extensive collection of fingerprints the FBI could maintain a steadily growing and elaborate network of contacts with foreign police. From 1928 onwards, the Bureau took steps to enable cooperation and exchange with police forces in Europe, and in 1932 an international exchange service of fingerprints was formally established in the Bureau. By 1936, police forces from seventy-three countries cooperated in the service, a number which had risen to eighty-nine in 1939.

The nationalization of international policing

This chapter has shown that the successful formation of an international organization of police cooperation does not imply that all internationally oriented police functions are channelled into such an organization to the exclusion of all other, transnational and bilateral plans. On the contrary, coinciding with the increase of successful as well as unsuccessful attempts to form an international police organization, other international police efforts were also on the rise during the first half of the 20th century. These developments, furthermore, followed paths that were influenced by nationally variable circumstances, again confirming a persistence of nationality in international developments.

The largely technical and descriptive nature of many of the police and criminal justice discussions in Germany as well as the United States betray the extent to which police and other institutions were bureaucratized across national states. Within those broad contours, however, markedly different political conditions and police traditions shaped international police developments in the United States and in Germany in distinct ways. Whereas political conditions in the United States only very gradually allowed for a federalization of policing, in Germany the Weimar Republic faced the problem of having to constitutionally curtail a traditionally powerful force. The pragmatic orientation and local organization of US law enforcement also needed to be transcended in order to allow for a more professional and nationally organized force. In Germany, however, a high degree of efficiency in policing organized under conditions of a strong nationalistic state had to be tempered during the democratic experiment of Weimar. Thus, while the theoretically well-developed tradition of police organization and activities in Germany during the 19th and early 20th century did not necessitate any borrowing of policing models from abroad, during the 1920s such importation, especially from the United States, became necessary inasmuch as democratic styles of policing had not developed internally (see, generally, Marx 1995b). German discussions of US criminal justice—originally confined to theoretical reflections on law and policy—therefore also shifted to practical policing matters. German officials travelled regularly to the United States and commented favourably on the US experience of policing traditions that protected the fundamental rights of the individual as a cornerstone of democratic policy, suitable for adoption in Weimar Germany (Waite 1992:192). Additionally, the German police entertaining international contacts with foreign police institutions and participating in international police meetings and organizations—notably the ICPC—also served to enhance the standing of the newly established Weimar institutions in the international community. Intended for the purposes of democratization during the Weimar years, however, these international connections would from 1933 onwards readily be invaded by a Nazi-controlled police, which retained a positive image only of the FBI and its powerful Director.

At the turn of the century, US involvement in international policing continued to a large extent on its path of insularity. US law enforcement was oriented pragmatically at local conditions, keeping its priorities in the United States (Nadelmann 1993:21), and likewise responded regionally to cross-border issues related to immigration, ethnicity, and narcotics, and other crimes of mobility (Friedman 1993:193–210). Furthermore, US law enforcement conditions also developed in relative isolation because of deep-rooted suspicions against the strongly centralized and powerful policing models of Europe. The high degree of efficiency characteristic of policing on the European continent and, especially, in Germany were generally favourably received in the United States, but they were not adopted in US law enforcement until the police reform movement recommended such adaptations in view of heightened professionalism and accountability. During the 1920s, especially, the US police eagerly imported European advances in police administration and methods of criminal investigation. But soon thereafter, these developments of importation would terminate, as international police duties with US involvement no longer needed assistance from abroad, especially because of the FBI's functional and organizational expansion and its technologically sophisticated means of policing. The duties which the Bureau acquired in connection with the precarious international situation in the years before World War II would propel the Bureau to become the leading federal US police agency and acquire a virtual monopoly in US involvement in international policing. At the same time, the police institutions of Nazi Germany had in the build-up and expansion of World War II begun to drastically refashion police duties to serve the dictatorship's nationalist agenda. On the international scene, Nazi police officials would soon find themselves on a collision course with their counterparts in the United States and many other parts of the world.

7

On the Road to War: The Control of World Policing

> It would be a pleasure for me to attend the meeting and I know that much valuable information could be obtained from the discussion of mutual problems. I find, however, that the pressure of my official duties require my constant presence in the United States.
> *J. Edgar Hoover to ICPC Secretary General Dressler, 1937.*

> Please, come over here.
> *Dressler to Hoover, 1939.*

Although the police institutions of national states continued to engage in international activities that were of a transnational or limited cooperative kind throughout the first half of the 20th century, the formation of a formal organization of cooperation in the International Criminal Police Commission was a major event in the history of international policing. The establishment of the ICPC showed that participating police institutions had attained formal separation from their respective governments so that a structural condition of institutional autonomy was created. The realization of formal bureaucratic autonomy is particularly clear from the fact that the ICPC was established independently at the initiative of police officials, who set up an autonomously cooperative structure of international policing which they thereafter sought to have politically and legally sanctioned. The Commission was also developed in response to an organizational myth of international crime that functioned as a motivational basis for cooperative work. Instrumental in achieving this form of operational bureaucratic autonomy were the professional police views on the rise and internationalization of crime after World War I and the expert, technologically sophisticated means the police suggested to control international crime efficiently beyond existing legal and political arrangements. Thus, despite its limited potential in terms of investigations and organizational infrastructure relative to many of the participating and other national police systems, the International Criminal Police Commission clearly emerged as the central organization through which international policing was formally structured throughout the first half of the 20th century. In this and the following chapter, I will concentrate on the development of the ICPC in the years leading up to, during, and shortly after World War II. In respect of political, economic, and other social developments, the centrality of World War II for 20th-century history is well recognized. In the case of modern international policing operations, also, as the final chapters of this book will show, the war had a major impact.

The fate of the International Criminal Police Commission in the years between 1939 and 1946 represents one of the most problematic periods in the history of international policing. I will therefore provide a carefully documented account of the relevant factors that shaped the course and outcome of the ICPC during World War II. I will first detail how the FBI became a member of the ICPC at roughly the same time when German participation in the Commission was affected more and more by the Nazi seizure of power. Next, I will discuss the confrontation between the FBI and the Nazi police as coexistent members of the ICPC and the implications thereof in terms of investigative policing activities and international cooperation.

The case of the Nazification of the International Criminal Police Commission will again show a persistence of national interests in international policing, which I discussed earlier in many other contexts. The US participation as well as the Nazi-German involvement in the international policing organization were intended to advance nationally defined interests. Of course, the motives of the Nazi police and the FBI in joining the ICPC were of a very different nature and ideological character, but formally they both indicate the persistence of nationality in international policing. Because of the uniqueness of the Nazi regime and the critical challenges it poses for sociological scholarship in coming to terms with this tragic period in history, I will also advance an explanatory model to account for the dynamics of the Nazi involvement in the ICPC. Relying on recent discussions in the sociology of Nazism (Brustein 1996; Anheier 1997), I will argue that the case of the evolution of the ICPC shows that competing sociological models of Nazification, emphasizing either the opportunism in, or the coherence of, the process of the Nazi seizure of power, should be transcended (Gamson 1997). Strategic shifts in the Nazification of the ICPC depended on changing historical conditions, especially world political and military developments before and during World War II. At the same time, I maintain, Nazification remained in tune with the broader goals of Nazi rule, especially in matters of foreign policy. As such, the perspective I will advance bridges rationalist and situational models of policy making and implementation.

'Official duties': the FBI and Nazi police join the ICPC

In the years before World War II, the ICPC continued to expand its membership and elaborate its organizational structures. The membership grew to some thirty-eight representatives by 1938 and, as before, most attention was devoted to the exchange of information through various ICPC publications (e.g. Adler 1937), the annual meetings (four of which were held between 1934 and 1938), and the international registers at the Vienna headquarters (AfK 1936b, 1937b, 1938a, 1938d; Kb 1935; Leibig 1936). Around 1936, the international registers reportedly contained information on 3,724 international criminals (Leibig 1936:266). In May of 1934, Antonio Pizzuto of the Italian Federal Police proposed that the ICPC Presidency should reside permanently with the Vienna Police Directorate. The suggestion was accepted and Michael Skubl, then Police President of Vienna, became the new ICPC President. The new selection procedure was confirmed few months later at the Commission's meeting in Vienna (Stiebler 1981:27). The ICPC had unknowingly reached one of its most consequential decisions. At the 14th ICPC ordinary meeting, held in Bucharest, Romania, in June of 1938, two proposals were considered for the next meeting site. A Hungarian delegate proposed Budapest, while Arthur Nebe, the head of the Nazi criminal police, suggested Berlin. After the Hungarian offer was withdrawn, the Commission members decided unanimously that the 15th ICPC meeting would be held in Berlin in 1939. The 15th ICPC meeting was held in Brussels in 1946.

The FBI's entry into the ICPC

Until the late 1930s, the US police had only been informally and irregularly represented in the ICPC. Although there had been some communications from the ICPC to the FBI in the 1920s and early 1930s, it was not until 1935 that the FBI was invited to participate in the Commission, when FBI Director J. Edgar Hoover authorized a Bureau representative to attend the ICPC meeting in Copenhagen.[1] The US

[1] My analysis of the FBI participation in the ICPC relies largely on a collection of all FBI documents and correspondence pertaining to the ICPC, which is available in the FBI Reading Room, see Federal Bureau of Investigation Headquarters, Washington, DC, Freedom of Information/Privacy Acts Reading Room, 'Interpol' files (hereafter:

presence at the Copenhagen meeting did not immediately lead the FBI to join the ICPC, but the Bureau did pass on information on fugitives—on at least seven occasions between 1935 and 1937—to the ICPC headquarters for publication in the periodical *International Public Safety* (1/11, 26–32, 2/32–36). A more formal initiative to have the FBI join the Commission was first taken in 1936 when FBI Director Hoover was invited to attend the next ICPC meeting. Characteristically, Hoover replied that he could not attend because of 'official duties in Washington' (1/17). But the following year, in June 1937, FBI Assistant Director Lester attended the ICPC meeting in London with approval of President Roosevelt (2/37, 49). Upon his return, Lester advised that the United States should become a permanent member of the ICPC and Hoover approved of the plan. On 10 June 1938, President Roosevelt enacted a bill that authorized the Attorney General to 'accept and maintain, on behalf of the United States, membership in the International Criminal Police Commission and to incur the necessary expenses therefor not to exceed $1,500 per annum' (US Congress 1938).

In December 1938, Hoover again declined with the familiar 'official duties' to attend the next ICPC meeting, which was planned to be held in Berlin in 1939 (5/186x). The Berlin meeting, however, was first postponed, then cancelled. In June of 1940, the FBI received an ICPC circular letter with the notice that Reinhard Heydrich, the Chief of the German Security Police, had accepted the Presidency of the Commission (5/196x2). A little over a year later, on 4 December 1941, Hoover issued an FBI memorandum stating it was 'desired that in the future no communications be addressed to the International Criminal Police Commission' (5/201x).

The invasion of the swastika

Nazi police officials did not participate in the ICPC until the 11th ICPC meeting in Copenhagen in 1935. Most of the German participants at the Copenhagen meeting, Arthur Nebe, Hans Palitzsch, Karl Zindel, Wolf von Helldorf, and Kurt Daluege, were not only members of a thoroughly Nazified German police, they counted among its main architects. Arthur Nebe, for instance, headed the Nazi criminal police office of the *Reichskriminalpolizeiamt* (RKPA), and *SS-Grupenführer*

FOIPA). References to these 1,758 pages of files, mostly containing correspondence as well as some investigative materials, include the section number followed by the page number. Unless otherwise stated, all references are to the FBI 'Interpol' files.

Kurt Daluege commanded the *Ordnungspolizei*, the Nazi police division that would rise to infamy because of its involvement in mass executions in the German occupied territories of Eastern Europe. At the Belgrade meeting, all resolutions were passed unanimously, except those that involved cooperation with the League of Nations from which the Germans abstained. The German delegates noted that Germany was not a member of the League and declared that they relied on 'a statement delivered by their *Führer*' (AfK 1936a:91).

At the 13th ICPC meeting in London in 1937, certain implications of the Nazi takeover in Germany were becoming clear to the Commission membership. Apparently, in order to avoid an overly pompous display by the Nazi police, the official invitation from the British organizers advised that no uniforms be worn at the meeting (FOIPA 2/44). Less because of the uniform restrictions and more because the meeting was held in Great Britain, no Nazi police attended the London meeting. Still, in London, the Commission reached certain decisions which were anything but detrimental to the securing of Nazi influence in the ICPC. In particular, it was affirmed that the function of the ICPC President would reside 'until the end of the year 1942' with the 'President of the Federal Police Directorate in Vienna' (AfK 1937b:102).

On 12 March 1938, German troops invaded Austria. At noon that day, the President of the ICPC, Michael Skubl, was called to the building of the Austrian federal chancellery where he was told that Himmler demanded his resignation. Skubl was arrested and imprisoned until he was freed by Allied Forces in 1945 (Greilsamer 1986:46–47). With the annexation of Austria, nothing would prevent the Nazis from taking control of the ICPC. By implication of the selection procedure for the ICPC Presidency decided in London, the newly, with Nazi approval, appointed President of the police at Vienna, Otto Steinhäusl, became President of the Commission in April 1938. Not only was Steinhäusl's loyalty to Nazi Germany ensured, the Germans also reckoned that he would be but an interim figure, as he was known to suffer from tuberculosis (Bresler 1992:50–51). The first meeting under Steinhäusl's Presidency, in Bucharest in 1938, produced only one unanimous decision: that the next meeting was to be held in Berlin. A preliminary programme for the Berlin meeting was drafted—a copy has survived in the FBI files on Interpol (FOIPA 5/179x)—but, as noted, the meeting was cancelled.

Following the death of Steinhäusl in June of 1940, Secretary General Dressler sent a report to all ICPC members that specified that he and other police officials, including Nazi police officers Nebe and Zindel, had decided 'to request the Chief of the German Security Police' to accept the Presidency of the ICPC (FOIPA 5/197). Reportedly, twenty-seven police officials representing fifteen states consented to the suggestion (Jeschke 1971:119). Because this was less than two-thirds of the total ICPC membership, the countries that could not be addressed were not counted and those that had abstained were considered as not voting against the motion, so that, the Nazi leadership reasoned, the necessary majority was reached. In a circular letter of 24 August 1940, Reinhard Heydrich declared—in a manner all too characteristic of Nazi officialdom—that he had been informed that his nomination for ICPC President had 'passed unanimously'. Heydrich stated that he would 'lead the Commission into a new and successful future' and that the ICPC headquarters would 'from now on be located in Berlin' (5/198x).

'The organization is an independent entity': Visions of a Nazified world police

Since it was several months after the '*Anschluss*' of Austria, in June of 1938, that the FBI formally joined the Commission, it could lead to the conclusion that the FBI willingly and consciously joined the ICPC when the organization was already under Nazi control. Some secondary studies on the ICPC and the FBI have defended such unfounded interpretations, often on the basis of distorted presentations of the evidence (e.g. Greilsamer 1986:55–63; Meldal-Johnsen and Young 1979:49–52; Schwitters 1978:25–26). To reach a more balanced conclusion, attention should be given to the increasing awareness among FBI officials of the growing Nazi influence in the ICPC. Also to be taken into consideration are the specific motives of the FBI in joining the ICPC, which related primarily to a nationally defined programme of law enforcement that also involved internationally oriented objectives.

From hesitation to awareness

Ever since the FBI was first contacted about the ICPC, the Bureau saw membership in the Commission largely as a technical matter on the basis of estimated benefits in terms of nationally defined goals for the control of federal crimes, for which the FBI was responsible. It was as a consequence of these national concerns that the FBI did not contemplate in the years before 1937 the Nazi presence in the ICPC, which at that time was relatively unpronounced. Although the FBI representative at the London meeting in 1937 had witnessed certain politically charged animosities among the European delegates, a more pressing matter for the Bureau was the cost of membership. Once Hoover had managed to get the necessary budget, the procedural requirements to have the matter approved by Congress took up so much time that when the appropriate bills were entered in Congress (April and May 1938) and enacted by President Roosevelt (June 1938), Nazi Germany had annexed Austria, and the ICPC Presidency was bestowed upon the Austrian Nazi Steinhäusl.

From 1938 onwards, the FBI leadership gradually became aware of the Nazi presence in the Commission. In March of 1939, the German question was brought up by the State Department, which contacted the FBI to ask if 'the German government intended to foster the International Crime Commission [*sic*], [and] whether it had taken over control of the same'. Hoover initially responded that the ICPC was an 'independent entity', but soon agreed that the Commission had assumed a 'distinctly Austro-German atmosphere' which was judged 'the principal objection to joining the Commission' (5/162, 184x).

From awareness to confrontation

Antagonisms between the FBI and the ICPC were to mount because of a newly instituted Commission policy on passports, strikingly a matter of investigative police tasks. In March and April of 1939, ICPC permanent reporters Florent Louwage and Bruno Schultz and Secretary General Dressler made requests to the FBI to send copies of all valid and cancelled forms of US passports to the ICPC headquarters. The passports were to be collected in line with the ICPC resolution reached at the London meeting that the refusal of the issuance and the annulment and withdrawal of passports were appropriate police measures in the fight against international crime (AfK 1937b:102). The ICPC had introduced, in other words, an important technique of policing inspired by the Nazi philosophy of so-called preventive policing based on an assumption of guilt. Aware of the unacceptability of such measures under US law, Hoover responded that individual case records concerning passports could not be transmitted and explained that under the US system 'the punishment for criminals is indicated in the laws, and additional punishment is not imposed through the refusal of passport facilities unless there is an outstanding reason for so doing' (5/195x). In April 1940, there was a final request, but then communications on the matter were discontinued (5/196x).

When from 1941 onwards, ICPC correspondence was sent from an address in Berlin, Germany, identified as 'Am Kleinen Wannsee 16' (5/201x), the FBI leadership recommended stopping all communications with the Commission headquarters. In December 1941, three days before the Japanese bombing of Pearl Harbor, Hoover circulated a memo that no FBI communications should be sent to the ICPC 'whose present location is Berlin, Germany' (5/201x). Clearly, concerns over the Nazi involvement in the ICPC were by now sufficiently developed so that FBI participation in the Commission had become impossible.

'The International Criminal Police Commission carries on': The path of Nazification

A gradual infiltration of the Nazi police in the ICPC is revealed in the activities of Nazi officials at the Commission's meetings, the transfer of the Presidency to the Nazi-appointed head of the Austrian police, and, ultimately, Heydrich's 'election' as ICPC President and the move of the International Bureau to Berlin. Analysing the trajectory of this process, Nazification can be conceived as either the manifestation of a preconceived and novel Nazi ideology (Brustein 1996, 1997) or as a more incoherent and opportunistic process (Anheier 1997). The former, rationalist perspective emphasizes the interest-based motivation of German society in adopting the Nazi manifesto and, organizationally, the logic and coherence in the making and implementation of Nazi policy. The latter, situational viewpoint hints at the eclecticism of the Nazi ideology built on commonplace nationalism and anti-Semitic cultural traditions and its *ad hoc* manner of implementation. Relying on William Gamson's (1997) suggestion to transcend these competing theoretical models, I propose a theoretical model that conceives of Nazification as a gradual process, involving deliberate goal-oriented efforts at implementing a particular policy that in itself was not especially novel and that could not and did not disregard changing societal conditions. In the case of the ICPC, specifically, the pattern of Nazification by and large followed a consistently implemented Nazi ideology, although the ideology itself was not entirely coherent and the strategies of implementation were shaped by internal as well as external societal conditions. Relevant conditions included not only a reorganization of the German police but also factors relating to the Commission's status as an international body with foreign membership.

Strategies of Nazification, Part I: Influence through participation

In the years immediately following Hitler's appointment, Nazi police officials did not seek to take control of the ICPC, but attempted to exert influence through participation in the organization. Mere participation, however, could very well prove beneficial for the Nazi police. The Copenhagen meeting was the first occasion where the Nazi presence in the ICPC could be felt. Shortly before the meeting, *SS-Gruppenführer* Kurt Daluege was interviewed about the ICPC for *Der Deutsche Polizeibeamte*, a police magazine published under the auspices of the SS (Daluege 1935). It was the intention of the National-Socialist delegates at the meeting, Daluege argued, to communicate their experiences to other countries and to promote the international fight against crime, the 'common enemy of every people' (p. 489). Daluege furthermore emphasized the unpolitical nature of the ICPC and attributed its success to the meetings, which, he argued, brought a 'personal touch' to an otherwise 'purely practical (*sachlich*)' matter (p. 490).

At the Copenhagen meeting, the Nazi representatives achieved some effective influence. Zindel delivered an address on the National Socialist fight against crime, which a report in *Die Polizei* referred to as 'the greatest result of the meeting' (*Die Polizei* 1935b:304; AfK 1935f:165, 166). The Commission elected Daluege as one of the ICPC Vice-Presidents, and a Nazi-supported plan for the creation of an 'International Central Office for the Suppression of Gypsies' was taken into consideration. At the Belgrade meeting in 1936, there was growing awareness among the participating police of the political sensibilities involved with the German participation. President Skubl in his opening speech to the meeting emphasized that the ICPC should serve 'the cause of peace' (in Leibig 1936:266). But during the discussions, the Nazi police delegates achieved relative success with their exposition on the National Socialist principles of policing. Daluege, in particular, argued for the effectiveness of the German measures on matters of 'preparatory actions of serious criminals' and other dangerous acts that betrayed a 'criminal will' (Leibig 1936:269). Also, an ICPC subcommittee 'on repressive and preventive measures against preparatory acts of serious crimes' was established at the recommendation of Daluege.

As discussed in Chapter 6, Nazi police reorganizations had led to a centralization of the various local police institutions in Germany. By 1935, the implications of the Nazification of police institutions in terms of international police activities included that all provincial and regional police were no longer allowed to entertain direct communications with foreign police (*Kriminalpolizei* 1937:22; Nebe and Fleischer 1939:166–170). Cooperation with the International Bureau in Vienna on matters of international investigations was still allowed, but all German police communications to the ICPC had to originate from the *Reich* Criminal Police Office (RKPA). The German police was allowed to send information abroad only with the approval of the Minister of the Interior, and a duplicate of all correspondence had to be sent to the RKPA. Centralization of German police institutions not only involved a transfer of police powers from local to national police institutions, but also implied that they were delegated to branches of the NSDAP. Police communications with German consuls abroad on matters that concerned the 'disposition and implementation of the party programme of the NSDAP' were not allowed, and any exchange with NSDAP representatives abroad had to be handled through the '*Auslandsorganization*' (Foreign Office) in the NSDAP (*Kriminalpolizei* 1937:24–25). In other words, not only were German criminal police institutions centralized and harmonized, they were also brought under the control of the Nazi Party.

At the London meeting in 1937, the ICPC Presidency was fixed for a period of five years with the President of the Federal Police of Vienna, a resolution which was to make way for the eventual Nazification of the Commission. There is no direct evidence to corroborate that the decision was reached because of pressure by the Nazi police, but it is to be noted that the resolution was made at the suggestion of a representative of the Italian fascist police, which was not unsympathetic to the Nazi cause. In 1936, Mussolini and Hitler had agreed on a formal treaty of alliance between Germany and Italy, and in a speech on 1 November 1936, the Duce announced the formation of an 'axis' running between Rome and Berlin (Morris 1982:252). The Italian initiative for the London resolution may have been suggested by Nazi police officials on the occasion of one of the international meetings the Italian fascist police organized in Italy in the 1930s or at a bilateral German–Italian police meeting in Germany in the same period.[2]

[2] Available evidence indicates that an international police meeting under Italian auspices was organized in Rome shortly before the ICPC meeting in London (FOIPA 3/90), and a German–Italian police meeting was planned to be held in March 1936 in Berlin (RLSS 20/2525494).

Strategies of Nazification, Part II: Command through control

The annexation of Austria left little in the way of the Nazification of the ICPC. Austrian police officials were either dismissed or allowed to remain in place when considered sufficiently loyal to the Nazis. For Oskar Dressler, Secretary General of the ICPC since 1923, the consequences of the '*Anschluss*' provided no main obstacles. He cooperated with the Nazi-appointed ICPC President and, editing the ICPC periodical, he contributed to the growing prominence of Nazi viewpoints. Since 1938, the renamed periodical '*Internationale Kriminalpolizei*' (*International Criminal Police*) published articles on racial inferiority and crime, praiseworthy reviews of books on racial laws, and reports concerning preventive arrests (Bresler 1992:53).

The ICPC meeting planned in Berlin was initially postponed until some time in February of 1940, but was eventually cancelled because of the outbreak of the war in Europe when on 1 September 1939, German troops invaded Poland (GFO 3262/E575156). Even then, Dressler wrote to FBI Director Hoover to affirm that despite the cancellation of the Berlin meeting, 'the International Criminal Police Commission carries on their activities' (FOIPA 5/194x). The relatively intense and cordial correspondence between a Nazified ICPC and the FBI in this period reveals how the Nazi regime was in the late 1930s still seeking to acquire the status of a respected nation and viable partner in international affairs. When in August 1940 Heydrich accepted the ICPC Presidency, he similarly expressed that he would continue the work of the ICPC 'in the interest of the peoples (*Völker*)' (5/198x). Notable for the manner in which the Nazi rulers sought to gradually invade existing political and bureaucratic structures in a pseudo-legal manner, Dressler's motion about Heydrich's nomination was careful to point out that the election procedure was in complete harmony with the ICPC statutes (Möllmann 1969:46–47).[3]

The aspiration of the Nazi police to fully control the ICPC was symbolized in the takeover of the Presidency and the placement of the headquarters in the RKPA offices in Berlin (Dressler 1943:30; Werner 1942:467). The Commission's new leadership had thus institutionally

[3] A report in the SS police magazine *Die Deutsche Polizei* went further and stated that the entire ICPC membership had 'delivered the request' to Heydrich to accept the Presidency (DDP 1940a). The Commission members, the report added, had also agreed that the headquarters should be moved to Germany, the country with the 'best-organized and most exemplary police organization' (p. 305).

linked the ICPC with the Nazi police structures. However, even then, Nazi officials remained eager to presume continuity in the Commission's goals and activities. A 1940 report in *Die Deutsche Polizei* declared that the ICPC had kept on functioning since the outbreak of the war in 1939, 'because all the states of the Commission—except of course England and France—continue international criminal-police collaboration in the frame of this Commission' (DDP 1940a:305). A 1942 article promoting the Nazi policing system still declared that 'despite the war, the international relationships, though often in different forms, could be maintained and furthered' (Werner 1942:467). And in a book published in 1943, Secretary General Oskar Dressler stated that no less than twenty-one countries—including Belgium, Switzerland, France, Great Britain, and the United States—were still cooperating with the ICPC headquarters in Berlin (Dressler 1943:69).

On 4 June 1942, ICPC President Reinhard Heydrich was assassinated and was provisionally replaced by Arthur Nebe (Dressler 1943:9, 120). A year later, Ernst Kaltenbrunner, the leader of the Austrian SS, acquired the post by virtue of his appointment as Chief of the German Security Police (DDP 1943d:193). In a letter of 29 May 1943, directed to 'all members' of the ICPC, Kaltenbrunner announced that he had accepted the ICPC Presidency 'conforming to the statutes (*satzungsgemäß*)' and expressed the hope that he could further the Commission's 'truly great work of civilization (*Kulturwerk*)' (in Dressler 1943:II, III). Later that year, Kaltenbrunner reaffirmed that he would maintain the activities of the ICPC, at least 'as far as this is at all possible during the war' (National Archives, Records of the *Reich* Leader SS [hereafter: RLSS] R450/4190151). In October 1943, Kaltenbrunner once again emphasized the ICPC's 'noble *Kulturwerk*' and asked 'all members of the Commission' for their continued cooperation (*ibid.*).

The rationality of a Nazified world police

The Nazification of the International Criminal Police Commission involved strategically a shift from seeking partnership to taking control. Nazification of the ICPC was practically achieved through Nazi police participants seeking to influence the Commission's agenda and by a mixture of manipulating legality and resorting to deceit in order to take control of the ICPC Presidency and headquarters. The various strategies in the Nazification of the ICPC always fitted the overall frame of National Socialist policy but were also adapted to specific needs and circumstances, largely determined by political and military developments. Below, I will offer a model to account for this two-staged development on the basis of theoretical insights in the sociology of Nazism. I will also discuss implications of the Nazification of the ICPC in terms of policing and international cooperation under conditions of increasing political hostility and warfare between the member-states.

The logic of Nazification

The strategic shift in the Nazification of the ICPC generally followed the foreign policy of National Socialist Germany which implied a transformation from international participation to global control (Fischer 1995:394–440, 473–476; Herzstein 1989; Hildebrand 1973). During the first phase of this '*Stufenplan*' (plan in stages), Nazi foreign policy sought mainly to abide by established diplomatic rules. To be sure, the Nazi regime had then already developed policies about foreign occupation and conquest, in particular the expansion of German '*Lebensraum*' in Eastern Europe, but the regime at first attempted to maintain acceptability and partnership in world affairs. Even when it became clear that the Nazis sought actively to achieve hegemony on the European continent, including the destruction of France, an alliance with Great Britain was still considered feasible. But although the Nazi plans for expansion through diplomacy had proven relatively successful (most notably at the Munich conference in 1938), a shift to global domination through aggressive imperialism and war was ultimately not avoided. Signalling the beginning of this second stage, Poland was invaded in September 1939, whereafter Great Britain and France immediately declared war on Nazi Germany. Once Nazi troops had swept into the low countries and France had fallen, Hitler's foreign policy still counted on neutrality from the United States, but those hopes could not be maintained after the Japanese attack on Pearl Harbor.

Corresponding to Nazi foreign policy, the first episode of the ICPC's Nazification entailed a strategy of influence through participation, best exemplified in the Nazi presence at the ICPC meetings from 1935 to 1938 and culminating in the planned organization of the meeting in Berlin in 1939. These seemingly innocent initiatives had the purpose of influencing the Commission's activities but also and at the same time were part of an effort to present a respectable Nazi nation and police.

As late as June of 1939, with tensions mounting in Europe (and the FBI already deeply involved in counter-espionage work against the Nazi movement), an invitation from Dressler to Hoover for the Berlin meeting still pleaded that the FBI Director should attend so he would become acquainted 'in Germany, with an excellent Criminal Police Organization, . . . with a people making progress and intending to come into friendly relations to all the nations' (FOIPA 5/179x).

The second episode of Nazification was launched when the ICPC Presidency was secured in Nazi hands—first with the Austrian Nazi Steinhäusl, then with Reinhard Heydrich—and when the headquarters were transferred to Berlin. Even then and throughout the war, there was still revealed an eagerness on the part of the Nazi police to uphold the Commission's continuity, at least in appearance. This presentation of continuity was also reflected in the manner in which the Nazis took control of the ICPC through pseudo-legal means, a tactic often preferred by the Nazi Party in its rise to power in Germany (Thamer 1996). There was, in fact, a clear obsession by the Nazi police to stress compliance with ICPC procedures, even if such compliance was fabricated, as when Heydrich was 'elected' President of the Commission.

The purpose of Nazification was regularly tuned to specific needs but always fitted the overall frame of the Nazi ideology, even those aspects of Nazi criminal justice which were racially motivated and lacked the protection of due process. This is not surprising considering the fact that Nazi criminal justice policies were partly continuations of existing measures, such as the policing of narcotics, passport forgery, the falsification of currencies, as well as the targeting of communist movements and other political opponents (see Chapter 1). Furthermore, German and other European police forces were experienced in targeting Jews and other ethnic groups as special categories of criminal suspects.[4] However, in most countries (except Nazi Germany), race-related police activities were not reflected in explicit policies and could therefore also not formally foster international collaboration. In fact, the formalization of racial policies signalled a separation between Nazi police and the other ICPC members. The so-called 'Nuremberg laws' of September

[4] Policies on the policing of gypsies were formalized in Germany since the late 19th century (Tenner 1918) and were on the ICPC agenda as early as 1931. The fact that the policing of ethnic minorities was not uncommon is also revealed from a search warrant, published in the February 1925 issue of the ICPC periodical, *Internationale Öffentliche Sicherheit*, that had been passed on by the Head of Police at Winnipeg, Canada (a country which at the time was not an ICPC member), requesting information about a swindler of 'Jewish nationality' (Bresler 1992:39–40).

1935 stripped Jews of civil rights and citizenship and introduced a system of criminal justice that broadened the definition of crime beyond legality and legitimated police arrests based on the suspicion of a crime.

The implications of this reorganization of criminal justice for the Nazification of the ICPC are not altogether clear. In terms of international cooperation, the Nazi discussions on so-called 'preventive' principles of policing and punishment were not widely adopted and did not seem to have influenced the investigative work in the Commission's member-states. Because of these issues there were mounting tensions among the police at the ICPC meetings from 1935 onwards. Nonetheless, the Nazis did achieve some results, such as the implementation of proactive passport measures and the control of the ICPC Presidency with the Austrian Police. During this period, Nazi police officials also organized international meetings with representation from several European countries independently from the ICPC network (National Archives, RLSS 20/2525494, 283/2777702).[5]

The fate of the ICPC reveals a mode of Nazification which indicates that various, not incompatible, intentions were reflected in different strategies of implementation, depending on preconceived planning in tune with National Socialist ideology but also responding to shifting historical conditions. This view of Nazification underscores, first and foremost, the consistent logic of the Nazi seizure of power in terms of its popular as well as institutional implications. This is reflected in the Nazis attempting to infiltrate the ICPC, first by seeking influence through participation, then by pursuing domination through control. Additionally, however, it is clear that the Nazi police in their involvement with the ICPC also responded to historical circumstances and shaped their plans to given opportunities (especially the outbreak of war). As such, the Nazification of the ICPC implies consistency in

[5] One such police meeting was held in Berlin from August 30 to September 10, 1937. The meeting was attended by representatives from fifteen countries (including Belgium, Brazil, Finland, the Netherlands, Japan, Uruguay, and Switzerland). Chaired by Heinrich Himmler, the meeting centred on the international fight against Bolshevism (RLSS 21/2525789). One more anti-Bolshevist police conference was organized by the Nazis in September 1938 and an additional one was planned by Heydrich as late as October 1941 (Van Doorslaer and Verhoeyen 1986:72–74; Fijnaut 1997:120–121). However, these meetings appeared to have had no practical implications. Other international police meetings with explicit political objectives during the 1930s—including efforts to establish anti-communist police cooperation organized by police from South-America, Nazi Germany, and fascist Italy—were likewise not successful (National Archives, Record Group 242, 21/2525789).

implementation of an established policy which was in itself not entirely novel but which did serve as a distinctive guide. Therefore, I argue in line with William Gamson's (1997) suggestion that the debate on the novelty (Brustein 1997) and the eclecticism (Anheier 1997) of the Nazi programme should be transcended. The decisive and goal-oriented path of the Nazification of the ICPC clearly hints at the coherence and consistency of a purposively directed plan, yet its various methods, opportunistic tactics, and strategic shifts at the same time reveal a contextuality that an interest-based rationalist explanation cannot adequately account for. What my analysis brings forth is the value of a theoretical perspective that recognizes the imbeddedness of the Nazification process in a more open-ended context of variably significant influencing factors. A distinction needs to be drawn between the formation of the Nazi policy and the implementation thereof in various institutional contexts. National Socialist policies consisted of partly new, partly re-assembled fragments from a 19th-century 'rubble of ideas' (*Ideenschutt*), couched in populist terms (Thamer 1996:13). However, the policy was consistently sought to be implemented in the various Nazi and Nazified institutions. In the case of the ICPC, this involved the two-fold strategies of influence through participation and command through control in fulfillment of implementing a police ideology which was only partly new.

My analysis of the Nazi takeover of the International Criminal Police Commission reveals a mode of Nazification which offers support for the viewpoint that Nazi officials strategically invaded, coordinated, and controlled existing social institutions, guided by concerns that were directed systematically at implementing a policy of nationalism and global domination. Corresponding to Nazi foreign policy, the Nazification of the ICPC shifted in strategy, from seeking influence through participation to striving for command through control. Strategies of Nazification were also influenced by shifting conditions and opportunity structures in relation to world-political and military affairs, but in terms of goal direction they were always attuned to Nazi ideology. This brings out the value of bridging rationalist and situational models of Nazification that argue for either an *ad hoc* opportunistic perspective or a highly (economic-) rationalist interpretation in favour of a more realistic perspective of historical developments in political and social control policy. The Nazification of the ICPC, moreover, was more ambivalent than the *Gleichschaltung* of German institutions (and the military conquest of enemy countries), because the Commission was an international organization with German as well as foreign participation. The status of the ICPC 'in-between' Germany and the world not only accounted for the fact that the Nazi police in an initial phase sought to influence the Commission's work more cautiously through participation, but also that imperialist Nazification directed at global control remained deceptively committed to uphold pseudo-legality.

Ideal and reality of a Nazi world police

There is considerable disagreement in the academic literature about the implications of the Nazification of the ICPC in terms of investigative work and international cooperation. In part, this confusion is a result of the uncertain destiny of the ICPC investigative files once the Nazi regime had taken control of the organization. Most often repeated in the secondary literature is the conjecture that the ICPC files were somehow destroyed or got lost at the end of the War (e.g. Duino 1960:140; Fooner 1973:21; Forrest 1955:31; Möllmann 1969:47; US House 1959:13). In the memoirs of Swedish police official Harry Söderman, an ICPC participant before as well as after the War, there is recounted a different story. According to Söderman, Nazi police official Karl Zindel left Berlin shortly before the fall of the city in 1945 and headed south in a car filled with ICPC documents. Zindel reported to the French authorities in Stuttgart, but what happened thereafter with the files he transported is unclear. Some have stated that those files survived (Fooner 1973:21), others that they were destroyed (Meldal-Johnsen and Young 1979:80–87).

Analysis of the FBI 'Interpol' files reveals a different destiny for the ICPC dossiers. At the end of the war in Europe, the FBI received a press release entitled 'World Police Files Found' that stated that on 2 August 1945, US army authorities had discovered in Berlin the ICPC records of 18,000 international criminals (5/end). In October 1945, the FBI leadership deemed the files not useful and recommended to take no further action (6/206). Not incompatible with the evidence from the FBI files, some commentators have claimed that part of the ICPC records were destroyed during the raids on Berlin, but that some were recovered from the ruins and were possibly taken to Moscow by Soviet military (Tullett 1963:30; Walther 1968:160–163). It has also been suggested that some of the Commission's documents were retrieved shortly after their discovery in Berlin (Forrest 1955:31) or later during the blockade of the airbridge from Berlin to Paris in 1948 (Möllman 1969:49–50). Based on the FBI 'Interpol' files, I could partly corroborate the recovery theory of the ICPC records. In a letter dated 4 December 1945, Director Hoover was informed about 'the recovery of the archives' of the ICPC (7/257). In May 1946, Hoover was again informed that Florent Louwage, the first President of the ICPC after the War, had been 'successful in hiding some of the records of the Commission in Germany' and had now 'in his possession at Brussels the files of some 4,000 criminals' (6/228). Two years later, the FBI attaché in Paris again confirmed that a portion of the files had been recovered (9/end).

Partly because of the confusion over the ICPC files, the fate of the organization immediately before and during World War II has been a topic of considerable controversy. Several commentators have suggested that the Commission no longer functioned after the '*Anschluss*' of Austria in March 1938, or that at least the nations of the free world then ceased participating in the organization (e.g. Fooner 1989:40; Lee 1976:19; Tullett 1963:27–29). Others, however, have argued that the Nazi regime took control of the ICPC with the express and consequential purpose of using the organization to further its own goals (e.g. Garrison 1976:63–85; Greilsamer 1986:45–88; Stiebler 1981:33). This debate was additionally fuelled when it was discovered in the early 1970s that Paul Dickopf, President of Interpol from 1968 until 1972, had been a member of the SS until 1943, when he fled to Switzerland and worked for the Office of Strategic Services, the forerunner of the CIA (Garrison 1976:66–73; Schwitters 1978:47–65). The Dickopf affair also led to questioning the involvement of other police officials in the years before 1945. Two of the post-war Presidents of the ICPC, the Belgian Florent Louwage and the Frenchman Jean Nepote, were especially targeted because they would have collaborated with the Nazis during the war (e.g. Garrison 1976:66–69; Wiesenthal 1989:254–255).[6] Others, however, have downplayed the role played by Louwage and other officials involved in the ICPC at the time of its Nazification (Fijnaut 1993a; Forrest 1955:24–26). Söderman (1956), for instance, described Arthur

[6] An FBI memorandum of 1 September 1950 mentions unspecified 'derogatory allegations' against Louwage, but the memo is otherwise favourable (FOIPA 17/102–127). Among the few corroborated facts can be mentioned that Louwage was once in 1943 in touch with Arthur Nebe in Berlin in order to rescue (successfully) two Belgian police officials from Nazi captivity, that he reaffirmed his position as ICPC Permanent Reporter in December 1942, and that he was confirmed in the position when Kaltenbrunner became President of the Commission (Fijnaut 1993a:197; IKP, 30 September 1943, in RLSS R450/4190151).

Nebe and Karl Zindel as 'professional policemen, . . . very mild Nazis' (p. 376). When in 1960, Oskar Dressler, the ICPC Secretary-General who had moved with the files to Berlin, died, the then Secretary-General of Interpol, Marcel Sicot, wrote in an obituary that Dressler had been 'the moving spirit of the ICPC' and that it was time 'that his name was brought out of the limbo of lost reputations' (in NCLESJ 1977: document #7).

In 1975, when the US Congress evaluated the US's participation in Interpol, the famous Nazi hunter Simon Wiesenthal declared that the ICPC had been used by the Nazis to track down fugitive criminals and force them to provide information on (fellow) Jews (Garrison 1976:79). In his memoirs, Wiesenthal repeated the allegation and also claimed that the ICPC files provided the Nazis with access to the identity and whereabouts of banknote forgers, who could be coerced into producing false foreign currency in the Sachsenhausen concentration camp (Wiesenthal 1989:253–255). Thus, argues Wiesenthal, the ICPC after Heydrich's ascension to the Presidency dealt with one more crime, 'the crime of being a Jew' (Letter to the author, 15 July 1996). The Nazi practice of coercing Jews to track down fellow Jews for extermination is confirmed by Tuviah Friedman, another holocaust survivor active in the post-war hunt for Nazi war criminals (E-mail to the author, 27 June 1996).[7]

Yet, what the presumed continuity of the ICPC during the war actually implied from the viewpoint of international cooperation and investigative police duties is not clear. Primarily, it seems, Nazification of the ICPC involved a mere presentation of a continuation of international police cooperation. Effective use of the ICPC headquarters to

[7] Wiesenthal and others have also claimed that the infamous conference at which Reinhard Heydrich and other Nazi officials discussed the implementation of the 'Final Solution' was held in the headquarters of the ICPC (Wiesenthal 1989:253; Krausnick et al. 1968:83). This is inaccurate, because the Wannsee Conference—as the meeting has come to be known—was held on 20 January 1942, in a villa located at 'Am Grossen Wannsee, No. 56–58'. It is true, however, that the meeting was originally planned by Heydrich to be held 'on 9 December 1941, at 12:00 p.m., in the headquarters of the International Criminal Police Commission, Berlin, Am Kleinen Wannsee No. 16' (Heydrich to Luther, in Friedman 1993). The meeting was postponed because of the Japanese bombing of Pearl Harbor and the United States entry in World War II. There is no evidence to determine whether Heydrich had scheduled the meeting in the ICPC headquarters because he conceived of the extermination of European Jewry as a matter of international criminal police. On the Wannsee Conference, see Breitman 1991:229–243; Dawidowicz 1986:136–139; Büchler 1995; Pätzold and Schwarz 1992; Duprat 1968:135–155.

advance the nationalist agenda of Nazi rule is improbable because the files were few in number—especially relative to the extensive collections of the national police systems in the Nazi-occupied countries—and could not have been of much practical benefit.[8] Also, based on available evidence, it is unlikely that the ICPC achieved any of the Nazi-aspired continuity in international cooperation and effectiveness. Among the few tangible achievements, the ICPC periodical, *Internationale Kriminalpolizei*, continued to be published regularly during the war years.[9] Yet, the publication mostly contained general interest articles and administrative notices, all authored by Nazi police or sympathizers (among them, Nebe, Kaltenbrunner, Dressler, and Schultz). In a 1943 issue, there was detailed a list of countries that had in recent years joined the Commission. The list still included the USA. In fact, the United States was formally a member of the ICPC throughout the war, for the enactment of membership in the Commission was never reversed. That this was a mere formal matter became clear when after the fall of Nazi Germany, it was discovered that the Nazi-controlled ICPC had after 1941 still forwarded about 100 wanted notices to the Federal Bureau of Investigation, an unidentified number of which had reportedly been forwarded to the FBI after the entry of the United States into the War (FOIPA 6/205). In the 29 February 1944 issue of the ICPC periodical, there appeared a short article on 'The Gathering of Members of the ICPC, in Vienna', held from 22 to 24 November 1943 (in RLSS R450). The meeting was likely the first held since 1938, but the article does not mention any noteworthy events or decisions reached at the conference.[10]

Regardless of whether the ICPC served investigative purposes for the Nazi regime, what the Nazification of the ICPC definitely entailed was a conscious attempt to maintain the appearance of 'at least the fiction of its ongoing existence' and 'the illusion of a normally functioning

[8] Before the war, the ICPC headquarters contained less than 4,000 investigative case files. And although the number rose rather dramatically to 18,000 at war's end (FOIPA 5/end), that is still negligible relative to the files available to the Nazis through the occupation of Europe.

[9] According to Bresler (1992:55–56), the periodical was published every month until April 1945. The Captured German Records at the National Archives contain an incomplete collection of *Internationale Kriminalpolizei* issues from the years 1942, 1943, and 1944. Only the German version is available (which was likely the only one printed during the war).

[10] At the Nuremberg trials in 1946, it was this meeting that Kaltenbrunner referred to when he attempted to defend Nazi police interrogation measures (International Military Tribunal, Vol. 11:312).

ICPC' (Jeschke 1971:118; Fijnaut 1997:118). The appearance of continuity in the ICPC may, towards the end of the war, in anticipation of a German capitulation, also have served purposes that took into account changing historical circumstances. An official Nazi '*Aktennotiz*' (file memorandum) of 2 May 1944, on the 'Activities of the ICPC after the War', states that it should be endeavoured to have as many countries as possible participate in the Commission during its control by the Nazis, so that participation of enemy countries could be used to reach more favourable peace settlements after the war had ended (Jeschke 1971:119; Walther 1968:160–163). The remarkable continuation of the appearance of diplomacy and pseudo-legality, even when Nazification had turned from participation to command, presents a case of institutional impression management that, I argue, can be attributed to the Commission's unique international character. Not an international organization perceived as a foreign threat to Nazi Germany (like the League of Nations), nor a German institution that could be taken control of without foreign interference, the ICPC was a network of national institutions that brought together police from Germany and other nations. Therefore, if the National Socialist cause was to be advanced in international police matters, the ICPC had to be invaded and managed, ideally with the approval—fabricated or enforced, real or imagined—of its international membership.

Finally, it is to be noted that Nazification of the ICPC was achieved swiftly, not only because of pseudo-legality, but also because novel Nazi principles of policing could be readily infused with existing police practices. After the headquarters had moved to Berlin, for instance, the ICPC search-warrant forms were altered in only one respect: the addition of the category '*RASSE*' ('RACE') next to the entry '*RELIGION*' (in Dressler 1943:53). Beyond such symbolic manipulation, with or without more than symbolic implications (Hughes 1955), all that had to be done to achieve Nazification of the Commission, at least organizationally, was placement of the ICPC headquarters in the Nazi criminal police, Office V of the *Reichssicherheitshauptamt*. The lack of any need for major revisions to the already existing ICPC structures in order to institutionally complete Nazification can be attributed to the fact that the international police organization provided for a purposive-rational machinery that could be used by any police force—loyal to whatever political purpose and ideological persuasion—that participated in, or had taken control of, the organization. As I argued in Chapter 5, the ICPC was founded as an expert technology of international crime control independent from legal and political contexts. The ironic consequence is that the ICPC became amenable to be politicized by whomsoever controlled the organization and wanted to use it to advance a particular ideology, precisely because the organization was established as an expert institution that brought together highly bureaucratized police institutions from different countries. Hence, the technical, formal-rational manner in which the ICPC structures were set up contributed to pave the way for its eventual Nazification and attempted use for political and nationalist purposes.

The persistence of nationality: From cooperation to espionage and warfare

In Chapter 5, I argued that the establishment of the International Criminal Police Commission implies a persistence of nationality in international policing, most clearly because the organization was conceived as a facilitating network for exchange and cooperation between national police institutions. The findings discussed in this chapter confirm the thesis of a persistence of nationality in that both the US as well as the Nazi-German participation in the international police organization were intended to advance nationally defined interests. Of course, the motives of the Nazi police and the FBI in joining the ICPC were of a very different character, but formally they both indicate persistence of nationality in international policing.

In the case of the Nazi infiltration of the Commission, national interests relating to the nationalist dictatorship were already apparent when the Nazi police officials sought to participate in the ICPC. In this seemingly benign way, it was endeavoured to have Germany accepted as a viable partner in international affairs, a nation among nations. This may also explain the anti-Bolshevist meetings Nazi police organized with the police from other European countries. Thereafter, in a second phase of Nazification, the Nazi attempt to take full control of the ICPC displays the aggressive nationalism of the Nazi dictatorship, implying the threat and reality of aggression and war.

The persistence of nationality in the Nazi infiltration and control of the ICPC is paralleled formally by the participation of the FBI. Initially, the FBI did not join the Commission because membership in the international police organization was not thought to have many practical benefits for the agency. When Director Hoover approved of FBI membership of the ICPC, he did so because he thought it would be 'helpful to *us* in *our* work' (FOIPA 3/54, my emphasis). Ironically, once the FBI had joined the Commission in June of 1938, the Bureau did not collaborate much in the international police organization, much less, in fact, than it had before membership was approved. The reasons for this lack of cooperation are twofold. First, the FBI had little practical need to join an international police organization because it had itself already established a vast cross-border system of policing. Especially through the FBI fingerprinting system, the Bureau had managed to expanded its powers not only nationally (and financially) but also internationally (see Chapter 6). A second reason for the FBI's reluctance to collaborate in the ICPC, especially after 1940, is the growing awareness among the Bureau's leadership of the increasing influence of the Nazi presence in the Commission. Particularly once the ICPC headquarters had been moved to Berlin, the FBI leadership was well aware of the intolerably tainted status of the ICPC and decided to terminate all communications.

A strong persistence of nationality in internationally oriented police practices, finally, is also revealed in the manner in which Nazi police institutions and the FBI were involved transnationally in counter-intelligence and espionage activities, at the same time as they collaborated in the ICPC, and how their functions were further restructured once the war had broken out. As with the reorganization of police duties during World War I (see Chapter 4), I cannot discuss these implications in detail in this book, but a few remarks may bring out the effect of the war for German and US police institutions, the involvement of which in international policing in the period following the war I will discuss in the next chapter.

A host of new, warfare-oriented police activities of a distinctly cross-border character accompanied Nazi domestic and foreign policy.[11] The promulgation of the Nuremberg laws in 1935, the persecution of political opponents and non-Aryans, and mounting hostilities between Germany and enemy nations meant that more intense and more aggressive duties than ever before were assigned to the Nazi-controlled German police agencies. The Nazi regime basically employed three strategies in terms of warfare-related police operations. First, in some

[11] On the espionage and war functions of the Nazi police institutions, see National Archives, *Records of the German Foreign Office Received by the Department of State* (GFO); *Collection of Foreign Records Seized, 1941- (Record Group 242): Records of the Reich Leader of the SS and Chief of the German Police* (RLSS); Deutsches Auswärtiges Amt (German Foreign Office), *Akten zur Deutschen auswärtigen Politik* (Documents on German Foreign Policy); Peterssen 1940.

countries the preferred strategy was to infiltrate popular movements and key military, political, and police posts. In police matters, these activities involved the use of foreign diplomats to watch over German émigrés and the placement of Nazi political police in foreign embassies (RLSS 199/2739630). Secondly, the Nazi police established contacts with the police in friendly countries, such as Italy, Japan, and Spain.[12] And thirdly, in the German-occupied countries, the existing host systems were linked to the Nazi police organizations (e.g. in the low countries) or violently destroyed and replaced (e.g. in Poland and Czechoslovakia) (Fijnaut 1979:256–307).[13]

The function and organization of law enforcement agencies in the United States also underwent changes during the build-up to World War II. US police and military agencies were involved in anti-Nazi espionage activities since as early as the 1920s, when military intelligence observed the Nazi movement in Germany (MID 2657-B–603). In May 1934, President Roosevelt secretly ordered the FBI to launch an investigation of the American Nazi movement.[14] The presidential order was twice renewed, and on 6 September 1939, three days after the British and French declaration of war on Germany, Roosevelt formally put the FBI in charge of police activities relating to espionage, sabotage, subversive activities, and violations of the neutrality laws (Ungar 1976:102). The FBI was also engaged in anti-communist operations in South America, where Gestapo forces, too, were investigating the communist movement (Huggins 1998:58–65; McKale 1977:84–85). However, there is no conclusive evidence that anti-communism forged a partnership between the FBI and the Nazi political police. The FBI was after all also heavily involved with the investigation of Latin-American Nazi groups. And while an international Anti-Comintern Pact was planned by the Nazis, the United States opposed the idea (Galvis and Donadio 1986; McKale 1977:86–93).

[12] In 1939 and 1940, for example, the Nazi police organized a reorganization of the Spanish political police (GFO 1026/406403–409; MID 2072–482/58).

[13] The repressive operations of the Nazi police also involved many activities related to the extermination programmes in the concentration camps, which I cannot discuss within the space allowed in this work (see, e.g. Burrin 1994; Dawidowicz 1986; Gilbert 1985; Krausnick and Wilhelm 1981; Lichtenstein 1990; Breitman 1991). I can also not discuss police reorganization in the colonial territories controlled by Nazi Germany (see, generally, Morlang 1994; and the Nazi-influenced presentations by Bremer 1941; Hecker 1938a, 1938b; Heindl 1935b; Schoenfelder 1937).

[14] On the espionage functions of the FBI, see National Archives, *Military Intelligence Division Correspondence* (MID); Federal Bureau of Investigation 1945b:6–13; Lowenthal 1950:425–443; Poveda 1990:29–42; and Ungar 1976:96–118, 23–245.

World War II was to benefit the Federal Bureau of Investigation as much as it had negatively impacted upon international cooperation in the ICPC. Whereas the FBI Identification Division possessed some thirteen million fingerprints in 1940, at the end of the war in 1945 the Bureau had no less than 92 million. During the war years, the FBI's budget rose from $8 million in 1940 to $44 million in 1945. And whereas in 1940 the Bureau counted 898 agents, in 1945 it numbered no less than five thousand. Thus, it was particularly because of the FBI's wartime duties that the Bureau would after the war become the most powerful federal law enforcement agency in the United States and, arguably, the world.

8

Policing the Peace and the Restoration of World Order

In 1946, when we began to reconstruct the files of the old Commission, we were not quite sure they would be of use . . . To our surprise, however, many of the old, familiar characters turned up again, starting their remembered tricks, apparently none the worse—nor more skilful—for their war experiences. The only difference was that now they had graying temples and were hard to recognize from their prewar photographs.
Harry Söderman, 1956.

Any world police organization which the Director does not head would place him in a subordinate position on a comparative basis as far as title is concerned, which would be ridiculous when considering police organizations of any country in the world.
FBI Assistant Director H.H. Clegg, 1946.

With the collapse of the Nazi Empire in May 1945, the fate of the Nazi police officials who had participated in the ICPC would be sealed.[1] Arthur Nebe, the head of the *Reich* Criminal Police Office, and Berlin police official Count von Helldorf, who had both been actively involved in the ICPC during the first period of the organization's Nazification, were executed in 1944 by fellow Nazis in retaliation for a failed assassination attempt on Hitler.[2] Kurt Daluege, the head of the Nazi Order Police and a former ICPC Vice-President, was executed in 1945 by a military tribunal in Prague. Karl Zindel, who had transported some of the ICPC files to the French headquarters in Stuttgart, felt he was 'badly treated' by the French and committed suicide (Söderman 1956:376). In May 1942, then ICPC President Reinhard Heydrich was killed in Czechoslovakia. In retaliation for Heydrich's assassination, the Nazis rounded up thousands of Czechs

[1] On the lives and times of the discussed Nazi police officials, see Aronson 1971; Bradley 1972; Black 1984; Calic 1985; Deschner 1977; Graber 1980; Garrison 1976:80–85; MacDonald 1989; Paillard and Rougerie 1973; Schwitters 1978:38–46.

[2] Arthur Nebe (whom Söderman [1956:376] described as a 'mild' Nazi) had as head of the *Einsatzgruppe B*, a police unit accompanying the invasions in Eastern Europe, been responsible for the killing of at least 45,000 people (*International Military Tribunal*, Vol. 12, p. 288).

and transported them to the extermination camps. In the Czech village of Lidice, Nazi troops killed all women, children, and males over fifteen. Eight children were spared because they were considered suitable for 'Germanization' in SS families. The village of Lidice itself was totally destroyed. Heydrich's successor in the ICPC, Ernst Kaltenbrunner, was sentenced to death by the International Military Tribunal in Nuremberg in 1946.

The destiny of the ICPC after World War II has been a source of considerable controversy and has provoked almost as much debate as the Commission's Nazification. Of particular concern have been the reasons for the ICPC's resurrection after the war, the political character of its organization and activities, and the involvement of the FBI (see, e.g. Möllmann 1969:47–49; Schwitters 1978:65–70; Stiebler 1981:34–42). In the years following the war, a reconstructed ICPC would indeed be more and more confronted by implications and tribulations surrounding the changing world-political scene. Based on the theory forwarded in this book, police organizations must be sufficiently autonomous from the political centres of their respective states to be in a position to cooperate across national borders, while historical conditions affect the degree of formal autonomy that the police can maintain. In a world characterized by intense political antagonisms in international affairs with the advent of the Cold War, the condition of formal bureaucratic autonomy would become problematic for several police institutions participating in the ICPC. To make sense of these post-war developments of the ICPC, I will first detail the manner in which the ICPC was refounded, and describe how the FBI first rejoined the Commission but soon thereafter discontinued membership. Then, I will argue that the problems that the ICPC was enduring in the post-war era cannot be interpreted in terms of a politicization of the organization. Instead, the Commission was, in the post-war years, affected by political conditions related to the proliferation of the Cold War that influenced the various participating police institutions in different ways.

'On the same basis as before': The reconstruction of an international police

About a year after the end of World War II, in June 1946, the International Criminal Police Commission was refounded at an international meeting in the building that housed the Belgian Justice

Department in Brussels.[3] The participants—some fifty officials from seventeen countries—decided to relocate the Commission's headquarters to Paris, where a Secretary-General would be in charge of the organization's daily affairs. The Belgian police official Florent Louwage, at whose initiative the Brussels meeting was held, was elected as the first post-war ICPC President. The statutes of the Commission were not changed from those already adopted in Vienna in 1923, except in one respect. The ICPC would continue to concentrate on the fight against ordinary crime, to which was now added explicitly that the objectives excluded 'all violations of a political, racial or religious character' (6/234). But apart from making the non-political aspiration of police cooperation explicit, the participants at the Brussels meeting stressed the continuity of the ICPC. As President Louwage emphasized at the meeting, the ICPC should 'function on the same basis as before the war' (6/228). Not accidentally, Louwage had organized the meeting in Brussels in his function of 'Permanent Recorder of the Commission,' and the gathering itself was referred to as the 15th general assembly meeting of the ICPC (6/228). The aspiration of the continuity of the ICPC was also reflected in the re-established organizational structure. The Commission was, as before, headed by a President, several Vice-Presidents, reporters, and a Secretary-General. The various ICPC leadership positions were, as before but now by formal statute, arranged to be assigned to officials from different countries. Only the Secretary-General would reside permanently with the Paris headquarters and always be selected from the French national police.

In terms of the objectives of international policing and investigative matters, also, it was planned to have the Commission operate as before. The participating police assumed that there would be a normalization of the international crime problem back to the conditions that justified the ICPC's activities before the war. As Swedish participant Harry Söderman (1956) claimed, the participating police believed that after the war 'many of the old, familiar characters [had] turned up again' (pp. 384–385). Referring to the targets of the ICPC's efforts, Söderman's statement was equally true with respect to the police officials participating in the Commission. The key delegates at Brussels had indeed already played a part in the ICPC before World War II

[3] This section relies largely on evidence available from the FBI 'Interpol' files (sections 6 and following). See also Anderson 1989:42–43; Garrison 1976:97–100; Walther 1968:164–170.

(FOIPA 6/237). The meeting organizer, Florent Louwage, had been involved in international policing since at least 1923 when he attended the International Police Conference in New York. In 1928, he joined the ICPC and in 1932 he became permanent reporter. Other participants, among them Ronald Howe of Scotland Yard, Harry Söderman of Sweden, Werner Müller of Switzerland, and Louis Ducloux of France, had also participated in the ICPC throughout the 1930s. Aptly, then, Söderman (1956) remarked of the officials gathered at Brussels, 'We were all old friends' (p. 384).

'A complicated international picture': The FBI and the re-formation of the ICPC

The first time the FBI was informed about the re-formation of the ICPC was in March of 1946, when the meeting in Brussels was brought up in a communication. But concerns were then raised in the Bureau over the fact that 'many of the countries participating are still in a very confused state' (6/215). Following an invitation from the Belgian ambassador, the State Department advised against participation because of the unstable state of organization of European police institutions and the 'complicated international picture' (6/219). Director Hoover decided not to send an FBI delegate to Brussels, arguing additionally that the Bureau had not been formally invited to the meeting (6/215).[4] Though no US delegate attended the Brussels meeting, the gathered officials did elect J. Edgar Hoover as one of the ICPC Vice-Presidents.

Soon after the Brussels meeting, on 26 June 1946, the FBI formally rejoined the Commission. There was some concern in the FBI that the ICPC could become an 'undesirable block of police organizations especially if Russia should gain dominance of the whole European continent' (6/243). Still, membership in the Commission was viewed favourably, mostly because it was believed that it enhanced the FBI's international prestige. Actual participation by the FBI in the ICPC in the post-war years, however, was minimal. Director Hoover sent some articles he had written to Paris for inclusion in the ICPC periodical, and in June 1947, the FBI joined the ICPC police radio system (7/264, 8/299). But when Hoover was invited to attend the next ICPC meeting in Paris in 1947, he declined because of the all too familiar 'previous

[4] The invitations for the Brussels meeting had been sent through formal diplomatic channels from the Belgian Foreign Office, which at the time was facing logistic difficulties, so that there had been a delay in the correspondence to the FBI (6/228).

commitments' (7/268). The FBI leadership also reaffirmed that the Bureau would continue to maintain outside of the ICPC direct contacts with foreign police, particularly through the division on International Exchange of Fingerprints (7/287). After rejoining the Commission, the FBI did not send any investigative requests to the ICPC headquarters, and the Bureau in turn received only some fifty to seventy-five inquiries from Paris.

The FBI would gradually break off ties with the ICPC not long after it had renewed membership in the organization. The Commission was judged to have little practical benefit for the Bureau and there were mounting concerns over the participation in the ICPC by police agencies from communist countries. Police from the Soviet Union had not joined the refounded ICPC, but some eastern European countries—including Bulgaria, Poland, Yugoslavia, and Czechoslovakia—were official members. Apprehension in the FBI about the communist presence in the Commission would rapidly increase. When in 1948 the FBI was invited to the ICPC meeting in Prague, Czechoslovakia, it was decided not to send a delegate because Czechoslovakia lay 'behind the iron curtain' and its government was 'under the domination of Russia' (10/407, 9/373). The FBI also decided to ignore all communications the Bureau would receive from eastern-European police and discontinued participation in the ICPC radio network (9/375, 395). An internal FBI report warned that the Bureau should not follow up requests from 'satellite agencies' in Bulgaria, Czechoslovakia, and other eastern-European communist countries (13/135). Having been ordered to 'discreetly ascertain the present status of efforts to have the Soviet Union join the organization', the FBI attaché in Paris concluded that the Bureau should discontinue membership in the ICPC (11/470). Among other reasons, the attaché mentioned that the Czech police had recently circulated search warrants through the ICPC channels for ten individuals who had in March 1950 fled from Czechoslovakia to Allied-controlled Germany. The refugees had in Germany received political asylum from the US government, but the ICPC had nonetheless circulated the wanted notices. This, the attaché concluded, meant that the Commission had been 'used by the communist States as an instrument of oppression against political enemies in non-communist countries' (17/11, 49–56).

In July 1950, Hoover informed ICPC President Louwage and Secretary-General Ducloux that the FBI would terminate membership in the ICPC effective 31 December 1950. Among the reasons, Hoover stated that membership in the Commission did not justify the financial expense and that it had come 'as a surprise when the Commission issued ten wanted circulars . . . for individuals wanted by another government on obviously political charges although the circulars indicated that the apprehensions were desired for vaguely described criminal charges' (17/23, 34–35). In a desperate attempt to have Hoover reconsider his decision, ICPC President Louwage in September and October 1950 met with the FBI attaché in Paris and twice thereafter with FBI Assistant Director Clegg in the United States, but to no avail (17/84, 89, 94). In November 1950, Hoover informed all ICPC members 'except those within the Iron Curtain' that the FBI was no longer a member of the Commission and should be contacted directly (18/155, 159).

The politics of international policing

Among the critical issues posed by the post-war reformation of the ICPC are the aspiration of continuity the participants attributed to the Commission relative to the structure that existed before World War II and the initial appeal to and ultimate withdrawal by the FBI. The normatively sensitive resonance of some of these developments has been especially strongly felt in the secondary literature on Interpol. The role played by the ICPC in response to the Cold War and other politically volatile issues, indeed, has been a ground for condemnation and praise alike, leading some observers to argue for the professionalism of the international police organization (e.g. Fooner 1975; Noble 1975; Tullet 1963) and others to rebuke the organization for its political involvements (e.g. Garrison 1976; Schwitters 1978). Debate on the status of the ICPC/Interpol has been particularly intense because of the FBI criticisms of the organization, the Dickopf affair and the questionable past of other police officials involved with the ICPC before 1945, and the attacks against the organization's supposed 'Orwellian' tendencies and attempt to create a global police organization, which have been launched by groups and individuals as varied as the Church of Scientology and Simon Wiesenthal (NCLESJ 1977; Wiesenthal 1989:253–255).

The analytical framework I introduced in this book may bring a proper perspective to this discussion and reorient some of the all too hastily advanced interpretations which appear guided by ideological persuasion more than by informed analysis. I will argue that the bureaucratic autonomy of modern police institutions continued to be a significant factor shaping international policing in the historically changing contexts of the period after World War II. Variable conditions affecting national police institutions in respect of formal bureaucratic autonomy, in particular, are to be held accountable for the pathways and turning points of the Commission after 1946.

A resurrection from war

Police officials involved with the re-formation the ICPC in 1946 were keen to project the continuity of the international police organization from the organizational and operational accomplishments that had been built up before World War II. The course and implications of the Commission during the war, particularly its Nazification, were not discussed or simply brushed aside as a temporary loss of control by the international community. However, the key implication of the end of the war in matters of crime—in particular a spectacular resurgence in international criminal activity—was seen as the principal ground for the ICPC's reformation. As Louwage stated in the invitation to the Brussels meeting, the ICPC had to be refounded because of the 'dangers resulting, since the cessation of hostilities, from the moving about of international criminals' (FOIPA 6/234). Moreover, Louwage added, these international criminals 'have more and more, a tendency to transport their criminal activities, successively, into different States' and they can rely on 'increased facilities of communication' (6/234, 228). Irrespective of empirical accuracy, the notion that turbulent social and economic changes at war's end (in addition to the expansion of technological means) had led to an increased internationalization of crime necessitating police cooperation across national borders clearly reflected the self-understanding of police, much like it had more than two decades before. The suggested rise in international crime in the days after World War II thus provided the motivational basis on which to operationalize international police cooperation, at least for those police institutions that were sufficiently autonomous to be in a position to transcend the borders of their respective national states.

The reappearance of the international criminal as the target of cooperation between police across national borders served as the primary justification for re-establishing the ICPC in much the same framework that had already been elaborated before the war. The Commission's activities in the post-war years again primarily involved the elaboration of structures and technologies intended to facilitate international communications between national police institutions in matters of non-political offences, specifically in the form of the central headquarters, an international radio network, publications, and annual meetings. Characteristically, as soon as Louis Ducloux took up the post of Secretary-General, he declared that the publication of an official ICPC periodical—now called *International Criminal Police Review*—would be 'one of the essential duties of the Secretary General's office' (6/235). The communication facilities were again, as was the case with the pre-war ICPC, structured in a collaborative model, also manifested in the distribution of the leadership positions across nationalities. Other organizational ambitions that already existed in the pre-war organization—specifically the Commission's a-political character and its broad international representation—were now made explicit. This was no doubt in response to the problems leading up to the Nazification of the ICPC, but may also already have anticipated the implications of the changing situation in world-political affairs immediately after the end of World War II.

Yet, the ambition to secure the organizational and operational continuity of the ICPC with its original structures had certain limitations, especially in terms of international representation. Although most countries participating in the post-war ICPC had been members of the Commission before the war, there were some police institutions that no longer participated. Specifically, police from Germany, Austria, Italy, and Spain had not been invited to the Brussels meeting and were not asked in the years immediately following World War II to rejoin the Commission. In a communication to the FBI, Louwage explained that the police agencies in these countries—several of which were occupied by the Allied Forces—were not 'sufficiently well organized and independent enough to participate in the Commission' (FOIPA 6/228). Louwage further explained that police from the Soviet Union had not been invited because the country had also not been a member of the ICPC before the war. However, Louwage added, should the Soviet police apply for membership, the request would be considered by the Commission (6/228).

I earlier defended the viewpoint that international representation in the ICPC was limited, not because of ideological–political motives, but because of the structural condition that non-participating national police institutions were too closely linked to their respective political centres to have the autonomy to engage in police operations beyond national jurisdictions. In the case of the re-formation of the ICPC after

World War II, this thesis is confirmed, as the causes that prevented certain police institutions from attaining formal bureaucratic autonomy related closely to the specific post-war circumstances. In particular, in the case of Germany, Austria, and Italy, a formal separation of the police as expert institutions was no longer accomplished because in the years following the war these countries were still under control of the Allied powers and had no independent police institutions. In the case of Spain, the circumstances were different in that the country had been formally neutral during World War II and continued an independent course in international affairs after the war. For reasons of isolationism, therefore, the Spanish police could not participate in multilateral international cooperation initiatives. As such, noted again are the political conditions preventing the police from attaining the formal bureaucratic independence necessary to engage in international police cooperation.

The thesis that political and other societal processes influence the degree of the formal bureaucratic autonomy of police can also explain the fact that the police from the Soviet Union did not acquire membership in the ICPC. The Soviet Union had not been a member of the ICPC before the war because, as I argued in Chapter 5, the Soviet police lacked formal autonomy from the political centre in Moscow. In this sense there was no discontinuity after 1945, as the conditions that prevented Soviet police from joining the ICPC in the 1930s would in the post-war period only intensify. For by 1946, when the ICPC was re-formed, the Soviet Union's alliance with the western powers during World War II had already and drastically been replaced by a renewed antagonism between the communist bloc and the democratic countries of the free world. In consequence of the changing political climate, there was surely among the ICPC European members also an anti-communist consensus. Yet, these ideological sentiments cannot be held accountable for the exclusion of the Soviet police for it was a fact that the police from other communist countries, in particular, Bulgaria, Czechoslovakia, Hungary, Poland, and Yugoslavia (13/135), did participate in the Commission—and actively too, as the Czech refugee incident revealed.[5] Instead of hinting at political motives, therefore, I argue that the police institutions of the participating eastern European

[5] Secretary-General Ducloux, in fact, argued that the search warrants for the Czech refugees had been distributed through the ICPC headquarters because not doing so would have constituted a political decision in violation of the Commission's statutes (Fijnaut 1997:125).

countries were, unlike their Soviet counterparts, still in a position to attempt to exert influence through cooperation in an existing international police network with broad representation (perhaps not unlike the participatory strategy of the first phase in the process of the Commission's Nazification). In that sense, it could additionally be suggested, that the Soviet police did not need to gain membership in the ICPC because police participation from several of the Soviet Union's satellite countries could also secure influence from Moscow.

My theoretical model acknowledges that the formal bureaucratic autonomy of the police is influenced by changing historical conditions. It is no surprise that political factors impeded the police of certain countries—particularly the Soviet Union and Spain—from participating in the ICPC. Under the totalitarian regimes of both countries, police institutions were too closely linked to their respective political centres to engage in international cooperation, at least beyond the boundaries determined by international diplomacy between politically aligned nations. The implications of an ever-intensifying Cold War would also impact upon the police from eastern Europe participating in the ICPC. Not long after the FBI had left the Commission, the eastern-European police agencies, too, terminated membership in the ICPC: Bulgaria resigned in 1951 and the other communist countries left the year thereafter (Fooner 1989:41; Greilsamer 1986:341). It is unlikely that police institutions from eastern Europe left the ICPC for the reason that they faced an anti-communist bloc in the Commission, because that was already the case in 1946 when they decided to join the organization. Instead, with the strengthening of communist control in the proliferation of the Cold War, the police from eastern Europe could by 1952 no longer maintain formal bureaucratic autonomy from their respective central governments, each of which were additionally directed by the central command at Moscow.

In sum, as was the case with the ICPC before World War II, it was a lack of formal separation of national police systems from politics that placed limits on the international participation in the Commission. Thus, while political–ideological motives were not constitutive of international police cooperation to create, as it were, an 'Interpol against Communism', changing historical conditions in respect of world-political affairs did determine the boundaries of international representation in police cooperation across nation-states. Also, as political contexts affected police institutions of different countries in variable ways, noted again is a persistent relevance of nationality over and against the international aspirations of police cooperation. In addition to refounding the ICPC as a collaborative facilitator between national police agencies and securing diverse international representation in the leadership positions, national persistence also applied to the conditions for police participating in as well as withdrawing from international cooperation, for it were nationally variable characteristics in respect of bureaucratic autonomy that allowed or prevented national police institutions from participating in the ICPC. Hence, the conditions that faced police institutions from eastern Europe and the Soviet Union are structurally similar to those that would influence the FBI to withdraw from the ICPC.

The FBI as international police

The re-formation of the ICPC was a predominantly European affair, with police officials from Europe eagerly appealing to the FBI to renew the Bureau's membership in the Commission, much like when the FBI was initially called upon to join before the war. Unlike the hesitant manner in which it acquired membership in the late 1930s, however, the Bureau readily resumed membership in 1947. Still, FBI participation in the post-war ICPC would never be an enthusiastic affair.[6] Preventing the FBI from ever fully embracing the cause of the Commission from the moment of its post-war reformation, there was, as mentioned, an awareness in the FBI of the influence, real or feared, of the police from communist countries in the post-war days of the ICPC. Already shortly after the Brussels meeting, the FBI attaché in Paris had remarked that the police from some eastern European countries had been present at the gathering. The attaché pointed out that Russia could therefore possibly join the ICPC and that cooperation between the Russian police and the FBI would require 'a considerable stretch of the imagination' (6/245).

Effectively substantiating the fear of a communist presence in the ICPC, the incident with the Czech refugees provided the Bureau with a concrete ground to leave the Commission. However, this should not lead to an acceptance at face value of the viewpoint defended by the

[6] The hesitation of the FBI to join the Commission in 1938 and its lack of involvement after 1946 are obscured in much of the popular literature, both in works critical (e.g. Meldal-Johnsen and Young 1979) and praiseworthy (e.g. Forrest 1955) of the Commission. In a very laudatory book on Interpol, Tom Tullett (1963:60) goes as far as to claim that Director Hoover was 'one of the first police officers to rally to the cause of Interpol in 1946'.

FBI leadership that the ICPC was an instrument of politically motivated oppression. On the contrary, I argue, the decision on the part of the FBI to terminate membership in the ICPC can be explained by the fact that the effective influence of the police from communist countries in the Commission—if only on one occasion—clashed with the Bureau's role in seeking to thwart the spread of communist ideas and influence. Conforming to my thesis on the possible influence of political conditions on the bureaucratic autonomy of the police, I maintain that the FBI, though surely an expert bureaucratic force *par excellence*, was in the years after World War II also closely associated with the political–ideological ambitions of US foreign (and domestic) policy, playing a leading part in US policies aimed at forging an anti-communist dam against the presumed spread of Soviet control. Importantly, the intimate association between the FBI and US politics was not achieved because the US government would have tightly controlled the FBI. The fact that many high-placed members of the government as well as dissenters across the ideological spectrum were under FBI surveillance points to a more generalized strategy of control. The Bureau was successful in establishing a leading role in the policing of US political–ideological affairs because of its expanded powers since World War II and, not least of all, the cunning schemes of its Director (Gentry 1991; Keller 1989; Ungar 1976). In this respect, the role of J. Edgar Hoover and the influence of his 'professional charisma' in targeting what the Director and others like him conceived to be un-American activities was indeed critical (Horobin 1983; Keller 1989). As such, bureaucratization and politicization were remarkably co-existing components of Hoover's FBI. Yet, irrespective of the dynamics that influenced the manner in which FBI and the centre of US political life were closely aligned in the decades after World War II, the fact remains that the structural conditions of the autonomy of police institutions (or the loss thereof) determined the likelihood of international cooperation rather than presumed political–ideological persuasions among the ICPC participants.

The thesis that the degree of the formal bureaucratic autonomy of the police determines participation in international cooperation, albeit under variable societal circumstances, is additionally supported by the fact that the European participants of the ICPC on the western side of the Iron Curtain were in ideological respects surely no less committed to an anti-communist agenda than Hoover and the FBI. However, unlike the FBI, police institutions in western-European and other democratic nations continued membership in the Commission despite the participation of the police from eastern Europe, indicating that they were less affected in respect of their autonomy by the political conditions of the Cold War. The fact that relevant characteristics in respect of bureaucratic autonomy are nationally variable reaffirms national police institutions as the central players in international affairs. And furthermore demonstrating that worldwide events impact upon nations differently, when the police agencies from the communist bloc left the ICPC, the remaining members were candid about the anti-communist sentiments they shared with the FBI. In his 1956 memoirs, Harry Söderman proudly reported that 'now, for several years, the Commission has had no members from the other side of the Iron Curtain' (Söderman 1956:385). But again indicating that political ideology is not constitutive of international police cooperation, the FBI did not resume membership in the Commission despite the resignation of police from the Eastern Bloc.[7] Thus, instead of political motives driving international police cooperation, political conditions relating to the proliferation of the Cold War limited cooperation across national states because of the differing impact of those global events across different countries. In the United States as well as in the Soviet Union and its satellite powers, police institutions withdrew sooner or later from the ICPC because they underwent a diminished autonomy in respects of the political dictates of their respective governments committed to deep-rooted ideological causes.

The relevance of bureaucratization processes is also shown from the fact that practical considerations of efficiency also played a central role in the FBI's withdrawal from the ICPC. For in addition to concerns over the communist participation in the ICPC, the FBI leadership indeed also lamented the lack of practical advantages of membership in the Commission in terms of its investigative objectives. This concern, not accidentally, preoccupied FBI officials throughout its involvement with the ICPC. When the FBI was contacted about the re-formation of the ICPC, an FBI memorandum prepared by Assistant Director Clegg stated that membership in the Commission required 'an exorbitant fee

[7] It was therefore also not surprising when some police officials participating in the ICPC countered the allegations against the ICPC's purported political bias by criticizing the FBI for its political motives and involvement in political policing in the United States. According to the FBI attaché in Paris, for instance, ICPC participant Söderman had once 'slyly observed that the Director expected his Agents to be paragons of virtue or downright "goodie-goodies" . . . [and] implied that the FBI is a political police' (17/11).

when compared with any benefits derived', that the ICPC had 'no record of accomplishment', and that it would be 'ridiculous when considering police organizations of any country in the world' for the FBI to join an international organization in which the Bureau did not have the leading role (6/243). In late 1949, an FBI report reaffirmed the necessity of international police cooperation but added that the FBI already did excellent work in this respect through its own fingerprint service (13/135). When the FBI attaché in Paris in 1950 advised the FBI to discontinue membership in the Commission, he likewise mentioned that the ICPC had not produced any impressive results and that the Bureau preferred 'to contact foreign police agencies direct[ly]' (17/11). Because of the perceived lack of practical advantages of ICPC membership and the relatively high cost of membership, Director Hoover and other FBI officials had already in June of 1950 expressed desire to withdraw from the Commission, a decision that was implemented swiftly once the Czech refugee incident was discovered (17/44–45). Practical considerations in terms of effectiveness of international police cooperation were prevalent concerns among the FBI leadership because participation in a multilateral organization was judged to be of only little value relative to the international police structures the Bureau had itself established. Direct contacts with foreign police, especially through the exchange of fingerprints, were the preferred strategy of international policing in the FBI. And not only was a system of direct police-to-police relations considered to be of practical benefit, it also positioned the FBI at the centre of an almost literally worldwide network, securing a privileged position for the Bureau relative to other police agencies in the United States. That the FBI considered it crucial to maintain the leading US role in international policing would again be revealed in 1957, more than six years after the FBI had decided to leave the ICPC, when it was brought to Director Hoover's attention that the Treasury Department had since 1952 been semi-officially involved in the organization which in 1956 was renamed the International Criminal Police Organization or Interpol (20/231–232). The FBI leadership realized that the Treasury Department's participation in Interpol would imply a relatively weakened position for the FBI in international police relations. Still, the FBI did not decide to rejoin the police organization. When in the following year the Treasury Department sought to acquire formal membership in Interpol and took steps to have legislation passed that would transfer US authority to maintain membership in Interpol explicitly and exclusively to the Secretary of the Treasury, the FBI leadership objected and argued that Interpol membership should remain with the Attorney General. FBI officials reckoned that this would allow the Bureau to decide 'at some future time' to again participate in the organization (20/250). On 27 August 1958, a bill was enacted that specified that the Attorney General was responsible for assigning membership in Interpol to a federal US law enforcement agency (21/269). The FBI was additionally assured that foreign police officials participating in Interpol would always be informed that they could continue to deal directly with the FBI 'in all matters in which [the] Bureau is interested' (20/254). In 1960, the FBI again declined a request to rejoin Interpol.

Conclusion
Patterns and Dynamics of International Policing

> The more the group is spread out, although densely concentrated, the more the collective attention, dissipated over a wide area, becomes incapable of following the movements of each individual . . . The surveillance is less careful, because there are too many people and things to watch.
>
> *Emile Durkheim.*

Historical antecedents of international police practices and organizations in the modern era are manifold and diverse in terms of functional objectives, fields of operation, organizational structure, and aspired and achieved extent of international participation. Having uncovered a multitude of instances and forms in the history of international policing, which until now had remained largely hidden from sociological scrutiny, clearly demonstrates that the internationalization of the police function is not the invention of a recent era of increased globalization. Also, the inclusion in this study of international policing efforts as varied as unilaterally conducted covert operations for a specific purpose and structured multilateral organizations reveals considerable empirical variability. Paralleling observations on the multidimensional nature of globalization in general (Kettner 1997), international policing covers many different dimensions—from temporary practices with restricted participation to relatively stable and multilateral organizations; from early developments during the 19th-century formation of national states to more recent efforts to establish technologically advanced models of international cooperation—that may defy a single propositional explanation. Ethan Nadelmann (1993:466) has indeed suggested that 'there is, clearly, no one explanation for the internationalization of US criminal law enforcement', while Gary Marx (1995:329) has similarly commented that 'it is far easier to ask questions about social control than to answer them'. However, to the extent that the theme of inquiry in research logically unites dimensions of investigation, it invites a general model of explanation. This work was not intended to present description without analytical significance, for beyond an interest in the disorder of events, as Durkheim (1908:224) already realized, sociological analysis must also explain the causes and functions of social facts and be able to order variation in reality. The intention of my study, therefore, was to show that for developments in the history of international policing, a Weberian theory of bureaucratization can account for the development of international police cooperation on the basis of a two-fold model of bureaucratic autonomy. First, police institutions must have attained a sufficient level of independence from their respective political centres to create a structural condition that allows for international cooperation beyond politically akin or aligned states. Secondly, international police cooperation efforts must additionally rely on myths or systems of knowledge related to the fight against international crime as the motivational basis for cooperation. Also, with respect to the forms under which international policing takes place, this study showed that there remained a strong persistence of nationally variable characteristics despite the development of international structures, even when they involved cooperation across nations. In this Conclusion, I wish to strengthen the analysis by discussing some analytically relevant implications of these issues.

The nationality of international policing

In terms of the form of police internationalization, the evidence shows that international policing strategies typically do not conflict with national tasks of policing because they are conceived as dimensions of the function of the police to enforce the 'laws of the land'. The primacy of national concerns in international initiatives is manifested in a preponderance of unilateral and bilateral police operations relative to multilateral forms of international policing. Also, in the attempts to form, and willingness to take part in, more permanently structured multilateral police organizations, nationally variable characteristics continue to be influential. This is especially clear in view of the critical differences between the German experience in international policing and the participation by US law enforcement agencies, differences, moreover, that also underwent critical changes over time. In 19th-century Europe, international police strategies were instigated mostly to suppress the political opposition to established regimes. The policing of criminality could occasionally accompany such high-policing initiatives, but it would not become a more explicit motive of international policing until the early 20th century. In the United States, police institutions were less concerned with political opposition and typically did not forge alliances with the European police even when there were similarities in objectives. Whatever policing of politics that had occupied US law enforcement would be restricted to the home front, targeting alien dissenters and un-American ideologies. In 19th-century Europe, also, international police practices were far more intensive than in the United States. This difference can cause little surprise given the geographical proximity in Europe of various political regimes and national cultures. There can be no international police activity, no need to cross or transcend jurisdictional boundaries, without nationally defined jurisdictions.

Although international developments in the 20th century gradually brought police institutions from both sides of the Atlantic into closer contact, national differences remained important. During World War I, the politically motivated antagonistic causes of the police in Germany and the United States brought police institutions in contact by opposition. Yet, this situation would quickly change, particularly as US law enforcement began to claim a more commanding role on the international scene. Shortly before the end of World War I, similar experiences in the suppression of communism were shared by the police from the United States, Germany, and other parts of Europe. But while it was a theme common to police agencies in both countries, the communist menace did not lead to any international agreements or otherwise collaborative police efforts across the Atlantic. Likewise, the perception of a dramatic influx in crime affected German and US police agencies alike, but although a distinctly criminal matter, the post-war rise in crime did not readily cement relationships among police. Instead, two separate initiatives, the International Police Conference and the International Criminal Police Commission, responded in distinct ways. Despite some institutional and personal connections, also, these initiatives remained largely disconnected from one another and met with different levels of success. Among the few unifying aspects of German–US policing during the first decades of the 20th century were various forms of diffusion of police methods. Especially through study trips abroad, police professionals studied one another's accomplishments for reasons, importantly, that were defined in terms of national objectives. In the United States, the importation of German and other European models served to enhance police professionalism. In Germany, similar initiatives were designed to learn from principles of democratic policing guaranteed under the US Constitution. Neither the German nor the US police institutions would ever successfully achieve these respective aims, as the tension between efficient police performance and democratic accountability remained a characteristic of policing on both sides of the Atlantic.

Nationally variable transformations in international police participation also occurred before, during, and after World War II. A dominance of different and contrasting national interests in international initiatives is revealed in particular in the case of the International Criminal Police Commission in the various phases of its evolution, from expanded international representation to the period of Nazi influence and control. The Federal Bureau of Investigation joined the Commission only after much hesitation, because membership in the international organization was not thought to have many practical benefits for an agency which had set up its own international system of policing. After the installation of the Hitler dictatorship in Germany, the Nazi police leadership immediately saw the potential of taking control of the international organization. Although the practical consequences are not altogether clear, the Nazification of the ICPC displays the dominance of nationalist concerns under conditions of the threat and reality of imperialism and war. In the period after World War II, similar national differences would continue to play a role, particularly when the FBI decided to leave the ICPC because of the organization's presumed political character, accusations which the organization has continued to face regularly since (Nadelmann 1993:184–186).

Theoretically, my analysis corroborates the viewpoint that global events and processes have different effects on nations and otherwise confined localities and their institutions. Available historical evidence indicates that no international police force in modern society has ever been modelled as a supranational force. On the contrary, whenever the idea of a supranational police was suggested, it received fierce opposition. Also, despite similarities in influencing factors (especially warfare and the increase in certain forms of crime), police systems across the world by and large maintained distinct traits based on national cultures and traditions and remained too varied in structure and activities to speak of a unifying trend of cross-cultural harmonization. The emergence of international police organizations with a broad participatory basis confirms the persistence of nationality. The International Criminal Police Commission, in particular, was set up as a network in which police institutions of different nations could cooperate with one another, facilitated by an international office that had no investigative powers of its own.

These findings suggest the value of a perspective of globalization that, more realistically than a globalized economic determinism (Marx 1946), hints at an enduring resistance of national structures and processes. Related to the foundational thought of sociology, this proposition supports Emile Durkheim's (1900:65–75) notion that the move towards a globalized world—what Durkheim labelled 'humanity in its entirety organized as a society' (p. 74)—is not fully achieved and accompanied by internal directions towards and within nations. This echoes a theme spelled out most clearly in the globalization theories of Roland Robertson (1992, 1995), who has argued that globalization refers to an ever-increasing interplay between local and global processes and events, not the creation of a monolithic cultural and social space. Against some continued Marxist resistance, scholars have recently likewise argued that even in the economic realm, globalization involves a linking of national economies, not the formation of a dislocated worldwide market (Hirst and Thompson 1996). Instead, globalization must be conceived to refer to an empirically variable degree of interrelatedness across national borders that is a complex process of interpenetration between universalism and particularism (Robertson and Khondker 1998). As such, Robertson accurately defines globalization as involving both processes of a universalization of particularism and, at the same time, a particularization of universalism (Robertson 1992:97–114). As Mike Featherstone (1995) aptly sums up, '[t]he process of globalization, then, does not seem to be producing cultural uniformity; rather it makes us aware of new levels of diversity. If there is a global culture it would be better to conceive of it not as a common culture, but as a field in which differences, power struggles and cultural prestige contests are played out' (p.14). Hence, it is important to note that processes of globalization—in the area of policing as elsewhere—are always uneven, with trends towards homogeneity counterbalanced by existing or new heterogeneity.

Corresponding to a realistic understanding of globalization, the history of the internationalization of the police function reveals an ever-increasing degree of density in police relationships across nations, but not the development of a monolithic global police. Instead, intranational and transnational actitivities are typically preferred over cooperation efforts which by necessity involve some surrendering of sovereign powers of decision-making. And even when police institutions decide to take part in bilateral and multilateral practices and organizations of cooperation, participation is largely determined by national and otherwise localized interests and anticipated outcomes. Thus, I agree with globalization scholars that we need to go beyond nation-state and market paradigms (Martin and Beittel 1998), but methodologically we should never lose sight of, and instead precisely incorporate, investigations of national (and local) structures and processes of policing. This neo-realist understanding is grounded in the fact that national interests always play an important role in international police strategies, even in those efforts that are driven by supranational concerns or involve international cooperation. The task is to analytically maintain accurate distinctions, in particular between nationality, internationality, and transnationality, that allows the empirical variation of globalization to be ordered precisely in a variety of social areas, past and present.

The rationality of international policing

I have in this book developed the theory that the extent to which national police institutions acquire formal bureaucratic autonomy or institutional independence presents structural conditions favourable for international cooperation, regardless of whether the nation-states of those police institutions approximate one another in political, cultural, legal, and other respects. Importantly, this perspective of bureaucratization recognizes the embeddedness of police institutions in broader societal contexts. During most of the 19th century, political policing initiatives dominated the international scene and by definition failed to forge international alliances beyond the police institutions of politically allied nations. However, as the century drew to a close, an international police culture began to develop that conceived of policing in a depoliticized manner both in terms of its means and objectives. In the earlier half of the twentieth century, the development of an international police culture continued, as manifested in an increasingly more influential conception of international policing in the form of a cooperative organization that should focus exclusively on criminal matters. Although World War I and the threat of communism presented a temporary break in this respect, a non-political cooperative structure was precisely what the International Criminal Police Commission successfully introduced in 1923. Even though the ICPC would also go through the turmoils of a world war and other periods of international political antagonism, the organization has remained in existence until this day, steadily expanding its membership to currently comprise representation from 179 countries.

The International Criminal Police Commission clearly emerges from this study as the central organization through which international policing was formally structured from the first half of the 20th century onwards. Despite its limited potential in terms of investigations and crime control relative to many of the participating and other national police systems, the case of the ICPC most clearly shows that participating police institutions had attained formal separation from their respective governments to create a structural condition of institutional independence. Formal bureaucratic autonomy was achieved as evinced by the fact that the ICPC was established independently at the initiative of police officials, who autonomously set up a structure of international cooperation, which they thereafter sought to have politically and legally sanctioned. To be sure, the ICPC could never fully insulate itself from socio-political influences over the years. A political dependency of policing could be observed most clearly in preparation for and during periods of warfare and other politically turbulent times and events. Then police institutions again draw closer to the political centres of their respective states to follow the patterns of cooperation or conflict as dictated by the international political scene. Police-external conditions are thus seen to influence the degree of institutional dependence of the police, in turn affecting the form and modalities of international policing.

Besides institutional independence, the formation of the ICPC also relied successfully on professional myths or systems of knowledge on international crime that police professionals had come to adopt and share. Particularly instrumental in achieving this condition of operational bureaucratic autonomy were the expert, technologically sophisticated means the police suggested to efficiently control international crime beyond existing legal and political arrangements, and the police views on the rise and internationalization of crime after World War I. Conditions favourable for international police cooperation were based on a mutual recognition of professional standards of policing, especially in technical respects of efficiency. Central among these accomplishments were organizational innovations (a functional division of labour, a structured chain of command, and other elements of formal rationalization) and enhanced skills and means in policing techniques (scientific methods of crime detection, and new technologies of communication and transportation). What these technologically driven arrangements have in common is that they enhance the opportunities for cooperation across national borders, showing the potential of technology to diminish the constraints of dependency on physical space (Marx 1997). Additionally, police technology was developed and implemented primarily in terms of the means of policing. As the application of knowledge, technology is inherently always more instrumental in nature. This emphasis on means explains that the origins of international policing activities revolved primarily around technical know-how and administrative methods, especially with respect to information exchange and direct ways of police communications. These technical achievements could at times even transcend strong political divisiveness. In the case of the 19th-century efforts to organize the fight against anarchism, for example, political–ideological sentiments could not prevent the successful implementation of administrative measures enabled by advances in policing techniques.

From a theoretical viewpoint, the primacy of means in the development of police technology offers support to the Weberian notion that technology is the embodiment of a means-oriented instrumental rationality (Weber 1922; see Shields 1997:193–194). Indeed, police expertise in means (technical know-how) developed before police institutions acquired knowledge (official information) about international crime. When the methods to respond to international crime were already in place, the incidence and nature of international crime was known as a possibility police bureaucracies could and should deal with. Then international police practices responded to this problem with a technical apparatus that was already developed, leading to dialectically reinforce the notion of an internationalization of crime. In other words, police systems of knowledge about international crime took on an actuarial form, as it presented an increased possibility of international crime as a risk (Ericson and Haggerty 1997; Simon 1988). In his writings on bureaucracy, Max Weber already recognized the relevance of knowledge systems for bureaucratic power, and he ultimately even defined bureaucracy as 'domination through knowledge' (Weber 1922:129). More recently, studies of social control have similarly indicated the relevance of expert cultures in terms of a tripartite relationship between theory (criminology), empirical knowledge (criminal statistics), and instrument of control (police) (Foucault 1978; see Garland 1992, 1997; Savelsberg 1994, 2000). Scholars of international policing have also argued for the relevance of knowledge systems for the diffusion of policing objectives and policing techniques in international partnerships (Nadelmann 1993; Sheptycki 1995). James Sheptycki (1998b, c) has described these knowledge systems usefully in terms of a transnational occupational subculture that the police across nations have come to develop through information exchange and practical arrangements of cross-border policing. Indeed, international crime functioned as a professionally defined construct that was real in its consequences of expanding international police organizations and facilities.

The emphasis on an efficiency of policing means has serious implications in terms of the legality and morality of policing. For as police agencies and international police organizations employ a technical apparatus of crime investigation and information exchange, normative questions of rights and legal matters of due process and constitutionally guaranteed rights are typically not, or at least not primarily taken into account. Some policing scholars have gone as far as to argue that the very practice of international policing lacks democratic accountability because it is unclear how citizens can have resource to necessary safeguards against these activities that by definition surpass the jurisdictions of national states and their legal guarantees (Sheptycki 1996, 1998b). International police strategies may be, and are often witnessed to be, conceived and implemented as efficient responses that are methodical and technologically sophisticated, but that fall short in terms of requirements of due process and human rights. The technologies of international policing are often precisely developed and implemented to bypass legal arrangements. Extradition procedures, in particular, were seen by police officials as time-consuming and unnecessarily restrictive arrangements that had to be replaced by ways to establish direct police communications across national borders. The systems of information exchange instituted by international police organizations were similarly intended to bypass the restrictions of legal provisions, anticipating the relevance of the international exchange of expert knowledge and technical know-how among police forces today.

The development of a technologically driven mode of policing implies a remarkable reversal from the highly politicized policing practices that dominated the 19th century. Indeed, the evolution of policing in the modern era reveals that police institutions that historically were very intimately connected with the governmental centres of states often lacked any legitimacy and, instead, were purely politicized instruments of violence. But modern bureaucratic police institutions can over time become so independent and efficiency-driven that they operate without due popular control and political-democratic oversight. Cyrille Fijnaut (1995:122–125) has in this respect spoken of the 'democratic deficit' of present-day forms of international police cooperation. Indicating one more manifestation of the ambiguity of societal rationalization (Habermas 1992), it is precisely in the modern era that policing becomes a balancing act, caught between unusually strong demands for job effectiveness in matters of crime control, on the one hand, and concerns for due process and respect for rights and liberties, on the other. It is also in this respect that state-centred and neo-Marxist perspectives fall short in not being able to critique developments of a highly bureaucratized police, while also recognizing the normative gains modern, democratic societies have accomplished. As such, the ambivalence of modernity is not even revealed in these perspectives (Habermas 1981).

What the bureaucratization perspective adopted here showed, is that expert police myths of international crime justified international cooperation practices, demonstrating that bureaucracies are driven significantly by internal dynamics related to organizational strength and professional expertise. Sociologists of formal organizations have in similar terms argued for the relevance of these developments in the broader context of societal bureaucratization. Comparative sociologist S.N. Eisenstadt (1956:69), for instance, explains the drift towards bureaucratic independence in terms of a development of official expertise and the bureaucracy's successful claim to build and defend a 'professional morale'. Wolfgang Mommsen (1989:112) likewise speaks of an 'inherent dynamism of bureaucratic institutions' that results in a 'self-propelling process', which further accelerates what Henry Jacoby (1969:156) calls the bureaucratic 'will to do everything'. Indeed, it was because of an organizationally developed system of knowledge on the cross-national rise and internationalization of crime that a successful international organization like the ICPC could found and expand its structure and facilities, despite the fact even that among the Commission members no clear-cut definition of international crime was ever attained. What did matter and what did motivate the ICPC was the notion—undisputed among the police—that crime was on the rise across the world and that it was of a more international nature.

My perspective entails no functionalist argument that international police cooperation is necessitated by an internationalization of crime. Such a narrow perspective has often been defended in the secondary literature on international policing (e.g. Duino 1960; Fooner 1975; Tullett 1963). The rise in international crime is then attributed to the expansion of advanced means of transportation, which are held accountable for 'an ever dwindling universe' (Forrest 1955:15) and the fact that 'the world is constantly getting smaller' (Walther 1968:7). Criminals, it is argued, take advantage of these opportunities, for 'then, as now, the tendency of the criminal was to put as great a distance as possible between himself and his victim—and those who wanted him for his crime' (Tullett 1963:22). Relatedly, the international criminal is also considered a particularly enterprising and intelligent person, who plans his deeds methodically 'with a perfection known to no railway in the world' (Tullett 1963:173). As noted throughout this book, these explanations reflect the internal rationalizations by the participants in international policing. What is seen to justify participation in international police cooperation is the threat of an extraordinarily cunning and bright class of criminals who take advantage of modern technologies to operate against society and, therefore, across national jurisdictions. The reliance on advanced technologies and the intelligence held as characteristic of international criminals echo a general theme of modernization. Under such circumstances of rapid and dramatic change, as Durkheim (1893:238–242) foresaw, the traditional means of social control are no longer considered sufficient.

The state of policing

Moving gradually towards the adoption of efficient means of investigation and a professional understanding of police objectives, there is revealed in the history of international policing a planning and execution of practices that extends beyond and purposely seeks to circumvent the requirements of state-sanctioned legality. During the 19th century, political dictates on police powers and national sovereignty concerns greatly impeded the internationalization of the police function. Hence, most 19th-century international police activities, including transnational operations as well as international structures like the Police Union of German States and the Anti-Anarchist meetings of Rome and St. Petersburg, were instigated for political purposes and remained limited in international appeal. But in the earlier part of the 20th century, the movement towards an independent and cooperative international criminal police progressed steadily. This development was reflected in a shift in the goals of international policing towards distinctly criminal concerns. The intergovernmental agreements on prostitution and narcotic drugs (1902–1911) and the First Congress of International Criminal Police in Monaco (1914) are exemplary in this respect. Yet, these initiatives were largely unsuccessful because they still operated on the basis of a legal model rooted in national jurisdictions. Although World War I and the communist menace were grounds for a temporary return to political policing duties, the early 20th century saw a veritable explosion of effort to foster international criminal police cooperation. A series of Latin-American meetings and projects failed to garner much support and were mostly instigated for reasons of advancing the adoption of policing techniques. Similar motives of self-presentation in the profession of policing were apparent in the International Police Conference of New York, which was organized independently by professional police agencies but lacked any realistic concern about an internationalization of crime. The International Criminal Police Commission of Vienna, however, could effectively rely on the twofold criteria of formal and operational bureaucratic autonomy and elaborate a considerable communications and investigative structure with wide international participation. The Commission also worked towards governmental and legal recognition of arrangements that the organization had already developed beyond state and law. As such, what is witnessed is an international police network seeking to obtain legal and governmental approval after the organization had already been established and elaborated independently on the basis of professional police conceptions and without regard for political and legal considerations.

The theory of bureaucratic autonomy underscores Weber's observation that bureaucracies can keep on functioning regardless of whether a society is organized economically along capitalist or socialist lines and regardless of the ideological nature of the political regime (Weber 1922:128–130, 560–579). Indeed, as this analysis has shown, once a police institution is sufficiently independent from its political centre, it functions as an expert apparatus that can engage in collaborative work with other, likewise highly bureaucratized police institutions. The institutional independence of the police accounts for the fundamental irony of international police cooperation: that police institutions transcend national jurisdictional competence and move beyond the function assigned to them by their respective governments. This confirms the Weberian viewpoint that relative to the bureaucrat, the political officeholder is always in the position of a 'dilettante'. Therefore, Weber argued, real authority in the modern state always rests in the hands of the bureaucracy (Weber 1918:32).

What this study has revealed is that—paralleling Foucault's provocative formula to 'behead the King' in political affairs (Foucault

1975:26)—international policing practices cannot be understood in terms of politics and law, for they do not follow government directives and do not target international criminals as legal subjects. On the contrary, the figure of the international criminal as the central motivator of international policing has an existence beyond, even against, law. The forms of behaviour controlled by formal systems of international law, indeed, are typically not the target of international policing, as these focus on crimes that have an international dimension, not necessarily coinciding, as in the case of genocide and war crimes, with behaviour regulated by international criminal law (Bassiouni 1997).[1] Illustrating nicely the extra-legality of international policing, Fooner (1975) reflects appropriately the professional understanding of the police when he remarks that international crime is 'technically, not a legal term, but it is a useful and handy phrase' (p. 4). The international criminal, Tullett (1963:22) notes similarly, 'is not based on any legal concept . . . but simply on practical convenience'. Not understood as explanations, but as reflections of the rationalizations of the participating police, such visions of the international criminal effectively inspired the notion that the police, too, should not care about legal arrangements or state control, relying instead on efficient means of policing. The case of international cooperation among police institutions thus illustrates Weber's (1922:128–129) argument that control of a bureaucracy is 'only limitedly possible for the non-specialist: the specialist is in the long run frequently superior to the non-specialist in getting his will done'.

Importantly, my analysis does not imply that international police organizations and their participating institutions can fully insulate themselves from concerns over legality and rights, nor that they are not or no longer related to state and market. Instead, as much as I argued that the development and justification of international policing practices in terms of professional expertise is itself political, so should it be noted that international policing is subject to criticisms in normative terms, especially with respect to finding new ways to guarantee human

[1] Max Weber's view of international law was in this respect still limited as a 19th-century perspective based on notions of sovereignty and national jurisdiction. For because Weber defined law as a normative order guaranteed by an enforcement apparatus that is especially designed for that purpose, he argued that 'international law' (*Völkerrecht*) is sociologically speaking not law, because it lacks 'a supra-national enforcement agency' (*überstaatliche[n] Zwangsgewalt*) (Weber 1922:18). Clearly, then, Weber did not recognize the possibility that international policing efforts may not be concerned with enforcing the regulations of international law at all.

rights and democratic accountability in the global age. Also, the relative lack of government control over police bureaucracies only refers to a formal separation of the police from the governments of states and is not meant to imply that police institutions are not related to the power of states. On the contrary, as a bureaucracy, police institutions are one component of the state, conceived as a multi-faceted state, the various institutions of which cannot simply be assumed to be tightly controlled by the state's political centre, but that may be relatively independent from and in conflict therewith as well as with one another. As such, it is important, both theoretically as well as empirically, to explore the specific mechanisms of 'structural coupling' between the institutions of police, politics, economy, and law, and to retrieve all, rather than expell any, by unravelling the linkages between them as well as their distinct functions and operations (see Hunt 1993; Hunt and Wickham 1994). My point here, therefore, is not to argue that the state and the public institutions of formal social control are not related, nor that the bureaucracies of social control are not part of state power, but only that the structures and mechanisms of international policing are not exhausted by reference to the ideological dictates of the political centre of states. An alternative perspective could hold that the elaboration of international policing, especially the formation of the International criminal Police Commission, was enabled by agreements between states upon the politically recognized utility of an international police organization. However, the evidence shows that such agreements only came after police experts had already formed such an organization with means and goals they had decided upon without political supervision and formal legal regulation. A related caveat to make here is that I do not argue that developments of law and international law are not relevant. On the contrary, formal legal systems can minimally redefine the disciplinary powers of policing in juridical terms, while developments of constitutionally protected rights can counteract the influences of disciplinary bureaucratic policing (Habermas 1985; Simon 1994; Smith 2000).

Thus, while recognizing the societal contexts of police bureaucratization and, at the same time, the relative autonomy of developments in international police (as much as in international law and politics), the perspective adopted in this book does not surrender to all too commonplace assumptions about the explanatory powers of state and market. I am led to reject state-centred and neo-Marxist arguments, not *a priori*, but because of their shortcomings with respect to empirical adequacy requirements. For although certain societal preconditions were significant in influencing the bureaucratization of the police, they cannot be considered constitutive of the dynamics of the internationalization of policing. Instead, once police institutions have gained institutional independence, expert knowledge systems about a cross-national rise and internationalization of crime provided the motivational basis for an operationalization of international police activities. The paradoxical implication of my theoretical model, then, can be summarized as follows: certain social preconditions favoured a trend toward a bureaucratization process which itself implied increasing independence on the basis of specialized skills and expertise. As such, this book has empirically grounded a Weberian perspective of international policing that is not reductionist in terms of developments of state politics and formal law, for what my analysis has shown is that international police organizations were not reflective of political and legal developments and did not target international criminals on the basis of political (intergovernmental) agreements, nor as subjects of formal systems of law.[2] On the contrary, the cross-national rise and internationalization of crime as the central motivator of international policing was constructed beyond, even against, politics and law. Only after police officials had established professional structures and facilities of international policing did they appeal to national and international bodies of government to formally sanction what had already been created under conditions of bureaucratic autonomy. To the extent that police institutions can make this claim effective, what is taking place is a re-alignment between the centre of the state and its various bureaucracies, involving an influence by the police on government in a manner that implies a technologization of politics (Dillon 1995; Dillon and Reid 2000; Halliday 1985)—or, indeed, a policecization of the state.

September 11

Although I have in this study strengthened the empirical foundations of my theoretical arguments by researching comparatively several

[2] My perspective is confirmed by recent studies which have found that intergovernmental initiatives between the governments of states, for instance in the contemporary context of the European Union, have by and large failed to influence the actual organization and practice of international policing (den Boer 1997; Guyomarch 1995; Sheptycki 1997).

instances in the history of international policing over a period of more than 100 years, my conclusions in this study may need to be qualified when considering other aspects of social control besides those involving public police institutions and more recent developments of international policing that may be qualitatively different from their historical antecedents. In terms of contemporary conditions, several scholars have defended competing theoretical models, specifically in their research on punishment (e.g. Goldstone and Useem 1999; Hochstetler and Shover 1997), the police use of force (e.g. Jacobs and O'Brien 1998), and dimensions of international policing (e.g. Gilboy 1997; Holden 1999; Stanley 1995). However, I have in ongoing research already made efforts to apply my theoretical model of bureaucratization to selected aspects of international policing in the contemporary context (Deflem 2002b, forthcoming). In particular, with respect to the counter-terrorist police measures that have been proposed and implemented since 11 September 2001, I argue that although September 11 was a highly transformative event in world affairs, it implies only in delineated ways a return to a politically directed policing. For in matters of international policing, accomplished developments in bureaucratic autonomy and the continued evolution of a global police culture for well over a century now have resisted a full and unhindered repoliticization. Indeed, on the one hand, worldwide responses to September 11 have influenced the institutional independence of police vis-à-vis the political centres of their respective national states. International terrorism presents a global battlefield on which many of the nations of the world are at war. In consequence, the events of September 11 have brought about a retreat of police institutions back to the political powers of national states. Strikingly, as was the case during the two world wars of the 20th century, the impact of September 11 has functionally and organizationally implied an expansion of police duties to include new tasks and new divisions designed specifically to combat terrorism. Resembling the conditions of World Wars I and II, police institutions across the world have again drawn closer to the political centres of their respective states to follow the patterns of cooperation and conflict as determined by the international political scene.

On the other hand, however, the political retreat of the police under conditions of terrorism today has not been complete, and it can no longer be as easily achieved as it was in the 19th century when police institutions were closely tied to the political dictates of states. For, unlike then, there is now a long-established global police culture that for many decades has forged cooperation on the basis of a shared professional expertise in terms of the means and objectives of policing. The degree to which bureaucratic autonomy has been accomplished during the periods of relative stability since World War II cannot be without consequences for international policing today, even during times of extreme upheaval. In this respect, it is striking that police institutions in the United States and Europe have been placing much emphasis on the efficiency of means to combat terrorism, rather than an appropriate definition of terrorism. New, high-tech solutions are proposed to combat terrorism as a crime that is stripped of its divisive ideological motives. At the international level, strikingly, a similar emphasis is placed on the technological means and a-political objectives of counter-terrorist policing. The current Secretary-General of Interpol, Ronald Noble, strikingly lamented his organization's technological backwardness and 'antiquated' communications systems (Agence Presse France 2001). Likewise, in a resolution at the General Assembly in Budapest just a few weeks after September 11, the members of Interpol agreed to define the terrorist attacks as nothing more nor less than 'a crime against humanity' (Interpol 2001). Such a de-politicized criminalization of terrorism enables police across the globe to rally around a common cause. Conversely, as a political issue, terrorism is unlikely to be able to function as a basis for international police cooperation on a broad multilateral scale.

In conclusion, although clearly more research is needed on the many aspects of international policing in the contemporary and historical context, what I hope my analysis in this book has demonstrated is the value of a sociological approach that transcends perceptions of policing in terms of the enforcement of laws or the control of crime. Gary Marx (1981) astutely described such narrow perspectives as 'trampoline-models' that view social control only in reaction to violations of formal laws and so fail to account for the many sociologically relevant complexities of social control. The bureaucratic model of policing which I developed in this book shows that international policing efforts can indeed not be viewed in terms of an enforcement of legal norms, but instead rely on expert systems of knowledge formulated beyond the realm of state-proclaimed laws. A theoretically founded approach beyond formal legality is precisely, I believe, what should be emphasized by sociological perspectives of policing and social control. Such an approach is readily counter-intuitive to an everyday understanding of policing (as the enforcement of law or the control of crime) and rectifies academic accounts that are dominated by such a misconception. The task for sociologists of social control is to develop and test theories that are rooted analytically in the sociological imagination in order to show the specific role played by police institutions in the construction of social order.

Appendix 1
A Chronology of International Policing

1851	On 9 April, police officials from Austria, Prussia, Sachsen and Hannover gather to create an international police organization for political purposes. Within a year, they are joined by police from Bavaria, Württemberg, and Baden to form the Police Union of German States.
	At least thirty-five foreign police officials, including several city police officers from the United States, attend the International Industrial Exhibition in London to investigate the activities of communists and liberals.
1851–1866	Members of the Police Union hold twenty meetings and establish direct police communications and systems of information exchange until the outbreak of the Austro-Prussian War (15 June to 23 August 1866).
1871	In October, a three-day National Police Convention is held in St. Louis, Missouri. Despite the fact that several European police were invited to attend the meeting, the convention remains an exclusively American affair.
1898	From 24 November to 2 December, the International Conference of Rome for the Social Defence Against Anarchists is held. The Conference is attended by fifty-four delegates from twenty-one European states. Police officials hold separate meetings at the Conference and agree to cooperate on selected matters of policing techniques.
1901	To broaden the scope of the National Police Chiefs' Union, the organization is renamed the International Association of Chiefs of Police.
	At the Second Latin-American Scientific Congress in Montevideo, Uruguay, Juan Vucetich, Police Chief in

La Plata, Argentina, proposes the establishment of an interconnected system of Intercontinental Offices of Identification in Europe, South America, and Northern America.

1902 On 15 July, the French government organizes an international conference in Paris to coordinate the suppression of prostitution and establish extradition procedures.

1904 As a follow-up to the Rome Conference of 1898, a second anti-anarchist meeting is organized by the Russian government in St. Petersburg, where ten governments agree upon a Secret Protocol for the International War on Anarchism.

As a follow-up to the conference of 1902, a second anti-prostitution meeting is held in Paris, where twelve European governments sign an International Agreement for the Suppression of White Slave Traffic.

1905 At a meeting in Hamburg, the International Union of Criminal Law (*Internationale Kriminalistische Vereinigung*) advocates the creation of interrelated central intelligence bureaux across nations.

Following a proposal at the Third Latin-American Scientific Congress in July in Rio de Janeiro, Brazil, an international police meeting is held in October in Buenos Aires, Argentina. The meeting leads to the signing of an International Police Convention by police from Buenos Aires, La Plata, Montevideo, Rio de Janeiro, and Santiago de Chile.

1909 An international police meeting is held in Madrid, Spain.

The governments of thirteen states convene at the International Opium Commission in Shanghai.

1910 In May, the International Convention for the Suppression of the White Slave Traffic is signed by the governments from thirteen nations at a meeting in Paris.

	The creation of a Universal Police Union is proposed at the International American Scientific Congress in Buenos Aires.
1911	The International Esperanto Society of Police Officials meets at an international meeting in Antwerp.
1912	Following the International Police Convention of Buenos Aires in 1905, an international meeting of Latin-American police is held in Sao Paolo, Brazil.
	Following the Shanghai meeting of 1909, a second Opium Conference in The Hague leads to the signing of a Convention for the Suppression of the Abuse of Opium and Other Drugs by the governments of fifty-seven countries.
1914	At the initiative of Albert I of Monaco, the '*Premier Congrès de Police judiciaire internationale*' is held in the Monegasque principality. The congress is attended by 300 delegates from twenty-four countries.
1917	The Bureau of Investigation in the US Justice Department is granted police powers against espionage and sabotage and the control of enemy aliens.
	Police institutions in Europe and the United States start engaging in transnational activities and limited multilateral arrangements to curb the communist threat following the revolution in Russia.
1919	The Versailles Treaty places formal restrictions on the number, functions, and military character of Germany's police.
	On 10 December, Captain M.C. van Houten of the Dutch criminal police sends out letters to police leaders of various countries to propose the establishment of an international police organization in the League of Nations.
1920	As a follow-up to the Latin-American police meeting of 1912, the '*Conferencia internacional sudamericana da policia*' (International South-American Conference of Police) is held in Buenos Aires from 20 to 27 February.

On 10 December 1920, German police officials convene a secret meeting, entitled 'The International Struggle Against Bolshevism: An International Trouble', in Munich, Bavaria. Attended by twenty-four police officials from six European countries, methods of information exchange and mutual support against the communist threat are discussed.

On 2 and 6 January, police raids across the United States lead to the arrest of some 10,000 people charged with violations of the Alien Act of 1918.

1922 Under direction of Richard Enright, the Commissioner of the New York City Police Department, a meeting of police in New York leads to the creation of the International Police Conference.

1923 From 3 to 7 September, the International Police Congress is held in Vienna. Attended by over 100 police officials from various countries, the Congress establishes the International Criminal Police Commission (ICPC).

1924–1938 The International Criminal Police Commission holds fourteen annual meetings in various capital cities across Europe.

1924 In July, the Police-Technical Exhibition in Zoppot, Poland, attracts police representatives from Germany, Hungary, and Warsaw.

1925 In June, the International Police-Technical Exhibition in Karlsruhe is attended by police from various European countries and the United States.

1926 German authorities organize the Great Police Exhibition in Berlin to promote international understanding among the police.

1931 In September, a joint meeting of the International Police Conference and the International Criminal Police Commission is held in Paris.

1932 The Bureau of Investigation formally establishes an international exchange service of fingerprints.

1934	In May, US President Roosevelt secretly charges the Bureau of Investigation to investigate the American Nazi movement.
	The International Criminal Police Commission accepts the proposal of the Italian Federal Police that the ICPC Presidency should reside permanently with the Viennese Police Directorate.
1937	Nazi police officials organize an anti-communist police meeting in Berlin, attended by representatives from fifteen countries. In the following years, Nazi authorities organize several similar international police meetings.
1938	In April, a few weeks after the German annexation of Austria, the Nazi-appointed Police President of Vienna, Otto Steinhäusl, takes over as President of the International Criminal Police Commission.
	At the ICPC meeting in June in Bucharest, Romania, the head of the Nazi criminal police successfully introduces the motion that the next ordinary meeting will be held in Berlin in 1939.
	On June 10, President Roosevelt enacts a bill which authorizes the Attorney General to arrange US membership in the International Criminal Police Commission, effectively securing FBI membership of the ICPC.
1939	On 6 September, the FBI is formally assigned investigative duties related to espionage, sabotage, and subversive activities.
1940	In June, Reinhard Heydrich, the Chief of the Nazi office of the German Security Police, assumes the Presidency of the ICPC. In August, he decides to relocate the ICPC headquarters from Vienna to Berlin.
1941	On 4 December, FBI Director J. Edgar Hoover decides to terminate all Bureau communications with the International Criminal Police Commission.
1943	In May, Ernst Kaltenbrunner succeeds Heydrich, who had been assassinated a year earlier, as ICPC President.

1946 In June, the International Criminal Police Commission is re-founded at an international meeting in Brussels, Belgium.

1950 In July, Director Hoover decides that FBI membership in the ICPC will be terminated effective 31 December that year.

Appendix 2
A German–US Dialogue on Policing and Criminal Justice

Accompanying the analysis in Chapter 6, I here list the references and a short description of a theoretical sample of articles published in the first half of the 20th century in German and US criminology and police journals that deal with aspects of crime and criminal justice in the United States and Germany, respectively. Papers specifically discussing policing issues are separated from those on other or more general aspects of criminal justice.

German Perspectives of US Criminal Justice

Police

1900 Hatscheck 1910, 1911 (comparison of US and Prussian police law); Heindl 1914a (methods of US police); Heindl 1914d (negroes as aides to police)

1919 Heindl 1922b (review of Fosdick's book on US police); Welzel 1922a (comparison between German and US police); Welzel 1922b (travel report on police in New York); Jörgensen 1923b (police conference in New York); Welzel 1925a (New York police conference); Welzel 1925b (comparison between German and US police); Vollmer and Schneider 1925 (police school in Berkeley); Welzel 1926 (organization of US federal police); AfK 1926a (police in New York); AfK 1926b (police relationships); Paetsch and Voit 1927 (travel report on police); Paetsch 1928a (organization of US police); Paetsch 1928b (police methods in the USA); AfK 1929b (fingerprinting at the FBI); Heindl 1930a (a new US journal on police science); Riege 1930b (police laboratories); Gerland 1930 (review of Sellin's book on police); *Die Polizei* 1931b (traffic control in Chicago); AfK 1931a (criminalistics in New York); AfK 1931c (New York; criminology courses); Riege 1931b, 1931c (New York); Ratcliffe 1932a, 1932c, 1932e (Chicago and Hoover); AfK 1932a (crime detection in Chicago); Heindl 1932c (national criminal police); Hartmann 1933 (US judgment on the German police); *Die Polizei* 1933f, 1933g (New York police)

1934 Heindl 1934 (federal police in the USA); AfK 1934 (municipal police and fingerprinting); Hartmann 1934 (German and US police); Exner 1935 (travel report on criminalistics); AfK 1935c (FBI fingerprinting); *Die Polizei* 1935c (police in Kansas); AfK 1936c (car theft); *Die Polizei* 1936a (fingerprinting at the FBI); *Die Polizei* 1936c (police in Hollywood); *Die Polizei* 1936d (fingerprints at the FBI); *Die Polizei* 1936e (traffic control); *Die Polizei* 1936f (the national guard); *Die Polizei* 1936g (police congress); *Die Polizei* 1936h (police in Chicago); *Die Polizei* 1937b (police in New York); Burchardt 1937a, 1937b, 1937c (New York, FBI, fingerprinting); Burchardt 1937e, 1937f, 1937g (police in the USA, FBI); Roenneke 1937a (police in New York); AfK 1937c (police statistics in New York); Meyer 1938 (story by a US police official); Hoover 1938b (FBI fingerprinting); Brasol 1939 (scientific criminalistics); AfK 1939a (New York police statistics; a US police magazine); Burchardt 1939 (police in New York)

1940 Burchardt 1940a (lie detector); Burchardt 1940b (crime-fighting in the USA); *Die Polizei* 1940a, 1940b, 1940c (Hoover); *Die Deutsche Polizei* 1943e (a US view of German police); *Die Deutsche Polizei* 1943f (the Jew and the Yankee); *Die Deutsche Polizei* 1943h (on the origin of the term Yankee)

Crime and criminal law

1900 Hintrager 1900 (travel report about prisons); Näcke 1903a (US view of Lombroso); Näcke 1903b (a criminal case); Spitzka 1903 (statistics on lynching); Witry 1903 (Elmira reformatory); Pinkerton 1905 (bank robbers); Fehlinger 1906 (negro criminality); Liszt 1906 (review of a book on US children's courts); Herr 1907 (travel report on prisons); Fehlinger 1908 (prison statistics); Hellwig 1909 (criminal superstition); Näcke 1909 (diversity of the negro); Fehlinger 1910 (marriage prohibitions); Mitteilungen der IKV 1910b (report of the US group of the IKV); Stammer 1911 (travel report on juvenile delinquents); Stammer 1912 (criminal policy); Rechert 1912 (theft in Chicago); Fehlinger 1912 (crimes of children and women); S. 1913 (prostitution); McMurtrie 1913 (sexual deviance among women); Hofman 1913 (sterilization in California); Näcke 1913 (white slavery); S. 1914 (arson); Struve 1914 (child reformatories); Fehlinger 1915 (sterilization of criminals in the USA); Schultze 1917 (murder statistics)

1919 Fehlinger 1919 (crime statistics); Heindl 1921 (number of murders, probation); Heindl 1922a (eugenics congress); Ranck 1926 (travel report on prisons); Heindl 1927a (prison society); Heindl 1927b (criminal statistics); AfK 1928a (criminal statistics); *Die Polizei* 1928 (traffic problems); Roesner 1928 (homicide statistics); *Die Polizei* 1929 (commercial air traffic); Foltin 1930 (travel report prisons); Baerensprung 1931a (crime in the media); Kraft 1931 (mass murderer in Chicago); Raper 1932 (lynching); AfK (1932b (crimes and prisoners); AfK 1932c (suicide); AfK 1933 (suicide and crime); Bartels 1933 (uniform criminal statistics); *Die Polizei* 1933b, 1933c, 1933d (lynching); Heindl 1933 (lynching)

1934 Heinrich 1934 (review of a German book on professional crime in the USA); AfK 1935a (sterilization, crime and prohibition); AfK 1935e (medical treatment of prisoners); Heindl 1935a (gangs in New York); *Die Polizei* 1935a (employment programme); *Die Polizei* 1935d (traffic); Anuschat 1936 (guns); AfK 1936d (burglary in New York); AfK 1936e (motives of homicides in New York); *Die Polizei* 1936b (air traffic); Roenneke 1937c (air traffic); Burchardt 1937d (crime statistics); AfK 1937a (decrease in crime in Chicago); AfK 1938b (crime slightly increasing in New York); Meinert 1939a, 1939b (criminal procedure); AfK 1939a (traffic accidents in New York); *Die Polizei* 1939b (crime in Chicago)

1940 AfK 1940a (punishment of homicide); AfK 1940b (juvenile delinquency); AfK 1940c (prevention of hereditary diseases); *Die Polizei* 1940c (negro criminality); Schneickert 1940, 1941 (Lindbergh baby kidnapping)

US Perspectives of German Criminal Justice

Police

1910 Andrews 1903 (travel report on police in Europe); Garner 1911 (method for crime detection in Berlin); Albrecht 1911a (review on criminal police); Fuld 1911 (review of police in Europe); Fuld 1912a (police magazine); Fuld 1912b (review of German book on British police); Fuld 1912c (review of book on police dogs); Borosini 1913b (police conference in Berlin); Fosdick 1915a, 1915c (travel report on police systems in Europe); Powers 1917 (costs of police compared with USA)

1919 Belton et al. 1924c (Berlin police); Gollomb 1926 (travel report on European police); Glueck 1926 (travel report on European police); JAICLC 1928, 1929 (reviews of books on police); Goddard 1930 (travel report on scientific crime detection laboratories in Europe); Kavanaugh 1933 (travel report on European police); Wilson 1933 (travel report on European police); Exner 1933 (criminal justice); Ploscowe 1936 (police in France, Germany, and England)

Crime and criminal law

1910 James 1910 (criminal code); MacDonald 1910 (criminal statistics); Healy 1910 (review of German book on juvenile delinquency in USA); Albrecht 1911b (review on criminalistics); Kuhn 1911 (review on international criminal law); Upson 1911 (review of German book on crime); Hartmann 1911 (reform of criminal law); Shepard 1912 (review of German book on crime); Meyer 1912 (review of German book on US criminal law); Fuld 1913 (review on criminal law); James 1913 (Prussian administration); Gault 1913 (treatment of criminally insane); Urban 1914 (review of book on crime); Gault 1914 (review on psychology of crime); Todd 1914 (review of German criminology bulletin); Todd 1915 (review of von Hentig book on crime); Gault 1915 (obituary Hans Gross)

1919 Kuhlman 1928 (review on crime); Heindl 1930b (a new US journal for police science); Sellin 1931 (review on German crime); Gehlke 1931 (review on crime and war in Germany); Viernstein 1932 (criminal-biological service Bavaria); Gentz 1932 (punishment)

1934 Cantor 1934a (review of German criminology dictionary); Cantor 1934b (prison reform); Preuss 1936 (Nazi penal law);

Honig 1936 (changes in criminal law); Cantor 1937 (criminology); Kirchheimer 1938 (juvenile delinquency); Leiser 1938 (Nazi prisons)

1940 Landecker 1941 (German criminology); Hoefer 1945 (the Nazi penal system)

Appendix 3
Archives and Libraries

Universität Hamburg, Germany: Staats- und Universitätsbibliothek Carl von Ossietzky, Von-Melle-Park 3; Bibliothek Seminar für Strafrecht und Kriminologie, Schlüterstraße 28; Sozialwissenschaftliche Bibliothek, Fachbereich 05, Allende-Platz 1, Hamburg 20146; Bibliothek Fachbereich Rechtswissenschaft II, Luruper Chaussee 149, Hamburg 22761

Archiv, Bürgerrechte und Polizei/CILIP, Freie Universität Berlin, Malteserstraße 74–100, Berlin 12249, Germany

Polizeibibliothek, Der Polizeipräsident in Berlin, Platz der Luftbrücke 6, Berlin 12101, Germany

Staatsbibliothek zu Berlin, Preußischer Kulturbesitz, Haus 1, Unter den Linden 8, Berlin 10117, Germany

Bibliothek, Polizei-Führungsakademie, Zum Roten Berge 18–24, Münster 48165, Germany

Katholieke Universiteit te Leuven, Belgium, Centrale Bibliotheek, Mgr. Ladeuzeplein; Bibliotheek Rechtsgeleerdheid, Tiensestraat 51; Bibliotheek Sociale Wetenschappen, Van Evenstraat 2B, 3000 Leuven

Library of Congress, Law Library of Congress, James Madison Memorial Building, 101 Independence Ave, SE, Washington, DC 20540–3000

National Archives, Military Reference Branch, Civil Reference Branch, National Archives Building, Pennsylvania Avenue, Washington, DC 20408 (Since June 1995 located at: National Archives at College Park, 8601 Adelphi Road, College Park, MD 20740–6001)

Federal Bureau of Investigation Headquarters, Freedom of Information/Privacy Acts (FOIPA) Reading Room, J. Edgar Hoover Building, 10th Street and Pennsylvania Avenue, NW, Washington, DC 20535

The University of Colorado, Norlin Library, Law Library, Boulder, CO 80309

The University of Chicago, Regenstein Library, 1100 East 57th Street, Chicago, IL 60637; D'Angelo Law Library, 60th Street, Chicago, IL 60637

Bibliography

Abbott, Andrew. 1988. *The System of the Professions*. Chicago: University of Chicago Press.

Abbott, Grace. 1915. 'Immigration and Crime (Report of Committee "G" of the Institute)'. *Journal of the American Institute of Criminal Law and Criminology* 6:522–532.

Abbott, Edith. 1918. 'Crime and the War'. *Journal of the American Institute of Criminal Law and Criminology* 9:32–45.

Abegg, Wilhelm. 1926. *Aufbau und Gliederung der Großen Polizeiausstellung Berlin 1926*. Berlin: Kameradschaft, Gersbach & Sohn.

Adler, Hans. 1937. *Handbuch der Banknoten und Münzen Europas*. Wien, Berlin: Internationale Kriminalpolizeiliche Kommission, Wirtschaftsgruppe Privates Bankgewerbe.

Agence France Presse. 2001. 'Interpol Needs Thorough Overhaul to Fight Terrorism'. *Agence France Presse*, International News, 26 September, 2001.

Albrecht, Adalbert. 1911a. [Review of A. Niceforo, *Die Kriminalpolizei und ihre Hilfsmittel*]. *Journal of the American Institute of Criminal Law and Criminology* 1:831–833.

—— 1911b. [Review of Hans Gross, 1908, *Gesammelte kriminalistische Aufsätze*]. *Journal of the American Institute of Criminal Law and Criminology* 2:314–316.

Albrow, Martin. 1970. *Bureaucracy*. New York: Praeger Publishers.

—— 1997. *The Global Age*. Stanford, Calif: Stanford University Press.

—— and John Eade. 1994. 'The Impact of Globalization on Sociological Concepts: Community, Culture and Milieu'. *Innovation: The European Journal of Social Sciences* 7(4):371–389.

Almandos, Luis R. 1931. 'Union internationale de Identification'. *Archiv für Kriminologie* 88:179.

American Journal of Police Science. 1930. 'Third International Congress of Criminal Police'. *American Journal of Police Science* 1(6):621.

Amin, Ash. 1997. 'Placing Globalization'. *Theory, Culture & Society* 14(2):123–137.

Anderson, Malcolm. 1989. *Policing the World: Interpol and the Politics of International Police Cooperation*. Oxford: Clarendon Press.

—— 1997. 'Interpol and the Developing System of International Police Cooperation'. Pp. 89–102 in *Crime and Law Enforcement in the Global Village*, edited by W.F. McDonald. Cincinnatti, Ohio: Anderson.

—— and Monica den Boer, eds. 1994. *Policing Across National Boundaries*. New York: Printer Publishers.

Anderson, Malcolm, Monica den Boer, Peter Cullen, William Gilmore, Charles Raab, and Neil Walker. 1995. *Policing the European Union*. New York: Oxford University Press.

Andreas, Peter. 1994. 'The Making of Amerexico: (Mis)Handling Illegal Immigration'. *World Policy Journal* 11(2):45–56.

—— 1996. U.S.-Mexico: Open Markets, Closed Borders'. *Foreign Policy* 69:51–69.

—— 2000. *Border Games: Policing the U.S.-Mexico Divide*. Ithaca: Cornell University Press.

Andrew, Christopher and Oleg Gordievsky. 1991. *KGB: The Inside Story of Its Foreign Operations from Lenin to Gorbachev*. New York: HarperPerennial.

Andrews, Avery D. 1903. 'The Police Systems of Europe'. *The Cosmopolitan* 34(5):495–504.

Anheier, Helmut K. 1997. 'Studying the Nazi Party: "Clean Models" versus "Dirty Hands".' *American Journal of Sociology* 103(1): 199–209.

Anuschat, Erich. 1936. 'Amerikanische Handfeuerwaffen'. *Die Polizei* 33:100–103.

Archiv für Kriminologie. 1924a. 'Ein internationales Polizeiblatt'. *Archiv für Kriminologie* 76:320.

—— 1924b. 'Internationale kriminalpolizeiliche Kommission'. *Archiv für Kriminologie* 76:74.

—— 1924c. 'Automatische Polizeimelder in Berlin'. *Archiv für Kriminologie* 76:74–75.

—— 1925a. [Review of *Festalbum der Internationalen Polizeitechnischen Ausstellung in Karlsruhe*, 1925]. *Archiv für Kriminologie* 77:320.

—— 1925b. 'Der 9. Internationale Gefängniskongreß'. *Archiv für Kriminologie* 77:146.

—— 1925c. 'Zeitschriften (Die Internationale Öffentliche Sicherheit)'. *Archiv für Kriminologie* 77:229.

—— 1925d. 'Deutsche Kriminalpolizeiliche Kommission'. *Archiv für Kriminologie* 77:301–304.

—— 1925e. 'Kriminalistisches Institut der Polizeidirektion in Wien; Der Erkennungsdienst beim Landespolizeiamt Karlsruhe'. *Archiv für Kriminologie* 77:64–66.

—— 1925f. 'Die Internationale Polizeitechnische Ausstellung zu Karlsruhe'. *Archiv für Kriminologie* 77:226.

—— 1925g. 'Internationale Polizeitechnische Ausstellung Karlsruhe 1925'. *Archiv für Kriminologie* 77:70.

—— 1926a. 'Die Vermißtenzentrale der Polizeibehörde New York'. *Archiv für Kriminologie* 78:69.

—— 1926b. 'Amerikanische Polizeiverhältnisse'. *Archiv für Kriminologie* 78:197–198.

—— 1928a. 'Vereinheitlichung der amerikanischen Kriminalstatistik'. *Archiv für Kriminologie* 83:73.

—— 1928b. [Review of Schmitz, H., 1927, *Das internationale Verbrechertum und seine Bekämpfung*]. *Archiv für Kriminologie* 883:84.

—— 1929a. 'Die Wiener Zentralstelle für Bekämpfung des Mädchenhandels'. *Archiv für Kriminologie* 85:249–251.

—— 1929b. 'Das Fingerabdruckverfahren in Amerika; Statistik des Erkennungsdienstes in Washington'. *Archiv für Kriminologie* 84:73.

—— 1930a. 'Preußen und die internationale Kriminalpolizei'. *Archiv für Kriminologie* 87:53–61.

—— 1930b. 'Internationaler Polizeikongreß und Tagung der Internationalen Kriminalpolizeilichen Kommission; Die "Commission Internationale Pénale et Pénitentiaire" '. *Archiv für Kriminologie* 87:76–77.

—— 1931a. 'Projekt einer "Kriminalistischen Klinik" in New York'. *Archiv für Kriminologie* 88:255.

—— 1931b. 'Die Kriminalität der in Deutschland sich aufhaltenden Ausländer im Vergleich zur Kriminalität der Inländer; Eine "neue internationale Gaunersprache" '. *Archiv für Kriminologie* 889:164–166.

—— 1931c. 'Überfüllung amerikanischer Gefängnisse; Die New Yorker Polizei sucht die Verbrechensverhütung zu Organisieren; Kriminologische Universitätskurse in Amerika; Die Sterilisation Anormaler in England'. *Archiv für Kriminologie* 89:248–249.

—— 1932a. 'Das Scientific Crime Detection Laboratory in Chicago'. *Archiv für Kriminologie* 91:190–191.

—— 1932b. 'Über die Zuhnahme der "Federal-Gefangenen" ' in den amerikanischen Gefängnissen; Auch sonst in Amerika Zuhname der Kriminalität; Und die Kriminalität in Deutschland?; Eine "Akademie für Kriminologie"; Selbstmorde in Amerika; Die New York Crime Commission; Der 86. Jahresbericht der "Prison Association of New York"; Waffenhandel in Frankreich; Jugendgerichte in Kanada; Mexiko; Polizeiliche Themen für Doktorarbeiten'. *Archiv für Kriminologie* 90: 85–88.

—— 1932c. 'Selbstmord in Amerika'. *Archiv für Kriminologie* 90:174.

—— 1933. 'Verbrechen und Selbtsmord in USA'. *Archiv für Kriminologie* 92:165.

—— 1934. 'Personalstärke der Grossstadtpolizei in Zentraleuropa und Nordamerika; Eine einfache Methode, Fingerabdrücke zu Identifizieren'. *Archiv für Kriminologie* 95:68–69.

—— 1935a. 'Sterilisationsgesetz für New York vorgeschlagen; Sterilisationsgesetzentwurf in Delaware; Abnahme der Verbrechen in USA seit Aufhebung des Alkoholverbots?' *Archiv für Kriminologie* 96:176–177.

—— 1935b. 'Der 11. Internationale Kongreß für Strafrecht und Gefängniswesen'. *Archiv für Kriminologie* 96:252–253.

Archiv für Kriminologie. 1935c. 'Die Fingerabdruckzentrale in Washington; Die Internationale Polizei im Luftraum: Ein Preisausschreiben; Kongreß der Internationalen Gesellschaft für Verbrechensverhütung; Die 6. Tagung des Bureau international pur l'unification du droit pénal'. *Archiv für Kriminologie* 97:79–81.

—— 1935d. 'Der 4. Intern. Strafrechtskongress'. *Archiv für Kriminologie* 97:168.

—— 1935e. 'Die ärtzliche Behandlung der Strafgefangenen in USA'. *Archiv für Kriminologie* 96:4.

—— 1935f. 'Die XI. ordentliche Tagung der Internationalen Kriminalpolizeilichen Kommission'. *Archiv für Kriminologie* 97:163–168.

—— 1936a. 'Die XII. ordentliche Tagung der Internationalen Kriminalpolizeilichen Kommission'. *Archiv für Kriminologie* 99:85–91.

—— 1936b. 'Eine "Internationale Zentralstelle zur Bekämpfung des Zigeunerunwesens"; Die XII. Tagung der "Internationalen kriminalpolizeilichen Kommission" '. *Archiv für Kriminologie* 98:257.

—— 1936c. 'Der Kampf gegen den Autodiebstahl in Amerika und die Versicherungsprämien'. *Archiv für Kriminologie* 99:78.

—— 1936d. 'Einbrüche in New York 1934'. *Archiv für Kriminologie* 99:84.

—— 1936e. 'Die Kriminalität der Frauen, Jugendlichen und Vorbestraften nach dem Kriege im In- und Auslande; Motive und Ausführungsart der Tötungsdelikte in New York'. *Archiv für Kriminologie* 98:167–171.

—— 1937a. 'Abnahme der Verbrechen in Chicago'. *Archiv für Kriminologie* 101:99–100.

—— 1937b. 'Die XIII. ordentliche Tagung der Internationalen kriminalpolizeilichen Kommission'. *Archiv für Kriminologie* 101:100–102.

—— 1937c. 'Polizeistatistik der Stadt New York 1934–1936'. *Archiv für Kriminologie* 101:167–169.

—— 1938a. 'Die XIV. ordentliche Tagung der Internationalen Kriminalpolizeilichen Kommission'. *Archiv für Kriminologie* 103:85–88.

—— 1938b. 'Kriminalitätskurve in den Vereinigten Staaten von Amerika 1937 etwas gestiegen; Der I. Internationale Kongreß für Kriminologie'. *Archiv für Kriminologie* 102:249.

—— 1938c. 'Internationaler Kongreß für Kriminologie'. *Archiv für Kriminologie* 102:92.

—— 1938d. 'Über Beschlüsse der Internationalen Kriminalpolizeilichen Kommission'. *Archiv für Kriminologie* 103:170.

—— 1938e. 'Die 3. Tagung der Internationalen Akademie für kriminalistische Wissenschaften'. *Archiv für Kriminologie* 102:172–173.

—— 1939a. 'Jahresbericht der New Yorker Polizei 1936 und 1937; Verkehrsunfälle in New York 1936 und 1937; Der I. Internationale Kongreß für gerichtliche und soziale Medizin; Neue amerikanische Polizeizeitschrift'. *Archiv für Kriminologie* 104:87–89.

—— 1939b. 'Ein polizeiliches Zentralbüro für Südamerika geplant; Fingerabdrucke durch Fernseher übermittelt'. *Archiv für Kriminologie* 105:42.

—— 1940a. 'Strafmaß der Freiheitsstrafen wegen mordes in USA'. *Archiv für Kriminologie* 106:47–48.

—— 1940b. 'Kriminalität der Jugendlichen in USA'. *Archiv für Kriminologie* 106:100.

—— 1940c. 'Verhütung erbkranken Nachwuchses in USA'. *Archiv für Kriminologie* 107:145.

Archivio di Antropologia Criminale. 1925a. 'La 2a conferenza della polizia Internationale: I metodi italiani illustrati dall'Ottolenghi'. *Archivio di Antropologia Criminale, Psichiatria e Medicina Legale* 45:404–405.

—— 1925b. 'La Conferenza internatiozale di Polizia di New York (12–16 maggio 1925)'. *Archivio di Antropologia Criminale, Psichiatria e Medicina Legale* 45:646–651.

Aronson, Sholomo. 1971. *Reinhard Heydrich und die Frühgeschichte von Gestapo und SD*. Stuttgart: Deutsche Verlags-Anstalt.

Auer, Georg. 1916. 'Über Verbrecher, Verbrechen und Strafen während des Krieges'. *Archiv für Kriminologie* 67:133–148.

Auerbach, Leopold. 1884. *Denkwürdigkeiten des Geh. Regierungsrathes und Polizeidirectors Dr. Stieber*. Berlin: Julius Engelmann.

Axelrod, Alan. 1992. *The War Between the Spies: A History of Espionage During the American Civil War*. New York: The Atlantic Monthly Press.

Baerensprung, Horst. 1931a. 'Ein Beispiel amerikanischer Berichterstattung'. *Die Polizei* 28:117–120.

—— 1931b. 'Die 8. Tagung der Internationalen Kriminalpolizeilichen Kommission'. *Der Gendarm* 29:521–522.

Barber, John R. 1993. *Modern European History*. New York: HarperPerenial.

Barlow, David E. 1994. 'Minorities Policing Minorities as a Strategy of Control: A Historical Analysis of Tribal Police in the United States'. *Criminal Justice History* 15:141–163.

Barnes, Harry E. 1931. *Battling the Crime Wave: Applying Sense and Science to the Repression of Crime*. Boston: The Stratford Company.

Barry, Andrew, Thomas Osborne, and Nikolas Rose, eds. 1996. *Foucault and Political Reason: Liberalism, Neo-Liberalism, and Rationalities of Government*. Chicago: University of Chicago Press.

Bartels, Ludwig. 1926. 'Die moderne deutsche Polizei im Spiegel des Auslandes'. *Die Polizei* 23:251.

—— 1933. 'Einheitliche Kriminalstatistik in den Vereinigten Staaten von Nordamerika'. *Archiv für Kriminologie* 92:162–165.

Bassiouni, M. Cherif. 1997. *International Criminal Law Conventions And Their Penal Provisions*. Irvington-on-Hudson, NY: Transnational Publishers.

Bassiouni, M. Cherif. ed. 1999. *International Criminal Law*. Second edition. Ardsley, NY: Transnational Publishers.

Bayley, David H. 1975. 'The Police and Political Development in Europe'. Pp. 328–379 in *The Formation of National States in Western Europe*, edited by Charles Tilly. Princeton, NJ: Princeton University Press.

—— 1985. *Patterns of Policing: A Comparative International Analysis*. New Brunswick, NJ: Rutgers University Press.

—— 1991. *Forces of Order: Police Behavior in Japan and the United States*. Second Edition. Berkeley, Calif: University of California Press.

—— 1995. 'A Foreign Policy for Democratic Policing'. *Policing & Society* 5:79–93.

—— 1996. 'Policing: The World Stage'. *Journal of Criminal Justice Education* 7:241–251.

—— 1997. 'Who Are We Kidding? or Developing Democracy Through Public Reform'. Pp. 59–64 in *Policing in Emerging Democracies: Workshop Papers and Highlights*. Washington, DC: US Department of Justice, Office of Justice Programs.

Beck, Friedrich, and Walter Schmidt, eds. 1993. *Die Polizeikonferenzen deutscher Staaten, 1851–1866: Präliminardokumente, Protokolle und Anlagen (Dokumente aus geheimen Archiven, Band 5)*. Weimar: Hermann Böhlaus Nachfolger.

Beck, Ulrich. 2000. 'The Cosmopolitan Perspective: Sociology of the Second Age of Modernity'. *British Journal of Sociology* 51(1)79–105.

Bellman, Elisabeth. 1994. *Die Internationale Kriminalistische Vereinigung (1889–1993)*. Frankfurt: Peter Lang.

Belton, Samuel G. 1924a. 'Inside Famous Scotland Yard: What an American Police Committee Saw of the Workings of London's Great Detective Bureau'. *Police Magazine* 1(1):30–31,38,40,42–44.

—— 1924b. 'European Chiefs Favor Clearing House: In Vienna Police Congress They Plan for Great International Bureau to Aid Work in All Countries'. *Police Magazine* 1(4):14–15,63.

—— William T. Davis, John A. Golden, and F.C. Kruse. 1924a. 'How London's "Bobbies" Work: Problems of the Uniformed Force in the English Metropolis as Seen by Visiting American "Cops"'. *Police Magazine* 1(2):46–49.

—— 1924b. 'Vienna Police Are Highly Popular: They Act as Counsellors and Friends as well as Guardians of the Populace'. *Police Magazine* 1(3):29–32.

—— 1924c. 'Berlin's New Safety Police: "Green" Force Has Many Tasks and "Carries on" Despite Great Obstacles Caused by War's Aftermath'. *Police Magazine* 1(4):29–32,45–46.

—— John A. Golden, F.C. Kruse, and William T. Davis. 1925a. 'The Uniformed Police of Rome: Administration of the Law and Order

Organization of the Eternal City Still Shows the Influence of the Mighty Ceasars'. *Police Magazine* 2(3):25–27,59–60.

—— 1925b. 'Belgium's Police Force: The Inside Workings of the Law and Order Organization of Europe's Most Progressive Kingdom'. *Police Magazine* 2(5):32–34,68,70–71,73–74.

—— 1925c. 'The Cops of Copenhagen: Throughout Denmark, as in the Capital City, the Police System Is Effective and the Men both Courteous and Efficient'. *Police Magazine* 3(1):25–28,91–93.

Benson, Bruce L., David W. Rasmussen, and David L. Sollars. 1995. 'Police Bureaucracies, Their Incentives, and the War on Drugs'. *Public Choice* 83:21–45.

Bentwich, Norman. 1943. 'Alien Enemies in the United States'. *The Contemporary Review* 163:225–230.

Benyon, John. 1996. 'The Politics of Police Co-Operation in the European Union'. *International Journal of the Sociology of Law* 24(4):353–379.

Berman, Jay S. 1987. *Police Administration and Progressive Reform: Theodore Roosevelt as Police Commissioner of New York*. Westport, Conn: Greenwood Press.

Bernard, L.L., and Jessie Bernard. 1934. *Sociology and the Study of International Relations*. Washington University Studies, New Series, Social and Philosophical Sciences, No. 4. St. Louis, WA: Washinton University.

Bessel, Richard. 1987. 'Problems of Policing in Weimar Germany'. Manuscript, The Open University.

—— 1992. 'Militarisierung und Modernisierung: Polizeiliches Handeln in der Weimarer Republik'. Pp. 323–343 in *'Sicherheit' und 'Wohlfahrt'*, edited by Alf Lüdtke. Frankfurt: Suhrkamp.

Best, Werner. 1941. *Die Deutsche Polizei*. Darmstadt: L.C. Wittich.

Beynon, Erdmann D. 1935. 'Crime and Custom among the Hungarians of Detroit'. *Journal of Criminal Law and Criminology* 25:755–774.

Bierstedt, Robert. 1966. 'Indices of Civilization'. *American Journal of Sociology* 71(5):483–490.

Bischoff, Marc A. 1931. 'The International Academy of Criminology'. *The Police Journal* 4(3):464–466.

Bittner, Egon. 1970. *The Functions of Police in Modern Society*. Chevy Chase, Md: National Institute of Mental Health.

Black, Donald. 1980. *The Manners and Customs of the Police*. New York: Academic Press.

Black, Forrest R. 1938. 'Interstate Rendition as Applied to a Person Brought Involuntarily into the Surrendering State'. *Journal of Criminal Law and Criminology* 29:309–328.

Black, Peter R. 1984. *Ernst Kaltenbrunner: Ideological Soldier of the Third Reich*. Princeton, NJ: Princeton University Pres.

Blau, Peter. 1955. *The Dynamics of Bureaucracy*. Chicago: University of Chicago Press.

—— (1964) 1976. 'Social Exchange Among Collectivities'. Pp. 55–68 in *Interorganizational Relations*, edited by William M. Evan. Harmondsworth: Penguin Books.

—— and Marshall W. Meyer. 1971. *Bureaucracy in Modern Society*. Second edition. New York: Random House.

Boli, John, and George M. Thomas. 1997. 'World Culture in the World Polity: A Century of International Non-Governmental Organization'. *American Sociological Review* 62(2):171–190.

—— eds. 1999. *Constructing World Culture : International Nongovernmental Organizations since 1875*. Stanford, Calif: Stanford University Press.

Bonfield, John. 1893. 'Police Protection at the World's Fair, II'. *The North American Review* 156:713–716.

Borgerhoff, Th. 1922. 'Die Fernidentifizierung nach dem System Hakon Jörgensen'. *Archiv für Kriminologie* 74:81–84.

Borosini, Victor von. 1913a. 'The School of Scientific Police in Rome'. *Journal of the American Institute of Criminal Law and Criminology* 3:881–889.

—— 1913b. 'Conference on Police Problems in Berlin'. *Journal of the American Institute of Criminal Law and Criminology* 4:123.

Bradley, John. 1972. *Lidice: Sacrificial Village*. New York: Ballantine Books.

Brasol, Boris. 1939. 'Die Entwicklung der naturwissenschaftlichen Kriminaluntersuchung in den Vereinigten Staaten'. *Archiv für Kriminologie* 104:131–135.

Breitman, Richard. 1991. *The Architect of Genocide: Himmler and the Final Solution*. Hanover: Brandeis University Press.

Bremer, Richard. 1941. 'Hüter des Imperiums: Die Schule der italienischen Kolonialpolizei in Tivoli'. *Die Deutsche Polizei* 9:22.

Bresler, Fenton. 1992. *Interpol*. Weert, The Netherlands: M & P.

Bristow, Edward J. 1983. *Prostitution and Prejudice: The Jewish Fight Against White Slavery, 1870–1939*. New York: Schocken Books.

Brodeur, Jean-Paul. 2000. 'Transnational Policing and Human Rights: A Case Study'. Pp. 43–66 in *Issues in Transnational Policing*, edited by J.W.E. Sheptycki. London: Routledge.

Broekhoff, K.H. 1933. 'The League of Nations and the Suppression of Currency Counterfeiting'. *The Police Journal* 6:10–25.

Browder, George C. 1990. *Foundations of the Nazi Police State: The Formation of Sipo and SD*. Lexington, Ky: University of Kentucky Press.

Brown, Anthony C. 1975. *Bodyguard of Lies*. New York: Harper & Row.

—— 1982. *The Last Hero: Wild Bill Donovan*. New York: Times Books.

Browne, Douglas G., and Alan Brock. 1953. *Fingerprints: Fifty Years of Scientific Development*. London: George C. Harrap & Co.

Brustein, William. 1997 'Who Joined The Nazis and Why.' *American Journal of Sociology* 103(1):216–221.

Bruun, Kettil, Lynn Pan, and Ingemar Rexed. 1975. *The Gentlemen's Club: International Control of Drugs and Alcohol*. Chicago: University of Chicago Press.

Büchler, Yehoshua. 1995. 'Document: A Preparatory Document for the "Wannsee Conference" '. *Holocaust and Genocide Studies* 9(1):121–129.

Burchardt, Hans H. 1937a. 'Von der Tätigkeit des Federal Bureau of Investigation in den Vereinigten Staaten'. *Die Polizei* 34:106–107.

—— 1937b. 'Polizei im Ausland: Vereinigte Staaten (Poland)'. *Die Polizei* 34:105–106.

—— 1937c. 'Polizei im Ausland: New York'. *Die Polizei* 34:128.

—— 1937d. 'Polizei im Ausland: Die Kriminalität in den Vereinigten Staaten (England)'. *Die Polizei* 34:216–217.

—— 1937e. 'Polizei im Ausland: USA (Soviet Union, Canada, China, Letland, New Sealand, Sweden, Netherlands, Austria)'. *Die Polizei* 34:260–261.

—— 1937f. 'Polizei im Ausland: USA (Austria, Rumania)'. *Die Polizei* 34:327.

—— 1937g. 'Polizei im Ausland: Vereinigte Staaten von Nordamerika (Csechoslovakia)'. *Die Polizei* 34:421–422.

—— 1939. 'Kurzergebnisse der Verbrechensbekämpfung in Neuyork (Polizei im Ausland)'. *Die Polizei* 36:25–26.

—— 1940a. 'Der "Lügenentdecker" (Polizei im Ausland)'. *Die Polizei* 37:255.

—— 1940b. 'Verbrecherbekämpfung in USA (Polizei im Ausland)'. *Die Polizei* 37:136–137.

Burrin, Philippe. 1994. *Hitler and the Jews: The Genesis of the Holocaust*. London: Edward Arnold.

Busch, Heiner. 1995. *Grenzenlose Polizei? Neue Grenzen und polizeiliche Zusammenarbeit in Europa*. Münster, Germany: Westfälisches Dampfboot.

Butler, Amos W. 1926. 'Ninth International Prison Congress'. *Journal of the American Institute of Criminal Law and Criminology* 16:602–609.

Cahnmann, Werner J. 1943. 'Concepts of Geopolitics'. *American Sociological Review* 8(1):55–59.

Calic, Edouard. 1985. *Reinhard Heydrich: The Chilling Story of the Man Who Masterminded the Nazi Death Camps*. New York: William Morrow and Company.

Cantor, Nathaniel. 1934a. [Review of Alexander Elster and Heinrich Lingeman, eds, 1933, *Handwörterbuch der Kriminologie*]. *Journal of Criminal Law and Criminology* 24:812–813.

—— 1934b. 'Prison Reform in Germany—1933'. *Journal of Criminal Law and Criminology* 25:84–90.

—— 1937. 'Recent Tendencies in Criminological Research in Germany'. *Journal of Criminal Law and Criminology* 27:782–793.

Carr, E.H. 1947. *International Relations Between the Two World Wars, 1919–1939*. New York: Harper Torchbooks.

Carr, William. 1991. *The Origin of the Wars of German Unification*. Longman: London.

Center for Research on Criminal Justice. 1977. *The Iron Fist and the Velvet Glove: An Analysis of the U.S. Police*. Berkeley, Calif: Center for Research on Criminal Justice.

Chan, Janet, David Brereton, Margot Legosz, and Sally Doran. 2001. *E-Policing: The Impact of Information Technology on Police Practices*. Brisbane, Australia: Criminal Justice Commission.

Clegg, Stewart R. 1994. 'Max Weber and Contemporary Sociology of Organizations'. Pp. 46–80 in *Organizing Modernity*, edited by Larry J. Ray and Michael Reed. New York: Routledge.

Cohen, Stanley. 1985. *Visions of Social Control*. Cambridge: Polity Press.

—— and Andrew T. Scull, eds. 1985a. *Social Control and the State*. Oxford: Basil Blackwell.

—— 1985b. 'Introduction: Social Control in History and Sociology'. Pp. 1–14 in *Social Control and the State*, edited by Stanley Cohen and Andrew T. Scull. Oxford: Basil Blackwell.

Comfort, Mildred H. 1959. *J. Edgar Hoover, Modern Knight Errant*. Minneapolis, Minn: T.S. Denison & Company.

Cole, Simon A. 2001. *Suspect Identities: A History of Fingerprinting and Criminal Identification*. Cambridge, MA: Harvard University Press.

Collier, Barron. 1932. 'International World Police'. *Journal of Criminal Law and Criminology* 23(3):545–548.

—— 1938. 'Progress in Cementing Foreign Police Relationships'. *Yearbook International Association of Chiefs of Police* (1937–1938):160.

Conquest, Robert. 1968. *The Soviet Police System*. New York: Frederick A. Praeger.

Conti, Ugo and Adolphe Prins. 1911. 'Some European Comments on the American Prison System'. *Journal of the American Institute of Criminal Law and Criminology* 2:199–215.

Cooley, Charles H. 1918. 'Social Control in International Relations (& Discussion)'. *Papers and Proceedings of the American Sociological Society* 12:207–232.

Coser, Lewis A. 1982. 'The Notion of Control in Sociological Theory'. Pp. 13–22 in *Social Control: Views from the Social Sciences*, edited by Jack P. Gibbs. Beverly Hills, Calif: Sage.

Cottam, Martha L., and Otwin Marenin. 1999. 'International Cooperation in the War on Drugs: Mexico and the United States'. *Policing and Society* 9:209–240.

Cowell, E.V. 1925. 'Hong-Kong Fashions in Crime: An Account of the Changes in Manners and Modes of Smugglers, Pirates, Robbers, and

Owners of Opium Dens in that Most Picturesque British Outpost. From the Address of Capt. E.D. Wolfe, Superintendent of Hong-Kong Police'. *Police Magazine* 3(3):14–16,57.

Crank, John P. 1994. 'Watchman and Community: Myth and Institutionalizing in Policing'. *Law & Society Review* 28(2):325–351.

—— and Robert Langworthy. 1992. 'An Institutional Perspective of Policing'. *American Journal of Criminal Law and Criminology* 18:338–363.

Crawley, Frederick J. 1929. 'Observations on American Police Systems'. *Journal of the American Institute of Criminal Law and Criminology* 20:167–178.

Critchley, T.A. 1967. *A History of Police in England and Wales, 900–1966*. London: Constable.

Daluege, Kurt. 1935. 'Die Zusammenarbeit der Polizei in der Welt. Interview mit Generalleutnant Daluege aus Anlaß der 11. Jahresversammlung der internationalen kriminalpolizeilichen Kommission in Kopenhagen'. *Der Deutsche Polizeibeamte* 3:489–490.

—— 1936. *Nationalsozialistischer Kampf gegen das Verbrechertum*. München: Zentralverlag der NSDAP, Franz Eher Nachf.

Dandeker, Christopher. 1992. 'The Causes of War and the History of Modern Sociological Theory'. Pp. 37–58 in *Effects of War on Society*, edited by G. Ausenda. San Marino, Italy: AIEP Editore.

Daranyi, Alexander and Oskar Daranyi, eds. 1927. *Große Polizei-Ausstellung Berlin in Wort und Bild: Internationaler Polizeikongreß*. Wien: Internationale Öffentliche Sicherheit.

Das, Dilip K., and Peter C. Kratcoski. 2001. 'International Police Cooperation: A World Perspective'. Pp. 3–27 in *International Police Cooperation: A World Perspective*, edited by Daniel Koenig and Dilip K. Das. Lanham, Md: Lexington Books.

Davies, Celia. 1983. 'Professionals in Bureaucracies: The Conflict Thesis Revisited'. Pp. 177–194 in *The Sociology of the Professions*, edited by Robert Dingwall and Philip Lewis. New York: St. Martin's Press.

Dawidowicz, Lucy S. 1986. *The War Against the Jews, 1933–1945*. Tenth anniversary edition. New York: Bantam Books.

Decker, John F. 1979. *Prostitution: Regulation and Control*. Littleton, Colo: Fred B. Rothman & Co.

Deflem, Mathieu. 1992. 'The Invisibilities of Social Control'. *Crime, Law and Social Change* 18(1–2):177–192.

—— 1994a. 'Law Enforcement in British Colonial Africa'. *Police Studies* 17(1):45–68.

—— 1994b. 'Social Control and the Theory of Communicative Action'. *International Journal of the Sociology of Law* 22(4):355–373.

—— 1996. 'International Policing in Nineteenth-Century Europe: The Police Union of German States, 1851–1866'. *International Criminal Justice Review* 6:36–57.

Deflem, Mathieu. 1997a. 'Surveillance and Criminal Statistics: Historical Foundations of Governmentality'. *Studies in Law, Politics and Society* 17:149–184.

—— 1997b. 'Policing International Society: Views from the United States'. Review Essay. *Police Forum* 7(3):6–8.

—— 2000. 'Bureaucratization and Social Control: Historical Foundations of International Policing'. *Law & Society Review* 34(3):601–640.

—— 2001. 'International Police Cooperation in Northern America: A Review of Practices, Strategies, and Goals in the United States, Mexico, and Canada'. Pp. 71–97 in *International Police Cooperation: A World Perspective*, edited by Daniel Koenig and Dilip K. Das. Lanham, Md: Lexington Books.

—— 2002a. 'The Logic of Nazification: The Case of the International Criminal Police Commission ("Interpol")'. *International Journal of Comparative Sociology* 43(1):21–44.

—— 2002b. 'International Terrorism: The U.S. Federal Law Enforcement Response', Paper presented at the Law & Society Association annual meeting, Vancouver.

—— forthcoming. 'The Boundaries of International Cooperation: Problems and Prospects of U.S.-Mexican Policing'. In *Corruption, Police, Security & Democracy*, edited by Menachem Amir & Stanley Einstein. Chicago: Office on International Criminal Justice.

—— and Fred C. Pampel. 1996. 'The Myth of Post-National Identity: Popular Support for European Unification'. *Social Forces* 75(1):119–143.

—— and Amanda J. Swygart. 2000. 'Comparative Criminal Justice'. Pp. 51–68 in *Handbook of Criminal Justice Administration*, edited by Toni DuPont-Morales, Michael Hooper, and Judy Schmidt. New York: Marcel Dekker Publishers.

—— and Kelly Henry-Turner. 2001. 'Smuggling'. Pp. 473–475 in *Encyclopedia of Criminology and Deviant Behavior*, Clifton D. Bryant, Editor-in-Chief. Volume 2, *Crime and Juvenile Delinquency*. Philadelphia, Pa: Brunner-Routledge.

Delarue, Jacques. 1962. *The Gestapo: A History of Horror*. New York: Dell Publishing.

De Lint, Willem. 1999. 'A Post-Modern Turn in Policing: Policing as Pastiche?' *International Journal of the Sociology of Law* 27(2):127–152.

den Boer, Monica. 1997. 'Justice and Home Affairs Cooperation in the Treaty on European Union'. *Maastricht Journal of European and Comparative Law* 4(3):310–316.

—— 1999. 'Internationalization: A Challenge to Police Organizations in Europe'. Pp. 59–74 *Policing Across the World: Issues for the Twenty-first Century*, edited by R.I. Mawby. London: UCL Press.

Der Deutsche Polizeibeamte. 1937. 'Aufschub der Durchführung einer Ausweisung'. *Der Deutsche Polizeibeamte* 5:672.

Deschner, Günther. 1977. *Reinhard Heydrich: Statthalter der totalen Macht. Biographie*. Esslingen am Neckar: Bechtle Verlag.

Deutsche Strafrechts-Zeitung. 1914. 'Der erste internationale Kongreß für Kriminalpolizei'. *Deutsche Strafrechts-Zeitung* 1(1–3):141.

Deutsches Auswärtiges Amt (German Foreign Office). 1950–1979. *Akten zur Deutschen Auswärtigen Politik, 1918–1945 (Aus dem Archiv des Deutschen Auswärtigen Amtes)* (ADAP). Serie D (1937–1945); Serie E (1941–1945). Several volumes. Baden-Baden: Imprimerie Nationale; Göttingen: Vandenhoeck & Rupprecht (Incomplete English translations published by US Department of State).

Dickens, Charles, and W.H. Wills. 1851. 'The Metropolitan Protectives'. *Household Words* 3(57):97–105.

Die Deutsche Polizei. 1940a. 'SS-Gruppenführer Heydrich Präsident der Internationalen Kriminalpolizeilichen Kommission'. *Die Deutsche Polizei* 8:305.

—— 1940b. 'Ordnungspolizei im Elsatz eingesetzt'. *Die Deutsche Polizei* 8:377.

—— 1941a. 'Die deutsche Grenzpolizei'. *Die Deutsche Polizei* 9:7.

—— 1941b. 'Der Ausweiszwang'. *Die Deutsche Polizei* 9:15.

—— 1941c. 'Blick in ein Juden-Getto; Juden arbeiten'. *Die Deutsche Polizei* 9.

—— 1943a. '10 Jahre Sicherheitspolizei und SD'. *Die Deutsche Polizei* 11:42–44.

—— 1943b. 'Polizei an allen Fronten'. *Die Deutsche Polizei* 11.

—— 1943c. 'Landwacht gegen englische Flieger'. *Die Deutsche Polizei* 11:156.

—— 1943d. 'Dr. Ernst Kaltenbrunner: Der neue Chef der Sicherheitspolizei und des SD; Deutsch als Weltsprache; Drüben liegt England'. *Die Deutsche Polizei* 11:193,196,198–199.

—— 1943e. 'Wie ein Amerikaner uns sieht'. *Die Deutsche Polizei* 11:263.

—— 1943f. 'Der Jude und der Yankee'. *Die Deutsche Polizei* 11:328.

—— 1943g. 'Die antijüdische Weltbewegung'. *Die Deutsche Polizei* 11:350.

—— 1943h. 'Der "Yankee" '. *Die Deutsche Polizei* 11:399.

Die Polizei. 1922a. 'Verkehr mit ausländischen Amtstellen'. *Die Polizei* 18(1921/1922):121.

—— 1922b. 'Ausweisung lästiger Ausländer'. *Die Polizei* 18(1921/1922):415.

—— 1924a. 'Die Ausweisung ausländischer politischer Agitatoren'. *Die Polizei* 20(1923/1924):363.

—— 1924b. 'Ausländische Landarbeiter; Aufhebung der Internierung ausgewiesener Ausländer'. *Die Polizei* 20(1923/1924):319.

—— 1925. 'Auslieferung an die Tschechoslowakei; Unmittelbarer Schriftverkehr zwischen deutschen und österreichischen Behörden in fremdenpolizeilichen Angelegenheiten'. *Die Polizei* 21:83.

—— 1926. 'Auslandsdienstreisen'. *Die Polizei* 23:366.

Die Polizei. 1922a. 1930. 'Aufenthaltserlaubnis für Ausländer; Internationale polizeiliche Zusammenarbeit'. *Die Polizei* 27:28,201.

—— 1932. 'Fürsorge für Ausländer'. *Die Polizei* 29:85–86.

—— 1933a. 'Polizei im Ausland: Vereinigte Staaten (USA) (England, India, France, Austria)'. *Die Polizei* 30:404.

—— 1933b. 'Polizei im Ausland: Vereinigte Staaten (USA) (France, Ireland, Rumania, Poland, Netherlands)'. *Die Polizei* 30:529.

Die Polizei 1933c. 'Aus fremden Polizeien: Lynchjustiz in den Vereinigten Staaten (Spain, Italy, France)'. *Die Polizei* 30:172.

—— 1933d. 'Aus fremden Polizeien (France, Austria)'. *Die Polizei* 30:145–146.

—— 1935. 'Polizei im Ausland (Austria, England, Switserland, France, Netherlands)'. *Die Polizei* 32:415.

—— 1936a. 'Polizei im Ausland: Vereinigte Staaten von Nordamerika (Ireland, Italy, Netherlands, Sweden, Switserland, Hungary, Czechoslovakia, Peru, South-Africa)'. *Die Polizei* 33:392–393.

—— 1936b. 'Omnibusverkehr in den Vereinigten Staaten (Polizeitechnik, Verkehr und Luftschitz)'. *Die Polizei* 33:108.

—— 1936c. 'USA (Umschau)'. *Die Polizei* 33:128–129.

—— 1936d. 'Polizei im Ausland: Vereinigte Staaten von Nordamerika (Poland, Australia, Argentine, China)'. *Die Polizei* 33:240.

—— 1936e. ' "Grüne Welle" in Chikago'. *Die Polizei* 33:240.

—— 1936f. 'Polizei im Ausland: Vereinigte Staaten (USA) (Hungary, Yugoslavia, Spain, Finland, Mexico)'. *Die Polizei* 33:84–85.

—— 1936g. 'Polizei im Ausland: USA'. *Die Polizei* 33:415.

—— 1936h. 'Amerika (Umschau)'. *Die Polizei* 33:107–108.

—— 1937a. 'Auslieferungsverträge'. *Die Polizei* 34:305.

—— 1937b. 'Polizei im Ausland: USA (Denmark, Ecuador, France)'. *Die Polizei* 34:309–310.

—— 1940a. 'Polizei im Ausland: USA'. *Die Polizei* 37:269.

—— 1940b. 'Polizei im Ausland: Vereinigte Staaten (Spain, Cuba, China)'. *Die Polizei* 37:104,128.

—— 1940c. 'Polizei im Ausland: USA (Hoover gegen das Begnadigungs-unwesen; Negerkriminalität; Frauenhandel)'. *Die Polizei* 37:243.

Die Polizeipraxis. 1933. 'Internationale Zusammenarbeit der Polizei'. *Die Polizeipraxis* 9:223–225.

Dillon, Michael. 1995. 'Sovereignty and Governmentality: From the Problematics of the "New World Order" to the Ethical Problematic of the World Order'. *Alternatives* 20(3):323–368.

—— and Julian Reid. 2000. 'Global Governance, Liberal Peace, and Complex Emergency'. *Alternatives* 25(1):117–143.

Doorslaer, Rudi van, and Etienne Verhoeyen. 1986. 'L'Allemagne Nazie, la Police Belge et l'Anticommunisme en Belgique (1936–1944)—Un Aspect des

Relations Belgo-Allemandes'. *Belgisch Tijdschrift voor Nieuwste Geschiedenis* 17(1–2):61–126.

Douglas, Mary. 1986. *How Institutions Think*. Syracuse, NY: Syracuse University Press.

Draper, D.C. 1931. 'International Co-operation (Address, "International Co-operation in Police Service", Paris)'. *The Canadian Police Bulletin* (December, 1931):3–5.

—— 1937. 'International Police Cooperation'. *Police Chiefs' News Letter* 4(10):5.

Dressler, Oskar. 1927. 'Der Internationale Polizeikongreß in Berlin'. Pp. 292–301 in *Große Polizei-Ausstellung Berlin in Wort und Bild*, edited by Alexander Daranyi and Oskar Daranyi. Wien: Internationale Öffentliche Sicherheit.

—— 1931. 'Die VIII. ordentliche Tagung der Internationalen Kriminalpolizeilichen Kommission in Paris'. *Internationale Öffentliche Sicherheit* 7:1–5.

—— 1933. 'Die internationale Zusammenarbeit der Kriminalpolizeibehörden'. Pp. 359–365 in *Der österreichische Bundes-Kriminalbeamte: Gedenkwerk anläßlich des 80jährigen Bestandes des Kriminalbeamtenkorps Österreichs*, edited by Oskar Daranyi. Wien: Verband der Bundes-Kriminalbeamten Österreichs.

—— 1943. *Die Internationale Kriminalpolizeiliche Kommission und Ihr Werk*. Berlin-Wannsee: Internationale Kriminalpolizeiliche Kommission (für den Dienstgebrauch).

Droz, Jacques. 1983. 'Die deutsche Revolutionen von 1848'. *Die deutsche Revolutionen von 1848/49*, edited by D. Nagewiesche. Darmstadt: Wissenschaftliche Buchgesellschaft.

Dunn, Timothy J. 1996. *The Militarization of the U.S.-Mexico Border, 1978–1992*. Austin, Tex: CMAS Books.

—— 1999. 'Military Collaboration with the Border Patrol in the U.S.-Mexico Border Region: Interorganizational Relations and Human Rights Implications'. *Journal of Political & Military Sociology* 27(2):257–277.

Duino, Michel. 1960. *Achter de Schermen van Interpol*. Utrecht: Maraboe Pockets.

Duprat, François. 1968. *Histoire des SS*. Paris: Le Sept Couleurs.

Durkheim, Émile. (1893) 1984. *The Division of Labor in Society*. New York: The Free Press.

—— (1900) 1992. *Professional Ethics and Civic Morals*. London: Routledge.

—— (1908) 1982. *The Rules of Sociological Method and Selected Texts*. New York: The Free Press.

—— (1915) 1991. *'L'Allemagne au-dessus de Tout': La Mentalité Allemande et la Guerre*. Paris: Armand Collin.

Eisenstadt, S.N. (1956) 1971. 'Tensions and Conflicts in Bureaucratic Societies'. Pp. 65–75 in *Bureaucracy in Historical Perspective*, edited by

Michael T. Dalby and Michael S. Werthman. Glenview, IL: Scott, Foresman and Company.

Eldefonso, Edward, Alan Coffey, and Richard C. Grace. 1982. *Principles of Law Enforcement: An Overview of the Justice System.* New York: John Wiley & Sons.

Eliot, Thomas D. 1953. 'A Criminological Approach to the Social Control of International Relations'. *American Journal of Sociology* 58(5): 513–518.

Endres, Hans Ulrich. 1991. *Internationale Verbrechensbekämpfung: Verfassungs- und Verwaltungsrechtliche Probleme.* München: Verlag V. Florentz.

Engel, Gloria V. 1969. 'The Effect of Bureaucracy on the Professional Autonomy of the Physician'. *Journal of Health and Social Behavior* 10(1):30–41.

Engelmann, Otto. 1949. 'Aus der Polizeigeschichte der Jahre 1932 und später'. *Polizei-Praxis* 3:35–164.

Enright, Richard E. 1925a. 'The Significance of the International Police Conference'. *Police Magazine* 3(3):21–22,88–89.

—— 1925b. 'Our Neighbors to the South: A Plea for a Better Understanding of and a Closer Relationship with the Great South American Republics'. *Police Magazine* 2(6):22–23,48–50.

—— 1925c. 'Below the Equator: A Comparison of South American Police Systems and Policemen with Those of Our Own Country'. *Police Magazine* 3(1):9–12,71–72.

Ericson, Richard V., and Kevin D. Haggerty. 1997. *Policing the Risk Society.* Toronto: University of Toronto Press.

Ethington, Philip J. 1987. 'Vigilantes and the Police: The Creation of a Professional Police Bureaucracy in San Francisco, 1847–1900'. *Journal of Social History* 21(2):197–227.

Exner, Franz. 1933. 'Development of the Administration of Criminal Justice in Germany'. *Journal of Criminal Law and Criminology* 24:248–259.

—— 1935. *Kriminalistischer Bericht über eine Reise nach Amerika.* Berlin, Leipzig: Walter de Gruyter.

Fallati. 1844. 'Die Genesis der Völkergesellschaft: Ein Beitrag zur Revision der Völkerrechtswissenschaft'. *Zeitschrift für die gesammte Staatswissenschaft* 1(1):260–328.

Farrell, Bill, and Larry Koch. 1995. 'Criminal Justice, Sociology and Academia'. *The American Sociologist* 26(1):52–61.

FBI Law Enforcement Bulletin. 1936a. 'Suggestion for Officials Transmitting Wanted Circular to Canada'. *FBI Law Enforcement Bulletin* 5(1):2.

—— 1936b. 'International Exchange of Fingerprints'. *FBI Law Enforcement Bulletin* 5(1):5–10.

—— 1937a. 'International Cooperation'. *FBI Law Enforcement Bulletin* 6(12):8.

—— 1937b. 'International World Police Convention'. *FBI Law Enforcement Bulletin* 6(12):9–11.
—— 1938a. 'Police Organization at Prague, Czechoslovakia'. *FBI Law Enforcement Bulletin* 7(9):21–25.
—— 1938b. 'The Police Organizations of Sweden'. *FBI Law Enforcement Bulletin* 7(11):14–17.
—— 1938c. 'The Police Organizations of Poland'. *FBI Law Enforcement Bulletin* 7(12):25–28.
—— 1938d. 'England and America Interchange Officers for Study'. *FBI Law Enforcement Bulletin* 7(10):11–14.
—— 1938e. 'The Scientific Police Laboratories of Belgium'. *FBI Law Enforcement Bulletin* 7(10):26–28.
—— 1939. 'Police Organizations of France'. *FBI Law Enforcement Bulletin* 8(2):32–36.
—— 1940. 'Attention All Law Enforcement Agencies: Cuban Police Request Any Information on Background of Murderer'. *FBI Law Enforcement Bulletin* 9(8):44–46.
Federal Bureau of Investigation. 1938. *Annual Report of the Federal Bureau of Investigation (July 1, 1937, to June 30, 1938)*. Washington, DC: Federal Bureau of Investigation.
—— 1939. *Annual Report of the Federal Bureau of Investigation (July 1, 1938, to June 30, 1939)*. Washington, DC: Federal Bureau of Investigation.
—— 1940. *Annual Report of the Federal Bureau of Investigation (July 1, 1939, to June 30, 1940)*. Washington, DC: Federal Bureau of Investigation.
—— 1941a. *Annual Report of the Federal Bureau of Investigation (July 1, 1940, to June 30, 1941)*. Washington, DC: Federal Bureau of Investigation.
—— 1941b. *The Federal Bureau of Investigation, United States Department of Justice (A Booklet)*. Washington, DC: Federal Bureau of Investigation.
—— 1942a. *War Duty Suggestions for Police Executives*. Washington, DC: Federal Bureau of Investigation, United States Department of Justice.
—— 1942b. *War Duty Suggestions for Police*. Washington, DC: Federal Bureau of Investigation, United States Department of Justice.
—— 1943. *Annual Report of the Federal Bureau of Investigation (Fiscal year 1943)*. Washington, DC: Federal Bureau of Investigation.
—— 1945a. *Annual Report of the Federal Bureau of Investigation (Fiscal Year 1945)*. Washington, DC: Federal Bureau of Investigation.
—— 1945b. *The Story of the Federal Bureau of Investigation*. Washington, DC: Federal Bureau of Investigation.
—— 1974. *The FBI Laboratory: A Brief Outline of the History, the Services, and the Operating Techniques of the World's Greatest Scientific Crime Laboratory*. Washington, DC: Federal Bureau of Investigation.
—— 1994a. *Overview of the Federal Bureau of Investigation*. Washington, DC: Office of Public and Congressional Affairs, Federal Bureau of Investigation.

Federal Bureau of Investigation. 1994b. *Abridged History of the Federal Bureau of Investigation.* Washington, DC: Office of Public and Congressional Affairs, Federal Bureau of Investigation.

Federal Bureau of Investigation Headquarters, Washington, DC, Freedom of Information/Privacy Acts (FOIPA) Reading Room, J. Edgar Hoover Building: Files on Interpol (21 sections, 1,758 pages); Hitler, Adolf (734 pages); Donovan, William J. (747 pages). Available online at: http://foia.fbi.gov.

Fehlinger, Hans. 1906. 'Die Kriminalität der Neger in den Vereinigten Staaten'. *Archiv für Kriminal-Anthropologie und Kriminalistik* 24:112–114.

—— 1908. 'Die amerikanische Gefängnisstatistik vom Jahre 1904'. *Archiv für Kriminal-Anthropologie und Kriminalistik* 30:352–364.

—— 1910. 'Über Eheverbote in Amerika'. *Archiv für Kriminal-Anthropologie und Kriminalistik* 39:29–33.

—— 1912. 'Erwerbsarbeit und Kriminalität von Kindern und Frauen in den Vereinigten Staaten'. *Archiv für Kriminal-Anthropologie und Kriminalistik* 49:196–203.

—— 1915. 'Sterilisation von Verbrechern usw. in den Vereinigten Staaten von Amerika'. *Archiv für Kriminal-Anthropologie und Kriminalistik* 61:285–290.

—— 1919. 'Die Kriminalität in den Vereinigten Staaten von Amerika'. *Archiv für Kriminologie* 71:170–175.

Featherstone, Mike, ed. 1990. *Global Culture: Nationalism, Globalisation and Modernity.* London: Sage Publications.

—— 1995. *Undoing Culture: Globalization, Postmodernism and Identity.* London: Sage.

Fijnaut, Cyrille. 1979. *Opdat de Macht een Toevlucht Zij? Een Historische Studie van het Politieapparaaat als een Politieke Instelling.* (2 volumes). Antwerpen: Kluwer.

—— 1987. 'The Internationalization of Criminal Investigation in Western Europe'. Pp. 32–56 in *Police Cooperation in Europe*, edited by Cyrille Fijnaut and R.H. Hermans. Lochem, The Netherlands: Van den Brink.

—— 1991. 'Police Co-operation within Western Europe'. Pp. 103–120 in *Crime in Europe*, edited by Frances Heidensohn and Martin Farrell. London: Routledge.

—— 1993a. 'Florent Louwage, 1888–1967'. Pp. 195–209 in *Gestalten uit het Verleden*, edited by Cyrille Fijnaut. Antwerpen, Belgium: Kluwer.

—— 1993b. 'The Schengen Treaties and European Police Co-operation'. *European Journal of Crime, Criminal Law and Criminal Justice* 1(1):37–56.

—— 1995. 'International Policing in Europe: Its Present Situation and Future'. Pp. 115–134 in *Comparisons in Policing: An International Perspective*, edited by Jean-Paul Brodeur. Aldershot, England: Avebury.

—— 1997. 'The International Criminal Police Commission and the Fight against Communism, 1923–1945'. Pp. 107–128 in *The Policing of Politics in the Twentieth Century : Historical Perspectives*, edited by Mark Mazower. Providence, RI : Berghahn Books.

—— and Gary T. Marx, eds. 1995. *Undercover: Police Surveillance in Comparative Perspective*. The Hague: Kluwer Law International.

Findlay, Mark. 1999. *The Globalization of Crime: Understanding Transnational Relationships in Context*. Cambridge: Cambridge University Press.

Finger. 1914. 'Der Erste Internationale "Congrès de Police Judiciaire" in Monaco'. *Deutsche Strafrechts-Zeitung* 1(4–5):268–269.

Fischer, Ben B. 1997. *Okhrana: The Paris Operations of the Russian Imperial Police*.

Fischer, Klaus P. 1995. *Nazi Germany: A new History*. New York: Continuum

Fogelson, Robert. 1977. *Big-City Police*. Cambridge, MA: Harvard University Press.

Foltin, Edgar M. 1930. *Amerikanisches Gefängniswesen*. Reichenberg: Gebrüder Stiepel.

Fooner, Michael. 1973. *Interpol: The Inside Story of the International Crime-Fighting Organization*. Chicago: Henry Regnery Company.

—— 1975. *Inside Interpol: Combatting World Crime Through Science and International Police Cooperation*. New York: Coward, McCann & Geoghegan.

—— 1985. *A Guide to Interpol: The International Criminal Police Organization in the United States*. Washington, DC: National Institute of Justice, US Department of Justice.

—— 1989. *Interpol: Issues in World Crime and International Criminal Justice*. New York: Plenum Press.

Forrest, A.J. 1955. *Interpol*. London: Allan Wingate.

Fosdick, Raymond B. 1915a. 'European Police Systems'. *Journal of the American Institute of Criminal Law and Criminology* 6:28–38.

—— 1915b. 'The Passing of the Bertillon System of Identification'. *Journal of the American Institute of Criminal Law and Criminology* 6: 363–369.

—— 1915c. *European Police Systems*. New York: The Century Co.

Foucault, Michel. (1974) 1994. 'La vérité et les formes juridiques'. Pp. 538–646 in *Dits et écrits, 1954–1988, Vol.II*, edited by Daniel Defert and François Ewald. Paris: Gallimard.

—— (1975) 1977. *Discipline and Punish*. New York: Pantheon.

—— (1976) 1978. *The History of Sexuality. Volume I: An Introduction*, translated by R. Hurley. New York: Pantheon.

—— (1978) 1991. 'Governmentality'. Pp. 87–104 in *The Foucault Effect: Studies in Governmentality*, edited by Graham Burchell, Colin Gordon, and Peter Miller. Chicago: University of Chicago Press.

Foucault, Michel. 1981. '*Omnes et Singulatim*: Towards a Criticism of "Political Reason" '. Pp. 223–254 in *The Tanner Lectures on Human Values*, Volume 2, edited by S.M. McMurrin. Salt Lake City: University of Utah Press.

—— (1982a) 1988. 'Technologies of the Self'. Pp. 16–49 in *Technologies of the Self*, edited by L.H. Martin, H. Gutman and P.H. Hutton. Amherst, Mass: University of Massachusetts Press.

—— 1982b. 'The Subject and Power'. Pp. 208–226 in *Michel Foucault: Beyond Structuralism and Hermeneutics*, by Hubert L. Dreyfus and Paul Rabinow. Chicago: University of Chicago Press.

Friedman, Lawrence M. 1993. *Crime and Punishment in American History*. New York: BasicBooks.

Friedman, Tuviah, ed. 1993. *Die drei verantwortlichen SS-Führer für die Durchführung der Endlösung der Judenfrage in Europa Waren: Heydrich-Eichmann-Müller. Eine dokumentarische Sammlung von SS-und Gestapo-Dokumenten über die Vernichtung der Juden Europas, 1939–1945*. Haifa (Israel): Institute of Documentation in Israel for the Investigation of Nazi War Crimes.

Fuld, Leonhard F. 1909. *Police Administration: A Critical Study of Police Organisations in the United States and Abroad*. New York and London: G.P. Putnam's Sons.

—— 1911. [Review of Gerhard Anschütz, 1910, *Die Polizei*]. *Journal of the American Institute of Criminal Law and Criminology* 2:306–307.

—— 1912a. 'Ein Musterhaftes Zentral Polizeiblatt'. *Journal of the American Institute of Criminal Law and Criminology* 2:768.

—— 1912b. [Review of C. Budding, 1908, *Die Polizei in Stadt und Land in Grossbritannien*]. *Journal of the American Institute of Criminal Law and Criminology* 2:796–797.

—— 1912c. [Review of Th. Zell, 1909, *Der Polizeihund als Gehilfe der Strafrechtsorgane*]. *Journal of the American Institute of Criminal Law and Criminology* 2:803.

—— 1913. [Review of Otto Lindemann, 1911, *Die Gesetzgebung über Polizeiverordnungen in Preussen*]. *Journal of the American Institute of Criminal Law and Criminology* 3:817–818.

Funk, Albrecht. 1986. *Polizei und Rechtsstaat: Die Entwicklung des staatlichen Gewaltmonopols in Preußen, 1848–1914*. Frankfurt: Campus.

Galton, Francis. 1892. *Finger Prints*. London, New York: Macmillan and Co.

Galvis, Silvia, and Alberto Donadio. 1986. *Colombia Nazi, 1939–1945: Espionaje alemán, La caceria del FBI, Santos López y los pactos secretos*. Bogotá, Colombia: Planeta.

Gamson, William A., and Ephraim Yuchtman. 1977. 'Police and Society in Israel'. Pp. 195–218 in *Police and Society*, edited by David H. Bayley. Beverly Hills, Calif: Sage.

Gamson, William A. 1997. 'On Coming to Terms with the Past.' *American Journal of Sociology* 103(1):210–215.

Garland, David. 1985. 'The Criminal and His Science: A Critical Account of the Formation of Criminology at the End of the Nineteenth Century'. *British Journal of Criminology* 25:109–137.

—— 1990. *Punishment and Modern Society*. Oxford: Clarendon Press.

—— 1992. 'Criminological Knowledge and Its Relation to Power: Foucault's Genealogy and Criminology Today'. *British Journal of Criminology* 32(4):403–422.

—— 1996. 'The Limits of the Sovereign State: Strategies of Crime Control in Contemporary Society'. *British Journal of Criminology* 36(4):445–471.

—— 1997. '"Governmentality" and the Problem of Crime: Foucault, Criminology, Sociology'. *Theoretical Criminology* 1(2):173–214.

Garner, James W. 1911. 'Apparatus for Detecting Crime in Berlin'. *Journal of the American Institute of Criminal Law and Criminology* 2:91.

Garrison, Omar V. 1976. *The Secret World of Interpol*. New York: Ralston-Pilot.

Gault, Robert H. 1913. 'The Method of Treating the Criminal Insane in Germany'. *Journal of the American Institute of Criminal Law and Criminology* 4:5–7.

—— 1914a. [Review of Max Kauffman, 1912, *Die Psychologie des Verbrechens*]. *Journal of the American Institute of Criminal Law and Criminology* 5:140–141.

—— 1915. 'Hans Gross'. *Journal of the American Institute of Criminal Law and Criminology* 6:639–642.

—— 1929. 'International Prison Congress'. *Journal of the American Institute of Criminal Law and Criminology* 20:488.

Gehlke, Charles E. 1931. [Review of Moritz Liepmann, 1930, *Krieg und Kriminalität in Deutschland*]. *Journal of Criminal Law and Criminology* 22:464–467.

Gellately, Robert. 1992a. 'Gestapo und Terror: Perspektiven auf die Sozialgeschichte des nationalsozialistischen Herrschaftssystems'. Pp. 371–392 in *'Sicherheit' und 'Wohlfahrt'*, edited by Alf Lüdtke. Frankfurt: Suhrkamp.

—— 1992b. 'Situating the "SS-State" in a Social-Historical Context: Recent Histories of the SS, the Police, and the Courts in the Third Reich'. (Review article). *Journal of Modern History* 64(2):338–365.

Gentry, Curt. 1991. *J. Edgar Hoover: The Man and the Secrets*. New York: W.W. Norton & Company.

Gentz, Werner. 1932. 'The Problem of Punishment in Germany'. *Journal of Criminal Law and Criminology* 22:873–894.

Gerland, Heinrich. 1930. [Review of Thorsten Sellin, 1929, "The Police and the Crime Problem"]. *Juristische Wochenschrift* 59:1853.

Gibney, Mark. 1990. 'Policing the World: The Long Reach of U.S. Law and the Short Arm of the Constitution'. *Connecticut Journal of International Law* 6:103–126.

Giddens, Anthony. 1990. *The Consequences of Modernity*. Stanford, Calif: Stanford University Press.

Gilbert, Martin. 1985. *The Holocaust: A History of the Jews of Europe during the Second World War*. New York: Holt, Rinehart and Winston.

Gilboy, Janet A. 1997. 'Implications of "Third-Party" Involvement in Enforcement: The INS, Illegal Travelers, and International Airlines'. *Law & Society Review* 31(3):505–529.

Gillis, A.R. 1989. 'Crime and State Surveillance in Nineteenth-Century France'. *American Journal of Sociology* 95(2):307–341.

Glueck, Sheldon. (1926) 1974. *Continental Police Practice in the Formative Years: A Report Made in 1926 to Colonel Arthur Woods, then Police Commissioner of the City of New York*. Springfield, Ill: Charles C. Thomas.

Goddard, Calvin. 1930. 'Scientific Crime Detection Laboratories in Europe'. (2 parts). *American Journal of Police Science* 1(1):13–37; (2):125–155.

Goldstone, Jack A. 1997. 'Methodological Issues in Comparative Macrosociology'. *Comparative Social Research* 16:107–120.

—— and Bert Useem. 1999. 'Prison Riots as Microrevolutions: An Extension of State-Centered Theories of Revolution'. *American Journal of Sociology* 104(4):985–1029.

Gollomb, Joseph. 1926. *Master Man Hunters*. New York: The Macaulay Company.

Goode, Matthew. 1994. ' "Obey the Law and Keep Your Mouths Shut": German Americans in Grand Rapids During World War I'. *Michigan History* 78(2):19–23.

Gordon, Colin. 1991. 'Governmental Rationality: An Introduction'. Pp. 1–51 in *The Foucault Effect: Studies in Governmentality*, edited by Graham Burchell, Colin Gordon and Peter Miller. Chicago: University of Chicago Press.

Graber, G.S. 1978. *History of the SS*. New York: David McKay Company.

—— 1980. *The Life and Times of Reinhard Heydrich*. New York: David McKay Company.

Graf, Christoph. 1983. *Politische Polizei zwischen Demokratie und Diktatur: Die Entwicklung der preußischen Polizei vom Staatsschutzorgan der Weimarer Republik zum Geheimen Staatspolizeiamt des Dritten Reichs*. Berlin: Colloquium Verlag.

Grauert. 1934. 'Die Entwicklung des Polizeirechts im nationalsozialistischen Staat'. *Deutsche Juristen-Zeitung* 39(15):965–968.

Greilsamer, Laurent. 1986. *Interpol: Le Siège du Soupçon*. Paris: Alain Moreau.

Groeben, Klaus von der. 1984. 'Die Erfüllung von allgemeinen und besonderen polizeilichen Aufgaben'. Pp. 435–451 in *Deutsche Verwaltungsgeschichte, Band 3. Das deutsche Reich bis zum Ende der Monarchie*, edited by Kurt G.A. Jeserich, Hans Pohl, and Georg-Christoph von Unruh. Stuttgart: Deutsche Verlags-Anstalt.

Gundlach, W. 1925. *Die Polizei der Gegenwart in Wort und Bild, nach den Darbietungen der Internationalen Polizeitechnischen Ausstellung in Karlsruhe, 1925*. Lübeck: Deutscher Polizei-Verlag.

Guyomarch, Alain. 1995. 'Problems and Prospects for European Police Cooperation after Maastricht'. *Policing & Society* 5(3):249–261.

Haalck, J. 1959. 'Die staatspolizeilichen Koordinierungsmassnamen innerhalb des Deutschen Bundes zwischen 1851 und 1866'. *Wissenschaftliche Zeitschrift der Universität Rostok* 9:99–105.

Habermas, Jürgen. (1962). 1990. *Strukturwandel der Öffentlichkeit*. Frankfurt: Suhrkamp.

—— 1985. *Der philosophische Diskurs der Moderne*. Frankfurt: Suhrkamp.

—— 1992. *Faktizität und Geltung*. Frankfurt: Suhrkamp.

—— 1998. *Die postnationale Konstellation: Politische Essays*. Frankfurt: Suhrkamp.

Hacker, Ervin. 1929. 'Criminality and Immigration'. *Journal of the American Institute of Criminal Law and Criminology* 20:429–438.

Haffner, Sebastian. 1989. *The Ailing Empire: Germany from Bismarck to Hitler*. New York: Fromm International Publishing Company.

Hagemann, Max. 1933a. 'Internationale kriminalpolizeiliche Zusammenarbeit'. Pp. 741–751 in *Handwörterbuch der Kriminologie, Erster Band*, edited by Alexander Elster and Heinrich Lingemann. Berlin, Leipzig: Walter de Gruyter.

—— 1933b. 'Internationale und reisende Verbrecher'. Pp. 728–741 in *Handwörterbuch der Kriminologie, Erster band*, edited by Alexander Elster and Heinrich Lingemann. Berlin, Leipzig: Walter de Gruyter.

Halliday, Terence C. 1983. 'Professions, Class and Capitalism'. *European Journal of Sociology* 24(2):321–346.

—— 1985. 'Knowledge Mandates: Collective Influence by Scientific, Normative and Syncretic Professions'. *British Journal of Sociology* 36:421–47.

—— 1987. *Beyond Monopoly: Lawyers, State Crises, and Professional Empowerment*. Chicago: University of Chicago Press.

Hanna, Francis D. 1927. 'Automobiles as a Factor in Crime'. *Journal of the American Institute of Criminal Law and Criminology* 18:116–120.

Harbord, J.G. 1924. 'Turning Pirates into Police: To Organize a Moro Constabulary the Americans Had to Reverse the Habits of a People'. *Police Magazine* 1(1):22–24,53–55.

Harnischmacher, Robert, and Arved Semerak. 1986. *Deutsche Polizeigeschichte: Eine allgemeine Einführung in die Grundlagen*. Stuttgart: W. Kohlhammer.

Hartmann. 1933. 'Die deutsche Polizei in einem amerikanischen Urteil'. *Der Deutsche Polizeibeamte* 1:305–308.

—— 1934. 'Deutsche und amerikanische Polizei im Urteil der Amerikaner'. *Der Deutsche Polizeibeamte* 2:305–307.

Hartmann, Adolf. 1911. 'Reform of the Criminal Law in Germany'. *Journal of the American Institute of Criminal Law and Criminology* 2:349–355.

Hatschek, Julius. 1910. 'Das Polizeirecht in den Vereinigten Staaten, auf der Grundlage des englischen und im Vergleiche zum preußischen Rechte dargestellt'. (Part 1). *Archiv für Sozialwissenschaft und Sozialpolitik* 31:67–101.

—— 1911. 'Das Polizeirecht in den Vereinigten Staaten, auf der Grundlage des englischen und im Vergleiche zum preußischen rechte dargestellt'. (Part 2). *Archiv für Sozialwissenschaft und Sozialpolitik* 32:433–495.

Healy, William. 1910. [Review of Hans Gudden, 1910, *Die Behandlung der jugendlichen Verbrecher in den Vereinigten Staaten von Amerika*]. *Journal of the American Institute of Criminal Law and Criminology* 1:674–675.

Hebenton, Bill, and Terry Thomas. 1995. *Policing Europe: Cooperation, Conflict and Control*. New York: St. Martin's Press.

—— 1998. 'Transnational Policing Networks'. *International Journal of Risk, Security and Crime Prevention* 3(2):99–110.

Hecker, Rolf. 1938a. 'Polizei in der Wüste'. *Illustrirte Zeitung* (September 15):344–345.

—— 1938b. 'Ägyptische Polizei'. *Illustrirte Zeitung* (August 4):147–148.

Heidensohn, Frances. 1997. 'Crime and Policing'. Pp. 81–103 in *The Future of Europe*, edited by Valerie Symes, Carl Levy, and Jane Littlewood. New York: St. Martin's Press.

Hein, Bruno. 1935. *Die Stellung der Polizei im Auslieferungswesen*. Dresden: Buchdruckerie M. Dittert & Co.

Heindl, Robert. 1914a. 'Die polizeiliche Überwachung der Pfandleiher in den Vereinigten Staaten von Amerika und in Canada'. *Archiv für Kriminal-Anthropologie und Kriminalistik* 56:266–268.

—— 1914b. 'Bericht über den I. Internationalen Kriminalpolizeikongreßs in Monaco'. *Archiv für Kriminal-Anthropologie und Kriminalistik* 58(3–4): 333–348.

—— 1914c. 'Bemerkungen zum I. Internationalen Kriminalpolizeikongreß in Monaco'. *Archiv für Kriminal-Anthropologie und Kriminalistik* 58(3–4):348–353.

—— 1914d. 'Neger als Spursucher im Dienst der Kriminalpolizei'. *Deutsche Strafrechts-Zeitung* 1(1–3):133–134.

—— 1914e. 'Internationale Kriminalpolizei'. *Deutsche Strafrechts-Zeitung* 1(12):647–652.

—— 1921. 'Die Zahl der Morde in Amerika, England und Deutschland; Das amerikanische Probationssystem'. *Archiv für Kriminologie* 73:289–291.

—— 1922a. 'Rückgang der Eigentumsdelikte bei der Eisenbahn; Der Nachrichtendienst der englischen Kriminalpolizei; Die Errichtung eines Zentralbüros zur daktyloskopischen Verbrecheridentifizierung in Stockholm; Strafgesetzreform in Italien; Abschaffung der Todesstrafe in Schweden; Kongresse (II. internationaler Eugenik-Kongreß, New York, 1921)'. *Archiv für Kriminologie* 74:59–66.

—— 1922b. (Review, R. Fosdick, 1920, *American Police Systems*). *Archiv für Kriminologie* 74:307.

—— 1924. 'Der internationale Polizeikongreß in Wien'. *Archiv für Kriminologie* 76:16–30.

—— 1926. 'Kriminalität und Krieg'. *Archiv für Kriminologie* 78:63–64.

—— 1927a. 'Der 55. Jahresbericht der Amerikanischen Gefängnisgesellschaft'. *Archiv für Kriminologie* 80:262.

—— 1927b. 'Amerikanische Kriminalstatistik; Nehmen die Mörde in Europa zu?' *Archiv für Kriminologie* 179–180.

—— 1928. 'Kriminalpolizei'. Pp. 799–806 in *Handwörterbuch der Rechtswissenschaft, Volume 3*, edited by Fritz Stier-Somlo and Alexander Elster. Berlin, Leipzig: Walter de Gruyter.

—— 1930a. 'A New American Journal for Police Science'. *American Journal of Police Science* 1(6):620–621.

—— 1930b. 'Eine neue amerikanische Zeitschrift für Polizeiwissenschaft'. *Archiv für Kriminologie* 86:175–176.

—— 1930c. 'Der Mädchenhandel'. *Archiv für Kriminologie* 87:266.

—— 1932a. 'Enorme Rückfallsziffern in England; Schober†'. *Archiv für Kriminologie* 91:77.

—— 1932b. 'Schober als Kriminalist'. *Archiv für Kriminologie* 91: 197–199.

—— 1932c. 'Landeskriminalpolizei in USA?' *Archiv für Kriminologie* 90: 256–257.

—— 1932d. 'Das 'Internationale Kriminalpolizeiliche Bureau'. Nachwort zum vorigen Aufsatz'. *Archiv für Kriminologie* 90:105–107.

—— 1933. 'Lynchjustiz in USA'. *Archiv für Kriminologie* 93:18.

—— 1934. 'Einführung einer "Reichskriminalpolizei" in den Vereinigten Staaten von Amerika?' *Archiv für Kriminologie* 95:64–65.

—— 1935a. 'Die Erpresserbanden von New York, Von Th. E. Dewey, New York'. *Archiv für Kriminologie* 97:233–234.

—— 1935b. 'Die Deportation von Verbrechern nach den Kolonien'. *Archiv für Kriminologie* 96:4–6.

Heinrich, Edward O. 1934. [Review of Ronald Grassberger, 1933, *Gewerbs- und Berufsverbrechertum in den Vereinigten Staaten von Amerika*]. *Journal of Criminal Law and Criminology* 24:823–824.

Hellwig, Albert. 1909. 'Krimineller Aberglaube in Nordamerika'. *Archiv für Kriminal-Anthropologie und Kriminalistik* 33:186–189.

Henderson, Charles R. 1910. 'The International Prison Congress; The Significance of the International Prison Congress'. *Journal of the American Institute of Criminal Law and Criminology* 1:132–137; 342–343.

Herbert, Steve. 1997. *Policing Space: Territoriality and the Los Angeles Police Department*. Minneapolis, Minn: University of Minnesota Press.

—— 1998. 'Police Subculture Reconsidered'. *Criminology* 36(2):343–369.

—— 1999. 'The End of the Territorially-Sovereign State? The Case of Crime Control in the United States'. *Political Geography* 18:149–172.

Herr, Paul. 1907. *Das moderne amerikanische Besserungssystem*. Berlin: W. Kohlhammer.

Herzstein, Robert Edwin. 1989. *Roosevelt & Hitler: Prelude to War*. New York: Paragon House.

Heydrich, Reinhard. 1941. 'Der Anteil der Sicherheitspolizei und des SD an den Ordnungsmaßnahmen im mitteleuropäischen Raum'. *Die Deutsche Polizei* 9:237–238.

Heyman, Josiah M. 1995. 'Putting Power in the Anthropology of Bureaucracy: The Immigration and Naturalization Service at the Mexico-United States Border'. *Current Anthropology* 36:261–277.

Hildebrand, Klaus. 1973. *The Foreign Policy of the Third Reich*. Berkeley, Calif: University of California Press.

Hintrager, Oscar. 1900. *Amerikanisches Gefängnis- und Strafenwesen*. Tübingen: J.C.B. Mohr (Paul Siebeck).

Hirsch, Max. 1916. 'Ueber Kriegspsychose des Weibes'. *Deutsche Strafrechts-Zeitung* 3(3–4):134–137.

Hirschfeld, H., and Karl Vetter, eds. 1927. *Tausend Bilder: Grosse Polizei-Ausstellung Berlin 1926*. Berlin: Gersbach & Sohn.

Hirst, Paul, and Grahame Thompson. 1996. *Globalization in Question: The International Economy and the Possibilities of Governance*. Cambridge: Polity Press.

Hochstetler, Andrew L., and Neal Shover. 1997. 'Street Crime, Labor Surplus, and Criminal Punishment, 1980–1990'. *Social Problems* 44(3):358–368.

Hoefer, Frederick. 1945. 'The Nazi Penal System—I & II'. *Journal of Criminal Law and Criminology* 35:385–393; 36:30–38.

Hofman, Geza von. 1913. 'Sterilisierung der Minderwertigen im Staate Kalifornien.' *Archiv für Kriminal-Anthropologie und Kriminalistik* 53:337–341.

Hoffmann, Walter. 1937. *Internationale Falschgeldbekämpfung*. Inaugural-Dissertation: Thüringischen Landesuniversität, Jena.

Holborn, Hajo. 1982. *A History of Modern Germany, 1840–1945*. Princeton, NJ: Princeton University Press.

Holden, R.H. 1999. 'Securing Central America Against Communism: The United States and the Modernization of Surveillance in the Cold War'. *Journal of Interamerican Studies and World Affairs* 41(1):1–30.

Honig, Freidrich. 1936. 'Recent Changes in German Criminal Law'. *Journal of the American Institute of Criminal Law and Criminology* 26:857–861.

Hoover, J. Edgar. 1937. 'Report of Committee on Foreign Relations'. *Yearbook International Association of Chiefs of Police* (1936–1937): 208–209.

—— 1938a. 'Report of the Committee on Foreign Relations'. *Yearbook International Association of Chiefs of Police* (1937–38):158–159.

—— 1938b. 'Die Fingerabdruckregistratur und das Laboratorium beim Bundeskriminalpolizeiamt zu Washington'. *Archiv für Kriminologie* 102:221–223.

—— 1938c. 'Mord in einem Goldsucherlager von Alaska. Ein Fall aus der Praxis des Laboratoriums beim Bundeskriminalpolizeiamt zu Washington'. *Archiv für Kriminologie* 102:224–225.

—— 1938d. 'Versuche, das Fingerabdruckverfahren zu vereiteln'. *Archiv für Kriminologie* 103:84.

Horobin, Gordon. 1983. 'Professional Mystery: The Maintenance of Charisma in General Medical Practice'. Pp. 84–105 in *The Sociology of the Professions*, edited by Robert Dingwall and Philip Lewis. New York: St. Martin's Press.

Hourwich, I.A. 1912. 'Immigration and Crime'. *American Journal of Sociology* 17(4):478–489.

Houten, M.C. van. 1923. 'Internationale Zusammenarbeit auf kriminalpolizeilichem Gebiet'. *Archiv für Kriminologie* 75:41–46.

—— 1930. 'The International Co-operation of Criminal Police: Its History and Aims'. *The Police Journal* 3(4):482–497.

Huber, Ernst R. 1967. 'Zur Geschichte der politischen Polizei im 19. Jahrhundert'. Pp. 145–167 in *Nationalstaat und verfassungsstaat: Studien zur Geschichte der modernen Staatsidee*, Stuttgart: W. Kohlhammer.

Hubert, Rainer. 1990. *Schober: 'Arbeitermörder' und 'Hort der Republik'. Biographie eines Gestrigen*. Wien, Köln: Böhlau Verlag.

Huggins, Martha K. 1998. *Political Policing: The United States and Latin America*. Durham, NC: Duke University Press.

Hughes, Everett C. (1955) 1994. 'The *Gleichschaltung* of the German Statistical Yearbook'. Pp. 200–207 in *Everett C. Hughes on Work, Race, and the Sociological Imagination*, edited by Lewis A. Coser. Chicago: University of Chicago Press.

Hughes, Michael. 1992. *Early Modern Germany, 1477–1806*. Philadelphia, Pa: University of Pennsylvania Press.

Hunt, Alan. 1993. *Explorations in Law and Society*. New York: Routledge.

—— and Gary Wickham. 1994. *Foucault and Law. Towards a Sociology of Law as Governance*. London: Pluto Press.

International Association of Chiefs of Police. 1924. *Proceedings, 31st Convention, Montreal Canada, July 14–17, 1924*. International Association of Chiefs of Police.

—— 1925. *Proceedings, 32nd Convention, Indianapolis, Indiana, July 13–16, 1925*. International Association of Chiefs of Police.

—— 1926. *Proceedings, 33rd Convention, Chicago, Illinois, July 19–22, 1926*. International Association of Chiefs of Police.

—— 1929. *Proceedings, Thirty-sixth Convention, Atlanta, Georgia, June 3–6, 1929*. International Association of Chiefs of Police.

International Military Tribunal, Secretariat of the Tribunal. 1947–1949. *Trial of the Major War Criminals Before the International Military Tribunal, Nuremberg, 14 November 1945–1 October 1946*. (42 Volumes). Nuremberg: International Military Tribunal, Allied Control Authority for Germany.

International Police Conference. 1923. *Report of the Proceedings of the Third Annual Meeting, International Police Conference, New York City, New York, U.S.A., April 30 to May 5, 1923*. New York: Police Department, City of New York, Bureau of Printing.

—— 1924. *International Police Conference Code*. New York: International Police Conference, American Code Company.

—— 1925. *Membership International Police Conference*. New York: International Police Conference, Executive Offices.

Internationale Kriminalpolizeiliche Kommission. 1923. *Der Internationale Polizeikongreß in Wien (3. bis 7. September 1923)*. Wien: Im Selbstverlage der 'Öffentliche Sicherheit' Polizei-Rundschau.

—— 1924. *Beschlüsse der Internationalen kriminalpolizeilichen Kommission in Wien (Gefabt in der I. ordentlichen Tagung vom 19. bis 21. Mai 1924)*. Wien: Internationale Kriminalpolizeiliche Kommission (Printed, German & French).

—— 1926a. *Internationaler Polizei-Telegraphencode*. Wien: Internationale Kriminalpolizeiliche Kommission.

—— 1926b. *Beschlüsse der Internationalen kriminalpolizeilichen Kommission in Wien (Gefabt in der II. ordentlichen Tagung vom 26. bis 29. April 1926)*. Wien: Internationale Kriminalpolizeiliche Kommission (Printed, German & French).

—— 1926c. *Der Internationale Polizei-Kongreß Berlin 1926 (27. September bis 3. Oktober 1926). Stenographisches Protokoll der Verhandlungen*. Wien: Im Selbstverlage der 'Internationalen kriminalpolizeilichen Kommission'.

—— 1927. *Resolutions Passed by the International Criminal Police Commission in Vienna. At the 4th Ordinary Meeting Held at Amsterdam on July 6th-8th, 1927*. Wien: Internationale Kriminalpolizieliche Kommission (Printed, German & English).

—— 1928a. *La Coopération Internationale dans le Domaine de la Police Judiciaire*. Wien: Internationale Kriminalpolizeiliche Kommission.

—— 1928b. *Resolutions Passed by the International Criminal Police Commission in Vienna. At the 5th Ordinary Meeting at Berne on September*

10th–12th, 1928. Wien: Internationale Kriminalpolizieliche Kommission (Printed, German & English).

—— 1934. *Die internationale Zusammenarbeit auf kriminalpolizeilichem Gebiete. Handbuch herausgegeben von der Internationalen Kriminalpolizeilichen Kommission (Zweite umgearbeitete und vermehrte Auflage)*. Wien: Im Selbstverlage der 'Internationalen Kriminalpolizeilichen Kommission'.

Interpol. 2001. 'Terrorist Attack of 11 September 2001'. Resolution No AG–2001-RES–05. General Assembly, 70th Session, Budapest, September 24–28, 2001 (http://www.interpol.int/).

Interstate Conference on Crime. 1935. *Proceedings of Interstate Conference on Crime, Held at the State House, Trenton, N.J., October 11 and 12, 1935*. Trenton.

Isay, Ernst. 1923. *Das deutsche Fremdenrecht: Ausländer und Polizei*. Berlin: Georg Stilke.

Iwasiuk, Viktor. 1915. 'Die Mordwaffen des Komplotts gegen Erzherzog Franz Ferdinand'. *Archiv für Kriminal-Anthropologie und Kriminalistik* 63:99–104.

Jacobs, David, and Robert M. O'Brien. 1998. 'The Determinants of Deadly Force: A Structural Analysis of Police Violence'. *American Journal of Sociology* 103(4):837–862.

—— and Ronald E. Helms. 1997. 'Testing Coercive Explanations for Order: The Determinants of Law Enforcement Strength over Time'. *Social Forces* 75(4):1361–1392.

Jacoby, Henry. (1969) 1973. *The Bureaucratization of the World*. Berkeley, Calif: University of California Press.

James, Herman G. 1910. 'Draft of a New Criminal Code for the German Empire'. *Journal of the American Institute of Criminal Law and Criminology* 1:657–658.

—— 1913. *Principles of Prussian Administation*. New York: The Macmillan Company.

Janowitz, Morris. 1960. *The Professional Soldier*. Glencoe Ill: The Free Press of Glencoe.

—— 1991. *On Social Organization and Social Control*. Chicago: University of Chicago Press.

Jensen, Richard B. 1981. 'The International Anti-Anarchist Conference of 1898 and the Origins of Interpol'. *Journal of Contemporary History* 16(2):323–347.

Jeschke, Jürgen. 1971. 'INTERPOL zwischen 1933 und 1945'. *Kriminalistik* 25(3):118–119.

Johnson, David R. 1981. *American Law Enforcement: A History*. Arlington Heights, Ill: Forum Press.

Johnston, Les. 1992. *The Rebirth of Private Policing*. New York: Routledge.

—— 2000. 'Transnational Private Policing: The Impact of Global Commercial Security'. Pp. 21–42 in *Issues in Transnational Policing*, edited by J.W.E. Sheptycki. London: Routledge.

Jones, Nigel. 1992. *Hitler's Heralds: The Story of the Freikorps, 1918–1923*. New York: Dorset Press.

Jörgensen, Hakon. 1922. 'Berlinographie und Fernidentifizierung'. *Archiv für Kriminologie* 74:255–261.

—— 1923a. 'Das drahtlose Telephon im Dienste der Kriminalpolizei; Shaw über das heutige Strafsystem'. *Archiv für Kriminologie* 75:156–158.

—— 1923b. 'Die Polizeikonferenz in New York und Boston'. *Archiv für Kriminologie* 75:153–154.

—— 1923c. 'Bericht über die II. Internationale Polizeikonferenz in New York'. *Archiv für Kriminologie* 75:310–311.

Journal du Droit International Privé. 1914. 'Congrès de police judiciaire internationale'. *Journal du Droit International Privé* 41:1416.

Journal of the American Institute of Criminal Law and Criminology. 1928. [Review of H. Hirschfeld and Karl Vetter, 1927, *Tausend Bilder*]. *Journal of the American Institute of Criminal Law and Criminology* 19:288.

—— 1929. '(Reviews, Verwaltungsbericht des Polizeipräsidiums Leipzig vom 1. Oktober 1922–31. Dezember 1927; Willy Gay, 1928, Die Preussische Landeskriminalpolizei)'. *Journal of the American Institute of Criminal Law and Criminology* 20:158–159.

Jung, Hermann. 1926. 'Das Ausland auf der Internationalen Polizeitechnischen Ausstellung in Karlsruhe 1925. Ein abschließender Rückblick'. *Deutsches Polizei-Archiv* 5:137–138.

Kamps. 1918. 'Das internationale Strafrecht und Strafverfahrensrecht im besetzten Gebiet'. *Deutsche Strafrechts-Zeitung* 5(11–12):342–347.

Kavanaugh, A.J. 1933. 'Police Organization'. *Public Management* 15(12): 363–364.

Kb. 1935. 'Polizeiarbeit von Staat zu Staat! Randbemerkungen zu einer internationalen Tagung'. *Der Deutsche Polizeibeamte* 3:888–889.

Keffer, Alfred. 1927. 'Organisation der Polizei in Belgien'. Pp. 71–73 in *Große Polizei-Ausstellung Berlin in Wort und Bild*, edited by Alexander Daranyi and Oskar Daranyi. Wien: Internationale Öffentliche Sicherheit.

Keller, William W. 1989. *The Liberals and J. Edgar Hoover: Rise and Fall of a Domestic Intelligence State*. Princeton, NJ: Princeton University Press.

Kettner, Matthias. 1997. 'Thesen zur Bedeutung des Globalisierungsbegriffs'. *Deutsche Zeitschrift für Philosophie* 45(6):903–918.

Kirchheimer, Otto. 1938. 'Recent Trends in German Treatment of Juvenile Delinquency.' *Journal of Criminal Law and Criminology* 29:362–370.

Klosek, Jacqueline. 1999. 'The Development of International Police Cooperation within the EU and Between the EU and Third Party States: A Discussion of the Legal Bases of Such Cooperation and the Problems and Promises Resulting Thereof'. *American University International Law Review* 14:599656.

Knemeyer, Franz-Ludwig. 1978. 'Polizei'. Pp. 875–897 in *Geschichtliche Grundbegriffe*, edited by Otto Brunner, Werner Conze, and Reinhart Koselleck. Stuttgart: Klett-Cotta.

—— 1980. 'Polizei'. *Economy and Society* 9(2):172–196.

Koenig, Daniel J., and Dilip K. Das, eds. 2001. *International Police Cooperation: A World Perspective*, edited by Lanham, Md: Lexington Books.

Kraft, B. 1931. 'Der Chicagoer Massenmord am 14. Februar 1929 ('The Valentine Day Massacre'). Ein Schießsachverständigengutachten von Oberst Calvin Goddard, Direktor des Scientific Crime Detection Laboratory, Northwestern University, Chicago, Illinois'. *Archiv für Kriminologie* 88:44–63.

Kraska, Peter B., and Victor E. Kappeler. 1997. 'Militarizing American Police: The Rise and Normalization of Paramilitary Units'. *Social Problems* 44(1):1–18.

Krausnick, Helmut, Hans Buchheim, Martin Broszat, and Hans-Adolf Jacobsen. 1968. *Anatomy of the SS State*. New York: Walker and Company.

Krausnick, Helmut, and Hans-Heinrich Wilhelm. 1981. *Die Truppe des Weltanschauungskrieges: Die Einsatzgruppen der Sicherheitspolizei und des SD, 1938–1942*. Stuttgart: Deutsche Verlags-Anstalt.

Kriminalpolizei. 1937. 'Kriminalpolizeiliche Zusammenarbeit, Mit dem Auslande'. Pp. 16–14 in *Kriminalpolizei: Sammlung für die kriminalpolizeiliche Organisation und Tätigkeit geltenden Bestimmungen und Anordnungen*, edited by Die Polizei und Der Gendarm. Berlin: Kameradschaft Verlagsgesellschaft Gersbach & Co.

Kuhlman, A.F. 1928. [Review of Walter Luz, 1927, *Das Verbrechen in der Darstellung des Verbrechers*]. *Journal of the American Institute of Criminal Law and Criminology* 19:106–109.

Kuhn, Arthur K. 1911. [Review of F. Meili, 1910, *Lehrbuch des internationalen Strafrechts und Strafprozessrechts*]. *Journal of the American Institute of Criminal Law and Criminology* 1:829–830.

—— 1934. 'International Cooperation in the Suppression of Crime'. *American Journal of International Law* 28(3):541–544.

La Fontaine, M.H. 1911. 'The Work Done by Private Initiative in the Organisation of the World'. Pp. 243–254 in *Papers on Inter-Racial Problems*, edited by G. Spiller. London: P.S. King & Son.

Lacombe, Dany. 1996. 'Reforming Foucault: A Critique of the Social Control Thesis'. *British Journal of Sociology* 47(2):332–352.

Lancaster, Lane W. 1932. [Review of William C. van Vleck, 1932, *The Administrative Control of Aliens*]. *Journal of Criminal Law and Criminology* 23:694–695.

Landecker, Werner S. 1941. 'Criminology in Germany'. *Journal of Criminal Law and Criminology* 31:551–575.

Langer, William L. 1971. *The Revolutions of 1848*. New York: Harper Torchbooks.

Langum, David J. 1994. *Crossing over the Line: Legislating Morality and the Mann Act*. Chicago: University of Chicago Press.

League of Nations. (1919a) 1936. 'Covenant of the League of Nations'. Pp. 159–168 in *A Brief History of the League of Nations*. 1936 Edition. New York: The League of Nations Association.

—— (1919b) 1924. 'Treaty of Versailles'. Pp. 3–263 in *The Treaties of Peace, 1919–1923*. Vol. I. New York: Carnegie Endowment for International Peace.

—— 1927a. *Report of the Special Body of Experts on Traffic in Women and Children. Part One*. Geneva: Publications of the League of Nations.

—— 1927b. *Report of the Special Body of Experts on Traffic in Women and Children. Part Two*. Geneva: Publications of the League of Nations.

Lee, Peter G. 1976. *Interpol*. New York: Stein and Day.

Leibig, P. 1936. 'XII. Ordentliche Tagung der Internationalen Kriminalpolizeilichen Kommission in Belgrad von 25. Mai bis 4. Juni 1936'. *Die Polizei* 33:266–270.

Leiser, Clara. 1938. 'A Director of a Nazi Prison Speaks Out'. *Journal of Criminal Law and Criminology* 29:345–352.

Leo, Richard A. 1996. 'Police Scholarship for the Future: Resisting the Pull of the Policy Audience'. Review Essay. *Law & Society Review* 30(4): 865–879.

Liang, Hsi-Huey. 1970. *The Berlin Police Force in the Weimar Republic*. Berkeley, CA: University of California Press.

—— 1992. *The Rise of the Modern Police and the European State System from Metternich to the Second World War*. New York: Cambridge University Press.

Lichtenstein, Heiner. 1990. *Himmlers grüne Helfer: Die Schutz- und Ordnungspolizei im 'Dritten Reich'*. Köln: Bund-Verlag.

Liepelt, Adolf. 1938. *Über den Umfang und die Bedeutung der Polizeigewalt im nationalsozialistischen Staat*. Würzburg: Konrad Triltsch.

Lind, John E. 1922. 'The Cross-Examination of the Alienist'. *Journal of the American Institute of Criminal Law and Criminology* 13:228–234.

Lindsey, Edward. 1910. 'International American Scientific Congress, at Buenos Aires'. *Journal of the American Institute of Criminal Law and Criminology* 1:464.

Liska, Allen E. 1997. 'Modeling the Relationships Between Macro Forms of Social Control'. *Annual Review of Sociology* 23:39–61.

Liszt, Elsa von 1906.'"Children" Courts in the United States (Samuel J. Barrows, 1904)'. *Archiv für Kriminal-Anthropologie und Kriminalistik* 26:81–92.

Locard, Edmond. 1914. 'Ier Congrès de Police Judiciaire Internationale (Monaco)'. *Archives d'Anthropologie Criminelle* 29:523–528.

Loening, Edgar. 1910. 'Polizei'. Pp. 842–851 in *Handwörterbuch der Staatswissenschaften*, Volume 6, edited by J. Conrad, L. Elster, W. Lexis and E. Loening. Jena: Gustav Fischer.

Loock, Walter. 1893. *Der strafrechtliche Schutz der Eisenbahnen im Deutschen Reiche*. Berlin: J. Gutentag.

Lowenthal, Max. 1950. *The Federal Bureau of Investigation*. New York: Harcourt Brace Jovanovich.

Lüdtke, Alf. 1982. *'Gemeinwohl', Polizei und 'Festungspraxis': Staatliche Gewaltsamkeit und innere Verwaltung in Preußen, 1815–1850*. Göttingen: Vandenhoeck & Rupprecht.

—— ed. 1992a. *'Sicherheit' und 'Wohlfahrt': Polizei, Gesellschaft und Herrschaft im 19. und 20. Jahrhundert*. Frankfurt: Suhrkamp.

—— 1992b. 'Einleitung: "Sicherheit" und "Wohlfahrt". Aspekte der Polizeigeschichte'. Pp. 7–33 in *'Sicherheit' und 'Wohlfahrt'*, edited by Alf Lüdtke. Frankfurt: Suhrkamp.

Lyon, F. Emory. 1931. 'Tenth International Prison Congress'. *Journal of the American Institute of Criminal Law and Criminology* 21:499–503.

Lyotard, Jean-François. (1979) 1984. *The Postmodern Condition: A Report on Knowledge*. Minneapolis: University of Minnesota Press.

Lyttleton, Edith. 1928. 'Der Frauen- und Mädchenhandel'. *Nord und Süd* 51:38–42.

McAdoo, William, 1909. 'The London Police from a New York Point of View'. *The Century Magazine* 78(5):649–670.

McCaffrey, George H. 1913. 'Report of the President of the International Association of Chiefs of Police'. *Journal of the American Institute of Criminal Law and Criminology* 3:803–804.

McClaughry, R.W. 1893. 'Police Protection at the World's Fair, I'. *The North American Review* 156:711–713.

MacDonald, Arthur. 1910. 'Criminal Statistics in Germany, France and England'. *Journal of the American Institute of Criminal Law and Criminology* 1:59–70.

MacDonald, Callum. 1989. *The Killing of SS Obergrupenführer Reinhard Heydrich*. New York: The Free Press.

Macdonald, Keith M. 1995. *The Sociology of the Professions*. London: Sage.

McDonald, William F., ed. 1997a. *Crime and Law Enforcement in the Global Village*. Cincinnati, Ohio: Anderson Publishing.

—— 1997b. 'Crime and Justice in the Global Village: Towards Global Criminology'. Pp. 3–22 in *Crime and Law Enforcement in the Global Village*, edited by W.F. McDonald. Cincinnatti, Ohio: Anderson.

—— 1997c. 'Illegal Immigration'. Pp. 65–86 in *Crime and Law Enforcement in the Global Village*, edited by W.F. McDonald. Cincinnatti, Ohio: Anderson.

—— 1997d. 'Crime and Illegal Immigration'. *National Institute of Justice Journal* (232):2–10.

McMurtrie, Douglas C. 1913. 'Die konträre Sexualempfindung des Weibes in den Vereinigten Staaten von Amerika'. *Archiv für Kriminal-Anthropologie und Kriminalistik* 55:141–147.

McRae, Rob, and Don Hubert. 2001. *Human Security And The New Diplomacy: Protecting People, Promoting Peace*. Montreal: McGill-Queen's University Press.

Maguire, Edward R, and Rebecca Schulte-Murray. 2001. 'Issues and Patterns in the Comparative International Study of Police Strength'. *International Journal of Comparative Sociology* 42(1–2):75–100.

Mander, Linden A. 1941. 'The International Prevention of Crime'. Pp. 38–103 in his *Foundations of Modern World Society*. Stanford, Calif: Stanford University Press.

Manning, Peter K. 1977. *Police Work: The Social Organization of Policing*. Cambridge, Mass: MIT Press.

—— 2000. 'Policing New Social Spaces'. Pp. 177–200 in *Issues in Transnational Policing*, edited by J.W.E. Sheptycki. London: Routledge.

Marabuto, Paul. 1935. *La Collaboration Policière Internationale en Vue de la Prévention et de la Répression de la Criminalité: Les Institutions Internationales de Police*. Nice: École Professionnelle Don-Bosco (Thèse pour le Doctorat en Droit, Université de Lyon).

Marenin, Otwin, ed. 1995. *Policing Change, Changing Police: International Perspectives*. New York: Garland Publishers.

Marenin, Otwin. 2001. 'United States International Policing Activities: An Overview'. Pp. 297–320 in *International Police Cooperation: A World Perspective*, edited by Daniel Koenig and Dilip Das. Lanham, Md: Lexington Books.

Martin, William G., and Mark Beittel. 1998. 'Toward a Global Sociology? Evaluating Current Conceptions, Methods, and Practices'. *Sociological Quarterly* 39(1):139–161.

Marx, Gary T. 1981. 'Ironies of Social Control'. *Social Problems* 28: 221–246.

—— 1988. *Undercover: Police Surveillance in America*. Berkeley, Calif: University of California Press.

—— 1993. 'The Neglect and Importance of Cross-Border Studies of Policing'. *Onati Proceedings* 14:77–88.

—— 1995a. 'Undercover in Comparative Perspective: Some Implications for Knowledge and Social Research'. Pp. 323–337 in *Undercover: Police Surveillance in Comparative Perspective*, edited by Cyrille Fijnaut and Gary T. Marx. The Hague: Kluwer Law International.

—— 1995b. 'Police and Democracy'. In *The Encyclopedia of Democracy*. Seymour M. Lipset, editor in chief. Washington, DC: Congressional Quarterly.

—— 1997. 'Social Control Across Borders'. Pp. 23–39 in *Crime and Law Enforcement in the Global Village*, edited by W.F. McDonald. Cincinnati, Ohio: Anderson Publishing.

—— and Mathieu Deflem. 1993. 'The Relevance and Irrelevance of Classical Theory to Cross-Border Social Control'. Paper presented at the annual meeting of the American Society of Criminology, Phoenix, November 1993.

Marx, Karl. (1846) 1978. 'The German Ideology: Part I' Pp. 146–202 in *The Marx-Engels Reader*, edited by Robert C. Tucker. New York: Norton.

—— (1853) 1979. 'The Berlin Conspiracy'. Pp. 28–31 in *Marx Engels Collected Works*, Volume 12. New York: International Publishers.

Maürer, W. 1925. 'Ausweisungsrecht gegenüber Ausländer'. *Die Polizei* 21:105–107.

Mawby, R I. 1990. *Comparative Policing Issues: The British and American Experience in International Perspective*. London: Unwi Hyman.

—— ed. 1999. *Policing Across The World: Issues for the Twenty-First Century*. London: University College London Press.

Mead, George H. 1929. 'National-mindedness and International-mindedness'. *International Journal of Ethics* 39(4):385–407.

Meinert, F. 1939a. 'Das Strafverfahren in England und in den Vereinigten Staaten von Nordamerika'. *Die Polizei* 36:29–30.

—— 1939b. 'Strafverfolgung und Starfverfahren im englischen, schottischen und nordamerikanischen Recht'. *Archiv für Kriminologie* 105:28–36, 90–97,133–139.

Meldal-Johnsen, Trevor and Vaughn Young. 1979. *The Interpol Connection: An Inquiry into the International Criminal Police Organization*. New York: The Dial Press.

Melossi, Dario. 1990. *The State of Social Control*. Cambridge: Polity Press.

Meyer, Fr. von. 1938. 'Ein amerikanischer Kriminalbeamter erzählt'. *Die Deutsche Polizei* 6:31–32.

Meyer, John W., and Brian Rowan. 1977. 'Institutionalized Organizations: Formal Structure as Myth and Ceremony'. *American Journal of Sociology* 83(2):340–363.

—— John Boli, George M. Thomas, and Francisco O. Ramirez. 1997. 'World Society and the Nation-State'. *American Journal of Sociology* 103(1):144–181.

Millspaugh, Arthur C. 1937. *Crime Control by the National Government*. Washington, DC: The Brookings Institute.

Möllmann, Heinrich. 1969. *Internationale Kriminalpolizei—Polizei des Völkerrechts? Zur Problematik der Abgrenzung öffentlicher und privater internationaler Organisationen am Beispiel der Internationalen Kriminal-polizeilichen Organisation (IKPO -Interpol)*. Inaugural-Dissertation: Julius-Maximilians-Universität, Würzburg.

Mommsen, Wolfgang J. 1989. *The Political and Social Theory of Max Weber*. Chicago: University of Chicago Press.

Monfigny, von. 1931. 'Aus fremden Polizeien. Reiseeindrücke von der finnischen Polizei'. *Die Polizei* 28:17–19.

Moore, Wilbert E. 1966. 'Global Sociology: The World as a Singular System'. *American Journal of Sociology* 71(5):475–482.

Morlang, Thomas. 1994. 'Die Polizeitruppe Deutsch-Neuguineas, 1887–1914'. *Archiv für Polizeigeschichte* 5(1):8–15.

Morris, Warren B. 1982. *The Weimar Republic and Nazi Germany*. Chicago: Nelson-Hall.

Müller, G. 1933. 'Die Ostjudenfrage als fremdenpolizeiliches Problem'. *Die Polizei* 30:230–232.

Murray, Topsy, Robert Dingwall, and John Eekelaar. 1983. 'Professionals in Bureaucracies: Solicitors in Private Practice and Local Government'. Pp. 195–220 in *The Sociology of the Professions*, edited by Robert Dingwall and Philip Lewis. New York: St. Martin's Press.

Näcke, P. 1903a. 'Ein interessantes amerikanisches Urtheil über Lombroso'. *Archiv für Kriminal-Anthropologie und Kriminalistik* 10:287–288.

—— 1903b. 'Ein amerikanischer Blaubart'. *Archiv für Kriminal-Anthropologie und Kriminalistik* 13:295–296.

—— 1909. 'Die Verschiedenartigkeit der Neger'. *Archiv für Kriminal-Anthropologie und Kriminalistik* 33:179.

—— 1913. 'Amerikanische Tricks beim Mädchenhandel'. *Archiv für Kriminal-Anthropologie und Kriminalistik* 55:364.

Nadelmann, Ethan A. 1990. 'Global Prohibition Regimes: The Evolution of Norms in International Society'. *International Organization* 44(4):479–526.

Nadelmann, Ethan A. 1993. *Cops Across Borders: The Internationalization of U.S. Criminal Law Enforcement*. University Park, Pa: Pennsylvania State University Press.

National Archives, Washington, DC, *Collection of Foreign Records Seized, 1941- (Record Group 242): Records of the Reich Leader of the SS and Chief of the German Police (RLSS)*. Microfilm T–175. 678 rolls (Room 400, cabinet U). Index: Guides to German Records Microfilmed at Alexandria, VA, Volumes No. 32, 33, 39 & 81, published by the American Historical Association, Committee for the Study of War Documents and National Archives and Records Service, Washington, DC, 1961–1982.

—— *Collection of Foreign Records Seized, 1941- (Record Group 242): Records of the German Foreign Office Received by the Department of State (GFO)*. Microfilm T–120. 5,779 rolls (Room 400, cabinet 158, drawer 6). Index: A Catalog of Files and Microfilms of the German Foreign Ministry Archives 1920–1945, 3 volumes, edited by George O. Kent, published by the Hoover Institution, Stanford University, Stanford, Calif, 1962.

—— *General Records of the Department of State (Record Group 59): Records of the Department of State Relating to Internal Affairs of Germany, 1910–1929 (IAG)*. Microfilm M–336. 955 rolls (Room 400, cabinet 555). Index: Records of the Department of State Relating to Internal Affairs of Germany, 1910–1929, published by National Archives and Records Service, Washington, DC, 1971.

—— *Records of the Federal Bureau of Investigation (Record Group 65): Investigative Case Files of the Bureau of Investigation, 1908–1922 (ICF)*.

Microfilm M–1085 (Room 400, cabinet 139, drawer 1). Index: Investigative Case Files of the Bureau of Investigation, 1908–1922, published by the National Archives Trust Fund Board, National Archives and Record Service, Washington, DC, 1983.

—— *Records of the U.S. Office of Strategic Services (Record Group 226): Foreign Nationalities Branch Files, 1942–1945 (FNB)*. Microfiche C0002. 2,450 fiche (Room 400, cabinet C, drawer 5). Index: U.S. Office of Strategic Services, Foreign Nationalities Branch Files, 1942–1945, 2 volumes, published by Congressional Information Service, Bethesda, Md, 1988.

—— *Records of the War Department General and Special Staffs (Record Group 165): Military Intelligence Division Correspondence, 1917–1941 (MID)*. Hard copy. Approximately 1,920 boxes (on request). Indexes: name index microfilm M–1194 (262 rolls, Room 400, cabinet 128, drawer 04); country index microfilm M–1271 (5 rolls, Room 400, cabinet 077, drawer 02); subject card index (900,000 cards, on request).

National Commission on Law Enforcement and Social Justice. 1977. *Interpol: Facts vs. Fallacies*. Toronto: National Commission on Law Enforcement and Social Justice.

National Police Convention. 1871. *Official Proceedings of the National Police Convention, Held at the City of Saint Louis, Missouri, on the 20th, 21st and 23rd Days of October, 1871*. St. Louis: R. & T.A. Ennis.

Nebe, Arthur and Willy Fleischer. 1939. *Organisation und Meldedienst der Reichskriminalpolizei*. Berlin: Kriminal-Wissenschaft und -Praxis Verlag Elise Jaedicke.

New York Times, The. 1909. 'Nations Uniting to Stamp Out the Use of Opium and Many Other Drugs'. *The New York Times* (July 25).

Ng-Quinn, Michael. 1990. 'Function-Oriented and Functionally Indirect Expansion as Bureaucratic Responses to Modernization: The Case of the Royal Hong Kong Police'. *Public Administration and Development* 10:101–117.

Noakes, John. 1996. 'The FBI and the Transition to Modern Means of Social Control.' Paper presented at the annual meeting of the American Sociological Association, New York, August 1996.

Noble, Iris. 1975. *Interpol: International Crime Fighter*. New York: Harcourt Brace Jovanovich.

O'Malley, Pat. 1997. 'Policing, Politics and Postmodernity'. *Social & Legal Studies* 6(3):363–381.

O'Reilly, Kenneth. 1987. 'Bureaucracy and Civil Liberties: The FBI Story'. Pp. 109–119 in *Bureaucracy Against Democracy and Socialism*, edited by Ronald M. Glassman, William H. Swatos, and Paul L. Rosen. New York: Greenwood Press.

Overstreet, Harry, and Bonaro Overstreet. 1969. *The FBI in Our Open Society*. New York: W.W. Norton & Company.

P.P.D. 1938. 'Existiert Paris eigentlich noch?; 2,36 Millionen Ausländer sahen Deutschland'. *Die Deutsche Polizei* 6:32,271.

Paetsch. 1928a. 'Die amerikanische Polizei'. *Die Polizei* 25:3942.

—— 1928b. 'Technische Ausrüstung der amerikanischen Polizei'. *Die Polizei* 25:113–115,141–142.

—— 1929. 'Ausbildungsfragen bei europäischen Polizeien'. *Die Polizei* 26:481–484.

—— and Voit. 1927. *Amerikanische Polizei: Erfahrungsbericht der Amerika-Reise des Ober-Regierungsrats Paetsch und des Polizei-Oberstleutnants Voit*. Original type-written manuscript.

Page, Edward C. 1985. *Political Authority and Bureaucratic Power*. Knoxville, Tenn: University of Tennessee Press.

Paillard, Georges, and Claude Rougerie. 1973. *Reinhard Heydrich (Protecteur de Bohême et Moravie): Le Violoniste de la Mort*. Paris: Fayard.

Palitzsch, H. 1926a. *Die Bekämpfung des internationalen Verbrechertums*. Hamburg: Otto Meissners Verlag.

—— 1926b. 'Internationale Verkehrssprache der Polizei'. *Die Polizei* 23:92.

—— 1926c. 'Die zweite ordentliche tagung der Internationalen kriminalpolizeilichen Kommission in Wien'. *Die Polizei* 23:353–354.

—— 1926d. 'Die Tagung der Deutschen kriminalpolizeilichen Kommission in Berlin'. *Die Polizei* 23:639–641.

—— 1927a. 'Die Internationale Kriminalpolizeiliche Kommission in Amsterdam'. *Die Polizei* 24:383–384.

—— 1927b. 'Internationale Verbrecher und ihre Bekämpfung'. Pp. 197–201 in *Große Polizei-Ausstellung Berlin in Wort und Bild*, edited by Alexander Daranyi and Oskar Daranyi. Wien: Internationale Öffentliche Sicherheit.

—— 1928. 'Die 5. Tagung der Internationalen Kriminalpolizeilichen Kommission'. *Die Polizei* 25:654–656.

—— 1930. 'Gibt as eine "Internationale Organisation der Verbrecher"?' *Die Polizei* 27:216.

Palm. 1934. 'Die Aufgaben der Polizei im Dritten Reich—ein Beitrag zum Kampf gegen die Reaktion'. *Der Deutsche Polizeibeamte* 2:366–368.

Parsons, Talcott. (1961) 1969. 'Order and Community in the International Social System'. In his *Politics and Social Structure*. New York: The Free Press.

—— (1964) 1967. 'Evolutionary Universals in Society'. Pp. 490–520 in his *Sociological Theory and Modern Society*. New York: The Free Press.

Pasquino, Pasquale. 1991a. 'Theatrum Politicum: The Genealogy of Capital—Police and the State of Prosperity'. Pp. 105–118 in *The Foucault Effect*, edited by Graham Burchell, Colin Gordon and Peter Miller. Chicago: University of Chicago Press.

—— 1991b. 'Criminology: The Birth of a Special Knowledge'. Pp. 235–250 in *The Foucault Effect*, edited by Graham Burchell, Colin Gordon and Peter Miller. Chicago: University of Chicago Press.

Pätzold, Kurt, and Erika Schwarz. 1992. *Tagesordnung: Judenmord. Die Wannsee-Konferenz am 20. Januar 1942: Eine Dokumentation zur Organisation der 'Endlösung'*. Berlin: Metropol.

Pearce, F., and M. Woodiwiss, eds. 1993. *Global Crime Connections: Dynamics and Control*. Basingstoke, England: Macmillan.

Pella, Vespasien V. 1928. *La Coopération des États dans la Lutte Contre le Faux Monnayage*. Paris: Rapport et Projet de Convention Présentés a la Société des Nation.

Perritt, Henry H. 1999. 'Policing International Peace and Security: International Police Forces'. *Wisconsin International Law Journal* 17:281–324.

Peterssen. 1940. 'Die Arbeit der Verwaltung eines Polizeibataillons in Polen'. *Die Deutsche Polizei* 8:23–24.

Petrow, Stefan. 1994. *Policing Morals: The Metropolitan Police and the Home Office, 1870–1914*. Oxford: Clarendon Press.

Pierhal, Armand. 1939. ' "G"-Männer gegen Gangster'. *Die Auslese* 13:29–31.

Pinkerton, Allan. (1883) 1989. *The Spy of the Rebellion*. Lincoln, NE: University of Nebraska Press.

Pinkerton, William A. 1905. 'Amerikanische Bankräuber'. *Archiv für Kriminal-Anthropologie und Kriminalistik* 18:223–234.

Ploscowe, Morris. 1936. 'The Organization for the Enforcement of the Criminal law in France, Germany and England'. *Journal of Criminal Law and Criminology* 27:305–327.

Poetzsch, Fritz. 1925. 'Vom Staatsleben unter der Weimarer Verfassung (vom 1. Januar 1920 bis 31. Dezember 1924)'. *Jahrbuch des Öffentlichen Rechts der Gegenwart* 13:1–238.

Police Chiefs' News Letter. 1934. 'Exchange of Criminal Data with Foreign Countries'. *Police Chiefs' News Letter* 1(7):1.

—— 1936. 'Deporting Criminal Aliens'. *Police Chiefs' News Letter* 3(1):1.

—— 1938. 'South Africa now Represented in IACP'. *Police Chiefs' News Letter* 5(4):4.

—— 1939. 'Trend and Distribution of IACP Memberships, May 1, 1939'. *Police Chiefs' News Letter* 6(5):1.

Police Magazine. 1925. 'A New Immigration Plan'. *Police Magazine* 2(6):62–64.

Polizei-Ausstellung Berlin. 1926a. *Almanach zum Polizeiball am 2. Oktober 1926*. Berlin.

—— 1926b. *Grosse Polizei-Ausstellung Berlin 1926: Prospekt*. Berlin: W. Büxenstein.

Polizeipräsident von Berlin, Der. *Amtliche Nachrichten*, 1899–1941. Printed internal reports ('nur für den Dienstgebrauch'). Published by Der Polizeipräsident von Berlin, Berlin.

Pounds, Norman. 1985. *An Historical Geography of Europe, 1800–1914*. Cambridge: Cambridge University Press.

Poveda, Tony G. 1990. *Lawlessness and Reform: The FBI in Transition*. Pacific Grove, CA: Brooks/Cole Publishing.

Powers, Le Grand. 1917. 'Comparative Costs of European and American Police'. *Journal of the American Institute of Criminal Law and Criminology* 7:918–919.

Powers, Richard G. 1987. *Secrecy and Power: The Life of J. Edgar Hoover*. New York: The Free Press.

Preston, William Jr. (1963) 1994. *Aliens and Dissenters: Federal Suppression of Radicals, 1903–1933*. 2nd edition. Urbana, Ill: University of Illinois Press.

Preuss, Lawrence. 1936. 'Punishment by Analogy in National Socialist Penal Law'. *Journal of Criminal Law and Criminology* 26:847–856.

Radzinowicz, Leon. 1991. *The Roots of the International Association of Criminal Law and Their Significance*. Freiburg: Max-Planck-Intsitut für ausländisches und internationales Strafrecht.

Raeff, Marc. 1975. 'The Well-Ordered Police State and the Development of Modernity in Seventeenth- and Eighteenth-Century Europe: An Attempt at a Comparative Approach'. *American Historical Review* 80(5):1221–1243.

Ranck, Chr. 1926. *Neuere amerikanische Gafängnisbauten: Bericht über eine im Jahre 1926 ausgeführte Studienreise*. Hamburg: Original manuscript.

Raper, A. 1932. 'Amerikanische Lynchjustiz neuerdings im Zunehmen?' *Archiv für Kriminologie* 90:22–23.

Ratcliffe. 1932a. 'Aus fremden Polizeien: Chicago kein Verbrecherparadies? (France, Netherlands, England)'. *Die Polizei* 29:240.

—— 1932b. 'Polizeiliches aus Afrika'. *Die Polizeipraxis* 8:437.

—— 1932c. 'Aus fremden Polizeien: Eine Akademie für Kriminologie in Chicago; Lehrgange für Polizeibeamte an der Universität von Süd-Kalifornien (England)'. *Die Polizei* 29:62–63.

—— 1932d. 'Aus fremden Polizeien (London, Hungary)'. *Die Polizei* 29:113.

—— 1932e. 'Aus fremden Polizeien: Ansprache des Präsidenten Hoover and die Jahresversammlung der amerikanischer Polizeiführer (Belgium, Paris, France)'. *Die Polizei* 29:209–210.

Rau, K.H. 1853. 'Ueber Begriff und Wesen der Polizei'. *Zeitschrift für die gesammte Staatswissenschaft* 1853(9):605–625.

Reader's Digest Association. 1982. *Great Cases of Interpol*. Selected by the Editors of Reader's Digest. Pleasantville, NY: The Reader's Digest Association.

Rechert, Emil. 1912. 'Ein Raubmord in Chicago vor den Wiener Geschworenen'. *Archiv für Kriminal-Anthropologie und Kriminalistik* 48:354–370.

Reiner, Robert. 1985. *The Politics of Police*. New York: St. Martin's Press.

Reinsch, Paul S. 1916. *Public International Unions: Their Work and Organization*. Boston: World Peace Foundation.

Reitlinger, Gerald. (1957) 1989. *The SS: Alibi of a Nation, 1922–1945*. New York: Da Capo.

Renborg, Bertil A. 1942. 'Narcotic Drugs—International Administration'. Pp. 99–111 in *World Organization: A Balance Sheet of the First Great Experiment*. Washington, DC: American Council on Public Affairs.

Rhee, C.H. van. 1999. 'Geschiedenis van het Deurwaardersambt: Van "Nederige Dienaar" tot Zelfbewuste Professional'. *Justitiële Verkenningen* 25(3):88–102.

Richter, Hans. 1941. *Einsatz der Polizei: Bei den Polizeibataillonen in Ost, Nord und West*. Berlin: Zentralverlag der NSDAP, France Eher Nachfolger.

Riege, Paul. 1930a. 'Aus fremden Polizeien (France)'. *Die Polizei* 27:202.

—— 1930b. 'Aus fremden Polizeien: Moderne Polizeieinrichtungen in Amerika (Memelland)'. *Die Polizei* 27:586–587.

—— 1930c. 'Aus fremden Polizeien (England, France, Holland, Austria, Yugoslavia, Czechoslovakia)'. *Die Polizei* 27:23–24.

—— 1931a. 'Aus fremden Polizeien (Spain)'. *Die Polizei* 28:40–41.

—— 1931b. 'Aus fremden Polizeien: Amerika (Vereinigte Staaten) (England)'. *Die Polizei* 28:90–91.

—— 1931c. 'Aus fremden Polizeien: New York (Denmark, England)'. *Die Polizei* 28:359–360.

—— 1966. *Kleine Polizei-Geschichte*. Lübeck: Georg Schmidt-Römhild.

Roberts, Gilmore. 1925. 'Some Immigration Facts: Controlling the Distribution of Aliens Has a Vital Bearing on All Plans for Preserving Law and Order'. *Police Magazine* 3(2):76–79.

Robertson, Roland. 1990. 'Mapping the Global Condition: Globalization as the Central Concept'. *Theory, Culture and Society* 7(2):15–30.

—— 1992. *Globalization: Social Theory and Global Culture*. London: Sage.

—— 1995. 'Globalization: Time-Space and Homogeneity-Heterogeneity'. Pp. 25–44 in *Global Modernities*, edited by Mike Featherstone, Scott Lash, and Ronald Robertson. London: Sage.

—— and Habib H. Khondker. 1998. 'Discourses of Globalization: Preliminary Considerations'. *International Sociology* 13(1):25–40.

Robinson, Cyril D., and Richard Scaglion. 1987. 'The Origin and Evolution of the Police Function in Society'. *Law & Society Review* 21(1):109–153.

Robinson, William I. 1998. 'Beyond Nation-State Paradigms: Globalization, Sociology, and the Challenge of Transnational Studies'. *Sociological Forum* 13(4):561–594.

Roenneke, Werner. 1936. 'Luftverkehr und Auslandsdeutschtum'. *Der Deutsche Polizeibeamte* 4:705–706.

—— 1937a. 'Polizeiliches aus USA'. *Der Deutsche Polizeibeamte* 5: 453–454.

—— 1937b. 'Bescheinigungen für das Ausland'. *Der Deutsche Polizeibeamte* 5:132–133.

—— 1937c. 'Mit Flugzeug und Luftschiff im Lande der Wolkenkratzer'. *Der Deutsche Polizeibeamte* 5:155–156.

Roesner, Ernst. 1928. 'Die Morde in den Vereinigten Staaten von Amerika'. *Archiv für Kriminologie* 83:196–197.

Röhl, Klaus F., and Stefan Magen. 1996. 'Die Rolle des Rechts im Prozeß der Globalisierung'. *Zeitschrift für Rechtssoziologie* 17(1):1–57.

Ronquillo, Remigio B. 1934. 'The Administration of Law among the Chinese in Chicago'. *Journal of Criminal Law and Criminology* 25:205–224.

Roosevelt, Theodore. 1897. 'The Ethnology of the Police'. *Munsey's Magazine* 17(3):395–399.

Roschorke, Helmuth, ed. 1937. *Die Polizei—Einmal anders!* München: Franz Eher Nachf.

—— 1939. *Jederzeit einsatzbereit. Ein Bildbericht von der neuen deutschen Polizei.* Berlin: Wilhelm Andermann.

Rose, Nikolas. 1999. *Powers of Freedom: Reframing Political Thought.* Cambridge: Cambridge University Press.

Rosenbaum, Hilda. 1917. 'Kriegskriminalität'. *Deutsche Strafrechts-Zeitung* 4(7–8):271–275.

Ross, Harold. 1937. 'Crime and the Native Born Sons of European Immigrants'. *Journal of Criminal Law and Criminology* 28:202–209.

Roux, Jean-André, ed. (1914) 1926. *Premier Congress de Police Judiciare Internationale, Monaco (Avril 1914). Actes du Congrès.* Paris: G. Godde.

Roxborough, Ian. 1994. 'Clausewitz and the Sociology of War'. *British Journal of Sociology* 45(4):619–636.

Rueschemeier, Dietrich. 1983. 'Professional Autonomy and the Social Control of Expertise'. Pp. 38–58 in *The Sociology of the Professions*, edited by Robert Dingwall and Philip Lewis. New York: St. Martin's Press.

Ruggie, John G. 1993. 'Territoriality and Beyond: Problematizing Modernity in International Regions'. *International Organisation* 47(1):139–174.

Ruggles-Brise, Evelyn J. 1924. *Prison Reform at Home and Abroad: A Short History of the International Movement since the London Congress, 1872.* London: Macmillan.

Rupieper, Hermann-Josef. 1977. 'Die Polizei und die Fahndungen anläßlich der deutschen Revolution von 1848/49'. *Vierteljahresschrift für Sozial- und Wirtschaftsgeschichte* 64:328–355.

S., E. 1913. 'Die Bekämpfung der Prostitution in Chicago'. *Archiv für Kriminal-Anthropologie und Kriminalistik* 52:87–90.

—— 1914. 'Brandstiftertrusts in Nordamerika'. *Archiv für Kriminal-Anthropologie und Kriminalistik* 56:19–190.

Santiago, Michael. 2000. *Europol and Police Cooperation in Europe.* Lewiston, NY: Mellen Press.

Sassen, Saskia. 1996. *Losing Control? Sovereignty in an Age of Globalization.* New York: Columbia University Press.

Savelsberg, Joachim. 1994. 'Knowledge, Domination, and Criminal Punishment'. *American Journal of Sociology* 99:911–943.

—— 2000. 'Kulturen staatlichen Strafens: USA und Deutschland'. Pp. 189–209 in *Die Vermessung kultureller Unterschiede: USA und Deutschland im Vergleich*, edited by Jürgen Gerhards. Opladen: Westdeutscher Verlag.

Schaefer, Kurt. 1977. *Internationale Verbrechensbekämfung*. Wiesbaden: Bundeskriminalamt, BKA-Schriftenreihe Band 14.

—— 1979. 'Internationale Verbrechensbekämpfung'. Pp. 46–80 in *Handwörterbuch der Kriminologie, Ergänzungsband*, edited by Rudolf Sieverts and Hans J. Schneider. Berlin, New York: Walter de Gruyter.

Schlanbusch. 1927. 'Kriminalität und Kriminalpolizei im Hamburger Hafen'. Pp. 98–100 in *Große Polizei-Ausstellung Berlin in Wort und Bild*, edited by Alexander Daranyi and Oskar Daranyi. Wien: Internationale Öffentliche Sicherheit.

Schmitz, Hans. 1927. *Das internationale Verbrechertum und seine Bekämfung*. Inaugural-Dissertation: Universität Köln (Selbstverlag des Verfassers).

Schneickert, Hans. 1904. 'Fernschrift und Fernphotographie; Geheime Verständigung durch telephonische Lichttelegrahie'. *Archiv für Kriminal-Anthropologie und Kriminalistik* 16:188–190.

—— 1911. 'Kinematographische Steckbriefe'. *Archiv für Kriminal-Anthropologie und Kriminalistik* 41:147.

—— 1912a. 'Die Ausbildung der Pariser Polizeibeamten'. *Archiv für Kriminal-Anthropologie und Kriminalistik* 50:244–246.

—— 1912b. 'Der deutsche Polizeikongreß'. *Archiv für Kriminal-Anthropologie und Kriminalistik* 47:363–364.

—— 1913. 'Die Polizeikonferenz der deutschen Bundesstaaten am 20. und 21. Dezember 1912 in Berlin'. *Archiv für Kriminal-Anthropologie und Kriminalistik* 51:169–171.

—— 1914. 'Der I. Kongress für internationales Kriminalpolizeiwesen in Monaco'. *Archiv für Kriminal-Anthropologie und Kriminalistik* 58:354–356.

—— 1921. 'Ein internationales Fahdungsbureau in Kopenhagen'. *Deutsche Strafrechts-Zeitung* 8(1–2):46–47.

—— 1940. 'Die Entführung des Lindbergh-Kindes und der Mordprozeß gegen Hauptmann'. *Archiv für Kriminologie* 107:125–138.

—— 1941. 'Die Entführung des Lindbergh-Kindes und der Mordprozeß gegen Hauptmann'. (several parts). *Archiv für Kriminologie* 108;109:27–33, 90–97;18–39,88–97,134–143.

Schober, Hans. 1925. 'Die Polizei-Internationale'. *Deutsches Polizei-Archiv* 4:116.

—— 1926. 'Der Internationale Polizeikongreß in Berlin 1926'. *Archiv für Kriminologie* 79:197–219.

—— 1928. 'Internationale Zusammenarbeit der Kriminalpolizei'. *Archiv für Kriminologie* 83:12–20.

Schober, Hans. 1930. 'Internationale Zusammenarbeit der Kriminalpolizei: Der Antwerpener Polizeikongreß'. *Archiv für Kriminologie* 87:88–100.

Schoenfelder, Roland. 1937. *Vom Werden der deutschen Polizei: Ein Volksbuch*. Leipzig: Breitkopf & Härtel.

Schultz, Bruno. 1930. 'Schober und Die Polizei'. Pp. 161 in *Schober*, edited by Oskar Kleinschmied. Wien: Manz-Verlag.

—— 1932. 'Das Internationale Bureau für die zwischenstaatliche Zusammenarbeit gegen das Verbrechertum. Eine Erwiderung'. *Archiv für Kriminologie* 90:97–104.

Schultze, Ernst. 1917. 'Das Mordrecht in den Vereinigten Staaten'. *Deutsche Strafrechts-Zeitung* 4(5–6):206–211.

Schwitters, Bert. 1978. *Dossier Interpol: De Verborgen Wereld van Interpol.* Amsterdam: Loeb & van der Velden.

Scruton, Roger. 1987. 'Notes on the Sociology of War'. *British Journal of Sociology* 37(3):295–309.

Scull, Andrew T. 1988. 'Deviance and Social Control'. Pp. 667–693 in *Handbook of Sociology*, edited by Neil Smelser. Newbury Park, Calif: Sage.

Sellin, Thorsten. 1931. [Review of Theodor Hampe, 1929, *Crime and Punishment in Germany*]. *Journal of Criminal Law and Criminology* 22:136–137.

Shearing, Clifford. 1996. 'Reinventing Policing: Policing as Governance'. Pp. 285–307 in *Policing Change, Changing Police*, edited by Otwin Marenin. New York: Garland Publishing.

Shepard, J F. 1912. [Review of Erich Wulffen, 1910, *Gauner und Verbrecher-Typen*]. *Journal of the American Institute of Criminal Law and Criminology* 3:326.

Sheptycki, J.W.E. 1995. 'Transnational Policing and the Makings of a Postmodern State'. *British Journal of Criminology* 35(4):613–635.

—— 1996. 'Law Enforcement, Justice and Democracy in the Transnational Arena'. *International Journal of the Sociology of Law* 24:61–75.

—— 1997. 'Transnationalism, Crime Control, and the European State System: A Review of the Literature'. Review Essay. *International Criminal Justice Review* 7:130–140.

—— 1998a. 'Reflections on the Transnationalization of Policing: The Case of the RCMP and Serial Killers'. *International Journal of the Sociology of Law* 26:17–34.

—— 1998b. 'The Global Cops Cometh: Reflections on Transnationalization, Knowledge Work and Policing Subculture'. *British Journal of Sociology* 49:57–74.

—— 1998c. 'Policing, Postmodernism and Transnationalization'. *British Journal of Criminology* 38(3):485–503.

—— ed. 2000a. *Issues in Transnational Policing*. London: Routledge.

—— 2000b. 'Introduction'. Pp. 1–20 in *Issues in Transnational Policing*, edited by J.W.E. Sheptycki. London: Routledge.

Shields, Mark A. 1997. 'Reinventing Technology in Social Theory'. *Current Perspectives in Social Theory* 17:187–216.

Siemann, Wolfram, ed. 1983a. *Der 'Polizeiverein' deutscher Staaten: Eine Dokumentation zur Ueberwachung der Oeffentlichkeit nach der Revolution von 1848/49*. Tübingen: Niemeyer Verlag.

—— 1983b. 'Einleitung'. Pp. 1–19 in *Der 'Polizeiverein' deutscher Staaten*, edited by Wolfram Siemann. Tübingen: Niemeyer Verlag.

—— 1985. *'Deutschlands Ruhe, Sicherheit und Ordnung': Die Anfänge der politischen Polizei, 1806–1866*. Tübingen: Max Niemeyer.

—— 1990. *Gesellschaft im Aufbruch: Deutschland, 1849–1871*. Frankfurt: Suhrkamp.

Siering. 1931. 'Internationaler Bund der Polizeibeamten'. *Der Gendarm* 29:530.

Silbey, Susan S. 1997. ' "Let Them Eat Cake": Globalization, Postmodern Colonialism and the Possibilities of Justice'. *Law & Society Review* 31(2):207–235.

Simon, Jonathan. 1988. 'The Ideological Effects of Actuarial Practices'. *Law & Society Review* 22:771–800.

—— 1994. 'Between Power and Knowledge: Habermas, Foucault, and the Future of Legal Studies'. *Law & Society Review* 28(4):947–961.

Skolnick, Jerome H. 1966. *Justice Without Trial: Law Enforcement in Democratic Society*. New York: John Wiley & Sons.

Skubl, Michael. 1937. 'Völkerbundidee und Polizei'. *Öffentliche Sicherheit* 17(1):1–3.

Smith, Carole. 2000. 'The Sovereign State v. Foucault: Law and Disciplinary Power'. *The Sociological Review* 48(2):283–306.

Smith, Phillip T. 1985. 'The Alien Question: The Metropolitan Police and Continental Refugees'. Pp. 79–112 in his *Policing Victorian London: Political Policing, Public Order, and the London Metropolitan Police*. Westport, Conn: Greenwood Press.

Söderman, Harry. 1956. *Policeman's Lot*. New York: Funk & Wagnalls Company.

Sorokin, Pitirim A. 1966. 'Comments on Moore's and Bierstedt's Papers'. *American Journal of Sociology* 71(5):491–492.

Spitzer, Steven. 1985. 'The Rationalization of Crime Control in Capitalist Society'. Pp. 312–334 in *Social Control and the State*, edited by Stanley Cohen and Andrew Scull. Oxford: Basil Blackwell.

Spitzka, E.A. 1903. 'Statistisches über das Lynchen in Nordamerika'. *Archiv für Kriminal-Anthropologie und Kriminalistik* 11:224–227.

Stammer, Georg. 1911. *Strafvollzug und Jugendschutz in Amerika: Eindrücke und Ausblicke einer Gefängnisstudienreise*. Berlin: R. v. Decker's Verlag.

—— 1912. 'Bemerkungen über amerikanische Strafpolitik'. *Archiv für Kriminal-Anthropologie und Kriminalistik* 47:79–109.

Stanley, William. 1995. 'International Tutelage and Domestic Political Will: Building a New Civilian Police Force in El Salvador'. *Studies in Comparative International Development* 30(1):30–58.

Stead, Philip J. 1983. *The Police of France*. New York: Macmillan.

Stenson, Kevin. 1993. 'Community Policing as a Governmental Technology'. *Economy and Society* 22(3):373–389.

Stieber, Wilhelm J.C.E. 1980. *The Chancellor's Spy: The Revelations of the Chief of Bismarck's Secret Service*. New York: Grove Press.

Stiebler, Georg W. 1981. *Die Institutionalisierung der internationalen polizeilichen Zusammenarbeit auf dem Gebiet der Verbrechensverhütung und -bekämpfung in der 'Internationalen Kriminalpolizielichen Organisation INTERPOL (IKPO-INTERPOL)'*. Bochum: Studienverlag Dr. N. Brockmeyer.

Struve, Karl. 1914. 'Kinderrepubliken in Amerika und England'. *Deutsche Strafrechts-Zeitung* 1(4–5):252–255.

Sullivan, John J. 1939. 'Policing a World's Fair'. *The Police Yearbook* (1938–1939):58–63.

Sullivan, John L. 1977. *Introduction to Police Science*. New York: McGraw-Hill Book Company.

Sumners, Anthony. 1993. *Official and Confidential: The Secret Life of J. Edgar Hoover*. New York: G.P. Putnam's Sons.

Sylvester, Richard A. 1912. 'The Co-operation of the International Police Association for Good Government'. *Journal of the American Institute of Criminal Law and Criminology* 2:822–824.

—— 1914. 'Convention of the International Association of Chiefs of Police'. *Journal of the American Institute of Criminal Law and Criminology* 5:300–301.

Teeters, Negley K. 1949. *Deliberations of the International Penal and Penitentiary Congresses*. Philadelphia, Pa: Temple University Book Store.

Tenner. 1918. 'Der Erkennungsdienst der Polizeidirektion München und die Zigeunerpolizeistelle München im Jahre 1917'. *Deutsche Strafrechts-Zeitung* 5(3–4):99–101.

Tenner, F. 1932. 'Das Internationale Bureau für die zwischenstaatliche Zusammenarbeit gegen das Verbrechertum'. *Archiv für Kriminologie* 91:21–23.

Thamer, Hans-Ulrich. 1996. 'Die nationalsozialistiche Bewegung in der Weimarer Republik; Beginn der nationalsozialistischen Herrschaft.' *Informationen zur politischen Bildung* 251:5–29, 29–56.

Theoharis, Athan. 1992. 'FBI Wiretapping: A Case Study of Bureaucratic Autonomy'. *Political Science Quarterly* 107(1):101–122.

—— 1995. *J. Edgar Hoover, Sex, and Crime*. Chicago: Ivan R. Dee.

—— and John S. Cox. 1993. *The Boss: J. Edgar Hoover and the Great American Inquisition*. London: Virgin Books.

Thomson, Basil H. 1923. 'Ein internationales Polizeibureau'. *Archiv für Kriminologie* 75:109–117.

Tilgner, Fritz. 1927. 'Das Interesse der Wirtschaft an der internationalen Zusammenarbeit der Polizei'. Pp. 247 in *Große Polizei-Ausstellung Berlin in Wort und Bild*, edited by Alexander Daranyi and Oskar Daranyi. Wien: Internationale Öffentliche Sicherheit.

Tilly, Charles. 1986. *The Contentious French*. Harvard, Mass: Harvard University Press.

—— Louise Tilly, and Richard Tilly. 1975. *The Rebellious Century: 1830–1930*. Harvard, Mass: Harvard University Press.

Tissot, Victor. 1884. *La Police Secrète Prussienne*. Paris: E. Dentu.

Todd, Arthur J. 1914. [Review of *Bulletin der Internationalen Kriminalistischen Vereinigung*, vol. XXI, no. 1, 1914]. *Journal of the American Institute of Criminal Law and Criminology* 5:307–311.

—— 1915. [Review of Hans von Hentig, 1914, 'Die Kriminalität der Verwitweten und Geschiedenen']. *Journal of the American Institute of Criminal Law and Criminology* 6:624–627.

Torpey, John. 2000. *The Invention of the Passport: Surveillance, Citizenship and the State*. Cambridge: Cambridge University Press.

Travers, J. 1915. 'Der Krieg und die Kriminalität'. *Archiv für Kriminal-Anthropologie und Kriminalistik* 62:393.

Tullett, Tom. 1963. *Inside Interpol*. London: Frederick Muller.

Tully, Andrew. 1980. *Inside the FBI*. New York: McGraw-Hill.

Turner, William W. 1993. *Hoover's FBI*. New York: Thunder's Mouth Press.

Ungar, Stanford J. 1976. *FBI*. Boston, Mass: Little, Brown and Company.

Upson, L.D. 1911. [Review of Paul Pollitz, 1909, *Die Psychologie des Verbrechers*]. *Journal of the American Institute of Criminal Law and Criminology* 1:825.

Urban, F.M. 1914. [Review of Adolf Merkel, 1912, *Die Lehre von Verbrechen und Strafe*]. *Journal of the American Institute of Criminal Law and Criminology* 5:142–143.

Useem, Bert. 1997. 'The State and Collective Disorders: The Los Angeles Riot/Protest of April, 1992'. *Social Forces* 76(2):357–377.

Usinger. 1929. 'Die polizeiliche Behandlung der Ausländer in Deutschland'. *Deutsches Polizei-Archiv* 8:326–329.

US Attorney General. *Annual Report of the Attorney General of the United States*. Several volumes (1918–1946).Washington, DC: Government Printing Office.

US Comptroller General. 1976. *Report of the Comptroller General of the United States: United States Participation in INTERPOL, The International Criminal Police Organization*. Washington, DC: United States General Accounting Office.

US Congress. 1938. 'International Criminal Police Commission' (House); 'Membership in International Criminal Police Commission' (Senate). 75th Congress, 3rd Session.

Vechten, C.C. van. 1942. 'The Criminality of the Foreign Born'. *Journal of Criminal Law and Criminology* 32:139–147.

Viernstein, Theodor. 1932. 'The Crimino-Biological Service in Bavaria'. *Journal of Criminal Law and Criminology* 23:269–275.

Voit. 1928. 'Die Nachrichtentechnik im Dienste der Berliner Polizei'. *Die Polizei* 25:142.

—— 1931. 'The International Police Radio'. *The Police Journal* 4(3): 467–469.

Vollmer, August. 1922. 'Aims and Ideals of the Police'. *Journal of the American Institute of Criminal Law and Criminology* 13:251–257.

—— 1930. 'The Scientific Policeman'. *American Journal of Police Science* 1(1):8–12.

—— 1932. 'Abstract of the "Wickersham" Police Report'. *Journal of Criminal Law and Criminology* 22:716–723.

—— 1933. 'Police Progress in the Past Twenty-Five Years'. *Journal of Criminal Law and Criminology* 24:161–175.

—— 1936. *The Police and Modern Society*. Berkeley, Calif: University of California Press.

—— and Albert Schneider. 1925. 'Die Polizeischule in Berkeley'. *Deutsches Polizei-Archiv* 4:3–4.

Waite, Robert G. 1992. 'Law Enforcement and Crime in America: The View from Germany, 1920–40'. *Criminal Justice History* 13:191–216.

Walker, Neil C. 1996. 'Policing the European Union: The Politics of Transition'. Pp. 251–283 in *Policing Change, Changing Police*, edited by Otwin Marenin. New York: Garland Publishing.

Walker, Samuel. 1977. *A Critical History of Police Reform: The Emergence of Professionalism*. Lexington, Md: Lexington Books.

—— 1980. *Popular Justice: A History of American Criminal Justice*. New York: Oxford University Press.

Walker, William O. 1991. *Opium and Foreign Policy*. Chapel Hill: University of North Carolina Press.

Wallerstein, Immanuel. 2000. 'From Sociology to Historical Social Science: Prospects and Obstacles'. *British Journal of Sociology* 51(1):25–35.

Walther, Hans (pseudonym for Hans Walter Gaebert). 1968. *Interpol auf Verbrecherjagd: Die Internationale Kriminalpolizeiliche Kommission im Einsatz*. Würzburg: Arena.

Warth. 1938. 'Die Neuregelung des Ausländerpolizeiwesens'. *Die Deutsche Polizei* 6:744.

Weber, Max. (1918) 1988. 'Parlament und Regierung im neugeordneten Deutschland: Zur politischen kritik des Beamtentums und Parteiwesens'.

Pp. 306–443 in his *Gesammelte Politische Schriften*. Tübingen: J.C.B. Mohr (Paul Siebeck).

—— (1919) 'Politik als Beruf'. Pp. 505–560 in *Gesammelte politische Schriften*. Tübingen: J.C.B. Mohr (Paul Siebeck).

—— (1920) 1976. *The Protestant Ethic and the Spirit of Capitalism*, translated by Talcott Parsons. New York: Charles Scribner's Sons.

—— (1922) 1980. *Wirtschaft und Gesellschaft: Grundriss der verstehenden Soziologie*. Tübingen: J.C.B. Mohr (Paul Siebeck).

—— 1958. *From Max Weber: Essays in Sociology*, edited by H.H. Gerth and C. Wright Mills. New York: Oxford University Press.

—— 1978. *Economy and Society: An Outline of Interpretive Sociology*, edited by Guenther Roth and Claus Wittich. Berkeley, Calif: University of California Press.

Weiß. 1919. 'Die kriminelle Bedeutung des Luftverkehrs'. *Deutsche Strafrechts-Zeitung* 6(5–6):181–182.

Weiß, Bernhard. 1927. 'Die Organisation der preußischen Polizei'. Pp. 101–102 in *Große Polizei-Ausstellung Berlin in Wort und Bild*, edited by Alexander Daranyi and Oskar Daranyi. Wien: Internationale Öffentliche Sicherheit.

Weiß, Curt. 1922. 'A World Bureau of Prosecution—New Methods of Identification'. *Journal of the American Institute of Criminal Law and Criminology* 13:272–274.

Welsh, Stephen. 2001. 'Ethical-Political Dimensions of Police Intervention: Domestic and International Contexts Compared'. *Civil War* 4(1):.

Welzel, Albrecht. 1922a. 'Die historische Entwicklung der amerikanischen Polizei'. *Archiv für Kriminologie* 74:210–223.

—— 1922b. 'Amerikanische Polizei'. *Die Polizei* 18(1921/1922):302–303.

—— 1925a. 'Die New Yorker Internationale Polizeikonferenz'. *Deutsches Polizei-Archiv* 4:147–148.

—— 1925b. 'Amerikanische Polizei der Gegenwart'. *Deutsches Polizei-Archiv* 4:331–332,353–354.

—— 1925c. 'The Chinese Policeman as I Know Him: Cops of the Celestial Empire Differ Vastly from Their Uniformed Brothers in Other Parts of the World'. *Police Magazine* 2(4):32–34,61.

—— 1926. 'Amerikanische Polizei der Gegenwart (Schluß)'. *Deutsches Polizei-Archiv* 5:46–49.

Werner, Paul. 1942. 'Aufbau und Aufgaben der Reichskriminalpolizei'. *Zeitschrift für die gesammte Strafrechtswissenschaften* 61:465–470.

Wiesenthal, Simon. 1989. *Justice Not Vengeance*. New York: Grove Weidenfeld.

Wigmore, John H. 1937. 'State Cooperation for Crime-Repression'. *Journal of Criminal Law and Criminology* 28:326–334.

Wilson, O.W. 1933. 'Police Selection and Training'. *Public Management* 15(12):364–365.

Winer, Jonathan M. 1997. 'International Crime in the New Geopolitics: A Core Threat to Democracy'. Pp. 41–64 in *Crime and Law Enforcement in the Global Village*, edited by W.F. McDonald. Cincinnatti, Ohio: Anderson.

Wirth, Louis. 1948. 'World Community, World Society, and World Government: An Attempt at a Clarification of Terms'. Pp. 9–20 in *The World Community*, edited by Quincy Wright. Chicago: University of Chicago Press.

Witry. 1903. 'Das reformatorium von Elmira'. *Archiv für Kriminal-Anthropologie und Kriminalistik* 12:130–133.

Woelfle, John W. 1939. 'Interstate Crime Control'. *The Police Yearbook* (1938–1939):171–173.

Wolz. 1926. 'Kriminaltechnische Neuerungen auf der Internationalen Polizeitechnischen Ausstellung Karlsruhe 1925'. *Archiv für Kriminologie* 78:94–104.

Wolzendorff, Kurt. 1905. *Die Grenzen der Polizeigewalt, Erster Teil. Über den Umfang der Polizeigewalt im Polizeistaat*. Marburg: Oskar Ehrhardt's Universitäts-Buchhandlung.

—— 1906. *Die Grenzen der Polizeigewalt, Zweiter Teil. Die Entwicklung des Polizeibegriffs im 19. Jahrhundert*. Marburg: Oscar Ehrhardt's Universitäts-Buchhandlung.

Wood, S.T. 1937. 'International Cooperation in Identification (Address before the 23rd Annual Convention of the International Association for Identification, Washington, September 29, 1937)'. *FBI Law Enforcement Bulletin* 6(12):3–8.

Zagaris, Bruce. 1996. 'International Criminal and Enforcement Cooperation in the Americas in the Wake of Integration'. *Southwestern Journal of Law and Trade in the Americas* 2:1–84.

—— and Jessica Resnick. 1997. 'The Mexico-U.S. Mutual Legal Assistance in Criminal Matters Treaty'. *Arizona Journal of International and Comparative Law* 14:1–96.

Zaika, Siegfried. 1979. *Polizeigeschichte—Die Exekutive im Lichte der historischen Konfliktforschung*. Lübeck: Schmidt Römhild.

Zaturenska, Marya. 1925. 'Policing Persia: An Account of the Introduction of Modern Western Police Methods into the Picturesque Land of the Rubiayat (Written from reports made by Abdollah Bahrami, Deputy Chief of Police of Persia, and Lieut.-Col. Seif, Chief of Police of Casnine)'. *Police Magazine* 3(4):14–16,83.

Index